Insights In Prophecy

Unlock The Ancient Mysteries Of Daniel & Revelation

BIBLE DISCOVERY SERIES

Kevin R. Swift

Insights In Prophecy
Unlock The Ancient Mysteries Of Daniel & Revelation
BIBLE DISCOVERY SERIES

A publication by Kevin R. Swift

Kevin R. Swift is founder of Focus On The Prophecies Ministry, a non-denominational resource devoted to the study of the ancient Hebrew prophecies of the Bible and the secrets God promised to unseal to the last generation of wise saints (Daniel 12:4, 9-10). The ministry goal is to help fulfill prophecy's primary intent: to guide and encourage "those who obey God's commandments and hold to the testimony of Jesus," (Revelation 12:17)—the followers of Christ who must remain faithful in spite of demonic signs, miracles, persecution and hardship, as they wait in anticipation for the approaching Day of our Messiah and His revelation in the heavens.

FOCUS ON THE PROPHECIES MINISTRY
5815 S.W. 29th Street
Topeka, Kansas 66614

A full-color copy of The Kingdom Calendar of the end-times
is available online.

Website: www.focusontheprophecies.org
Email: kevin.r.swift@gmail.com

Library of Congress Cataloging in Publication Data
Swift, Kevin
        Insights in Prophecy: Bible Discovery Series/ Kevin R. Swift
        ISBN-13: 978-1479101146
        ISBN-10: 1479101141
        Bible--Prophecies. 2. End of the world. 3. Good and evil.

PRINTED IN THE UNITED STATES OF AMERICA

Insights In Prophecy
Unlock The Ancient Mysteries Of Daniel & Revelation
BIBLE DISCOVERY SERIES

CONTENTS

Insights In Prophecy
Unlock The Ancient Mysteries Of Daniel & Revelation
BIBLE DISCOVERY SERIES

Insights In Prophecy
Unlock The Ancient Mysteries Of Daniel & Revelation
BIBLE DISCOVERY SERIES

Lesson Introduction

The Scriptures forecast, and believers anticipate the end of this present evil age, and the dawning of God's Eternal Kingdom of justice and peace. The Hebrew prophets, through the visions and dreams they received from the Spirit of God and Heaven's messengers, forewarned in the written Scriptures about a series of earth-shattering events lasting several years that will bring the planet, as we know it, to the brink of annihilation just before Yeshua our Messiah's return as King of kings. These events likely include in modern terms the escalation of terrorism, nuclear holocaust, chemical and/or biological warfare and bloodshed, along with increased disasters such as hurricanes, tidal waves, earthquakes, tornadoes, uncontrollable fires and diseases in epidemic proportions... and many other forms of human suffering and devastation. But still, we have hope!

From a series of quick and abrupt catastrophes and global upheaval of World War III, an individual will arrive on the world scene through miraculous displays. His arrival will be so magnificent and so grand that the prophet John wrote, "The whole world was filled with wonder and followed the beast [Antichrist]. People worshiped the dragon [Satan] because he had given authority to the beast, and they also worshiped the beast and asked, "Who is like the beast? Who can wage war against it?" The beast was given a mouth to utter proud words and blasphemies and to exercise its authority for forty-two months [1,260 days]," Revelation 13:3-5. Daniel earlier wrote about this man who will rise from the cryptic ashes of war to unprecedented power: "He will speak against the Most High and oppress His holy people and try to change the set times [of worship, including "the feasts"—Wycliffe Bible] and the laws [of God]. The holy people will be delivered into his hands for a time, times and half a time [1,260 days]," Daniel 7:25. His time to rule, written about in the prophecies, is now on the horizon, and global chaos and demonic displays will take the world captive under the Beast/Man of Sin's satanic spell.

However, God is still in control; He even allows the global delusion. Why? "The coming of the lawless one will be in accordance with how Satan works. He will use all sorts of displays of power through signs and wonders that serve the lie, and all the ways that wickedness deceives those who are perishing. They perish because they refused to love the truth and so be saved. For this reason, God sends them a powerful delusion so that they will believe the lie and so that all will be condemned who have not believed the truth but have delighted in wickedness," 2 Thessalonians 2:9-12. The masses take pleasure in sin, refusing to learn the truth about the modern-day travesties the Hebrew prophets forewarned about in God's Word. They refuse to acknowledge Jesus as their personal Savior and the soon arrival of His Kingdom. Only Yeshua can save mankind and this planet, not men in flowing robes, demonic powers disguised as intelligent life forms, governments, treaties or armies. Still, the world's population will adore the religious leader and nearly all will accept the mark of the Beast so they can buy and sell; and thereby, many will deny Christ, revealing their unfaithfulness and sealing their eternal doom—for that is how the Scriptures portray the final decision we all must make (Matthew 10:33; Revelation 13:16-18; 14:10-12; 15:2).

In contrast, Daniel was promised at "the time of the end... many will go here and there" in the pages of Daniel's scroll "to increase knowledge" (Daniel 12:4) of just how and when final events will play out. These wise individuals—who understand the Word of God does provide answers to life's complexities—will search through the ancient predictions of Daniel and Revelation with a sincere desire to understand God's plan for the end of the ages and His faith pathway to Glory. How do we distinguish authentic believers? Genuine followers of Christ "keep God's commands and hold fast their testimony about Jesus" (Revelation 17:12), and they demonstrate the fruit of the Holy Spirit, including "love, joy, peace, forbearance, kindness, goodness, faithfulness, gentleness and self-control," Galatians 5:22-23. Those who display hatred, violence and anger, and who foster the extermination of others who don't agree with them, are not to be believed or followed. These men and women are instruments of Satan in his attempt to overthrow God and His Kingdom; the Kingdom which is not of this world—but the world to come. Jesus said, "My kingdom is not of this world. If it were, My servants would fight... But now My kingdom is from another place," (John 18:36)—the New Jerusalem above (John 14:1-3; Hebrews 8:8-10; Hebrews 11:16; Hebrew 12:22). The King and the Kingdom of Heaven is our hope, not Jerusalem, this earth and those who control it.

Daniel 12:10 states clearly "none of the wicked will understand, but those who are wise will understand" final events, if they are attentive to the prophetic warnings. God gave His prophets various counting time periods, patterned by way of the Calendar of annual Biblical Festivals, which will guide His people through untold adversity to the revelation of Messiah. Jesus said "*all men will hate you* because of Me, but he who stands firm to the end will be saved," Matthew 10:22. He also promised, "*Surely I will be with you always, to the very end of the age,*" (28:20); He will never leave or forsake His faithful, but God expects us to perseverance through the storm all the way to the end, whether it means life or temporary death.

Paul, the other apostles, and the early congregations believed the writings of Daniel to be a book about the end. By all accounts, they expected the immediate, literal fulfillment of the "appointed time of the end" and God's Kingdom in their day. However, as time moved on and the long delay set in, the believers became discouraged—and understandably so. "How long, LORD?" Psalm 94:3. Teachers and scholars in the Dark Ages tried to make sense of the centuries of postponement. They found encouragement from the book of Daniel through applying his predictions to historical events, and by transforming the 24 hour "days" (Hebrew: *yom*) in the prophecies (Daniel 7:25; 12:11-12) to "years"—giving the believers some calculative reasoning for the delay in Messiah's return. These old and mistaken views, handed down through the centuries, have reached our modern commentaries as scholars assign nearly all of Daniel's visions to various military activities and political events in the past.

However, as the last generation, we are revisiting Daniel's predictions and time periods in view of current events and reclaiming what is promised to be ours—the unsealing of the scroll. God assures us that the *sealed* book of Daniel would be *unlocked* at the *time of the end*. Once Daniel is studied alongside Revelation as complimentary end-time books of prophecy, parallel predictions about our future begin to emerge that paint an accurate account of events that are playing out in our day.

Also, in this series we will apply the long-recognized principle of Biblical study—of looking first to the "literal-straightforward" meaning before turning to any "interpretive-figurative" explanation. The five prophetic time periods found in the book of Daniel will be considered 24-hour days, for that is exactly what the original Hebrew word "yom" means, and how the early church would have understood them. These include the 70 weeks (*490 days*) of Daniel 9:24; 2,300 evenings and mornings (*1,150 days*) of 8:14; the time, times and half (*1,260 days*) of 7:25 and 12:7; and the *1,290 days* and *1,335 days* of Daniel 12:11, 12. Although they seem ancient, these prophetic periods and the events surrounding them are given to help us make real life decisions as end-time events unfold. They represent counting periods for the last-day believers, so we can know where we are in time; and that we, by faith, might hold onto Jesus all the way to the end during this very difficult period in human history. This involves persistence and stamina, as we wait for our LORD's triumphant revelation in the sky (Psalm 37:7-11; Revelation 13:10; 14:12).

The five periods in the book of Daniel, combined with the *1,260 day* period repeated five times in the book of Revelation (11:2; 11:3; 12:6, 12:14 and 13:5), create a last-day Calendar of events that is packed full of insight. The events of both Daniel and Revelation are collected and merged into one overarching presentation of the future. From this emerges **The Kingdom Calendar** that combines all these time periods into an end-time counting chart of the last days, which lines up between the Festivals to prove both its authenticity and reliability.

The **Insights in Prophecy Bible Discovery Series** will help you dig deeper into the Biblical predictions. It will challenge your thinking, as we investigate the prophecies about the soon return of Yeshua our Messiah. In the search we'll discover Daniel's unlocked warnings, and with them the meaning of the mysterious symbols and intent of the book of Revelation. Today, because our generation faces the end of the age, spiritual knowledge is on the increase; there is a renewed interest in the prophetic visions of the ancient Hebrew prophets. A large portion of God's Sacred Word is devoted to future and end-time events, and is worth our undivided attention.

Therefore, our hope is that you will take the necessary time to study these spiritual warnings. Prophecy, by its very nature, is mysterious and will take effort on your part to comprehend the various elements. Remember our Creator is the source of all these prophecies, and His Spirit will teach us as He makes known to us His final work: "Remember the former things, those of long ago; I am God, and there is no other; I am God, and there is none like Me. *I make known* the end from the beginning, from ancient times, *what is still to come*. I say: My purpose will stand and I will do all that I please," Isaiah 46:9-10. And, "Surely the Sovereign LORD does nothing without revealing His plan to His servants the prophets," Amos 3:7.

Despite the insights gained from the study of the books of Daniel and Revelation, there are still unknowns; God has not revealed every detail about the future. Not until the Archangel's trumpet is heard will all mystery be finished: "But in the days when the Seventh Angel is about to sound His trumpet, the mystery of God will be accomplished, just as He [Michael] announced to His servants the prophets" (Revelation 10:7) on the banks of the Tigris River many years earlier (Daniel 12:5-7). However, God has provided enough understanding to give us the hope needed to endure until we reach the Kingdom, and in Him we can trust day by day until He returns.

This we know so far, Biblical evidence indicates the pattern of the numbered days of prophecy fall within the framework of the Festivals starting with Purim and Passover, and culminating three and one-half (3½) years later during Rosh Ha-Shanah (Feast of Trumpets), Yom Kippur (Day of Atonement) and Sukkot (Feast of Tabernacles). The Jerusalem devastation event could occur at any moment, but the numbered days will most likely start precisely at Purim. Nevertheless, God has certainly established the counting pattern; the "three and one-half years" represent the primary length of end-time prophecy. The Hebrew prophets repeated this *precise* period seven times—more than any other prophetic period, as though the Holy Spirit (Hebrew: *Ruach haKodesh*) is leading us to focus on and consider this timeline—the "time, times and the dividing of time," the "42 months," equaling "1,260 days," as found in Daniel and Revelation.

We will learn the "seven year" tribulation period—a view of recent history made popular among evangelicals by the Scofield Reference Bible—is a contrived view of Daniel 9:27, which holds little merit. Prophecy grants Antichrist 3½ years to rule and persecute, and no more. The dispensationalist view increases his rule to *seven years*, against the clear evidence of God's Word. When the 3½ year period of last-day authority, blasphemy and persecution by the Man of Sin comes to an end, when God's last two prophets complete their rule for 3½ years, and when Gentile armies reach the end of their 3½ year occupation of Jerusalem, a very short but brutal "Great Tribulation" will commence (Daniel 12:1; Matthew 24:15-22), lasting 40 days as the timelines and historical pattern reveals (Genesis 7:4, 12, 17). Rome's plunder of Jerusalem in 70 A.D.—as illustrated by the 82 A.D. Roman built victory Arch of Titus (book cover image)—was accomplished with a vast Roman army. However, according to the Bible prophecies, Rome's final victory over the Holy City during the last appointed times will be realized through Papal flatteries and the setting up of his Temple Mount abomination, followed by the judgment of Almighty God and Jerusalem's fiery desolation by Gentile armies (Luke 21:20-22; Matthew 24:15-22; Daniel 9:26-27).

Jesus said, "Now *learn this lesson from the fig tree*: As soon as its twigs get tender and its leaves come out, you know that summer is near. Even so, when you see all these things, you know that it is near, right at the door. Truly I tell you, this generation will certainly not pass away until all these things have happened. Heaven and earth will pass away, but My words will never pass away," Matthew 24:32-25. Psalm 90:10 says, "Our days may come to seventy years, or eighty, if our strength endures." In 1948 Israel became a nation once again and the fig tree bloomed; and now, that generation is about to pass. We are saddened by the Scriptural warnings that Jerusalem is a doomed city, because her leaders will ultimately reject and then rejoice in the death of God's two last prophets—as they did Yeshua at the end of His 3½ years of ministry on earth long ago (Matthew 21:12-20; Revelation 11:7-10). The Word warns in no uncertain terms, "When you see Jerusalem being surrounded by armies, you will know that its desolation is near. Then let those who are in Judea flee to the mountains, let those in the city [Jerusalem] get out, and let those in the country not enter the city [of Jerusalem]. For this is the time of punishment in fulfillment of all that has been written," Luke 21:20-22. However, soon thereafter the Commander's angels will gather His elect—the chosen from the twelve tribes living in the land of Israel and around the world, who will trust in the true King (Matthew 24:29-31; Romans 11:25-27). Our hope is in Messiah and the New Jerusalem, which He has built and prepared for His people (John 14:3).

Prophecy's predictions have been given to us by God to guide the believers past some of the most tragic events to engulf the planet, and the most overwhelming deceptions ever to confront mankind. Visitations, demonic miracles and apparitions will escalate... a series of "great signs and wonders" (Matthew 24:24) on earth and in the skies that will lead to idolatry and demonic worship (Revelation 9:20). Even the most ardent students of God's Word—church members, religious professors, teachers, scholars and ministers—will be surprised by global events that will challenge views they now hold. There will be no early rapture to escape the last-day troubles, nor are Daniel and Revelation relics of the past as historicists and preterists presume. The very foundations of our Christian faith will be shaken beneath us that we might learn to trust in God and His Son alone.

We must recognize the recklessness of blindly handing over our God-given responsibility to study God's Word to the clergy (all faiths have their scholars, who cannot agree on the simplest of matters). Some religions boast of popes and prophets whose teachings and writings they consider infallable and irrefutable. However, we must in good faith challenge all teachings other than the Word of God. Absolutely everything must be tested against the inspired Scriptures, including the views expressed in this lesson series.

When a new perspective is introduced, and long-held views are challenged, it's the teacher's obligation to present comprehensive proof from God's Word; then, to back it up with real-life evidence through matching world events to the prophetic warnings of Daniel and Revelation. At that point, when the proof has been delivered, whether it is received or rejected is determined by you and you alone. As followers of Christ, we have two choices: to be open-minded or empty-minded. To reject insights, when Scriptural facts are presented with sound reasoning, is to be empty-minded. *The Kingdom Calendar* may be a supernatural sign of divine origin, given as God's gift to the last generation of believers; if proven true over time, it should not be rejected to preserve false doctrines or to protect popular ideologies, which are merely inventions of previous generations from men and women who, doing the best they could in their day, are now dead and gone. They simply lived too early to be a part of the last generation... the only generation promised the final unsealing.

Just as in days of old, God reveals His truths through the Holy Spirit to the humble, who are considered foolish in the eyes of others; common men and women without the social status, labels and influence that normally impress the masses. And, in the end who gets the glory? The Father and His Son, through the work of the Holy Spirit. "Not by might nor by power, but by My Spirit,' says the LORD Almighty," Zechariah 4:6. For, "God hath chosen the foolish things of the world to confound the wise; and God hath chosen the weak things of the world to confound the things which are mighty," 1 Corinthians 1:27.

Because we face the end of the age, it is our privilege and moral responsibility to study the Biblical prophecies, particularly Daniel and Revelation, and to search for the final unsealing of the prophecies that is promised to the last generation at the end of time (Daniel 12:4, 10). Thank you for joining this growing movement in the study of God's end-time predictions through the 30 lesson series, Insights in Prophecy. Soon, global deception will be rampant through the powers of darkness. Therefore, you must learn from the prophetic pages of Scriptures who is involved, what events will transpire, as well as when and where. It is worth your undivided attention, for you and your family's destinies are at stake. Unwavering faith in Jesus our Messiah is your only hope.

My prayer is that God's prophetic truths will shine brighter, highlighting our Savior's love for you, for He alone gives your life eternal purpose and clarity. For, that is the reason the prophecies were penned long ago as God's final warnings to humanity, and made discernable in these last days. May we be found faithful, for the Day of the LORD is fast approaching—the return of the KING OF KINGS, AND LORD OF LORDS. He will split the sky wide open to reveal Himself, and the universe will never be the same again.

The Kingdom Calendar

Divine Dates of End-Time Disaster & Deliverance

FESTIVAL YEARS
2019-2022

The Kingdom Calendar reveals the pattern, and possibly the starting point when the prophetic counting days of Daniel and Revelation may begin.

The way the counting periods align, as one interconnected whole, is verified by the precision in which they connect "to the day" between the Festivals. The timelines start with the Purim celebration noted in the book of Esther, Passover of Leviticus 23, and the annual Tisha B'Av Fast of the 5th month referred to in Zechariah 7 and 8, with all ending precisely at the Day of Atonement (Yom Kippur) of Leviticus 16 and 23 over a three and one-half (3½) year period; but, for two of those periods the match would not be possible without the inclusion of those very small but all-important 3½ days discovered in Revelation 11 and Daniel 9.

The Kingdom Calendar is either a human invention of grand luck or ordained from the beginning of time as God's ancient end-time Calendar, to be unsealed just before events occur. Time will be the judge on this matter. I certainly did not seek this out or labor to create an end-time chart; nor, did I expect to uncover this unique connection 30 years ago in my mid-30s. What happened, happened. I'm just an ordinary man, who has experienced a few extra-ordinary events. Miracles, by all accounts, a visitation and calling, although these matters are personal in nature; family connections to historical events, and various signs and happenings. I'm still learning what all this means. In the meantime, let's consider the evidence.

First, no time chart published in the last 2,000 years comes close to the degree of verification illustrated by the Biblical facts, mathematics, history and matching current events. This will become clearer as proof continues to build. Second, no other chart employs *every significant counting period in Daniel and Revelation*. Third, having accounted for all the major timelines, no other chart aligns from beginning to end directly between the Biblical Festivals, celebrations and annual fasts, still observed today by Jews and Gentiles alike, to prove its authenticity.

As mentioned, if God follows the Festival pattern, the 1,290 counting days of Daniel 12:11 would begin at Purim, commemorative of Jewish survival despite Persian (Iranian) threats to destroy the Jews (which dangers are bound to escalate in the last days) and will end with the abomination being set up exactly 3½ days before Yom Kippur. That, by itself, would be amazing. However, following the same pattern the reoccurring 1,260 counting days, found seven times in Daniel 7:25; 12:7; and, Revelation 11:2; 11:3; 12:6; 12:14; 13:5 (indicating this period to be the primary length of final events), begin at Passover and end as well exactly 3½ days before Yom Kippur—the exact point the two witnesses (referred to as the two anointed ones—Zechariah 4:1-14) are martyred in Jerusalem's streets and remain unburied for 3½ days, according to Revelation 11:9-11 and Daniel 9:25-27. It's interesting to note that Judaism teaches Elijah will arrive at Passover to announce redemption, the precise point the two witnesses are to begin their 1,260 days of ministry, as shown on *The Kingdom Calendar*.

In addition to these two Biblical timelines, we discover the 2,300 evenings and mornings—which in the lesson series will prove to be 1,150 counting days associated first with Satan and his army desecrating Heaven's Sanctuary by war; and second, creating the need to surrender the Temple for an end-time courtroom judgment during this period (Daniel 7:9-10; Daniel 8:9-14, 26; Revelation 12:7-9). This 1,150 day counting period fits precisely between Tisha B' Av and Yom Kippur—bracketed by two of the most significant and solemn annual fasts in Judaism and the Scriptures. Satan's army will battle against Michael and His host of angels but will be defeated. This will force an official review of Satan and the Man of Sin's evil activities, leading to the verdict that Yeshua Messiah must reign supreme over all the universe henceforth, followed by His coronation as KING. The 1,150 days culminate with the Temple's reconsecration at Yom Kippur, when all sins were dealt with annually in the ancient Sanctuary services and verdicts for life or death are determined. Final events relate to historical patterns and Temple ceremonies both in timing and occurrences: Tisha B'Av is the fast of the 5th month referred to in Zechariah 7:3,5 and 8:19, still observed religiously, commemorating war and the desolation of Solomon's Temple by the Babylonians. The Day of Atonement (Yom Kippur) is the holiest day of the year, and an annual fast occurs on this day of judgment to "afflict your soul" (Leviticus 16:29-31). Jews fast and pray that God will "accept our repentance, forgive our sins, and seal our verdict" for life, and not for death. "But the court will sit, and his power will be taken away and completely destroyed forever. Then the sovereignty, power and greatness of all the kingdoms under heaven will be handed over to the holy people of the Most High. His kingdom will be an everlasting kingdom, and all rulers will worship and obey Him,' Daniel 7:26-27.

The 490 days begin with the declaration to rebuild a devastated Jerusalem and will end according to Daniel with one final week (of seven days), that is also split into two 3½ day periods, at which time the two anointed ones are killed in Jerusalem's streets. Then, the evil ruler will stop daily sacrifices and set up the abomination on the Temple Mount in either a partially or fully rebuilt Temple. What follows is the total and final desolation of the beloved City and Temple structures by the armies of the nations, claims the prophecies of Daniel 9:27 and Yeshua's prediction in Luke 21:20-22, to name just two of many.

Despite all this mounting evidence, doubt about *The Kingdom Calendar* is to be expected until the prophetic timelines begin to match world events and march toward completion; even then, many will not believe. The future shaking in Israel will cause terrible devastation to the City, and the loss of treasured lives. The Temple Mount with Islamic structures will fall in ruins and the Western Wall will collapse, taking away daily worship/pilgrimage (Daniel 12:11). "Jesus left the Temple and was walking away when His disciples came up to Him to call His attention to its buildings. "Do you see all these things?" he asked. "Truly I tell you, not one stone here will be left on another; everyone will be thrown down." Matthew (24:1-8) continues, "As Jesus was sitting on the Mount of Olives, the disciples came to Him privately. "Tell us," they said, "when will this happen, and what will be the sign of Your coming and of the end of the age?" Jesus answered: "Watch out that no one deceives you. For many will come in My Name, claiming, 'I am the Messiah,' and will deceive many. You will hear of wars and rumors of wars, but see to it that you are not alarmed. Such things must happen, but the end is still to come. Nation will rise against nation, and kingdom against kingdom. There will be famines and <u>earthquakes in various places</u>. All these are the beginning of birth pains."

Many will come in the name of Jesus, advancing deceptive and unscriptural views to the masses. Sights and sounds will hold higher value than "thus says the LORD". Conflict will escalate between the nations, initiating the end-time events Messiah foretold in Matthew 24 and the mysterious counting periods written in the Book of Truth (Daniel 10:21). Once the Jerusalem tragedy occurs, we are to begin counting the prophetic days of Daniel and Revelation, which will lead day by day to the return of Messiah and His Eternal Kingdom.

At the end of the 1,290, 1,260, 1,150 and 490 counting days, Michael—the Seventh Angel will stand and descend with shofar blast, and His thunderous ear-piercing Archangel's voice will reverberate around the globe (Daniel 12:1; 1 Thessalonians 4:16; John 5:25). The martyred saints will be raised along with the two witnesses to ascend to Heaven, while the great tribulation of plagues against the rebellious will commence. Starting at Purim, every one of the counting periods of *The Kingdom Calendar* will march to their conclusion on schedule including the 1,335 days (Daniel 12:12) with no further delay, based on Messiah's sworn statement to His two witnesses—His "servants the prophets"—Moses and Elijah on the banks of the Tigris river: They were told, "It will be for a time [one year], times [two years] and half a time [half a year]. When the power of the holy people has been finally broken, all these things will be completed," Daniel 12:7. The mystery of God will be accomplished.

As noted, this is the first end-time chart in which *all* the significant prophetic timelines (3½ days; 490 days; 1,150 days, 1,260 days, 1,290 days and 1,335 days) revealed in the books of both Daniel and Revelation are included; not one is missing, including the 490 days found in Daniel 9—also known as 70 weeks (which represents *70 literal weeks*—just as the Hebrew reads, about one year and four months). The periods were first chronologically aligned into a chart almost 30 years ago in 1990 based on the study of the books of Daniel and Revelation, with no realization there was or could be a connection to the Biblical Festivals. Two years later, after learning more of the Festivals' importance to final events, it was discovered the charted timelines of Daniel and Revelation fit between the Biblical Festivals *to the day* over a typical three and one half (3½) year Festival period, using the commonly accepted Jewish calendar observed today and established by

Hillel II around 359 A.D., well after the timelines in Daniel and Revelation were penned. Either I was incredibly lucky, or I had stumbled across, by God's grace, an ancient mystery.

The Western Wall, Wailing Wall or Kotel is the last standing remnant of the Second Temple, and this ancient 62' high limestone wall in Jerusalem's Old City became a place of Jewish worship and prayer following the Roman destruction in 70 A.D. Daily, thousands of Jews and Gentiles visit the Wall in reverence and awe; more than 10,000,000 visitors each year. However, a Jerusalem quake will take away the "daily" worship at the Western Wall and Temple Mount. The loss of the Temple Mount structures and toppled Wall will immediately initiate the 1,290 and 1,335 day counting periods. Simultaneously, we will see Middle-East upheaval, an Iranian confrontation and the escalation of events leading to World War III. Global tragedies and pandemonium would rise, leading to the arrival of Satan's Man of Sin and the beginning of the 1,260 day counting period, followed shortly after by the start of the 1,150 counting days. The 490 days (70 Weeks) will come into focus later during the end-times. The 490 days represent the final counting period specific to the *nation of Israel*: *"Seventy weeks are determined for your people [Israel] and for your holy city [Jerusalem],"* which includes a decree to rebuild an earthquake, war torn and devastated Jerusalem (Daniel 9:24-27), during a period when the holy sites, for the most part, are under Gentile control (Revelation 11:1-3).

To better appreciate why the match between the prophetic timelines and the Festivals is significant, establishing the Calendar's authenticity, consider this: The Biblical Festivals are not stationary, as for example birthdays, which fall on the same day each year, or the Christian holiday of Christmas that is celebrated every year on December 25. The Festivals shift to different dates each year. Let's consider Passover; this Festival was observed on April 23, 2016, on April 11, 2017, followed by March 31, 2018, and, in 2019 on April 20. This fluctuation of the Biblical Festivals is due to a complex lunar/solar calendar. Just imagine the outer ring of Jewish Festivals on the graph floats back and forth independently from the inner January—December Gregorian calendar ring; moreover, the Festivals can also have varying days between them.

At creation God said, "Let there be lights in the firmament of the heavens to divide the day from the night; and let them be for signs and seasons ["*moedim*"—Festivals], and for days and years," Genesis 1:14. When Moses received instructions from Jehovah, the command in Deuteronomy 16:1 was to "observe the month of Abib, and keep the Passover." This made it necessary to become acquainted with the position of the sun; and, the command to offer sacrifices according to the "new moon" (2 Chronicles 2:4; 8:13; Ezra 3:5) made it necessary to watch the phases of the moon. However, today's Festival schedule culminates from debate, disagreements and adjustments through the course of Jewish history. The Jewish calendar can be divided into three periods—the Biblical, the Talmudic, and the post-Talmudic—all effecting the timing of the annual Festival observations and celebrations. The study of astronomy is largely attributed to the need of fixing the dates of the Festivals due to the Diaspora (scattering of Jews worldwide), which calendar was established by Rabbi Hillel II several centuries after the prophet Daniel and John the Revelator penned the end-time timelines.

We understand the fulfillment of God's appointed times is in His hands. We have seen and know of many signs (tetrad blood moons, Shemitah years, the Jubilee cycles, Israel's 50, 70, 100, and 120 year historical connections, and global events) pointing to this current Festival cycle as a significant watch period. However, we don't know God's timing; any match of *The Kingdom Calendar* to events would be ordained by Almighty God as a gift of "*wisdom to the wise*"... from an all-knowing Father who "*reveals deep and hidden things*" (Daniel 2:22). God will fulfill His appointed times according to His divine purposes and on the schedule of His choosing, and through the means of His own divine will. The Jerusalem event could occur on any given day, on any given month... then, the counting would begin. *The Kingdom Calendar* may simply be a template, and therefore events may not begin exactly on the Festival schedule. On the other hand, God may have ordained in ancient times the Purim connection to the Jerusalem disaster, just as the Calendar shows, and other starting points connected to His Festivals. However, we can have confidence that final events are tied to the fall Festival season, just as the spring Festivals were fulfilled during the Passover crucifixion week and at Shavuot (Pentecost). God can change time; as He controls the earth, sun and the moon, and His times and seasons. We are told, there will be a "sudden" and unexpected Day of the LORD event for those who are not anticipating His return: "I will send My messenger [Elijah, the anointed one], who will prepare the way before Me [for 1,260 days]. Then **suddenly** the LORD you are seeking will come to His Temple; the Messenger of the Covenant, whom you desire, will come," says the LORD Almighty. But who can endure the Day of His coming [down]?" Malachi 3:1-2.

Therefore, we can be assured based on God's Word the sorrowful Jerusalem disaster will truly come to pass, when the prophetic counting periods will begin—providing curious and wise students of the Word divine dates of end-time disaster and deliverance. Messiah's sworn promise to the final generation is that He will open the minds of those who seek prayerfully wisdom from God, and from His inspired Word and prophecies (Daniel 12:9-10). With the devastation in Jerusalem, daily worship at the Western Wall and Temple Mount will be taken away, which will also coincide to some degree with the prophetic war foretold in Daniel 8 with Iran (Persia/Elam). When Israel's citizens are shattered from the Jerusalem quake, the wise will begin counting, day by day; and, the counting days will ultimately end on schedule with amazing accuracy. God will not lead us astray, my friends.

In summary, God's Word reveals His Yearly Festivals established around the 15 century B.C. at Mt. Sinai and recorded in Leviticus, followed by the annual Fasts in Zechariah founded around the 6th century B.C. with the destruction of Solomon's Temple and the Babylonian exile. The annual Purim celebration was inaugurated during the 4th century B.C., as recorded in Esther 9:1, 17, 22. From there, we add the prophetic counting periods revealed in the books of Daniel (5th century B.C.) and Revelation (1st century A.D.). These very precise counting periods in Daniel are the "seventy 'sevens'"—490 days; "2300 evenings and mornings"—1150 days; "time, times and a half"—1260 days; 1290 days; and 1335 days; followed by the five-time repeated 1260 days in the book of Revelation, known also as "42 months" and "time, times and a half". The pivotal three and one half (3½) days that just precede the Day of Atonement (Yom Kippur), which are essential for **The Kingdom Calendar** to align, are found in both Daniel 9:27 and Revelation 11:7-12. Finally, we add the Festival Calendar Hillel II established during the 4th century A.D., hundreds of years after the books of Daniel and Revelation were written, which Festival schedule is still in use today in Judaism. All these factors, both Biblical and historical, spread out over two millennia, must miraculously intersect to bring about **The Kingdom Calendar** we see today. Its purpose? To reveal the timing of modern-day events centered on Israel, Jerusalem and the epicenter of prophecy— the Temple Mount, to offer hope to stand firm in confidence by knowing the end is fast approaching when Messiah will rule and reign; this, at a time when many others are giving up their faith during a tumultuous period of deception, imprisonment, hatred, persecution and death.

Jesus warned of these matters, "Then you will be handed over to be persecuted and put to death, and you will be hated by all nations because of Me. At that time many will turn away from the faith and will betray and hate each other, and many false prophets will appear and deceive many people. Because of the increase of wickedness, the love of most will grow cold, but the one who stands firm to the end will be saved. And this gospel of the kingdom will be preached in the whole world as a testimony to all nations, and then the end will come," Matthew 24:9-14.

The Kingdom Calendar

FOR A FREE, HIGH RESOLUTION PDF COLOR
KINGDOM CALENDAR
GO TO:

WWW.FOCUSONTHEPROPHECIES.ORG

g Periods 2019-2022 ☙ Divine Dates of Disaster & Deliverance

Daniel 12:12

the end of the 1,335 days," Daniel 12:12.
to All Nations—Mat. 24:14; Rev. 14:6

Three Final Warning Messages Proclaimed
By Three Messengers:
1) Judgment is Come
2) Babylon is Fallen
3) Beware of the Mark of the Beast
Harvest Time Has Arrived
Revelation 14:6-12
6th
Seal

YOM KIPPUR
RESURRECTION AND TAKING OF PROPHETS & OVERCOMERS TO OPENED TEMPLE
Oct 5
2022
10 Tishri
Lev. 23:26-32

THE DAY OF THE LORD
19

GREAT DAY OF THE LORD
MESSIAH'S RETURN WITH OVERCOMERS
GATHERING OF HIS 144,000 ELECT
Matt. 24:30-31

Daniel 12:11

causes desolation is set up, there will be 1,290 days," Daniel 12:11.

ABOMINATION
Set Up On Temple Mount
18

THE GREAT TRIBULATION
Global Destruction
21

Elul Month of Repentance
Ten Days of Awe

; Revelation 11:2; 11:3; 12:6; 12:14; 13:5

ss His saints and try to change the set times and the laws. The
m for a time, times and half a time," Daniel 7:25.

then All Prophetic Events will be Completed—Dan. 7:25 / 12:7
Spiritual-Political Authority for 1,260 Days—Rev. 13:5
Arrive at Passover to Proclaim the Future Redemption,
es of Warning for 1,260 Days—Rev. 11:3
or by Gentile Armies for 1,260 Days—Rev. 11:2
cpared and Persecuted. Many Are Martyred,
Elect are Protected—Rev. 12:6, 14

30 Days   6 ½   3 ½

ROSH HA-SHANAH
15
Sep 26
2022
1 Tishri
Lev. 23:23-25

17

7th Seal
7th Trumpet
7th Vial

1st Trumpet, 1st Vial
2nd Trumpet, 2nd Vial
3rd Trumpet, 3rd Vial
4th Trumpet, 4th Vial
5th Trumpet, 5th Vial
Time of Jacob's Trouble
Jer. 30:7-8
144,000 Elect Scattered
Mat. 24:15-16

6th Seal
6th Trumpet
6th Vial

1,150 Days – Daniel 8:14

and mornings; then the Sanctuary [in Heaven] will be reconsecrated," Daniel 8:14.
ed. Judgment Court Convenes in Heaven to Review Evidence & End the Great Rebellion

Anointed Ruling Prophets, Elijah and Moses, Arrive at Jerusalem Dan. 8:26

Two Anointed Prophets Killed & Power Broken Rev. 11:7-8

J E R U S A L E M   D E S T R O Y E D

Messiah's Wedding to New Jerusalem
Rev. 19:7

A R M A G E D D O N

DECREE TO REBUILD JERUSALEM
13
June 2
2021
Dan. 9:25

14

TZOM Gedaliah
16

Sacrifice/Offering Stopped
Dan. 9:27

SUKKOT
20
Oct 10-16
2022
15 Tishri
Lev. 23:33-44

Shemini Atzeret Simchat Torah
Oct 17/18
Lev. 23:36

TISHA B'AV   SHABBAT NACHAMU

490 Days – Daniel 9:24   3 ½   3 ½

5   35

49 Days
7 Weeks
July 21 2020

434 Days
62 Weeks

7 days
1 Week

40 Days of God's Wrath
Days Will Be Shortened
"The people of the [evil] ruler who will come will destroy the city and the sanctuary," Daniel 9:27. "For the sake of the elect those days will be shortened...No one knows that day or hour...the coming of the Son of Man," Mat. 24:22, 36.

70 Weeks Decreed for Israel and Jerusalem
"Seventy 'sevens' are decreed for your people and your holy city to finish transgression, to put an end to sin, to atone for wickedness, to bring in everlasting righteousness, to seal up vision and prophecy and to anoint the Most Holy. Know and understand this: From the time the word goes out to restore and rebuild Jerusalem until the anointed one [Elijah] the ruler comes, there will be seven 'sevens,' and sixty-two 'sevens.' It will be rebuilt with streets and trench...In times of trouble...[then] the anointed one will be put to death," Dan. 9:24-26.

ABOUT THE KINGDOM CALENDAR

45th Year Anniversary ♦ Yom Kippur War (Oct 6-25, 1973)

For Calendar purposes, God's Festivals begin on Jerusalem time. Events could occur the day before, on or soon after the dates indicated. However, despite the efforts reflected in this Calendar, any attempt to establish the timing of final events is against all human odds; and, any match would be a God-ordained miracle above and beyond any genius of man. God will fulfill His appointed times in keeping with His divine purposes and on the schedule of His choosing. A full listing of Jewish Festival celebrations can be found from various sources. THE KINGDOM CALENDAR is not to scale. This Calendar may be duplicated if copied in its entirety and without any alteration of any kind. Copyright © 2018 by Kevin R. Swift

APITAL & RESTORATION
War + 50 Full Years = 2018

M I L L E N N I A L   R E I G N   F R O M   N E W   J E R U S A L E M

IEL & REVELATION

ere I will enter into judgment   against them... for they scattered My people among the nations and divided up My land," Joel 3:1-2.

Insights In Prophecy

Unlock The Ancient Mysteries Of Daniel & Revelation

BIBLE DISCOVERY SERIES

Lesson 1

BOUNDARIES OF THE APPOINTED TIMES & SEASONS

Read Daniel 12

- **Discover The Primary Elements Of The "Collective Futurist" View**
- **Unlock The 1,290 Days and 1,335 Days of Bible Prophecy**
- **Understand The Precise Timing Of End-Time Events**

Our first lesson in the **Insights In Prophecy** series delves right into the predictions of Daniel 12. It may seem odd that we would start with the last chapter first. However, in this chapter we will discover three important time periods of the final great conflict. If we grasp the importance of these three and their connection, we will find the other chapters and their timelines begin to line up, one by one, into a charted pattern. The first period in chapter 12 is well-known and discussed among prophetic students—the "time, times and a half," meaning, 1,260 days. However, two other time periods—1,290 days and 1,335 days— are nearly always neglected or given very little commentary, because scholars and teachers have not been willing or able to offer plausible explanations for them. Those who hold to the "historicist" view of prophecy cannot find any valid dates in the past for their fulfillment, and "futurists" in most cases simply suggest they somehow extend beyond the 1,260 days at the end of time.

Names have meaning. Our names are given to us at birth, and often reflect our personality or tell a story. My name **Kevin** means "beloved" and **Swift** means "one who is fast, a messenger". You might enjoy checking out your own name. Jesus—known in Hebrew as "Yeshua" means "salvation". Names are

important to God. In fact, He promises to give you—if you persevere faithfully through severe trial—an intimate name that only you and the Divine will know: *"To him who overcomes... I will give him a white stone, and on the stone a **new name** written which no one knows except him who receives it,"* Revelation 2:17. The new name is likely the name of adoption; adopted persons took the name of the family into which they were adopted.

In the Word of God, our Creator reveals Himself with over 200 names and titles. This brings home the fact that there is no one "who is like God"; He is indescribable and multi-faceted. However, God attempts to help us know Him more fully with names such as "Advocate, Almighty, Alpha & Omega, Ancient of Days and Prince of Peace". He also refers to Himself as earth, food and liquid--"the Rock, Bread of Life and Living Water" and even animals--the "Lion and the Lamb". All these have spiritual meaning and offer insight into the One who loves us. However, creature names do not diminish or lower God, but raises Him to the Highest and Holiest above all. He is all things to all of His creations in Heaven and on earth.

Our first lesson will focus on Daniel 12, where ***Michael--the Prince*** *"shall stand up"* from a seated position— a position of authority and thrones, and what follows is both earth-shaking and life-giving. In this regard, Messiah is the ultimate "mal'akh" (מַלְאָךְ) in Hebrew—meaning "messenger"—the Messenger the Covenant (Malachi 3:1) at Mt. Sinai—the Messenger of our Salvation.

In this series, we will look closely at the "Collective Futurist" view of Bible prophecy, which combines the times and events of both Daniel and Revelation into one interconnected whole. Both the historicist and futurist views apply many of Daniel's prophetic passages to events in the past; however, the view

Insights In Prophecy
Unlock The Ancient Mysteries Of Daniel & Revelation
BIBLE DISCOVERY SERIES

introduced in this lesson series contends that Daniels four visions, which he personally received (chapters 7-12), are to find fulfillment during the final conflict, which Daniel 8:19 calls "the appointed time of the end."

Daniel 12 is a chapter associated with the *mystery* of prophecy. How? Daniel was told to seal up the words. The times and events would be understood *only* at the time of the end. All attempts in the last two thousand years to fully understand prophecy has been thwarted by God. Only at the time of the end when the clock nears midnight and predictions begin to meet reality will the final unsealing come.

Daniel 12 portrays final events and times associated with those events and are a summation of the previous chapters of Daniel; that is, an overview of the book and the prophetic warnings written therein. If we become familiar with chapter 12, we have a chance of understanding the remainder of the visions. The times and events of this chapter represent the *overarching support* of the end-time prophecies given in Scripture, as prophecy hangs on these three major lengths of time. Daniel writes that the wicked will not understand, but the wise will; then he reveals the mysterious 1,290 and 1,335 days. Therefore, we can know that we are nearing the end of the age when there is a focus upon and a grasp of these time periods.

Michael—The Archangel

Considering the language of Daniel 12:1-3, we know that this chapter of prophecy refers to the future at the very end of time. Once the Man of Sin enters Jerusalem, between the Dead Sea and Mediterranean Sea, the holy mountain of God (Daniel 11:45), prophecy promises he will quickly come to his end. Antichrist will set up his pavilion, followed by his abomination, which will bring about Michael's decided and immediate response. The name Michael is not mentioned often in the Bible but, by comparing texts, we can learn the Messenger's identity.

1. What titles and activities are assigned to Michael that helps identify who He is (Daniel 10:13, 21; Jude 9)? _____

Michael is a powerful military commander, called "Chief Prince", and then Daniel was told in a more personal way, he is "*your* Prince". He is also associated with the dispute over the bodily resurrection of Moses in Jude 9; and, in fact is the only Archangel mentioned in the Scriptures. Michael would not argue with the Devil, who evidently believed Moses was unworthy of a resurrection back to life because of his sin (Deuteronomy 32:44-52). Michael did not get into a lengthy debate, but the Bible says that He quickly reprimanded Satan, and raised Moses to life. Why would Satan argue over the body of Moses? Satan doesn't want anyone resurrected; the death of the believers is his delight. How he must have trembled when our Messiah rose from the tomb! The religious leaders who sent Jesus to the cross were clearly inspired by Satan. Their idea of sealing the tomb (Matthew 27:64) was likewise inspired by the Adversary. He thought himself victorious at Christ's death in securing his position of power.

At the end of Moses' term of service, the prophet went to "the mountain of Nebo, to the top of Pisgah" across the Jordan Valley from Jericho. There the LORD showed him the Promised Land. "And Moses the servant of the LORD died there in Moab, as the LORD had said. He buried him in Moab, in the valley opposite Beth Peor, but to this day no one knows where his grave is," (Deuteronomy 34:5-6). Connecting this with what we learned from Jude 9, we see that the same LORD who buried him raised him to life again and took him to Heaven. Therefore, we find Moses with Elijah in the transfiguration (Mark 9:1-7). If he could, Satan would keep his victims eternally in the grave. Praise God for the One who is our Life-giver, too. Moses' resurrection was based on Christ's future victory on the cross (Revelation 1:18).

Insights In Prophecy
Unlock The Ancient Mysteries Of Daniel & Revelation
BIBLE DISCOVERY SERIES

From A Scholar's Point Of View

Matthew Henry's Commentary on the Whole Bible (1706-1721)
Daniel 12:1

I. Jesus Christ shall appear his church's patron and protector: *At that time,* when the persecution is at the hottest, *Michael shall stand up,* v. 1. The angel had told Daniel what a firm friend Michael was to the church, ch. 10:21. He all along showed this friendship in the upper world; the angels knew it; but now *Michael shall stand* up in his providence, and work deliverance for the Jews, *when he sees that their power is gone,* Deu. 32:3. 6. Christ is *that great prince,* for he is the *prince of the kings of the earth,* Rev. 1:5. And, if he stand up for his church, who can be against it? But this is not all: *At that time* (that is, soon after) Michael shall stand up for the working out of our eternal salvation; the Son of God shall be incarnate, shall be *manifested to destroy the works of the devil.* Christ *stood for the children of our people* when he was made sin and a curse for them, stood in their stead as a sacrifice, bore the cure for them, to bear it from them. He stands for them in the intercession he ever lives to make within the veil, stands up for them, and stands their friend... Christ shall *stand at the latter day upon the earth,* shall appear for the complete redemption of all his.

II. When Christ appears he will recompense tribulation to those that trouble his people. There shall *be a time of trouble,* threatening to all, but ruining to all the implacable enemies of God's kingdom among men, such *trouble as never was since there was a nation.* This is applicable. 1. To the destruction of Jerusalem, which Christ calls (perhaps with an eye to this prediction) such a *great tribulation as was not since the beginning of the world to this time,* Mt. 24:21. This the angel had spoken much of (ch. 9:26, 27); and it happened about the same time that Christ set up the gospel-kingdom in the world, that Michael our prince *stands up.* Or, 2. To the judgment of the great day, that day that shall *burn as an oven,* and consume the proud and all that do wickedly; that will be such a *day of trouble* as never was to all those whom Michael our prince stands against.

III. He will work salvation for his people: *"At that time thy people shall be delivered,* delivered from the mischief and ruin designed them... even all those that were marked for preservation, that were *written among the living,"* Isa. 4:3. When Christ comes into the world he will save his spiritual Israel from sin and hell, and will, at his second coming, complete their salvation, even the salvation of as many as were given him, as many as have *their names in the book of life,* Rev. 20:15. They were written there before the world, and will be *found written* there at the end of the world, when the books shall be opened.

Henry, M. 1996, c1991. *Matthew Henry's Commentary on the whole Bible : Complete and unabridged in one volume* . Hendrickson: Peabody

---

2. What titles and activities are assigned to the One named Michael (Revelation 12:7; 1 Thessalonians 4:16; John 5:25)? _____

_____

As shown in the box above, Matthew Henry shows Michael is another name for Jesus. Hel is the Prince of the host, or angels, the Archangel, and One associated with raising the dead. His name means "who is like God?" There is none like God!

Jews believe Michael to be their great protector and one of seven angels who surround God's throne. The Hebrew word for *angel* is not identifying creatures with wings; "mal'akh" (מַלְאָךְ) is primarily the standard Hebrew Bible word for "messenger", both human and divine, though it is less used for human messengers. He is first introduced in this vision at Daniel 10:5-6: "I [Daniel] looked up and there before me was a Man *dressed in linen*, with a belt of the finest gold around His waist. His body was like chrysolite, His face like lightning, His eyes like flaming torches, His arms and legs like the gleam of burnished bronze, and His voice like the sound of a multitude." Sacred linen garments were worn by the High Priest on the Day of Atonement (Leviticus 16:4) upon entrance into the Holy of Holies (the inner room of the Temple where the Ark of the Covenant was set in place). Michael's linen garment signifies His priestly activities relating to Yom Kippur—the Day of Atonement—the day associated with ushering in the Day of the LORD. Messiah is granted authority to rule forever. Michael represents, in title only, the great Messenger to mankind... the living eternal Son of God, who was with the Father from the beginning—the Alpha and Omega. Revelation 22:12-23 says, "Look, I am coming soon! My reward is with Me, and I will give to each person according to what they have done. I am the Alpha and the Omega, the First and the Last, the Beginning and the End."

Great Giants Of Faith Believed Michael Represented Jesus

The view that Michael could not possibly represent Jesus is a modern anomaly that should be discarded. In this lesson we are simply harking back to the accepted view not more than a couple of centuries ago, which assessment the Scriptures clearly prove to be true. Theologian and the Protestant reformation pastor **John Calvin** wrote, "As we stated yesterday, Michael may mean an angel; but I embrace the opinion of those who refer this to the *person of Christ*, because it suits the subject best to represent him as standing forward for the defense of his elect people." The great theologian, **John Wesley,** wrote in his commentary on Daniel 10:21, "*Michael - Christ* alone is the protector of his church, when all the princes of the earth desert or oppose it." And, the **Geneva Bible Commentary** says, "The angel here notes two things: first that the Church will be in great affliction and trouble at Christ's coming, and next that God will send his angel to deliver it, whom he here *calls Michael, meaning Christ*, who is proclaimed by the preaching of the Gospel." The Geneva Bible was produced by John Calvin, John Knox, Myles Coverdale, John Foxe and other English refugees in Geneva, Switzerland... fleeing the persecution of Roman Catholic Queen "Bloody" Mary in England. Mary would not tolerate the Protestant Geneva Bible, which proclaimed the Pope an "antichrist" in its commentary notes. Printed from 1560 until 1644, the Geneva Bible is the only Bible to ever surpass the 1611 King James Bible in popularity among the people of its day.

3. Daniel 12:1 indicates that when Michael stands up there is a Great Tribulation. Compare this with Bible passages that reveal when God arises His wrath begins. How are they the same?

Psalm 3:7-8 _____

Psalm 9:19-20 _____

Psalm 10:12-16 _____

Psalm 17:13-15 _____

Psalm 68:1-3 _____

Isaiah 14:22-24 _____

4. This time of trouble will be greater than any other proceeding in world history according to Matthew 24:21-22. The Man of Sin brings about the Great Tribulation because of his actions. What is it (Matthew 24:15)? _____

The setting up the abomination in Jerusalem (The Kingdom Calendar—Pt. 17).

5. Who are delivered at the time Michael stands in Daniel 12:1? _____

Daniel's people—Israel, are delivered, both natural (Jews) and spiritual (grafted in Gentiles).

6. Daniel introduces a "special" resurrection in verse 2 when Michael stands. What two classes are raised (Daniel 12:2)? _____

Some to life (the saved), and some to everlasting contempt (the lost). Revelation 1:7 mentions those who crucified Messiah and who most opposed the Savior may indeed see Him return in His glory. And surely those who have died for the cause of Christ will be raised to experience His glorious appearing.

7. What will the raised and living believers, the "wise" (margin says "teachers") who are a part of this special group, look like (Daniel 12:3)? _____

God's faithful, the wise teachers of truth, will literally shine with brilliance brighter than anyone could imagine—like the stars above. Their radiance will glow throughout the eternal ages, and when the believers travel, they may be seen as stars streaking across the heavens. "No eye has seen, no ear has heard, no mind has conceived what God has prepared for those who love him," I Corinthians 2:9. What a glorious future for the believers who remain faithful to the end (Matthew 24:13).

"They that be *teachers* shall shine as the brightness of the firmament." That is, of course, in the context of the chapter; those who teach the prophetic truths that will be unsealed at the time of the end (Daniel 12:9-10), and who lead others to a knowledge of the book's revealed truths at the time when the events recorded are being fulfilled. As the world estimates loss and profit, it will no doubt be costly to be teachers of truth in the last days. Speaking out for the Master will cost reputation, ease, comfort and prosperity. Teaching unpopular truths in order that others might be saved will involve labors, crosses, sacrifices, loss of friendships, ridicule and persecution; and, even life itself. However, through the prophet Daniel's written testimony these servants of God are promised life without end, as the stars forever.

Someone wrote long ago that in only a matter of a few years, all things gather the mold of age and the odor of decay. But the stars shine on in their glory as in the beginning of time. Centuries and cycles have come and gone, and kingdoms have risen and slowly passed away. We go back even to the earliest moment when order was evoked out of chaos, and "the morning stars sang together, and all the sons of God shouted for joy" (Job 38:7), and there the stars were shining. How long before this we do not know. Astronomers tell us of nebulae lying on the farthest outposts of telescopic vision, whose light in its never ceasing flight would consume five million years in reaching this planet. Yet their brightness is not dimmed. These glorious lights shine on in undiminished glory. Likewise, this collection of teachers will shine—those who turn many to righteousness. They shall bring joy even to the heart of the Redeemer; therefore, these teachers of righteousness will receive reward and positions for their servant-heart.

8. When will the prophecies about end-time events be truly understood (Daniel 12:4)?_____
_____

9. What kind of chaos can we expect in this world as we enter the three and one-half years of trouble, according to Matthew 24:6-8? _____

Insights In Prophecy
Unlock The Ancient Mysteries Of Daniel & Revelation
BIBLE DISCOVERY SERIES

The unimaginable holocaust of wars, bloodshed, social disorder, diseases, famine, earthquakes and natural disasters will usher in massive human losses and property damage. Jesus said these events would set in motion the great sorrows of the end, and with it a frantic search for truth and understanding of God's prophetic Word.

The escalation of bloodshed and nature's wrath are provoked by principalities and powers in high places (Ephesians 6:12), so that Satan's evil scheme for world dominion might unfold. Once pandemonium breaks out, demonic apparitions (2 Corinthians 11:13-14), signs and wonders (Matthew 24:24) in the heavens will be revealed around the globe. Planet Earth will never be the same again, and its days as the planet of peace and safety, will be numbered.

The Two Anointed Witnesses

Daniel 12:5 reveals that Daniel the prophet saw in vision two individuals, one on each side of the river. It would seem that these two holy ones play an important role in final events, for they are present witnesses to the vision, and they are asking the all-important question, "how long?" We can identify these *two witnesses* to the events by comparing the similarities between Daniel 12 and its counterpart, Revelation 10:1-7.

The Man clothed in linen (a priestly robe), identified as Michael, the Archangel, makes a declaration in Daniel 12:7 that when the three and one-half years (or three and a "part" years—KJV reference) are completed and the holy people (believers) are scattered, all prophecy will be "completed".

Joining John Calvin, John Wesley, Matthew Henry and countless other historical church leaders, many commentators also agree that in Revelation 10:1-7, the Mighty Angel (Archangel) is representative of Christ because of the description the prophet John gives. The Cruden's Concordance confirms that oftentimes the usage of "*angel*"—meaning "messenger" in the Bible is referring to Christ, as in the passage in Revelation 10. *"A messenger, or bringer of tidings, and is applied, [2] To Christ, who is the Mediator and Head of the church, Zech. 1:12, Revelation 10:1."* Seven verses later (Revelation 10:7) the Mighty Angel is declared to be the "Seventh Angel" who makes the same promise as Michael did centuries before. In the days of His voice, "the mystery of God should be finished, as He hath declared unto His [Christ's] servants the prophets." And, when did He declare it? Many centuries earlier, two men stood on each bank of the river described in Daniel 12:5. When Daniel saw the vision, he encountered these two witnesses who heard the same declaration of time with their own ears.

10. Who did Peter, James and John see with Yeshua in His future glory (Matthew 17:1-3), one on each side of Him? _____

Moses and Elijah were seen and identified as standing with Jesus in His future glory. Likewise, in Daniel 12, the two witnesses to Michael's declaration, one on each side of this Man in linen, are no doubt Moses and Elijah, Christ's "servants the prophets" who would be intimately involved in the final appointed time. They certainly would want to know about the final conflict, which is why one of the two asked the probing question.

11. What does one of the two witnesses ask the "Man" in linen, Michael, in Daniel 12:6 about the end of time? _____

How long before these astonishing events are fulfilled? Michael holds up both hands in Daniel 12:7 and swears by Heaven a specific time when all the prophetic events will be completed. And, not surprisingly, the 1,260 days, or three and a part years is the exact amount of time the two witnesses in the book of Revelation are assigned to minister on earth during the last appointed time.

Earlier in time Messiah came to Abraham and was referred to as the "Angel of the LORD" (Hebrew "malak"—again, which simply means "messenger"). He swore by oath a blessing on his seed (Genesis 22:15-18). Hebrews 6:13 clarifies that when Messiah made His promise to Abraham, since there was no one greater for Him to swear by, *He swore by Himself,* saying, "I will surely bless you and give you many descendents." Only God can swear a promise and know for sure it will come to pass. In fact, there are around 50 references in Scripture to God vowing a promise by His own Name. Here we have evidence that Jesus is referred to as an "angel". We need to suppress our misguided Western views; an angel is simply a "malak"—"messenger" from Heaven, and not always a description of winged creatures.

According to Daniel 12:7-8, at the completion of the "time" (one year), "times" (two years) and "part" (half, or part of a year) and the breaking apart or scattering of God's people, which will be finalized at the death of God's two last-day witnesses (in the example of Zechariah 13:7; and, Matthew 25:26), prophecy will be fulfilled and finished. Daniel was greatly disturbed and desired to understand the outcome.

12. In Daniel 12:7 the "man in linen" (priestly garments—Michael) restates a key time frame that was first mentioned in Daniel 7:25, which we will look at in our studies on this chapter. This same period is repeated many times in the book of Revelation, which signifies it to be the primary end-time period. How is it described? _____

Daniel 7:25 says, "He [Man of Sin] will speak against the Most High and oppress His holy people and try to change the set times and the laws. The holy people will be delivered into his hands for a time, times and half a time." A "time" equals one year; "times" equals two years, and "half" equals half a year—a total of 3½ years. The book of Revelation helps clarify the length of this period; it is referred to as 1,260 days (Revelation 11:3; 12:6). Therefore, Michael swore on His good Name that once the 1,260 days are completed—when "the power of the holy people has been finally broken, all these things [foretold in the prophecies] will be completed."

Daniel heard, but was confused; he wrote, "I heard, but I did not understand. So I asked, "My LORD, what will the outcome of all this be?"

13. What answer did Daniel receive to his question (Daniel 12:9)? _____
_____

"Go your way, Daniel, because the words are closed up and sealed until the time of the end." There was no use for Daniel to continue his questions; he would not understand what he has seen and written about.

14. Why would the mysteries be closed and sealed until the time of the end? _____

Of necessity, much of prophecy would remain hidden, that the work of God may be revealed at the appropriate time and only to the wise—those who love God and teach righteousness (Proverbs 1:5-7). Jesus often used parables so that only His disciples (those who really desire, and who had "ears" of interest) could truly understand His work (Matthew 13:9-11). We serve an awesome God who knows all things before they occur, but who has hidden prophecy's details until the time foretold—the time of its completion.

The prophet Daniel offered praised to God when he wrote in Daniel 2:20-22, "Praise be to the name of God for ever and ever; wisdom and power are His. He changes times and seasons; He deposes kings and raises up others. He *gives wisdom to the wise and knowledge to the discerning. He reveals deep and hidden things*; He knows what lies in darkness, and light dwells with Him." He reveals the deeper things to the individuals of His choosing.

15. Daniel 12:10 says what concerning the wisdom seekers? _____

The wise will understand, although at great price; they will be tried as by fire but made spiritually white and pure (2 Peter 3:12-14), while the wicked continue in sin.

By Daniel's desire to understand fully all that had been shown him, we are reminded of Peter's words (1 Peter 1:10-11) where he speaks of the prophets and angels inquiring and searching diligently to understand the predictions concerning the sufferings of Christ and the glory that should follow. How little of what they wrote were some of the prophets permitted to understand! They did not refuse to write, even though they long to grasp it, but could not. If God required it, they knew that in due time He would see that His people derived from their writings all the benefit that He intended.

So, Daniel and all the faithful up to the end of time, are being told that when the right time comes the wise will understand the meaning of what he had written. The time of the end was the moment in which the Spirit of God was to break the seal of the scroll. Consequently, this was the time during which the wise will understand, while the wicked, lost to all sense of the value of eternal truth, with hearts callous and hardened in sin, will grow continually more wickedly and more blind. None of the wicked will understand. The efforts the wise put forth to understand, the wicked call foolishness; and they continue to ask in critical questioning, "Where is the promise of His coming?" (2 Peter 3:4).

The phraseology of Daniel 12, verse 10 seems at first sight to be rather peculiar: "Many shall be purified, and made white, and tried." The language doubtless describes a process which is many times repeated in the experience of those who, during the time of the end, are being made ready for the coming and Kingdom of the LORD. They are purified and made white, as compared with their former condition. Then they are again tried. Greater tests are brought to weigh upon them. If they endure these, the work of purification is carried on to a still greater extent until they attain to a purer character. After reaching this state, they are tried again, and further purified and made white. Therefore, the process goes on until characters are developed which will stand the test of the Day of Judgment, and a spiritual condition is reached which needs no further trial.

The "Daily"

16. Daniel 12:11 declares an additional time period and more events, which might be of help to our understanding. What begins the 1,290 days? _____

"From the time that the daily *sacrifice* is abolished." The word *sacrifice* was not in the original text. Translators have not improved the passage by adding a word that Messiah did not give to Daniel. The original language simply reads the "daily" or "*tamid*"; meaning "*continual*," is to be abolished. The question remains, what is the daily?

During the Six-Day War in 1967 between Israel and the three countries that surrounded them (Syria, Jordon and Egypt), the Israelis captured Old Jerusalem from the Jordanians. On June 7, 1967, the army marched

into the Old City and took over the Western Wall and Temple Mount for the first time since 70 A.D. From that day forward, the faithful have worshiped day and night at the Wall, praying continually. The "daily" on earth speaks of the continual worship at the Temple Mount and Western Wall in Jerusalem. Through a series of events, quite possibly a strong earthquake, the daily flow of worshipers at the Temple Mount will be stopped. The Middle East will erupt, and the nation of Israel will be drawn into the escalating conflicts. Chaos and bloodshed will reign in the Middle East. According to prophecy,

daily worship at the Western Wall and Temple Mount will be taken away by unforeseen calamities. *The Kingdom Calendar* shows that the taking away of the daily occurs at Purim/Shushan Purim, which will usher in the 1,290 counting days of the appointed times and the believers' treacherous march towards the Kingdom of God. Jerusalem and the world will be turned upside down. Tragedies, unimaginable human loss and blood will flow, and the flames of World War III will erupt in a blaze of sudden release in the early part of the year.

Daniel 8:9-12 speaks of the powerful "little horn" (representing the evil ruler of the last days, through whom Satan will speak to mankind) and an end-time battle on earth that expands to a connected war that reaches Heaven and brings a great host of angels into the conflict. In verses 11-12 (KJV) the prophet wrote, "he [Satan/Evil Ruler] magnified himself even to the Prince [Michael] of hosts [angels], and by him [Satan/Evil Ruler] the daily... [worship/sanctuary activities in Heaven] was taken away, and the place of His [God's] Sanctuary [in Heaven] was cast down [trampled upon]."

17. What does Revelation 12:7-9 tell about this future confrontation in Heaven? _____

_____

Hebrews 8:1 says that Christ [High Priest—the Man clothed in linen] has been "sitting at the right hand of the throne of the Majesty in the heavens" (KJV). However, Satan will make one last attempt to overthrow Heaven; however, Michael and His angels will fight off Satan and his army, but not before it reaches the very throne-room of Heaven.

Daniel saw this confrontation (Daniel 7:9-10), "I beheld till the thrones were cast down," (KJV) in battle. The New International Version (NIV) notes an opposite effect: the thrones are "set up" (7:9-10) for courtroom testimony and books of evidence will be opened. The original word can be translated as both "cast down" and "set up"; and, for good reason.

The Throne Room Turned Into A Courtroom

The "daily" that is taken away represents tragedy on earth, as well as Heaven. The daily taken away above will be the "continual" sanctuary activities of Heaven (*The Kingdom Calendar*—Pt. 8 or soon after). When Satan and his armies attack Heaven, the Holy Temple will be trampled underfoot. Messiah's communion at the right hand of the Father will be stripped away. Once Satan is expelled, the Father and Son surrender the Sanctuary to Courtroom use, and this place of holiness will be trampled underfoot. Father and Son are separated for a period during the Court of Judgment (Daniel 8:13-14; Pt. 12). Near the end of this judgment the Son of Man will step before the Father to receive His coronation and kingdom (Daniel 7:13-14), while Satan and his subjects are sentenced to destruction (Daniel 7:26-27). At the end of the Courtroom Judgment, Revelation says the Temple door will be opened, revealing the Holy of Holies (Revelation 11:15-19) where the Ark of the Ten Commandments resides. The Moral Law is the basis of worldwide judgment—the moment when the Day of the LORD begins, and angels are sent out (Pt. 18) to deliver God's final plagues upon mankind (Revelation 15:5-6).

The Abomination

18. What event ends the 1,290 days (Daniel 12:11)? "The abomination that causes desolation is _____ _____."

Returning to Daniel 12, on earth the abomination (detestable act) that brings final desolation to Jerusalem and the world will be set up. In Ezekiel 5:8-11, the prophet speaks of the past and future judgment of God against Jerusalem for defiling the Temple with the abomination: "I will inflict punishment on you in the sight of the nations. Because of all your detestable idols."

19. What does Revelation 9:20 affirm on this subject of punishment and idols? _____
_____

20. What brings about *the end* and the Great Tribulation according to Matthew 24:14-15? _____
_____

When Antichrist sets up the abomination (idolatrous worship) on the Temple Mount in Jerusalem, then we can know "the end" is about to commence. Mark 13:14 clarifies that when you see the abomination spoken of by Daniel standing where "it" ought not... then let those in Israel flee for their lives because of great destruction about to fall upon Jerusalem and Israel, followed by the world, which culminates at Armageddon's battle.

Matthew 24:14-15 states that before the Great Tribulation begins the gospel will go to all the nations, and when the abomination is set up, then *the end* will come. It is very interesting to find the Jewish Encyclopedia says that Armilus [Anti-Messiah] "is to be the horrendous offspring of evil men, or Satan, coupled with a beautiful marble statue of a girl in Rome." Could the abomination involve a statue of the Virgin Mary?

We now have a connection between the abomination Jesus described to His disciples in Matthew 24 that will be set up in Jerusalem to a specific counting period—the timeline in Daniel 12:11—1,290 prophetic days.

21. How does Paul describe this evil act by the lawless leader at the Temple near the end of his rule in 2 Thessalonians 2:3-4? _____
_____

The Great Tribulation

Continuing at Daniel 12:12, the prophet heard Michael relay one more time frame that extends beyond the 1,290 days. There is a blessing for those who wait until the 1,335 days are complete.

22. How does the following verses describe the blessed Day of waiting (Matthew 24:13; Isaiah 25:9; Isaiah 40:31)? _____

The elect who by faith, and because of their deep love and trust in the LORD, endure to the end without yielding to Antichrist/Satan will receive eternal reward and blessings.

23. How many days are there between the 1,290 and 1,335 days? _____

There are 45 days between the abomination and the Day of blessing. This would tell us that between the setting up of the abomination on the Temple Mount and the visible return of Messiah is a short time of God's wrath known as the Great Tribulation"—a time that Jesus said, "except those days should be shortened, there should no flesh be saved," (Matthew 24:22).

The Great Tribulation does not last for many months, for three and a half years, or for seven years, but must be completed within a period represented by days! When we study the book of Revelation and the great devastating plagues that destroy so much of the ecological system of our planet, particularly fresh water supplies, it will be clear why the Great Tribulation could last only in terms of days or weeks, not months or years.

24. Evidence is given in the Scriptures that the Great Tribulation will last only a short span of time—weeks rather than years. What does each verse say that proves this point through the Word of God?

Psalm 2:12 _____
Psalm 30:5 _____
Psalm 37:9-10 _____
Isaiah 26:20-21 _____
Isaiah 54:7-10 _____
Mark 13:19-20 _____
Luke 21:25-28 _____
Romans 9:27-28 _____

---NOTES---

THE CREATOR

היוצר

Insights In Prophecy
Unlock The Ancient Mysteries Of Daniel & Revelation
BIBLE DISCOVERY SERIES

Lesson 2

EVENTS OF THE APPOINTED TIMES & SEASONS

Read Matthew 24 & Luke 21:5-28

- Discover How Jesus, In His Own Words, Confirmed Daniel's Predictions
- Unlock The Schedule of End-time Events
- Explore How Perilous Events Of The Last Days Line Up With Prophetic Time Lines

In Lesson 1 on Daniel chapter 12 we discovered three time periods of the appointed time of the end (1,260 days, 1,290 days and 1,335 days). The 1,260 day counting period, repeated seven times in the books of Daniel and Revelation, focuses on the period when the Little Horn Beast will rule over the earth (Daniel 7:25; Revelation 13:5), and when the woman (representative of God's chosen) will be protected (Revelation 12:6, 14) seemingly under the watch-care of the two witnesses (Revelation 11:3). The 1,290 days and 1,335 days are two counting periods, which to date have not been adequately explained in the popular views of prophecy. However, we learned in Lesson 1 that by simply allowing God's Word to *reveal itself* without preconceived notions, the appointed time of the end time periods and events associated with those periods begin to take shape. Now we are ready to build upon what we have discovered so far.

The problem with popular interpretations is that teachers have applied the "daily" and "abomination" in the visions of Daniel (Daniel 8:11-13; 9:27; 11:31; 12:11) to scattered historical events. However, we are

not going to look back, but look forward. As God's servants at the end of time we must ask, what does the predictive counting periods and prophetic events tell us about our future?

Lesson 2 compares similarities between the warnings Messiah gave His disciples in Matthew 24 and Luke 21, as they overlooked the beautiful Temple Mount 2,000 years ago, and the prophecies Daniel received in chapter 12 a few centuries earlier. Both speak of the great time of trouble, the end of time, the persecution of the believers, and the abomination of desolation that will be set up on the Temple Mount in Jerusalem—the epicenter of Bible prophecy. We will find the commentary of the final days, which Yeshua advanced in the Gospels (Matthew, Mark & Luke), align perfectly with the time lines that Michael gave to Daniel. Should this surprise us? God is the source of all prophecy revealed; therefore, all the timelines and events of the end from all the prophetic books of the Bible should merge together into one interconnected presentation.

1. Compare Daniel 12:1 and Matthew 24:21. What similarities are found? _____
_____

Both speak of the worse tribulation in human history and monumental events surrounding the last days.

2. Compare Daniel 12:6 and Matthew 24:3, 14. How do we know both speak of the final days? _____
_____

3. Compare Daniel 12:7, 10 and Matthew 24:9. Describe the persecution and the positive results of end-time difficulties? _____
_____

4. Waiting for deliverance, especially during periods of trial, takes perseverance. Daniel 12:12 assigns a counting period for salvation's culmination: "Blessed ["happy"] is the one who waits for and reaches the end of the 1,335 days." Matthew 24:13 also encourages believers to stand "firm to the end". Isaiah 25:9 reminds God's people to wait patiently for the LORD, which will pay big dividends. How? _____

_____

Isaiah 25:9 says, "And it will be said in that Day: "Behold, this is our God; we have waited for Him, and He will save us. This is the LORD; we have waited for Him; we will be glad and rejoice in His salvation." These passages relay words of encouragement for those who must endure the last trial period that ends this age. Happy are those who wait patiently through the affliction and loss in anticipation of the return of the LORD, who arrives offering victory and joyous salvation.

Yeshua clearly laid out for His disciples the events of the counting days that lead up to the abomination that ultimately destroys Jerusalem, Judea and then the world. In the questions that follow, we will begin the process of determining the sequence of events that will march mankind to Armageddon and the climax of Messiah's fiery return.

5. List what specific events begin the appointed time of the end and the 1,260, 1,290 and 1,335 days of prophecy (Matthew 24:4-8 and Luke 21:10-11)? _____

_____

At God's appointed time, the Devil will incite war, bloodshed and global catastrophes that force mankind into a state of panic. In quick succession, he will utilize fearful sights and great signs of demonic miracles that will introduce the false messiah—the supernatural rise of Antichrist, who will usher in temporal peace and cast humanity under his demonic but religious spell (Luke 21:10-11).

6. Describe the trial that continues for believers during the counting days of prophecy (Matthew 24:9-12)? _____

7. What does Messiah promise to be completed before the Great Tribulation arrives (Matthew 24:14; Revelation 14:6-7)? _____

Now we will look closer at the horrendous event that will destroy the rebuilt city of Jerusalem, which will usher in the most severe period of devastation ever experienced in human history.

8. Jesus specifies the event, and with it the turning point in the great controversy, which will mark the end of the 1,290 days and the beginning of the Great Tribulation. What is it (Matthew 24:15)? _____

_____

9. Compare Matthew 24:15 with the timeline in Daniel 12:11. What is the key similarity here? _____

_____

Both speak of the "abomination" that ushers in final desolate and utter destruction to Jerusalem, followed by the entire Planet Earth.

Jesus referenced the scroll of Daniel when announcing final events, offering a personal endorsement of Daniel's visions, where we first learn about this outrageous move on the part of the world's evil religious leader.

10. According to Daniel 12:11, when will the abomination be set up; at the *beginning* or *end* of the 1,290 days? _____

At the end of 1,290 counting days the Man of Sin, with the support of Israel's leaders and the Gentile governments of the world, will enter onto the Temple Mount in Jerusalem and will set up the idolatrous worship. By this abominable act he will go too far, and Heaven will respond. The Day of the LORD's wrath will commence with God's plagues, while military powers unleash their own destruction that brings the final and horrendous desolation forewarned throughout Scripture, and the end of the world as we know it. Jesus said whoever reads, let him understand (Matthew 24:15). That's the purpose of this lesson series.

11. What *must* the people in Israel (who believe the prophecies) do when the abomination is set up in Jerusalem (Matthew 24:16-19)? _____
Why (Luke 21:20)? _____

Judea is southern Israel, including Jerusalem, Bethlehem and the surrounding region. Danger abounds and this area must be evacuated with speed by heading to the mountains.

12. Jesus said to pray that God's chosen ones will not need to run during what periods (Matthew 24:20)?
_____

Winter travel would be difficult in the escape, and flight for your life on the seventh day of Sabbath rest (sundown Friday to sundown Saturday) would not be the day of choice.

13. Why must God's elect run for their lives (Matthew 24:21)? _____

14. How devastating will this dreadful span of time be—the Great Tribulation (Luke 21:22-23)? _____
_____

15. How does Daniel 12:1 describe this period? _____

16. Daniel and other Hebrew prophets describe this short period in time. How do the following Scriptures depict events that will follow the three and one-half years (1,260 days) of global famine and turmoil, during the 40 days of Great Tribulation?

Malachi 3:1-2 _____
Malachi 4:1-5 _____
_____
Jeremiah 50:27-28 _____
Psalm 18:6-15 _____
_____
Psalm 47:5-9 _____
Psalm 97:1-7 _____
_____
Joel 3:14-16 _____
Amos 1:2 _____
Amos 5:17-21 _____

Ezekiel 32:7-8 _____
Revelation 10:1-7 _____
_____

God will send His messenger Elijah to prepare the way 1,260 days before Messiah's dramatic visitation to Jerusalem. Elijah will be killed, and Antichrist will step onto the Temple Mount to set up his abomination and proclaim himself "God". Jesus—Hebrew "Yeshua"--the Messenger of the Covenant, will stand up in response to the Little Horn's defilement of the Jerusalem Temple, and descend in the cloak of darkness to "visit" Jerusalem and the Temple. The Archangel's voice will be heard throughout the earth, and He will raise to life Elijah and his companion, along with a great multitude of tribulation martyrs to be taken to Heaven for the duration of the short but dramatic Great Tribulation, while the elect (144,000) who are alive and sealed for protection will remain.

For additional study on Messiah's mysterious Day of Visitation to Jerusalem under the cloak of darkness (not to be confused with the very visible Second Coming at Armageddon) see Isaiah 10:30; Jeremiah 8:12; Jeremiah 10:15; Jeremiah 11:23; Jeremiah 46:21; Micah 7:4; Luke 19:44; 1 Peter 2:12—particularly the King James Version translation of the Scriptures focuses on the visitation *language.*

17. Why does Messiah promise the 24-hour day will be shortened during the Great Tribulation (Matthew 24:22)? _____

18. How do the following passages describe this global-wide, earth-shaking, rotation-altering event at the voice of God that will begin the Great Tribulation?

Job 9:5-8 _____
Isaiah 13:13 _____
Isaiah 24:18-21 _____
Daniel 2:21-22 _____
Revelation 16:18-21 _____

The whole planet will be moved off its axis and normal rotation by the massive worldwide earthquake. The rocks will cry out in response to the voice of God. This makes the final period difficult for the 144,000 elect (Revelation 7:1-8) to count the days, who are alive and remain on earth during the outpouring of the final plagues as they wait for Messiah's visible return and salvation.

19. How much time might the day and night be cut back (Revelation 8:12)? _____

One-third could be a real possibility; however, the exact time cannot be known for only the Father knows that future day and the hour! He will speed up the planet rotation to shorten time by His own determination.

20. What counterfeit will Satan employ against the 144,000 elect during this final hardship (Matthew 24:23-26; 2 Corinthians 11:14; Revelation 17:8-11)? _____
_____

The Antichrist "Beast" will fall in the destruction of Jerusalem; this "beast that was [alive], and is not" [alive] will return by satanic power to become the eighth ruler (Revelation 17:10-11). He will continue "a short space" of time before Christ returns with the great multitude for Armageddon's confrontation. Satan's melodious words of love, his signs and miracles, will test the elect (Matthew 24:24); but they will endure without yielding to his deceptions during the 40 days of Jacob's Trouble, just as Jesus endured His 40 days of testing long ago.

For further study about the 40 days periods found in the Scriptures, consider Moses (Exodus 24:18; Deuteronomy 9:9; Exodus 34:28) and Elijah's (I Kings 19:8) 40-day experiences, along with Jesus (Matthew 4:1-11). Jesus, Moses, Elijah and the 144,000 elect will sing a song specific to their personal victories (Revelation 14:1, 3). Only this group can rejoice with the Song of Deliverance, for they all endured 40 days of trial and severe testing, in want of food and water.

21. How will the 144,000 elect distinguish between the false messiah's (Satan's hoax) arrival, and the true return of Christ (Matthew 24:27; Revelation 1:7)? _____

While Satan may attempt to impersonate Christ with appearances here and there, Jesus said His coming is visible from the eastern sky, with lightning and great display of Messiah's power. This involves waiting patiently. Daniel 12:12 says, "Blessed is he that waits, and comes to" day 1,335.

22. How does the Word describe this waiting time and those blessed individuals who run for their lives during the great trial?

Isaiah 40:31 _____
Psalms 30:5 _____
Psalms 37:38-40 _____
Zephaniah 3:8 _____

23. How is the widespread death at Christ's return described (Matthew 24:27-28)? _____

24. Immediately after the Great Tribulation what happens (Matthew 24:29)? _____
_____

The lights of heaven will turn dark, and stars (meteors/asteroids) will fall to the earth. The planet and powers of the heavens will be shaken out of their places.

25. How do the following passages describe the events just preceding the Great Day of the LORD?

Luke 21:25-26 _____
Joel 2:30-31 _____
Zephaniah 1:14-18 _____
Revelation 6:12-14 _____

Next in the sequence of events, the Son and Father, along with the army of overcomers and angels—having returned from the New Jerusalem wedding (Luke 12:35-36), are seen as a mass speeding towards Planet Earth. The kings of the earth—not knowing the Scriptures—may interpret this approaching threat as an extinction event that must be stopped before it destroys the planet, and weapons of mass destruction will be turned against the Father and Son, and the approaching armies of Heaven.

26. The global leaders respond in what way, as it becomes clearer what and who they are attacking without success (Matthew 24:30; Revelation 6:15-17)? _____

27. What people are gathered up together to meet the LORD in the cloud of believers and angels (1 Thessalonians 4:17) at this time (Matthew 24:31)? _____

The "elect" or "chosen" are gathered—those who remained alive and on earth during the Great Tribulation, having been sealed for their protection against Satan and the plagues just before the Tribulation begins (Revelation 7:1-4).

28. What is the last segment of prophetic time called in Scripture besides the Great Tribulation (Jeremiah 30:7)? _____

29. What race are the "elect" in prophecy, who will be protected by the seal of God against the devastation and plagues of the Great Tribulation (Revelation 7:1-8)? _____

The 144,000 from the twelve tribes of Israel, chosen by Messiah and sealed for protection, will be the only ones to survive the Time of Jacob's trouble.

30. Describe why the 144,000 are left behind to experience such trial, and describe their assured safety (Jeremiah 30:11; Isaiah 54:6-10; Psalm 91:7-12, 15)? _____
_____

The elect are forsaken for this short period of time that they might be corrected in heart, and that they might know by personal experience God's mercy and salvation.

31. Where are the overcomers of all other Gentile nations who have already been resurrected at the voice of God, and taken out of the midst of Great Tribulation—those who precede the elect (the twelve tribes) left behind (Revelation 7:9-10, 14-15)? _____

The 144,000 represents a specific and "countable" number—all of Jewish heritage, while this "uncountable" faithful group of all nations (mainly Gentiles), who offer their lives for the cause of Messiah, will be raised and taken to Heaven as the Great Tribulation begins to stand before God's throne, clothed in victorious white robes.

32. How does Paul and others distinguish between the great multitude of overcomers—those raised at the shout of the Archangel's voice and taken on home (whom God will bring with Him a short time later at the Great Day of the LORD)—from those who are alive and remain on earth during the Great Tribulation until the visible return of the LORD (1 Thessalonians 4:13-17; 1 Thessalonians 3:13; Jude 14-15)? _____
_____

This great multitude of all nations (mainly Gentiles, but also Messiah believing Jews) that no man could number stands before God having been taken out of the midst of the Great Tribulation, just as it begins.

33. How does John identify this large sacrificial group who will not give up their faith even when facing death, and who will serve in God's temple forever (Revelation 7:13-17; Revelation 20:4)? _____
_____

Insights In Prophecy
Unlock The Ancient Mysteries Of Daniel & Revelation
BIBLE DISCOVERY SERIES

Lesson 3

BIBLICAL FESTIVALS—THE APPOINTED TIMES & SEASONS

Read Leviticus 23

- **Discover Why God Established His Festivals Over 3,000 Years Ago**
- **Probe How The "Appointed Times & Seasons" Foretell Final Events**

In this lesson we will discover God's great plan of redemption foreshadowed long ago in the appointed times and seasons. Gentile Christians have little appreciation of the Holy Days (also known as *Festivals* and *Feast Days*) established by God at Mount Sinai. It's sad their meaning and purpose has been lost to New Covenant thinking. The Scriptures boldly declare the Festivals foreshadow events to come at the end of time. When this lesson guide is completed, hopefully you will have a new or renewed perspective on God's Festivals, which Messiah Himself established for His divine purposes.

We are not to judge one another in respect to their commemoration. In the strictest sense, the Festivals cannot be observed without a Jerusalem Temple and without animal and grain sacrifices. Therefore, many

today celebrate with activities, meals, Scripture readings, prayer, fasting, repentance, gatherings and giving, while others simply acknowledge and rejoice in their predictive relevance to the end of this age. One is not saved by their keeping, nor lost by their disregard. Nonetheless, we must be clear that Paul did not bring God's appointed times under derision, as is often taught, when he attempted to dismiss "manmade regulations" of observance that were being forced upon the converts to Messiah (Colossians 2:16-17). The Festivals themselves were not under scrutiny, but their imposed mode of observance. Paul later wrote, "Do not handle! Do not taste! Do not touch!"? These are all destined to perish with use,

because they are *based on human commands and teachings*. Such *regulations* indeed have an appearance of wisdom, with their self-imposed worship, their false humility and their harsh treatment of the body, but they lack any value in restraining sensual indulgence," Colossians 2:21-23.

God's Festivals can be a wonderful source of encouragement, offering insight into our frailties and fostering spiritual renewal through their annual return each spring and fall season. They remind us that our sacrificed Redeemer lives (Passover), to humbly ask for God's forgiveness and His presence in the power of the Holy Spirit (Pentecost), to consider our need for repentance because of the approaching judgment of God (Feast of Trumpets) and the promised Day of the LORD (Day of Atonement); and finally, that we are but strangers on earth in need of God's protective care (Feast of Tabernacles). May we never discourage anyone from celebrating God's appointed times, as they see fit. This is especially true for Gentiles who, without hesitation, celebrate pagan days with zeal and fanfare, and who give very little consideration, if any, to the spiritual times God established long ago. The same holds true in reverse; let no one demand Festival celebrations of others, stating that God's approval only comes with their strict observance; let everyone be persuaded in their own minds (Romans 14:5).

With this, we are going to learn how God marvelously designed the "end of time" counting periods and events to follow His pattern of annual Festivals instituted over 3,000 years ago at Mount Sinai, and through significant historical events of His people Israel. The focus of prophecy is Jerusalem (the old one in Israel,

Insights In Prophecy
Unlock The Ancient Mysteries Of Daniel & Revelation
BIBLE DISCOVERY SERIES

and the New Jerusalem in Heaven), and the Scriptures were written by Hebrew prophets. So, let's step into the mind of God through His chosen Hebrew writers, inspired by the Holy Spirit to offer insight into our Savior and His salvation plan.

1. When the disciples asked Jesus about the kingdom to be set up in Acts 1:6-7, what did He relate to the closing periods? _____

The generation of Christ's day was not to know the "times or dates." The KJV reads, "times or the seasons."

2. How does Paul reaffirm the Day of the LORD is connected to "times and dates," or "times [and] the seasons," (1 Thessalonians 5:1-3)? _____

3. The Day of the LORD should not surprise God's people. What are the believers to be doing (1 Thessalonians 5:4-6)? _____

4. Daniel 8:19 also indicates at a set time in the future the end will come. What does he call this scheduled time? _____

The Bible defines the "appointed time" or "times and seasons." The first reference is found in Leviticus 23. At Mount Sinai God instituted this series of seasonal observances, called in Hebrew "moedim", which would unite His people in celebrations throughout the generations until the great Messianic age.

5. When are the Festivals to be observed, or "proclaimed," according to Leviticus 23:4? _____
_____

Leviticus 23 describes the Feasts, the "appointed times," based on a solar (sun) and lunar (moon) calendar. These Feasts are seasonal, celebrated in the spring and fall of each year as follows.

The Appointed Times & Seasons: God's Festival Days
Found in Leviticus 23

Spring Holy Days
Passover (Pesach)—23:5-14
Feast of Unleavened Bread
Feast of First Fruits
Pentecost (Shavuot)—23:15-21

Fall Holy Days
Feast of Trumpets (Rosh Hashanah)—23:23-25
Day of Atonement (Yom Kippur)—23:26-32
Feast of Tabernacles (Sukkot)—23:33-43

In addition to the Feast Days of Leviticus 23, three other annually celebrated events are found in the Scriptures—*Purim*, the celebration of the Jews' victory over their Persian (Iranian) oppressors—recorded in the Book of Esther. The Scriptures also reference a particularly sad historical day called in Israel *Tisha B'Av*, based on Zechariah 8:19—"fast of the fifth" month—an annual day of fasting commemorating the destruction of the Jerusalem Temple that occurred on this day in both 586 B.C. and again in 70 A.D., and other tragic events in Jewish history. *Hanukkah*, also called the Festival of Lights and Feast of Dedication, is found in John 10:22-23, "Then came the Feast of Dedication at Jerusalem. It was winter, and Jesus was in the Temple area walking in Solomon's Colonnade," (NIV). As a Jew, Jesus would have participated in the annual Feast of Dedication.

The Kingdom Calendar incorporates the Purim celebration and Tisha B'Av fast, while the eight-day celebration of Hanukkah also holds prophetic significance. Festivals play a vital role in setting a pattern for the unfolding of end-time events. It is written, "Now all these things happened unto them for examples and they are written for our admonition, upon whom the ends of the world are come," 1 Corinthians 10:11. To this we learn the annual observances "are a shadow of things to come" at the end of time, Colossian 2:16-17.

6. The Scriptures indicate the Festivals are connected to the final days. How does the following two verses connect the "appointed times" to the end of the age (Daniel 11:27, 35)? _____

_____

The end will occur at a very specific time, centered on the autumn Biblical Festivals—the appointed times and dates.

Books written by Jewish scholars hold a wealth of information concerning the Holy Days, as well as calendar dates when the Festivals will be observed in the coming years. Judaism anticipates Messianic end-time events on and during the Festivals, which the Word of God confirms as well. For example, Passover celebrates the great exodus from Egypt of God's people, and the central theme is *redemption*. Observers set an extra cup of wine at the special table in celebration of Passover called the Seder (meal), because it has been taught for centuries that Elijah will arrive to announce the final redemption of God's people at the end of the Passover meal. It is noteworthy that *The Kingdom Calendar* shows the patterned arrival of Elijah at Passover, just as Jews expect, as the end-time counting periods and events begin to unfold.

One prominent rabbi in the American Jewish community wrote, "God promises: 'And I will take you to be My people, and I will be your God, And you shall know that I, the LORD, am your God who freed you from the burdens of the Egyptians' (Exod. 6:7). This covenantal relationship lies at the heart of the celebration of Passover. We rejoice for the past liberation from Egypt and for other redemptions by God since then. And because of the fulfillment of past promises, we anticipate at Passover the future final redemption. We create a special role for the prophet *Elijah* at the seder [the family meal and home ritual for Passover] as the symbol of our faith in the redemption soon to come." *The Jewish Holidays: A Guide & Commentary, 1985, by Michael Strassfeld, p 7.*

Another Jewish writer adds, "After the blessing the wine is drunk. Before anyone drinks, however, some is spilled into a plate or tray. This gesture symbolizes sadness and loss; as *Shabbat* ends, so ends it glimpse of redemption, of a world made whole. Havdalah expresses a longing for a never-ending Shabbat, which for Jews is expressed in the image of the Messiah and, because according to Talmudic legend *Elijah will come after havdalah* [a recited blessing at the end of the celebration], it is traditional to sing "Eliyahu Hanavi" [which words are—*Elijah the prophet, Elijah the Tishbite, Elijah from Gilad, Come to us soon in our days with Messiah child of David*]." *Living A Jewish Life, 1991, by Anita Diamant and Howard Cooper, p 63.*

7. Upon what Biblical statements do Jews and Christians alike expect the prophet Elijah's arrival during the final days (Malachi 3:1; Malachi 4:5)? _____
_____

8. How long a period does the prophet John appoint to the two witnesses who will testify during the last days (Revelation 11:3)? _____

9. The prophet John—writer of Revelation revealed that two witnesses (Elijah and one other) would "prophesy" for exactly 1,260 days. In addition to the 1,260 days they speak for God, how many days will the two witnesses lie in the streets of Jerusalem after being martyred (Revelation 11:9, 11)? _____

When you add 3 ½ days onto the 1,260 days of Elijah's ministry, this equals 1,263 ½ days (1,260 days + 3 1/2 days = 1,263 1/2 days). During most Jewish calendar cycles there are exactly 1,264 days between Passover and the Day of Atonement. *Coincidental, or a divine pattern?*

10. Malachi 3:1-2 declares the LORD will arrive just after Elijah has prepared the way for Him. Where does Messiah first visit upon His arrival to Planet Earth? _____

Messiah will suddenly come to His Temple in Jerusalem to clear out the abomination. Yeshua has done this before: "Then Jesus went into the temple of God and drove out all those who bought and sold in the temple, and overturned the tables of the money changers," Matthew 21:12.

11. Immediately after Elijah's ministry and martyrdom, Christ will suddenly return to the Temple Mount in Jerusalem. What does Messiah warn the believers in Israel to do (Matthew 24:15-21 and Luke 21:20-22)? _____ **Why?** _____

Jesus warned that those in Israel must run for their lives into the mountains because the "great tribulation" is at the door, and Jerusalem's final demise is forthcoming.

12. Revelation 11 reveals that when the Seventh "Malak"—the Archangel sounds His trumpet; the kingdom of this world is turned over to whom (v. 15)? _____

13. Once the kingdom is given to Messiah, then God's wrath will be unleashed upon whom (vs. 16-18)?
_____

The nations of unrepentant are to be judged, who are angry at God; and, Jesus our Messiah will destroy those who destroy the earth. Elijah and his witnessing partner will be resurrected at His trumpet blast as well, along with other martyred overcomers. We know "because You [Messiah] have taken Your great power and reigned. And the time of the dead, that they should be judged, and that You should reward Your servants the prophets [two witnesses] and the saints, and those who fear Your name, small and great." The dead will be judged--who will live and reign with Christ, and reward will be given to God's servants the prophets— Elijah and his witnessing partner.

Revelation 20:4-5 focuses directly on the tribulation overcomers, who did not accept the mark of the beast, when it says," and I saw thrones, and they sat on them, and judgment was committed to them. Then I saw the souls of those who had been beheaded [martyrs] for their witness to Jesus and for the word of God, who had not worshiped the beast or his image, and had not received his mark on their foreheads or on their hands. And they lived and reigned with Christ for a thousand years. But the rest of the dead [all others who have died; whether good or bad] did not live again until the thousand years were finished."

More About The Biblical Festivals

From the beginning of creation God instituted the daily, weekly, monthly and yearly cycles that separate the four Festival seasons of the earth (Genesis 1:14-16). This was accomplished through the continual movement of the moon around Planet Earth, and the movement of the planet around the sun.

This cycle of time that divides spring, summer, autumn and winter also unites the seasons in a beautiful orchestrated production of God's creative marvel. From the new life of spring's budding plants and the beautiful blooms of summer to the palette of autumn colors which paint the landscape and the chill of winter with her glistening blanket, all these periods reveal a Divine epoch blueprint. The four repetitive seasons build within mankind a sense of stability as the globe rotates in precision and each season gives way to the next, right on schedule.

Our Maker has united the earth and sea with atoms and organisms into one well-balanced cycle of life, which sustains countless living creatures in an incredibly complex arrangement—all dependent upon one another. For this reason, the unseen God can be clearly witnessed in the marvelous revelation of nature's evidence, so that each of us are without excuse for having ignored and disobeyed Him (Romans 1:20). Added to the physical evidence, the same Designer has fashioned a spiritual and prophetic pattern of counting periods connected to His *appointed cycles of time—His Festivals*, which also prove that He is indeed the Supreme God whose knowledge surpasses all human understanding.

Egyptian Slaves Free To Rest

When the Holy One of Israel delivered the Israelites from their Egyptian slavery at the great Exodus nearly 3,500 years ago, God guided them to the foot of Mount Sinai. There the Messenger of the Covenant (Angel of the LORD—Acts 7:30-38; Deuteronomy 33:2) revealed to Moses and the people of Israel the Everlasting Covenant, which He had promised to Abraham and his descendants (Genesis 17:7). Deuteronomy 4:13 says, "He [the Messenger] declared to you His Covenant, the Ten Commandments, which He commanded you to follow and then wrote them on two stone tablets," as found in Exodus 20:1-17.

Also revealed through Moses were God's laws concerning conduct, worship and community. God's chosen people and their descendants, along with the Gentile converts who joined them, were introduced to a whole new way of living as described in Leviticus 23. In verse 3 the Israelites were reminded of the seventh-day Sabbath, which Messiah our Creator had given to all mankind as a day of rest the first week of creation (Genesis 2:2-3); for it was Jesus Himself who created all things (John 1:1-3; Hebrews 1:2; Col. 1:15-16), and why He clarified His intent and claimed for Himself ownership of the Sabbath during His earthly ministry (Mark 2:27-28). Now that they were freed from slavery, the re-introduction to the seventh-day was freely offered as a gift of rest and repose to the great multitude of Israelites. No longer would they be forced as slaves to work seven days a week—freedom from slavery was God's miracle to redeem His chosen people.

The reason earth's population lives on a seven-day week is because our Creator—the Word (John 11-3) instituted the seventh day and a seven-day week at creation. A seven-day week does not correlate to the movements of the planets, or a prophetic month of 30 days. Five weeks of six work days (30 days) would have better fit the original monthly cycle; however, Messiah saw man's need of rest, and therefore freely offered one additional day per week—the seventh day—as a gift to anyone who would "remember" to take Him up on His divine arrangement.

Insights In Prophecy
Unlock The Ancient Mysteries Of Daniel & Revelation
BIBLE DISCOVERY SERIES

God Set the Appointed Festivals In Motion For His Divine Purposes

Leviticus 23:4 begins the introduction to the "appointed feasts, the sacred assemblies you are to proclaim at their appointed times"; or as the King James Version reads, "ye shall proclaim in their [spring and autumn] seasons." Today, calendars establish uniform segments of time to help mankind know when to work, play, worship and to celebrate anniversaries, birthdays and national holidays. However, before the invention of printed calendars, the world's population used the rotation of earth and moon in relation to the sun to mark off time; the first sliver of the new moon heralded the new month. According to God's design, each day begins with the evening at sunset and ends the following day at sunset (Genesis 1:5); therefore, to this day many who observe the seventh-day Sabbath do so from Friday "evening... until the following Saturday evening," Leviticus 23:32.

Leviticus 23:4-22 introduces the first set of Festivals. We are told the Biblical religious year begins in the spring (around March/April—Nisan 1; for instance, the evening of March 16, 2018, and the next year on the evening of April 5, 2019). The first Festival two weeks later is Passover (Israel's *Pesach*) with its evening meal called the Seder, prepared before sunset on the fourteenth day of the first month. As the sun drops in the west the fifteen day begins, and God commanded that the Feast of Unleavened Bread be observed as a full day of rest with no eating of bread made with yeast as part of the celebration. Passover is a seven-day holiday with the first and last days observed as legal holidays, involving abstention from work, special prayer services, and holiday meals. The Seder evening meal of Passover at the beginning of the Day of Unleavened Bread is followed next by the Day of Firstfruits, when the Israelites were to assemble at the Temple and bring in the first grains of the harvest as an offering of thanksgiving to Yahweh. This day begins

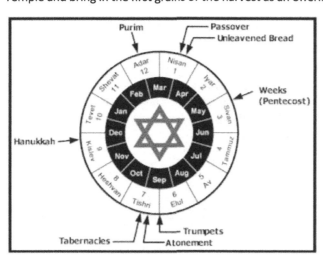

the counting of seven weeks of seven days (49 days), that leads to Pentecost (*Shavuot*), or Feast of Weeks. On day fifty, another day of rest is observed. Pentecost arrives in late May or early June each calendar year.

The fall observances later in the year described in Leviticus 23:23-44 are identified as the Feast of Trumpets (*Rosh Ha-Shanah*)—a day of rest and assembly with judgment as the them, which falls on the first day of the seventh month (around September/ October); followed ten days later by the Day of Atonement (*Yom Kippur*)—a solemn day of rest and repentance with the theme of a closing gate and end of the opportunity to repent or be cut off; therefore, each person is to examine himself/herself as to their relationship with God—are they living for Him, or against Him. Five days later the Feast of Tabernacles (*Sukkot*)—or Booths arrives, when celebrants are to build leafy booths (sukkah) and reside in them for several days of celebration. Although these Festivals were once centered on Temple rites and ceremonies, many in Israel today—along with Messianic Jews and some Gentiles, gather and observe the annual Holy Days in homes, churches and in local synagogues around the world.

As mentioned earlier, in addition to the spring and autumn Festival Days, the prophet Zechariah (8:19) introduces four fasts of mourning. Jewry anticipates future calamities could occur on some of these fast days. Of greatest concern is the most solemn period called the *Three Weeks,* which begins annually on the seventh day of Tammuz (fast of the fourth month; around June/July) and ends on the ninth day of Av (fast of the fifth month), on a critical July or August fast called *Tisha B' Av*.

Why Should Gentiles Care?

Gentile believers can gain insight into God's final plan by understanding God's Festivals, which He established long ago. The Sacred books were written by men chosen of God, and through these *Hebrew prophets* Yahweh first announced the future "Day of the LORD" to mankind. Only when Christians understand that all prophetic truths are built upon this Biblical historical foundation of faith will Heaven's end-time plan, which leads up to the Day of the LORD, be fully grasped; it is our heritage.

Christians have often misapplied the prophecies for our own sense of purpose. For example, some suggest their denomination should be identified as the "remnant" in Revelation, and that Gentiles make up the 144,000 elect, even though this group is *clearly identified* as from the *twelve tribes of Israel*. The only way for such Gentile teachings to flourish is that the simple language of prophecy is interpreted in a "spiritual" sense without regard for the Hebrew and Greek words inspired by the Holy Spirit, and that God has discarded His people—the Jews. This is known as "Replacement Theology", and nothing could be further from the truth.

The apostle Paul eloquently wrote, "I ask then, Did God reject His people? By no means! I am an Israelite, a descendant of Abraham, from the tribe of Benjamin. God did not reject His people, whom He foreknew," Romans 11:1-2. In fact, Paul wrote to the Gentile church at Rome, "I do not want you to be ignorant of this mystery, brothers, so that you may not be conceited: Israel has experienced a hardening in part until the full number of the Gentiles has come in. And so all Israel [of all twelve tribes] will be saved," Romans 11:25-26.

The Festivals have a direct fulfillment in the last days, when type (form) will meet antitype (reality). Looking for the establishment of the kingdom in their day, Christ's disciples asked the probing question, "LORD, at this time are you going to restore the kingdom to Israel? He said to them: It is not for you to know the [appointed] times and dates ["times or the seasons"—KJV] the Father has set by His own authority," Acts 1:6-7. In other words, it was not for that generation to know the annual Festival Days and holy dates when the final events will transpire. However, the last generation of overcomers is promised an unsealing of how and when final events will occur, on divine dates of end-time disaster and deliverance (Daniel 12:4, 9). This pattern is established by *The Kingdom Calendar*, bracketed by God's Festivals. And, on Purim or whatever day of the year "daily" worship is taken away at the devastation of Jerusalem, the Western Wall and Temple Mount, we can begin the counting days according to the Festival pattern.

Paul also connected the annual Festivals to the Day of the LORD. He wrote, "Now brothers, about the times and dates [spring and fall observances] we do not need to write to you, for you know very well that the Day of the LORD will come like a thief in the night [to sinners]. While people are saying, Peace and safety, destruction will come on them, as labor pains on a pregnant woman, and they will not escape... *but you, brothers, are not in darkness so that this day should surprise you like a thief*. You are all sons of the light and sons of the day... let us be alert" (1 Thessalonians 5:1-6) to the teachings of God's prophetic Word.

In other words, the events that precede the Day of the LORD are connected to and will occur based on the Biblical Festival pattern; and, God's people should not be surprised, because we will have the opportunity to understand the prophetic roadmap that will guide us through overwhelming demonic miracles, signs and wonders.

A Shadow of Things to Come

Paul's insight is this: the annual Festivals are "a shadow" of events "to come" at the end of time. Paul understood precisely the connection between the Feast days and the end, which he derived at least in part from the book of Daniel. God has an unalterable set time, an "appointed time," in which events of the final days will be played out in minute detail. Four times the Word associates the *appointed times*–the Festivals to *the end of time:*

- "I am going to tell you what will happen later in *the time of wrath*, because the vision concerns the *appointed time* of the *end*," Daniel 8:19.
- "The two kings, with their hearts bent on evil, will sit at the same table and lie to each other, but to no avail, because an *end* will still come at the *appointed time*," Daniel 11:27.
- "Some of the wise will stumble, so that they may be refined, purified and made spotless until the time of the *end*, for it will still come at the *appointed time*," Daniel 11:35.
- "For the revelation awaits an *appointed time*; it speaks of the *end* and will not prove false. Though it lingers, wait for it; it will certainly come and will not delay," Habakkuk 2:3.

The annual Festivals marked important events during Messiah's ministry. For instance, He may have been born on the Feast of Tabernacles, of which "water" plays a significant role, and ceremonies involving processions of water were common on this Festival. During His ministry, "on the last and greatest day of the Feast [of Tabernacles], Jesus stood and said in a loud voice, If anyone is thirsty, let him come to Me and drink. Whoever believes in Me, as the Scripture has said, streams of living water will flow from within him," John 7:37-38.

Six months later the Lamb of God was crucified at Passover; then, 50 days later His fiery Spirit was poured out at Pentecost. No less than *forty* such events in Israel's history have occurred on the annual Holy Days, according to some researchers. We find Yeshua personally involved for He first introduced their celebration many centuries ago at Mount Sinai; then, He celebrated them during His lifetime. He will someday bring the Festivals to a complete fulfillment during the end of days. No doubt with this divine plan, we can expect end-time prophecies to be fulfilled either on the Festivals or based on the pattern of the Festivals during the "appointed time", which leads up to Messiah's autumn visitation and visible return, when He shakes the earth and changes the calendar—the times and seasons (Daniel 2:21-22).

To summarize, we know from the Scriptures that Elijah will prepare the way for the returning King for 1,260 days; then the prophet will be killed. After three and one-half (3½) days, Messiah will "suddenly come to His Temple" at Jerusalem in the darkness of storm and earthquake (Amos 8:8-10; Isaiah 13:13; Ezekiel 32:7-8; Joel 2:31; Micah 3:6; Zephaniah 1:15). There He will deal severely with the Man of Sin who "opposes and exalts himself over everything that is called God or is worshipped, and even sets himself up in God's Temple, proclaiming himself to be God," 2 Thessalonians 2:4. The prophet Malachi asks the poignant question, "Who may abide the Day of His coming?"

Insights In Prophecy
Unlock The Ancient Mysteries Of Daniel & Revelation
BIBLE DISCOVERY SERIES

Lesson 4

FOUR WORLD MILITARY POWERS OF THE APPOINTED TIMES—PART I

Read Daniel 7:1-5; Revelation 6:1-4

- **Learn How The Animal Creatures Of Prophecy Represent Modern Nations**
- **Discover Where America Is Found In The Prophecies**

The participants and events which Daniel saw in vision are often repeated in the book of Revelation in sometimes similar, but more often different, symbolism. We might even think of Revelation as a commentary on Daniel's four visions of chapters 7-12. For example, we will teach that Revelation chapter 6 offers John's first description of *earth-bound events*, which are also found in the first few verses of Daniel chapter 7. Revelation chapters 4 and 5 give account of proceedings in Heaven's Temple—just as we'll discover later in Daniel 7.

So, let's set the stage for understanding Daniel 7 by first looking at Revelation 6; and, consider how Heaven connects the two prophetic visions. Here we see the Lamb (Messiah) opening the first seal of the divine

scroll and one of the four living creatures summons the White Horse, which gallops onto the world stage. The second living creature introduces the Red Horse, the third a Black Horse and the fourth living creature summons the Pale Horse. The four horses of Revelation are John's counterpart to the four animal creatures of Daniel 7, all of which represent modern-day governments.

In our attempt to understand what or who is represented in the four animals of Daniel 7, let's consider the parallel Biblical references to the four horses. The scroll of Revelation gathered much of its symbolism from the ancient Scriptures, also known in Judaism as the *Tanakh*. Primarily, the book of Zechariah contains fourteen chapters filled with end-time

language and predictions. It's here we find the four colored horses first mentioned prophetically, representative of military powers that are later discovered in Revelation 6, which John used to illustrate world forces on earth just before the return of Jesus our Messiah.

Four Colored Horses & The Four Winds

1. According to Zechariah 6:2-5, what are the four colors of the four horses? _____
_____

2. Zechariah asked, "What are these, my LORD?" The angel replied, "These are the four _____ of heaven, going out from *standing in the presence* of the LORD of the whole world."

In both the NIV and KJV translations of the Bible, the reference margins give the alternate reading "winds". In other words, the "four winds" are four heavenly intelligences that stand beside God in a holy alliance. The cross symbolism connects the four horses as being the same four "spirits" or "winds" of Heaven. Chariots and horses denote military maneuvers, so this moves the four spirits of Heaven into the governmental realm.

3. Another prophet—Ezekiel wrote that the four living creatures he saw with chariot-like wheels were extremely loud (3:12-13). What did the prophet associate with the noise? _____

The prophet Isaiah (6:2-4) also saw the four creatures in Heaven's Temple, but he called them four "seraphs"—or four angels, each with six wings. He described the creatures as each having four heads and they could travel in any direction without turning. As they rose in flight carrying God's throne, their massive wings stirred the air with awesome force creating turbulent winds and a loud roar.

4. Revelation 4:6-8 describes the same four-headed angelic creatures. What are their most identifiable characteristics? _____

John later described these four creatures when he wrote in Revelation 7:1-3, "I saw four angels standing at the four corners of the earth, holding back the four winds of the earth to prevent any wind from blowing on the land or on the sea or on any tree. Then I saw another angel coming up from the east, having the seal of the living God. He called out in a loud voice to the four angels who had been given power to harm the land and the sea: Do not harm the land or the sea or the trees until we put a seal on the foreheads of the servants of our God."

We know from this passage that just before the Great Tribulation, God's 144,000 elect will be sealed for protection as the world's great militaries marshal their forces for the last great battle. These four powerful creatures symbolize heaven's restraining control over earth's governments and armies.

5. How do we know God Almighty maintains restraining control over earth-bound powers (Daniel 2:21)? _____

God removes leaders and sets up leaders that His plan will eventually be accomplished.

6. What does the *sea* and *water* represent in prophecy (Isaiah 17:12-13; Jeremiah 6:23; Revelation 17:15? _____

Various nations and peoples of the world are portrayed. Therefore, Daniel recognizes the four political/military powers will emerge out of populated regions of the world. The "great sea" is symbolically stirred to bring about four powerful end-time governmental beasts.

7. What are the four living creatures that have power over land and sea called in Daniel 7:2-3? _____
_____

The Word depicts the four powerful living creatures with four heads and six massive wings as surrounding the throne and ready at a moment's notice to follow God's commands. The Father instructs them to stir up the political powers of the earth in Daniel 7:2. In similar fashion, when the four horses of Revelation 6 are introduced we find the same four living creatures summoning horse and rider into view.

We are left with this conclusion: the four horses of Revelation 6:1-8 represent the same end-time governments that the four animals of Daniel 7:1-7 symbolize, *because* both sets of animals are introduced by the same four mighty creatures—the "four winds of heaven"; and, in both prophetic books this is the first introduction to four animal creatures whose activities play out on Planet Earth just before the return of Jesus Christ. With this Biblical background established, let's begin to correlate the animals both Daniel and John in Revelation saw to four potential end-time governmental power-bases of our day.

Lion With Eagle's Wings

8. In Daniel 7:4, the first animal creature Daniel saw, described as the noblest of beasts and birds, might represent what county (or countries) based on the known symbols of nations in today's world? _____

The lion could represent the United Kingdom, which is closely connected historically and strategically to the world's mightiest power with eagle's wings—the United States. Prophecy is illustrating their historical relationship and today's dominant alliance between these two modern countries.

9. What happens to the eagle wings attached to the lion? _____

The wings will be torn off. This indicates America's collapse as the primary superpower, with the United Kingdom's simultaneous downgrade of power as well. Their sudden downfall may occur by several means— terrorism, military defeat, natural disasters, financial collapse and social disorder. No doubt, great perils will take down America due to her spiritual and moral decay over the last several decades, which decline has accelerated.

10. Daniel 7:4 indicates after the wings are torn off, what happens? _____

The lion is lifted from the ground so that it stands on two feet like a man, and the heart of a man is given to it.

In our study of Bible prophecy, we would not want to overlook critical details that might seem on the surface to be insignificant. Commentators have often thought the symbolism of prophecy too mysterious to offer relevance to our day, but in this lesson series we will attempt to explain the unexplainable by comparing Daniel, Revelation and other astute predictions in the Word of God. Our endeavor is to always provide reasonable and thoughtful interpretations.

Daniel saw the wings being torn off the lion, then the lion is made to stand up on two human feet and a man's heart is given it. This is by design. Prophecy declares "take notice!"—there is a cruel tearing off of the wings followed by symbolism involving human characteristics. This implies an end-time personality who will rise to power from the United Kingdom/United States alliance. He could be a famous individual or a mysterious personality. However, we know that when an animal, or animal parts, take on human qualities, the Hebrew prophet is introducing a person of prominence. We know this because Daniel also introduces the "little horn" in similar fashion (Daniel 7:8)—the animal's horn that acquires human "eyes" and man's "mouth". And, we know this represents a powerful religious leader of the last days.

In both cases (Daniel 7:4, 8), the animals take on human characteristics; and here, Daniel is describing the two evil, end-time personalities just as found in the prophecies of Revelation 13—the False Prophet and

Antichrist Beast. Therefore, it is our view that Daniel's prophecy is pointing out in subtle terms the False Prophet will emerge from this English alliance.

America's Jewish population (5,700,000) is just under the Jewish population in the land of Israel (6,446,000) as of 2018. America has long enjoyed divine protection against powers in high places, even though many nations have desired her demise. However, this is changing. The United States was once a nation built on the principles of religious freedom and morality. Even among the secular minded, there were standards of decency and respect for the basic commandments of God. However, decades ago a blight of corruption began to gain momentum, which now permeates American society like a disease. Pornography is rampant, and adultery, homosexuality and gay marriages are celebrated norms, with sexual immorality flouted in prime time. Innocent children are sacrificed daily to the god of convenience at abortion clinics. Crime and drug use reigns. Sin, mischief and immorality are unbridled, and nothing less than national catastrophe and revival can halt the tide. God's wise prophet warned long ago, "Woe to those who call evil good and good evil, who put darkness for light and light for darkness," (Isaiah 5:20). Sin and compromise have reached into our hearts, homes, churches and synagogues.

God's principles are scoffed at as antiquated ideas, but His Word warns nations who once served Him, "If you ever forget the LORD your God... I testify against you today that you will surely be destroyed. Like the nations the LORD destroyed before you, so you will be destroyed for not obeying the LORD your God," (Deuteronomy 8:19-20). The Israelites thought Elohim would protect them as His chosen nation despite their national rebellion; after all, they had experienced a miraculous deliverance from Egyptian slavery. History proves otherwise, with that generation dying in the wilderness. Many Americans also believe God will protect this "Christian" nation, with our own extreme national apostasy. Not so. Americans' love for their homeland cannot change the consequences of sin left unchecked and unrepented.

As we have found, the first animal that Daniel saw in vision was the Lion with Eagle's Wings. In Revelation 6:1-2, the first animal John viewed after the first of the seven-sealed scroll was broken open is the White Horse with a rider who has a bow of strength and crown of dominion. He gallops as a warrior and conqueror. This certainly is true of the American/British alliance for the last 100 years—their notable military supremacy and superpowers of the world for the short time that remains of their glory years. Now we will consider the second animal that Daniel saw in vision.

Bear With Three Ribs

Daniel 7:5 introduces the second animal—the Bear, which is inferior to the first, but next in the list of formidable beasts.

11. How is this creature described? _____

The Bear was raised up on one of its sides, and it had three ribs in its mouth between its teeth. It was told, "Get up and eat your fill of [human] flesh!"

The Bear was raised up on one side, indicating either a lopsided injured animal, unstable and unbalanced, or a mad fighting Bear rising to strike; quite possibly both. Symbolized in the Bear is a national power to be reckoned with in our modern world—the Russian Federation.

The collapse of the Soviet Union in December 1991 left the Russian Federation with the bulk of the massive Soviet weapons and a mass destruction complex. This legacy has allowed Russia to retain its power status even as its economy collapsed, but the burden of supporting its large military apparatus has strained the Russian political and economic system.

Russian President Vladimir Putin is attempting to restore confidence in Russia by rebuilding its military prowess and restoring pride through its show of force. Russia conducts increasing more bomber flights and nuclear exercises each year, and Putin personally supervises many of these maneuvers. Even today, he appears eager to demonstrate the Russian Bear has not gone to sleep and is quite capable of handling any threats to his nation and allies. Military demonstrations have involved launches of intercontinental ballistic missiles, including some from Russian nuclear submarines. Russia has also simulated enemy missile attacks and tested Moscow's missile defense system against strike. Involved in the exercises was Russia's Tu-160 strategic bombers and the test-firing of cruise missiles over the northern Atlantic.

Most experts agree Russia is preparing for a potential all-out war with other nuclear powers. This has some Western experts concerned. The United States and Russia's relationship after September 11, 2001, could be described as a period of cooperation, with the Bear supporting the American war on terrorism and a mutual nuclear arms reduction deal. However, the West expanded its military presence in the former Soviet republics of Central Asia instead of withdrawing, as expected by the Russians. Washington has also been moving elements of its strategic missile defense system closer to Russia's western borders as the U.S. military abandons traditional bases in old Europe in favor of friendlier eastern nations. Tensions seem to continue a steady path of escalation, month after month.

Daniel saw three *ribs* in the Bear's mouth. This reminds us of Amos 3:12, where a shepherd is said to recover bones from the mouth of a lion. The Bertholdt Commentary notes on Daniel 7:5, "fangs or tusks - or fangs crooked or bent like ribs." The Pulpit Commentary adds, "What is meant by these three ribs has been much debated... Havernick thinks that it is a mistake to translate עלעין ('il'een) "ribs;" he maintains the true rendering to be "tusks." Nonetheless, what would the three bones indicate? Since horns in prophecy represents countries, this symbolism likely denotes that the Old Soviet Bear will destroy three nations; and, by doing so will devour much human flesh.

This would indicate a massive calculated assault—likely nuclear; the Bear will rise in attack mode to abruptly destroy three countries in a short period of time. In Lesson 5 we will closely examine why the devastation will likely occur among the 10 voting Member-States of the former Western Europe Union (WEU) military alliance first established in 1948 (the same year Israel became a nation), which in recent times merged into the European Union of nations.

12. In Revelation 6:3-4 we find John's counterpart. What is the horse's color and what does the rider do?

_____

The red horse and rider are given power to take peace from the earth. He is given a "great sword". Russia's great sword could level thousands of structures in a moment of time and leave behind unimaginable death and suffering. World peace would be forever shattered.

As noted, for decades during the Cold War the Soviets were believed to be a threat to global peace. After the dissolution of the Soviet Union in 1991, many politicians proclaimed post-Cold War peace. However, this hope has been dashed in recent years, and Russia is once again an eminent threat. The Bear is divided and suffering anew from economic pressures, but Putin will not allow another national collapse without lashing out at the West.

The prophetic Word points to the Russian Federation as the primary instigator of end-time holocaust. The Bear will attack in anger as a powerful grizzly strikes its prey and will *uproot* (Daniel 7:8) three countries. To tear three horns out by their roots takes massive force. The human cost can be lost in the symbolism, but the price might be counted in the millions. Daniel's dream drives home a grim reality for our future: the flesh-eating bone-crushing Bear "was told, 'Get up and eat your fill of flesh!' (7:5). Out of what looks to be World War III the "little horn"—a little nation among the ten other European horns—will rise up with boastful "mouth" and traveling "feet" to rule with great authority.

In review, Daniel introduced two animal creatures that represent end-time powers in our modern world: the British/American alliance—Lion With Eagle's Wings, and the Russian—Bear. Apprehension grows when we realize that America's wings will be torn off, and the Russian Bear will rise and devour immeasurable human flesh.

Many people, including religious leaders, sneer that the world is just like it's always been (2 Peter 3:3-4). Every day is just another day; and, we pursue our normal lives eating, drinking, celebrating weddings, engaged in careers and climbing the ladder of success. But suddenly and without warning, sirens will blare, and indescribable chaos will mushroom. From that day forward, survival will be the primary concern of every man, woman and child on Planet Earth. Knowing Christ personally and His prophetic warnings will provide the one and only source for spiritual survival during this perilous period when demonic powers will be released to deceive and destroy.

Could Russia's Putin cause such unspeakable holocaust? The Word of God registers a resounding "YES!" Not only does the Bear have the power, but Heaven warns she will use it and lash out. Weapons of mass destruction have been held in check for decades, but Satan will release his buried weapons of genocide and the world will never be the same again.

Out of the holocaust, a boastful leader will emerge on the world stage with mysterious signs and wonders, supported by the false prophet. Delusions will capture the hearts and minds of the nations and will seduce nearly the whole world into eventually taking the mark of the beast. Many religious leaders will succumb to the craftiness of Satan, while disregarding the clearest warnings in the books of Daniel and Revelation. By doing so, the masses will enter through the broad gate and go to their destruction without God, the Creator and King—the true Savior of mankind. Yeshua warned, "Enter through the narrow gate. For wide is the gate and broad is the road that leads to destruction, and many enter through it. But small is the gate and narrow the road that leads to life, and only a few find it." Matthew 7:13.

Will you follow the crowd, or will you wait with patient endurance by faith to the end for the returning King of kings? Only He deserves our worship and alliance.

Lesson 5

FOUR WORLD MILITARY POWERS OF THE APPOINTED TIMES—PART II

Read Daniel 7:6-7; Revelation 6:5-8

- **Examine The Identity Of The Leopard With Four Heads**
- **Establish The Global Location Of The Terrible 10 Horn Beast**

In Lesson 4 we discovered how Heaven controls human governments. The Scriptures link modern militaries to the four powerful angels that surround God's throne. These four unique creatures each have four heads of sight and six massive wings, referred to as "the four winds of Heaven" (Daniel 7:2) who move upon the great sea of peoples to establish the earth-bound powers of Daniel 7—the Lion with Eagle's Wings, the Bear, the Leopard and the Terrible Beast.

The four, earthbound power-bases of Daniel 7 are not relics of the past as many commentators claim (i.e., Babylon, followed by the Medes and Persian, followed by Greece, followed by the Roman Empire; or similar grouping), but rather contemporary end-time contenders for world dominance. We know because near the end of prophetic time one of the four political powers is destroyed by the "blazing fire" (7:11-12), while the remaining three are stripped of their authority but are allowed to live for a short period longer (indicating their eventual and simultaneous demise). Daniel 7:26-27 also declares the final end of Antichrist and all world governments that have submitted to him once the Court of Heaven pronounces judgment against them all. This proves they are on the world scene at the same time and are not ancient powers that conquered and superseded each other.

In Revelation 5 we find the same four magnificent angels each with four heads and six wings standing in the presence of God. In Revelation 6 they also introduce four governmental horses, one at a time. And, just as Daniel confirms, all four will be overthrown by the triumphant King of kings.

We know the horses represent world governments and their military hierarchies because later in the chapter we read, "the *kings* of the earth, the *princes*, the *generals*" will call to the mountains to cover them for fear of what's coming upon the earth at Christ's return (Revelation 6:14-17).

As we merge Revelation's predictions with Daniel's, we will more accurately comprehend prophecy's true intent. In this lesson we will continue to look for similar events and parallel powers in the two books, and we will discover two more global authorities who align themselves with the last great global ruler of Planet Earth.

Insights In Prophecy
Unlock The Ancient Mysteries Of Daniel & Revelation
BIBLE DISCOVERY SERIES

Leopard With Four Heads

1. The third animal creature Daniel saw in vision (7:6) is what? _____

2. How many heads did the Leopard have? _____

The dictionary states concerning the leopard, "A large feline mammal, Panthera pardus, of Africa and Asia." China, and other Asian nations (including many Muslim countries) are likely represented in the Leopard animal. The cat has four heads while the other beasts in Daniel 7 sport only one. This may signify that although China and other Asian countries are territorially linked together, they still remain divided politically. The fact that the four-headed Leopard needs four wings to lift it in flight may denote the sheer size of the beast in geographical land mass.

3. John's counterpart horse in Revelation 6:5-6 is what color? _____

The rider of the Black Horse was holding a pair of balances in his hand, and John hears a voice among the four living creatures saying, "A quart of wheat for a day's wages, and three quarts of barley for a day's wages, and do not damage the oil and the wine!" Wheat and barley are basic food crops.

4. What would working all day for one day's worth of food communicate? _____

Draught and food shortages will be a devastating reality during the last days, causing the price of food to skyrocket. People may have to work all day just to pay for a day's worth of essential food.

In Matthew 24:7, Jesus warned the earth would suffer severe famine; however, Asia, which produces large amounts of barley, second only to rice, will likely supply commodities to the world at inflated prices.

History attests to the fact that war can erupt between nations at any time as a devastating surprise. Prophecy does not disclose with whom China and the Asian nations will become embroiled in local or international warfare. However, we know with certainty China and the other Eastern Asian countries will be found at Armageddon's battle, when that day arrives. Until then, the Asian Leopard will continue to play a strategic role in food supplies and world affairs and will remain a military threat not only in their region, but to the United States, Europe, Japan and other countries.

Terrible Beast With Ten Horns

5. The fourth and most terrifying creature has no zoological classification. What did Daniel see in the vision (7:7)? _____

6. What are the Beast's identifying traits? _____

This governmental beast-monster sports large iron teeth and it will crush and devour its victims and stomp underfoot whatever was left (Job 39:15; Isaiah 25:10).

7. This creature is different from the previous three in what ways? _____
_____

It was unusual in its form, strength and use of power. This creature was so hideous and grotesque that even Daniel could find no parallel in the natural world. The Beast tore to pieces and devoured its prey with its massive fangs of iron (Psalms 79:7; Jeremiah 10:25).

The King James Version of Daniel 7:7 says the beast "stamped the residue" with its feet. This implies the persecution of the "remnant" of God's people—*the remainder* of a larger group. Revelation 12:17 reinforces Daniel's vision with this dire warning, "The dragon [Satan] was enraged at the woman and went off to make war against the *rest of her offspring*—those who obey God's commandments and hold to the testimony of Jesus." The Commandments of God and testimony of Jesus counter the deceptions of Satan and the false religion of the Man of Sin. To hold to the testimony of Jesus is to believe and follow the counsel of the prophecies in the book of Revelation—the declarations of truth that the Messenger gave to His prophet John (Revelation 1:1-2).

8. Daniel 7:25 notes the "little horn" will use the fourth Beast's power to "oppress His [God's] holy people". We should consider, "What part of the world has historically brought holocaust to God's people in the past two thousand years?" _____

From Rome's tyranny during the Crusades of the Dark Ages, on street corners, in prison houses, attached to the fiery stakes and in the death camps of the Hitler, Western Europe has been a seed-bed for religious killings and anti-Semitism. History may be repeated; religious persecution could rise once again from the nations of the European Community. But what do the 10 horns represent?

Insights In Prophecy
Unlock The Ancient Mysteries Of Daniel & Revelation
BIBLE DISCOVERY SERIES

Western European Union Union de l'Europe occidentale	
Defensive alliance	
 Flag	
Members • Associate members • Observers • Associate partners	
Capital	Brussels
Political structure	International organisation
Historical era	Cold War
- Treaty of Brussels	17 March 1948
- London and Paris Accords	21 October 1954
- Treaty of Lisbon	1 December 2009
- Abolition	30 June 2011
Today part of	▣ European Union

**The Ten Horns
Western European Union (WEU)**

The Brussels Treaty of 1948

Treaty of Economic, Social and Cultural Collaboration and Collective Self-Defense

The Brussels Treaty was signed on 17 March 1948 by five nations--Belgium, France, Luxembourg, the Netherlands and the United Kingdom, and was the beginning of the unification of Europe. The Brussels Treaty Organization – as it was then called – provided for collective self-defense and economic, social and cultural collaboration between its signatories. On 23 October 1954, the Brussels Treaty was modified to include two more nations--the Federal Republic of Germany and Italy, thus being named the Western European Union (WEU). The aims stated in the preamble were:

"to afford assistance to each other in resisting any policy of aggression"
"to promote unity and to encourage the progressive integration of Europe"

Its two most important provisions are contained in Articles V and VIII.3:

"If any of the High Contracting Parties should be the object of an armed attack in Europe, the other High Contracting Parties will, in accordance with the provisions of Article 51 of the Charter of the United Nations, afford the Party so attacked all military and other aid and assistance in their power." (Article V)

"At the request of any of the High Contracting Parties, the Council shall be immediately convened in order to permit them to consult with regard to any situation which may constitute a threat to peace, in whatever area this threat should arise, or a danger to economic stability." (Article VIII.3)

In November 1988, a Protocol of Accession was signed by the WEU Member States adding Portugal and Spain, and the ratification process was completed in March 1990, thereby growing the WEU to 9 members--just one nation shy of the ten required in the prophecy.

Greece followed a similar process in 1992 and 1995 thus bringing the total WEU membership to exactly 10 Member Voting States. Decades after the Brussels Treaty was initially signed, and at its dissolution, the voting nations remained at 10, just as prophecy predicted.

The original formation of the Western European Union (WEU) represented by the blue logo of stars was, in fact, another piece of the end-time puzzle slipping into place. Even secular observers have tapped into the prophetic undertones that can be traced back to the idea that the Western European Union (WEU), which began with the Brussels Treaty in 1948—just two months before Israel became a nation, was a step toward the fulfillment of prophecies about the ten-horned political beast in Daniel 7 and Revelation 13. The treaty started with five-member nations, and eventually grew to ten Member Voting States. Although today the WEU has been absorbed into the European Union, the most power ten nations represent the whole of Europe and this prophecy. To visit the original Western European Union website, go to www.weu.int where you will find the original treaties, the articles and the list of 10 Member States and the other associated nations, now part of the 27-member European Union. For additional information on the modern Western European Union, visit http://en.wikipedia.org/wiki/Western_European_Union

WEU (Western European Union)—10 Member Voting States (Also members of the EU and NATO)	
Belgium (1948)	Germany (1954)
France (1948)	Italy (1954)
Luxembourg (1948)	Portugal (1990)
Netherlands (1948)	Spain (1990)
United Kingdom (1948)	Greece (1995)

9. John's counterpart animal in Revelation 6:7-8 is what color horse? _____

10. The Pale Horse's rider is given a name. What is it, and what follows him? _____
_____

Its rider was named Death, and hell [or "hades"—the grave] follows close behind him. As in Daniel 7:7 where the fourth Beast is dreadful, terribly strong and deadly, John emphasized the appalling acts of the fourth Pale Horse and its rider; they are the most dreadful of the four horses and riders. This fourth military Beast, identified as the Western Europe Union, kills and destroys. Wherever horse and rider go, death and the grave follow close behind.

11. How much of the earth is this military horse and rider given power over (Revelation 6:8)? _____

Notice the horse and rider rules over one-fourth of the earth, which signifies the rider dominates from a large geographical area.

12. What four elements of punishment are assigned to the rider, as seen in the verse above? _____
_____

This terrible power kills with four judgments—the same four judgments which in the ancient Scriptures warned the people of Israel they would face if they ever forget God's Covenant: sword, hunger, death and wild animals. It would be easy to overlook the four judgments as unimportant details, but they are vital to our understanding of last-day events.

"How much more when I send my four sore judgments upon Jerusalem, the sword, and the famine, and the noisome beasts, and the pestilence, to cut of from it man and beast? Yet, behold, therein shall be left a remnant that shall be brought forth, both sons and daughters... they shall come forth... and you shall be comforted concerning the evil that I have brought upon Jerusalem," (Ezekiel 14:21-22, KJV).

The four judgments warning of Leviticus 26:14-16-32 starts with these words, "If you [the Israelites] will not listen to Me and carry out all these commands, and if you will reject My decrees and abhor My laws and fail to carry out all My commands and so violate My Covenant [Ten Commandments—Deuteronomy 4:13], then I will do this to you," (NIV).

The four judgments against Israel are clearly laid out in Leviticus 26, as God's means of turning His people from sin to save the few who will respond in repentance. When God's chosen fail to listen to His instructions, which includes the divine evidence that Yeshua is Messiah (Matthew 23:37-39) to follow after Antichrist (and sadly, most will continue in their rebellion), He promises desolation and to multiply their affliction "seven times over" (vs. 18, 21), which in the book of Revelation seems to point to the seven trumpet punishments.

However, God is committed to saving a remnant of Israel who will listen, obey and accept Messiah's kingship: "When thou art in tribulation, and all these things are come upon thee, even in the latter days, if thou turn to the LORD thy God, and shall be obedient unto His voice. For the LORD thy God is a merciful God; He will not forsake thee," (Deuteronomy 4:30-31, KJV).

13. Daniel was troubled by the vision, so he asked the true meaning (Daniel 7:16-17). What does verse 17 clarify about the four beasts? _____

They are four kings, or kingdoms, that will rise from the earth.

14. What is the promise given in behalf of the faithful believers, despite the persecution that comes from the four governmental creatures (Daniel 7:18)? _____

We have discovered that both Daniel 7 and Revelation 6 employ symbolic animal creatures. The fourth and most dangerous creature is called the "Beast" in Daniel, while the fourth and most dangerous Pale Horse sports a Rider named "Death" in Revelation) to represent the four global regions of end-time governments around the globe, separate and distinct from one another.

In Revelation 13:1-2, John also relates seeing "a Beast coming out of the sea. He had ten horns and seven heads, with ten crowns on his horns, and on each head a blasphemous name. The *Beast* I saw resembled a *Leopard*, but had feet like those of a *Bear* and a mouth like that of a *Lion*." So, what Daniel saw as separate and distinct in Daniel's vision, in the book of Revelation we find a combination of the animal creatures of Daniel 7:1-7 working as one monstrous political *Beast*.

In today's world, we might hear this global alignment of nations called the *New World Order*, the *Grand Design*, the *Society of Nations*, or a similar name. How do we know for sure the prophet John is describing the same government creatures Daniel saw? Not only are they the same animals (Beast, Leopard, Bear and Lion), but we can also count the identical number of heads and horns found in both visions—the separate beasts of Daniel 7:1-7, compared to the combined beast of Revelation 13:1-2. This again shows that the book of Revelation is an enlargement of Daniel's mysterious scroll, written centuries before. The box below visually depicts the harmony between the two prophetic books.

The New World Order in Daniel *Before* the Global Upheaval of World War III

Daniel 7:1-7
Four Beasts Out of the Sea

Lion With Eagle's Wings ....1 Head......0 Horns
Bear With Three Ribs ....1 Head......0 Horns
Leopard With Four Heads/Four Wings ....4 Heads.....0 Horns
Terrible **Beast** With Ten Horns ....1 Head.....10 Horns
Total: New World Order ....7 Heads...10 Horns

----

The New World Order in Revelation *After* the Global Upheaval of World War III

Revelation 13:1-2
One **Beast** Out of the Sea
Like A **Leopard**, Feet of a **Bear**, Mouth of a **Lion** With
Seven Heads and Ten Horns ....7 Heads...10 Horns
Total: New World Order...................................7 Heads...10 Horns

While Daniel describes the four end-time powers as separate and distinct beasts, five hundred years later the prophet John saw all four in vision combined and working as one. This is the New World Order (Grand Design) described in both prophetic books. In both Daniel and Revelation, the emergence of the beasts from the sea heralds the world leader who will rise out of the war and chaos of World War III to rule for 1260 days.

Lion With Eagle's Wings represents ....United Kingdom/ United States
Bear With Three Ribs represents ....Russian Federation
Leopard With Four Heads/ Four Wings ....China & Asian Nations
Terrible Beast With Ten Horns ....Western European Union

In the fascinating book, The Keys Of This Blood, published by Simon and Schuster in 1990 and written by the former Dr. Malachi Martin, eminent theologian, former Jesuit and professor at the Vatican's Pontifical Biblical Institute and devout Roman Catholic, the author offers a behind the scenes look at what the Vatican considered a race for world dominance. Dr. Martin wrote of John Paul's conviction that one day the Papal leader will rule worldwide as the moral and spiritual leader of mankind, resulting from a great crisis of which the Soviet Union would be the instigator. We will study this subject further in Lesson 6.

Concerning the division of world powers, Dr. Martin wrote on page 349, "In the arena of the millennium end-game... in the Pontiff's geopolitical reckoning, there are chiefly *four regions* in which the near-future society of nations will be fashioned: the *United States*, the *Soviet Union*, mainland *China* and *Western Europe*," (emphasis added). Intellectuals in high places long ago had their finger on the pulse of the nations and the global political landscape and noted this four-way division of power in the world, having publicly stated so.

Insights In Prophecy
Unlock The Ancient Mysteries Of Daniel & Revelation
BIBLE DISCOVERY SERIES

Even today, the status of "great powers" is formally recognized in conferences such as the Congress of Vienna and the United Nations Security Council, which is made up of the most lethal world powers: United Kingdom and the United States—(the Lion with Eagle's Wings), Russia—(the Bear), China—(part of the Leopard), and France—(part of the European Beast), which serve as the body's five permanent members. As we have studied the four, world power-bases in both Daniel and Revelation, we see the exact four regions that secular sources point out as divisions of global strength. And, "great powers with United Nation P5 membership, and recognized nuclear weapons status are 1) the United Kingdom and the United States, 2) Russia, 3) China, and 4) France," according to Wikipedia.

We serve an all-knowing awesome God, who gave His prophet Daniel a vision of the worldwide political panorama thousands of years in advance and relayed that information through symbolism—the British Lion, American Eagle, Russian Bear, Asian Leopard and 10 Horn European Beast—known to represent the most influential powers of the 21st Century around the globe.

Let these holy words of wisdom guide and encourage you in the many decisions must face in the final days. "We have also a more sure word of prophecy... whereunto ye do well that ye take heed, as unto a light that shines in a dark place, until the day dawn, and the day star arise in your hearts: Knowing this first, that no prophecy of the Scripture is of any private interpretation. For the prophecy came not in old time by the will of man; but holy men of God spoke as they were moved by the Holy Ghost," (2 Peter1:19-21, KJV).

Jesus adds, "Howbeit when He, the Spirit of truth, is come, He will guide you into all truth: for He shall not speak of Himself: but whatsoever He shall hear, that shall He speak: and He will show you things to come. He shall glorify Me; for He shall receive of mine, and shall show it unto you." Yeshua finished with these words, "These things I have spoken unto you, that in Me you might have peace. In the world ye shall have tribulation; but be of good cheer; I have overcome the world," (John 16:13-14, 33, KJV).

---NOTES---

Insights In Prophecy
Unlock The Ancient Mysteries Of Daniel & Revelation
BIBLE DISCOVERY SERIES

Lesson 6

ANTICHRIST OF THE APPOINTED TIMES—WHO, WHEN & WHERE?

Read Daniel 7:8-28

- **Study When The Man Of Sin Will Emerge**
- **Discover What Small Nation Fosters Antichrist's Rule**

In Lessons 4 and 5, we discovered the four major global regions of power that prophecy indicates will influence world events during the final conflict of the ages. Secular sources back up the governmental predictions of Daniel—Great Britain (Lion) in alliance with the United States (Eagle's Wings), Russia (Bear), Asia (Leopard) and Western Europe (Terrible Beast). In Lesson 6 we are ready to examine the "little horn" power (Daniel 7:8), which will rise out of the Terrible Beast (7:7) region that has ten horns. We equate this Beast creature with the European Union, and the ten prominent horns as the ten Member-States of the Western European Union—the first organization to create a European military alliance starting in 1948—the year of Israel's birth as a nation. This is the best option we have to date.

Since horns in prophecy represent countries, we can rightly assume that a "little horn" represents a very small country. The smallest country in the world happens to be in Western Europe  and sits on just over 100 acres, with a population around 450 people. The Holy See is an independent papal state and territory of the Church of Rome, situated in Rome, Italy, under the terms of the Lateran Treaty, as concluded by the Italian government and the Papacy.

The Vatican has its own Diplomatic Corps—representatives of the government *permanently posted abroad* to foster relations with governments around the world. The New Catholic Encyclopedia reads, "The Pope alone has the fullness of legislative, executive, and judicial power and represents Vatican City in international relations." In other words, the Pope rules in absolute authority with his own diplomatic policies, laws and judicial power. The "little horn" of Daniel represents a leader who rules over a small country, but who will gain great worldwide authority during the appointed time of the end.

This study is not to disparage the faithful. Undoubtedly, many in Catholicism have great devotion to God and love for Jesus. On the other hand, there are many Protestants that have form of godliness, but deny its power (2 Timothy 3:5). However, false teachings are prevalent in world religions, and apostasy (the abandonment and renunciation of Biblical truths) is not that uncommon among the masses, whether Protestant or Catholic. The once-beloved Lucifer, an angel of high authority, was disloyal to the Father; and Judas—one of the disciples and inner circle of twelve—betrayed Jesus. Some priests have abused children, and renowned Protestant leaders have betrayed the trust of the Christian community. We all sin and fall short of the glory of God. Therefore, should we be surprised that prophecy exposes an end-time "religious" ruler, whom Satan will propel into the political and religious limelight—a man who will come in the name of Jesus Christ, but who will deceive the masses?

Insights In Prophecy
Unlock The Ancient Mysteries Of Daniel & Revelation
BIBLE DISCOVERY SERIES

Prophecy points to the "little horn" of Western Europe as the focal point of power just following pronounced global chaos, and out of catastrophes of global war and upheaval Satan will—with "seducing spirits, and doctrines of devils" (1 Timothy 4:1)—raise up his counterpart for the promotion of his idolatrous practices by means of the office and platform of the Papacy. This man will rise from the ashes of World War III as a *messenger of hope* to the masses. However, he will deceive the nations into following a pagan religion of compromise, devoid of God's blessing. The current Vatican leader is not the Man of Sin foretold in prophecy; his arrival on the world scene will be sudden, spectacular and miraculous.

Let's look closer at the vision Daniel received, starting with Daniel 7:8, which seems to point to the Vatican in Rome.

1. Daniel was considering the ten horns (modern nations of Western Europe) and then he saw a "little horn" emerge. How many horns, or countries, are uprooted as the small country rises to global dominance? _____

2. In prophecy when an animal—or in this case animal parts—the "horn" takes on human characteristics, it is indicating that we watch for a personality. What human features are associated with the horn?
_____

In Lesson 4 we studied Daniel 7:4; there, the Lion with Eagle's Wings (United Kingdom/United States) is found. When its wings are torn off and the Lion stands up, Daniel wrote that "human feet and a man's heart" is given to it; thereby, prophecy has given the animal *human* characteristics. So, this is prophecy's tool of warning to *watch for a powerful individual to emerge from the United Kingdom/United States alliance*. While Daniel 7:4 (the Lion) points to the "False Prophet" of Revelation 13:11-18, Daniel 7:8 (the Horn) points to the "Beast" (Antichrist) of Revelation 13:1-8.

3. The "eyes and mouth" of a man speaking great or boastful things may indicate what? _____
_____

The eyes may represent a proud and lofty attitude (Isaiah 2:11; Psalms 101:5). The Little Horn will magnify himself, speaking words of deception (Psalms 12:2-4; Obadiah 12)—boastful words about his origin and his future. He will speak words of blasphemy against God, says Revelation 13:5; his words will exceed what any man has the right to pronounce. Eventually, in a show of adoration he will be allowed by the leaders of Israel to enter onto the Temple Mount in Jerusalem (2 Thessalonians 2:3-4) to set up an abomination (sacrilegious idol).

4. Three horns (countries) are destroyed just as the little horn Vatican comes into power. What prophetic animal causes the devastation (Daniel 7:5)? _____

The Russian Bear has three ribs in its mouth equal to the three horns that are uprooted. It looks as though Russia will launch a nuclear attack on Western Europe and will "eat [its] fill of flesh" by killing countless individuals and uprooting cities and nations. Such terrible loss of human souls in mass. So sad.

From the catastrophe of World War III, Antichrist will rise into power through magnificent sky signs and miraculous demonic events. The whole world will exalt him his supernatural arrival on the world scene will be awe-inspiring. However, the world peace he will offer will come at a price; it will be a peace based on false religion, the adoration of the Virgin Mary, idol worship, and worship of demonic spirits and apparitions.

5. In spite of the Beast's successes through his three and one-half years in power from Western Europe, what does Daniel 7:11-12 say about the demise of his region of power? _____

While the governmental Beast (Western Europe) is destroy, given to the "burning flame'" the rest of the creatures—Lion, Bear and Leopard have their dominion taken away by the declaration of the Court of Heaven (Daniel 7:26), but live for a short time longer until Messiah returns to finalize God's wrath (Revelation 19:19).

6. How do we know the four creatures of Daniel (Lion, Bear, Leopard and Terrible Beast—UK/US, Russia, Eastern Asia, and European Union) are modern powers of our day, according to Daniel 7:11-12, 17-18?
_____

First, we know because all four are alive at the same time; the most powerful is destroyed first, while the remaining three live slightly longer. Second, the four arise to power just before the overcomers take the kingdom and possess it. The animal creatures are not historical relics of the past as commonly taught, but end-of-the-world nations… first at war with each other, but then at least temporarily aligned in support of the Man of Sin and his New World Order.

7. Daniel 7:21-22 says the "little horn" Papacy does what to the holy people? _____

8. How long does the Papacy make war with Yeshua's dedicated followers? _____

He persecutes the commandment-keeping believers who oppose him "until the Ancient [Father] of Days" takes His throne in the Courtroom, and the judgment of the Heavenly counsel announces the demise of Antichrist and Satan. Notice the verdict comes prior to the believers possessing the kingdom, as Daniel 7:22 indicates—a short delay between the announcement and actual possession. This Courtroom drama will be covered in our next lesson.

9. What distinguishes the many religious-minded people of the world from the faithful followers of Messiah, according to Revelation 12:17? _____

The genuine followers of Messiah hold to His testimony—His prophetic warnings, which the prophet John saw and wrote down in scroll of Revelation (1:1-3). Furthermore, they keep God's commandments while the world at large disregards the Commandments of the Word (Exodus 20). In times past, opponents persecuted and killed commandment-keepers for observing the Sabbath, for celebrating the Festivals or for simply being a Jew (anti-Semitism). Persecution to this degree will emerge once again as the appointed time of the end arrives and will crescendo until the Day of the LORD.

10. How do we know the Ten Commandments are central to the final conflict (Daniel 11:30)?_____
_____

The Evil Ruler will vent his fury against the Holy Covenant as given on Mt. Sinai by God, by showing favor to those who forsake the Commandments of God.

11. How do we know the Covenant is the Ten Commandments (Deuteronomy 4:13)? _____

Revelation 11:19 also focuses on the Law of God. John saw that at the very end of time the Ark of the Testimony—the depository of the Ten Commandments—will be revealed as the measure of judgment against mankind.

The former Dr. D. James Kennedy, well-known writer and host of the television program *The Coral Ridge Hour*, said that "our morally sick society needs the antidote found in God's law." In his book called *Why the Ten Commandments Matter*, Kennedy begins by explaining why the "Ten Commandments remain relevant: they summarize God's timeless moral law, convince people that they are sinners, and teach believers what pleases God," (Publishers Weekly).

In contrast, the Pope will attempt to turn Covenant-keepers into idol worshipers, which is really devotion to evil spirits (Revelation 9:20), and away from the Law of God as written by His own finger on Mt. Sinai.

12. Daniel 7:25 offers more identifying traits of "little horn" Papal power. What are they? _____
_____
_____

He will speak great words against God through a mixture of truth and lies. Secondly, he will persecute the believers who hold to God's commandments. Third, he will think to "change [Festival] times and [God's] laws."

Commandments Of God

Source: The Catholic Encyclopedia

Called also simply THE COMMANDMENTS, THE TEN COMMANDMENTS, or THE DECALOGUE (Gr. *deka*, ten, and *logos*, a word), the Ten Words of Sayings, the latter name generally applied by the Greek Fathers.

The Ten Commandments are precepts bearing on the fundamental obligations of religion and morality and embodying the revealed expression of the Creator's will in relation to man's whole duty to God and to his fellow-creatures. They are found twice recorded in the Pentateuch, in Exodus 20 and Deuteronomy 5, but are given in an abridged form in the catechisms. Written by the finger of God on two tables of stone, this Divine code was received from the Almighty by Moses amid the thunders of Mount Sinai, and by him made the ground-work of the Mosaic Law. Christ resumed these Commandments in the double precept of charity--love of God and of the neighbour; He proclaimed them as binding under the New Law in Matthew 19 and in the Sermon on the Mount (Matthew 5). He also simplified or interpreted them, e.g. by declaring unnecessary oaths equally unlawful with false, by condemning hatred and calumny as well as murder, by enjoining even love of enemies, and by condemning indulgence of evil desires as fraught with the same malice as adultery (Matthew 5). *The Church, on the other hand, after changing the day of rest from the Jewish Sabbath, or seventh day of the week, to the first, made the Third Commandment refer to Sunday as the day to be kept holy as the LORD's Day. The Council of Trent (Sess. VI, can. xix) condemns those who deny that the Ten Commandments are binding on Christians.* (emphasis added).

Several possibilities should be considered here. He may change the calendar to try to emphasize Sunday as the seventh day, and/or Antichrist will attempt to change the Jewish Festivals schedule and other recognized religious observances. In Daniel 2:21 the prophet writes it is God alone who "changes times and seasons," and "removes kings and sets up kings". The Beast's attempt to "change the times" is to fly in the face of providence and to assert that he can act as God in decreeing divine laws.

He will likely promote the Ten Commandments as found in Catholicism. The fourth commandment simply reads, "Remember to keep holy the LORD'S Day," but gives no mention to the seventh day, which God "blessed" and set aside as holy during the week of creation as a blessing for all of mankind—even before sin raised its ugly head (Genesis 2:2-3).

As noted in the Catholic Encyclopedia, "The Council of Trent (Sess. VI, can. xix) *condemns those who deny that the Ten Commandments are binding on Christians*." In other words, Catholicism condemns those who "deny" their shortened version of the Ten Commandments (see below), which erases the seventh day Sabbath and elevates Sunday as the LORD's "Day of rest" and allows the worship of idols (Blessed Virgin Mary, deceased saints blessed by the Vatican, etc.).

The Ten Commandments As Found In Catholicism

I
I am the LORD your GOD; you shall not have strong God's before me.

II
You shall not take the name of the LORD your GOD in vain.

III
Remember to keep holy the LORD'S Day.

IV
Honor your father and your mother.

V
You shall not kill.

VI
You shall not commit adultery.

VII
You shall not steal.

VIII
You shall not bear false witness against your neighbor.

IX
You shall not covet your neighbor's wife.

X
You shall not covet your neighbor's goods.

St. Augustine

13. We know by the evidence of Scriptures the ten precepts as written by God on tablets of stone at Mt. Sinai are still binding. How long would the Law remain unchanged (Matthew 5:18)? _____

First, Yeshua—Jesus is the Creator of Genesis 1: John 1:1-3 says, "In the beginning was the Word, and the Word was with God, and the Word was God. He was with God in the beginning. Through Him [Jesus] all things were made, *without Him nothing was made that has been made*." Hebrews 1:2 confirms, "In these last days He has spoken to us by His Son [Jesus], whom He appointed heir of all things, *and through whom He made the universe*." "He is the image of the invisible God, the firstborn over all creation. For *by Him [Yeshua] all things were created*: things in Heaven and on earth... all things were created by Him and for Him," Colossians 1:15-16.

Second, Jesus added the Sabbath day and declared it holy from the first week of creation: "By the seventh day God [Yeshua] had finished the work He had been doing; so on the seventh day He rested from all His work. And God [the Son] blessed the seventh day and made it holy, because on it He rested from all the work of creating that He had done," Genesis 2:2-3.

Third, when the abomination is set up by the Little Horn on the Temple Mount towards the end of the counting periods, Jesus said His people were to pray that they would not have to flee "in the winter, neither on the Sabbath day" (Matthew 24:20), proving beyond doubt the seventh-day Sabbath would remain until the end of the age.

Fourth, Messiah stated that His Law would endure until heaven and earth disappeared. He said unequivocally, "until heaven and earth disappear, not the smallest letter, not the least stroke of a pen, will by any means disappear from the Law, until everything is accomplished." Not "until heaven and earth disappear," no human—neither pope nor religious council of men—can change the smallest letter of the Law.

14. How long will the Lawless One rule according to Daniel 7:25? _____

He will be in control three and one-half years. A "time" equals one year; "times" equals two; and "dividing of time" equals one-half year. Nowhere in prophecy is the Man of Sin ever given more than three and one-half years, or 1260 days, to accomplish his plan of domination.

15. Revelation 13:5 gives a specific period when the Beast will rule. What is it? _____

Forty-two months of 30 days, equaling 1,260 days.

His three and one-half years will be much different than Yeshua's ministry 2,000 years ago. While the Son of Man came as a humble servant to die for mankind, the evil ruler will arrive exalting himself and ready to inflict laws of punishment against all who oppose him. For this reason, God will not allow the Lawless One to rule any longer than foretold. In fact, Jesus swears on His good name that at the end of the "times, times and an half... all these things will be finished," (Daniel 12:7). When the Divine speaks an oath of time, we can stake our lives on it! After three and a half years of Antichrist's reign, our Messiah will stand up with lifted hands to deliver His people.

In the St. Augustine Catholic version of the Ten Commandments the law against idolatry is deleted, and the seventh-day Sabbath is erased, with emphasis on the LORD's Day. However, the LORD's Day from a Biblical perspective is not the first day of the week. Even if Sunday is called the LORD's Day, it would not destroy or change God's seventh-day commandment of rest. Jesus Himself stated, "the Sabbath was made for man[kind], and not man for the Sabbath [see Genesis 2:2-3]: Therefore, the Son of man is LORD also of the Sabbath," Mark 2:27-28. The seventh-day Sabbath is truly the "LORD's Day" on a Biblical basis.

We are reminded of the words of Jesus in Revelation 22:19, that if any man takes away from the words of prophecy God will take his name out of the Book of Life. Why would anyone think to tamper with God's Law, considering the words of warning directly from Jesus that not the smallest letter or least stroke of a pen will disappear from the Law—not until heaven and earth pass away (Matthew 5:18). His Word remains unchanged, and God's Covenant will be become the focal point of contention at the end of the age between Jews, between Jew and Gentile, righteous and unrighteous, father and son.

In the book, The Keys Of This Blood, published in 1990 by the former Dr. Malachi Martin, theologian, former Jesuit and professor at the Vatican's Pontificate Biblical Institute and devote Catholic, the author wrote that

John Paul II (before his death) foresaw great disaster looming on the horizon, and that Russia would be the primary instigator of tragedy. Likewise, John Paul *"is waiting... for an event that will fission human history, splitting the immediate past from the oncoming future. It will be an event on public view in the skies, in the oceans, and on the continental landmasses of this planet. It will particularly involve our human sun, which every day lights up and shines upon the valleys, the mountains and the plains of this earth for our eyes. But on the day of this event, it will not appear merely as the master star of our so-called solar system. Rather, it will be seen as the circumambient glory of the Woman [whom Catholicism interprets to be the Virgin Mary] whom the apostle describes as 'clothed with the sun' and giving birth to 'a child who will rule the nations with a scepter of iron'... his ministry as the Servant of the Grand Design will then begin... he claim[s] the authority and the duty to advise, admonish and exhort all men, regardless of creed, race or ideology, on their duties to God and their due place in God's Grand Design for the society of nations,"* pages 639, 641.

Dr. Martin continues, *"The Fatima message (of 1917)... predicts that a catastrophic change will shortly shatter any plans or designs that men may have established. This is the era of the Fatima... This is why John Paul is waiting. God must first intervene, before John Paul's ministry to all men can start. In [his] outlook, therefore, the Grand Design of which he is the nominated Servant is the design of divine providence to recall men to the values that derive on from belief, from religion and from divine revelation. His is an unpleasant message and, for the moment, a thankless job. He has to warn his contemporaries of his conviction that human catastrophe on a world scale—according to his information—is impending,"* pages 656-657. To learn more about the Catholic Fatima event of 1917, see http://en.wikipedia.org/wiki/Our_Lady_of_Fatima.

Although John Paul believed he was to be the "child who [would] rule the nations" and lead the society of nations, he did not fulfill his vision as the moral and spiritual leader of mankind. This work will no doubt be given to another, and with it the great errors of Roman Catholicism, which include the pope's infallibility, purgatory, the Eucharist, the rosary, the worship of the dead, worship of Mary, plus other cultic religious activities that disagree to the Word of God.

However, Pope John Paul's relentless pursuit in worldwide travel and public addresses during his pontificate, and his outspoken devotion to Mary, brought the Papacy and Marian worship to the forefront of minds everywhere. As a government, the Holy See gained greater world influence through John Paul's untiring efforts—a cause he believed was worthy of his busy traveling schedule prior to his death.

Indeed, disaster on a worldwide scale is impending (Matthew 24:6-8) and the Russian Bear will be one of the key instigators of human tragedy, likely destroying three countries in Western Europe (Daniel 7:5, 8). However, these predictions were penned over 2,000 years ago in the prophecies of Daniel, and again hinted at in the book of Revelation, and are not new or divine divinations received from the Virgin Mary.

These Marian apparitions look beautiful and angelic, speaking sacred words to engage the religious heart of man, but only for the purposes of deception. They speak of Jesus and His love, but then add requirements to honor Mary, to pray the Rosary, and so forth. Her ghostly images, seen by thousands from all faiths and nationalities in locations around the globe, promote goddess worship and false teachings. Her words, although sweet to the ear, contradict the clear teachings of God's Word. The wise must know the testimony of Jesus, delivered through God's prophets. In the last days, error will be adored, and truth ignored, and the whole world will wonder after the Beast.

The last-day Antichrist, highly intelligent and artful in words and conversation (Daniel 7:20; Ezekiel 28:1-10), will likely call for a return to conservative values, which will intrigue the religious masses. We desire to live our lives "under God", to know that unborn babies are protected, and to be a nation that lives by the God's standards of morality. However, the Papacy will be against the Holy Covenant (Daniel 11:28) as revealed at Mt. Sinai, and Sunday laws will no doubt be enacted that will require first day observance as Sabbath rest.

No matter the terrible state of affairs in the appointed time of the end, "Christianity" cannot be legislated or required; our faith must be voluntary. The great commission says to teach, not demand. Jesus did not use government and powerful leaders to promote the kingdom of God, but kings and religious leaders demanded the crucifixion of this humble teacher. Religious edicts cannot be used to establish a worldwide religion or preside over the population. The Dark Ages attest to the evils of Christianity backed by laws and the state.

However, Satan will stir up international strife and unleash one disaster after another. World War III, nature's wrath, disease and other calamities will bring mankind to the brink of annihilation; then the world will be taken captive by Satan (Revelation 13:8). The Queen of Heaven will be exalted, and demonic deception will overtake Planet Earth. On the heels of church and state intervention, reverence for idols will increase (Revelation 13:14-15) and the worship of demons who seemingly bring them to life (Revelation 9:20), even though prophecy warns in no uncertain terms that idols of gold, silver and stone neither see, nor hear, nor walk. Don't believe talking or bleeding idols to be messengers from God.

In summary, there is a Catholic teaching that before the great climax of human history a righteous Pope will first rule the world, turning many to Christianity, followed by an evil Pope or Antichrist who would emerge to fulfill the apocalyptic predictions of Revelation.

The Bible reveals the Wicked One will rule the world. He will at first "come in [Christ's] name" (Matthew 24:5) but will then blaspheme God. And, at the apex of his rule he will step onto the Temple Mount in Jerusalem and declare himself God (2 Thessalonians 2:3-4). His abomination will be complete, and God's patience exhausted.

It is interesting to note that in the Jewish commentary—*Encyclopedia Judaica*, the legendary name given to the antichrist is Armilus. It says, *"This Armilus will deceive the whole world into believing he is God and will*

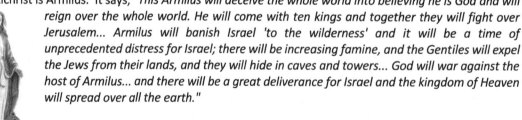

reign over the whole world. He will come with ten kings and together they will fight over Jerusalem... Armilus will banish Israel 'to the wilderness' and it will be a time of unprecedented distress for Israel; there will be increasing famine, and the Gentiles will expel the Jews from their lands, and they will hide in caves and towers... God will war against the host of Armilus... and there will be a great deliverance for Israel and the kingdom of Heaven will spread over all the earth."

In his book, *In Search of Temple Treasures*, Dr. Randall Price wrote that other references, *"Describe Armilus as arising from the Roman Empire, having miraculous powers, and being born to a stone statue of a virgin (which is why he is called "the son of stone"). It is also interesting that he makes this statue "the chief of all idolatry" with the result that "all the Gentiles will bow down to her, burn incense and pour out libations to her."*

Insights In Prophecy
Unlock The Ancient Mysteries Of Daniel & Revelation
BIBLE DISCOVERY SERIES

Historic Men of Faith Who Believed The Pope To Be Antichrist

Although a less popular view today among Protestant teachers and leaders, these Protestant reformers and historic men of faith all held the doctrine that the Church of Rome and the Pope is the Antichrist prophesied in Scripture.

From the Reformation
Huss, Wycliffe, Luther, Melancthon, Zwingli, Calvin, Beza, Bucer, Knox, Ferrar, Hooper, Latimer, Ridley, Cranmer, Ussher, Firth, Barnes, Philpot, Becon, Turner, Cartwright, Barrow, Jewel, Coverdale, LORD Cobham, Hooker, Ainsworth, Dent, Foxe, Fulke, Bradford, Bullinger, Rogers, Hutchinson, Whitgift, Sir Francis Drake and a host of others.

Post-Reformation Personalities
Sir Isaac Newton, Sir Henry Vane, Brightman, Milton, Beard, Baxter, Bishop Newton, John Bunyan, Fleming, Wesley, Matthew Henry, Jonathan Edwards, Gill, Clarke, Trapp, Brown, Toplady, Pool, Clarkson, Swimmock, Brooks, Chamock, Sibbs, Goodwin, Owen, Hall, Cunningham, Manton, Smith, Adams, Perkins, Gilpin, Field, Durham, Willet, Rainolds, Cotton, Gauge, Burroughs, Carter, Ames, Bridge, Marshall, Potter, Thomas Fuller, Twisse, Keith, Hales, Chalmers, Spurgeon, Wylie, Elliott, Cumming, Goode, Ryle, Candlish, Albert Bames, Wordsworth, Birks, Hislop, A. J. Gordon often called the Father of Fundamentalism, Moody, Hudson Taylor, Guinness, Salmond, Dinsdale Young, Horn, Close, T. T. Shields, Kensit, Baron Porceli and a host of others.

Names & Titles Of Antichrist In The Scriptures
From the Book, The Antichrist, by Arthur W. Pink

Antichrist, "opposed to / instead of Christ"
1 John 2:22: Who is the liar? It is the man who denies that Jesus is the Christ. Such a man is the antichrist — he denies the Father and the Son.

Man of Sin, Son of Perdition
2 Thessalonians 2:3: Let no one deceive you by any means; for that Day will not come unless the falling away comes first, and the man of sin is revealed, the son of perdition.

The Lawless One
2 Thessalonians 2:8: And then the lawless one will be revealed, whom the LORD Jesus will overthrow with the breath of his mouth and destroy by the splendor of his coming.

The Beast
Revelation 11:7: Now when they have finished their testimony, the beast that comes up from the Abyss will attack them and overpower and kill them.

Bloody and Deceitful Man
Psalm 5:6: You destroy those who tell lies; bloodthirsty and deceitful men the LORD abhors.

The Wicked One
Psalm 10:2, 4: In his arrogance the wicked man hunts down the weak, who are caught in the schemes he devises. In his pride the wicked does not seek him; in all his thoughts there is no room for God.

The Man of the Earth
Psalm 10:18: ...defending the fatherless and the oppressed, in order that man, who is of the earth, may terrify no more.

The Mighty Man
Psalm 52:1: Why do you boast of evil, you mighty man? Why do you boast all day long, you who are a disgrace in the eyes of God?

The Enemy
Psalm 55:3: ...at the voice of the enemy, at the stares of the wicked; for they bring down suffering upon me and revile me in their anger.

The Adversary

Psalm 74:8-10: They said in their hearts, "We will crush them completely!" They burned every place where God was worshiped in the land. We are given no miraculous signs; no prophets are left, and none of us knows how long this will be. How long will the adversary mock you, O God?

Isaiah 59:18: According to what they have done, so will he repay wrath to his enemies and retribution to his foes; he will repay the islands their due.

Head over Many Countries

Psalm 110:6: He shall judge among the nations, he shall fill the places with dead bodies, he shall execute the heads of many countries.

The Violent Man

Psalm 140:1: Deliver me, O LORD, from evil men; preserve me from violent men.

King of Babylon

Isaiah 14:4: Take up this proverb against the king of Babylon, and say: "How the oppressor has ceased, the golden city ceased!"

Lucifer, Son of the Morning

Isaiah 14:12: "How you are fallen from heaven, O Lucifer, son of the morning! How you are cut down to the ground, you who weakened the nations!"

The Spoiler

Isaiah 16:4, 5: Let My outcasts dwell with you, O Moab; be a shelter to them from the face of the spoiler.

The Nail

Isaiah 22:25: In that day, says the LORD of hosts, 'the nail that is fastened in the secure place will be removed and be cut down and fall, and the burden that was on it will be cut off; for the LORD has spoken.'

The Branch of the Terrible Ones

Isaiah 25:5: You will reduce the noise of aliens, as heat in a dry place; as heat in the shadow of a cloud, the branch of the terrible ones will be diminished.

The Profane and Wicked Prince of Israel

Ezekiel 21:25-27: Now to you, O profane, wicked prince of Israel, whose day has come, whose iniquity shall end....

The Little Horn

Daniel 7:8: I was considering the horns, and there was another horn, a little one, coming up among them, before whom three of the first horns were plucked out by the roots. And there, in this horn, were eyes like the eyes of a man, and a mouth speaking pompous words.

The Prince that shall come

Daniel 9:26: And after the sixty-two weeks Messiah shall be cut off, but not for Himself; and the people of the prince that shall come shall destroy the city and the sanctuary....

The Vile Person

Daniel 11:21: And in his place shall arise a vile person, to whom they will not give the honor of royalty; but he shall come in peaceably, and seize the kingdom by intrigue.

The Wilful King

Daniel 11:36: Then the king shall do according to his own will: he shall exalt and magnify himself above every god, shall speak blasphemies against the God of gods.

The Worthless Shepherd

Zechariah 11:16,17: For indeed I will raise up a shepherd in the land who will not care for those who are cut off, nor seek the young, nor heal those that are broken, nor feed those that still stand. But he will eat the flies of the fat and tear their hooves in pieces. "Woe to the worthless shepherd who leaves the flock! A sword shall be against his arm and against his right eye; his arm shall completely wither, and his right eye shall be totally blinded."

Insights In Prophecy
Unlock The Ancient Mysteries Of Daniel & Revelation
BIBLE DISCOVERY SERIES

Lesson 7

THE INVESTIGATIVE COURT DURING THE APPOINTED TIMES OF THE END

Read Daniel 7:9-28; 8:10-14

- Probe Heaven's Response To The Little Horn's Evil Activities
- Investigate The Seven-Division Outline Of Daniel's Courtroom Prophecies

Lesson 7 provides the opportunity for us to study the courtroom judgment in detail, which is clearly revealed in the Scriptures, but universally ignored or assigned to events over 2,000 years ago. Whenever the Man of Sin's deceitful actions are revealed in Daniel, we will discover the verses that *immediately follow* describe Heaven's response, through the drama of courtroom events. The Court sits in direct response to Antichrist's last-day deceptive practices on earth, and Satan's vicious attack against the LORD of Hosts and His army (Revelation 12:7-9). It's a contemporary courtroom event in Heaven that parallel's earth's final

activities that unfold during the appointed time of the end, although commentaries have wrongly assigned these activities to historical events involving Antioachus IV Epiphames' sacrilegious activities in the Jerusalem Temple around 167 B.C.

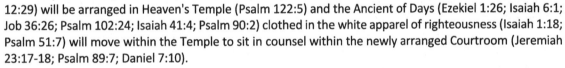

Thrones, like a wheel intersecting a wheel (Ezekiel 1:15-26; 10:2), ablaze with fire (Exodus 3:2; Psalm 97:3; Deuteronomy 4:24; Daniel 7:9; Hebrews 12:29) will be arranged in Heaven's Temple (Psalm 122:5) and the Ancient of Days (Ezekiel 1:26; Isaiah 6:1; Job 36:26; Psalm 102:24; Isaiah 41:4; Psalm 90:2) clothed in the white apparel of righteousness (Isaiah 1:18; Psalm 51:7) will move within the Temple to sit in counsel within the newly arranged Courtroom (Jeremiah 23:17-18; Psalm 89:7; Daniel 7:10).

Innumerable angels will be attending the proceedings (1 Kings 22:19; Daniel 7:10; Revelation 5:11), for the holy ones watch earthly affairs and proclaim announcements of the Court (Daniel 4:17). A small select group of humans are involved in the Courtroom drama (Revelation 4:4) for the redeemed will be given the power of decision in the future Kingdom of God (1 Corinthians 6:2-3; Revelation 20:4).

In vision Daniel saw that "the judgment was set, and the books were opened," (Daniel 7:9-10). The investigative court will proceed with opened books (Isaiah 65:6; Malachi 3:16; Psalm 56:8; Jeremiah 17:1), which will lead to the Judge's sentence of death against the rebellious nations (1 Kings 22:19; Joel 3:2; Psalm 72:2-4).

In each of the prophetic passages in Daniel's scroll, which deal with the Courtroom setting, we find the same elements of a modern courtroom. God *will not* forcibly reclaim earth's territory from Satan and his subjects without proper proceedings in the presence of jury and witnesses. In contrast, Yeshua underwent a sham trial spurred on by hatred and lies, which ended His three-and-one-half year ministry with a shameful and bloody execution on the cross. However, the Father will not seek the reversal of Satan's authority, the death sentence for the global leader who reigns supreme over the planet (Luke 4:6) and the demise of his rebellious subjects (Ezekiel 28:18-19; Revelation 19:20) without first allowing the case and evidence to be reviewed for the sake of every concerned onlooker.

Nonetheless, God knows the end from the beginning and His Word spells out Lucifer's doom that will end his three-and-one-half year cruel pursuit of the righteous, as well as the demise of the Wicked One and the False Prophet and those who have aligned themselves with him, and who receive his mark.

Opening Scene Of The Court

1. Daniel has just described the Little Horn's uprising in Daniel 7:8. Now Daniel takes us to a scene in Heaven. What does he see taking place after Antichrist comes into power (Daniel 7:9-10)? _____

_____

The prophet sees the thrones are "set in place" (N.I.V).

We should note, however; the King James Version reads the opposite—Heaven's thrones "were cast down". The original Hebrew word: רְמָה "remah"—according to Strong's Concordance 7412, means "to cast, throw" or "hurled by violence". However, both translations reveal truths that surround the courtroom drama. *Remah* was used to describe the casting of the three Hebrews into the fiery furnace, and of casting Daniel into the den of lions. The original language indicates although the thrones will be cast down in a cosmic battle that will occur in Heaven at the time of the end, they will soon thereafter be set back up for the end-time Court proceedings that will bring about the final solution to the great controversy. Satan and his angels will reach Heaven, even the very throne room of the Most High, in an attempt to overtake God's Kingdom. Despite this violent battle, Satan will not prevail; he and his army will be cast out of Heaven (Revelation 12:7-9).

Several versions, including the NIV Bible translation, have opted to translate the language as "to set or place in order," as in the placing of the judgment seats for the courtroom work. Another example is the "setting" or "placing" of the throne in Revelation 4:2, in which the Greek carries the same meaning: *"a throne was set in heaven, and One sat on the throne."* This throne rearrangement in the courts of Heaven set the stage for the opening of the recorded books of evidence so that all testimony might be examined as to whose kingdom will prevail—that of Messiah or Satan.

2. In Revelation 4:2-11 the prophet John is transported to the throne room in Heaven. How does he describe the One sitting on the throne and those who surround Him? _____

_____

The prophet describes the magnificent throne room and the Ancient of Days sitting on the throne. A rainbow encircled Him. Twenty-four elders, "purchased men" according to Revelation 5:9, who will eventually reign on earth with the believers, surround the throne.

In Daniel we are told "thrones" (plural) are set alongside God's throne. This could indicate the reigning of a group (possible jury) who will hear the evidence and may render importance decisions about the nations and about God's Kingdom. However, attention is focused on God the Father as Judge. He is described as One "advanced in years"—a picture not of senility but of venerability. It is He who existed before the worlds began (Isaiah 44:6; Psalm 55:19), who exemplifies wisdom as well as might. His raiment, like His hair, is the purist white, reflecting that dazzling brightness, which is a mark of divine or celestial beings (Matthew 28:3). In the counsel of the holy ones, God is greatly revered (Psalm 89:7). The picture of God as the arbiter and judge of all the earth is a common one in Hebrew writings.

3. Daniel saw the fiery throne, and its wheels were blazing (7:9). How does Ezekiel describe the four living creatures (Ezekiel 1:4-21)? _____

The throne has burning wheels, reminding us of the chariot throne of Ezekiel's vision from which fire came flashing (Ezekiel 1:4; 13-15). These fiery creatures are four massive angels who each have six wings. They stand before Almighty God, and are known in the Scriptures as the "four winds" (Zechariah 6:2-5). These four magnificent creatures are also closely associated with the four horses of Revelation 6:1-8, and the emergence of earthly powers (Lion, Bear, Leopard and Beast) in Daniel 7:2-3.

4. How many angels did Daniel see in the throne vision (7:10)? _____

There were millions of angels witnessing the proceedings. John likewise saw the vast number of angels in his vision (Revelation 5:11).

We do not see Jesus sitting on His throne next to the Father in either Daniel's vision or John's description of the Heavenly Sanctuary. Hebrews 8:1-2 says Christ is sat down at the right hand of God as the High Priest, so we want to examine why He is not at this moment sitting in His position of power.

5. Daniel 7:13-14 depicts the one "like a son of man," the Messiah, as separated from the Father but eventually stepping before the Ancient of Days to receive His Kingdom. Why? _____

_____

Messiah approaches the Father with many angels (clouds of heaven) for His official Kingship coronation, when He is given complete authority over the entire universe—including Planet Earth. Revelation 11:15-19 pinpoints this ceremony just before the blowing of the seventh trumpet near the end of time.

6. What event during the appointed time of the end initiates the separation between Father and Son (Revelation 12:7-9)? _____

A great war will ensue in Heaven between Michael—the LORD of hosts (His army)—the starry host (Daniel 8:10) and Satan and his fallen rebels (Isaiah 14:13-14). Satan attempts to be as great as the Prince ("sar"—"chief"; Joshua 5:13-15; Daniel 10:13; 20; 12:1) of the angelic host. His assault is designed to take away the daily ("tamid"—Exodus 29:38; Numbers 28:3) activities of the Heavenly Sanctuary (Daniel 8:11-13); and therefore, the Temple of God is brought low. Although Messiah and His angels successfully defend the Kingdom, a "third" of righteous angels are "cast down" to earth in conflict and trampled upon, according to Revelation 12:4. Once Satan and his army are defeated and the battle is won, the Courtroom thrones are set in place and the books of evidence are opened.

"LORD of hosts" occurs some 261 times in the Scriptures. God is first called the "LORD of hosts" in 1 Samuel 1:3. The word LORD, capitalized, refers to Yahweh, the self-existent, redemptive God. The word hosts is a translation of the Hebrew word sabaoth, meaning "armies"—a reference to the angelic armies of heaven. Thus, another way of saying "LORD of hosts" is "God of the armies of heaven." The NIV translates YHWH saboath as "LORD Almighty." This kingship of the LORD of hosts is vividly expressed in Psalm 24:10: "Who is this King of glory? The LORD of hosts, He is the King of glory!" (ESV). He is the glorious King of Israel, and Zechariah 14:6 tells us that He will be King of the world, over all the kingdoms of the earth (Isaiah 37:16). The only reason for an army is the threat of future conflict.

Jurisdiction Of The Court

7. In Daniel 7:13-14 the prophet saw "one like a son of man"; in other words, a benefactor of human descent will come before the Father to receive full authority. How does John the Revelator depict Messiah (1:13)? _____

John also speaks of Him as one "like a son of man." He is dressed in a robe and golden sash with white hair depicting His eternal age and eyes of penetrating glow, bronze feet and very loud voice. He comes transported by the clouds of heaven (Psalm 104:1-4) on wings of wind (Psalm 18:10; Matthew 26:64), subordinate only to the Ancient of Days. The Messiah King will be inaugurated by this ceremony of investiture.

8. How is the magnificent "Man" Daniel saw described in Daniel 10:4-6? _____

This Messiah Man is nearly identical with linen robe (the priest's attire), belt, eyes like flaming torches, and legs of bronze and very loud voice. His identity is later disclosed as Michael in Daniel 8:13, the protector of Israel and Angel of the LORD throughout the ancient Hebrew writings.

9. Daniel 7:14 offers the full realm of Heaven's authority. How widespread is the jurisdiction of the Court and how long will Heaven rule? _____

The jury completes the judgment. The Son of Man deserves sovereign control over the whole realm—"all peoples, nations and men of every language worship Him," whose kingdom will last for all eternity. The Scriptures foretell in the final days of the widespread conversion to Israel's King and faith in the sovereign God (Isaiah 2:2; Isaiah 49:6; Zechariah 8:21; Zechariah 14:9, 16-21).

10. Read Revelation 11:15-17. How does it compare to the declaration of the Court described in Daniel?
_____

Verdict Of The Court

11. The world's Papal leader will be wagging war against the faithful during his three and one-half year rule (Daniel 7:25), according to Daniel 7:21-22. What stops his onslaught against the people of God? __
_____

The Ancient of Days moves within the Temple: He "came" Daniel says, and "pronounced judgment in favor of the holy people." Only then will the overcomers possess the Kingdom.

The last days represent a time of decision for the followers of Messiah. The authentic Word-followers will not accept the mark of the beast or give credence to the Man of Sin but will by faith hold on to the Savior and keep His Commandments. They will commit to the instructions (testimony) from Jesus (Revelation 12:17) and never give up, even if facing persecution or death (Matthew 24:13). They realize at the end of the counting days the verdict will be issued against Satan and his world leader, and the faithful ones will victoriously possess the Kingdom!

Sentence & Punishment Of The Court

12. Read Daniel 7:25-27. How do the verses describe the outcome of the Court proceedings? _____
_____

Although the Lawless One will rule for a "time, times and half a time", the Court in Heaven will convene during this same period in Heaven and his power will ultimately be stripped away.

13. Besides Yeshua, who is also awarded sovereignty, power and greatness in the future Kingdom? _____
_____

The steadfast overcomers who endure to the end (Matthew 24:13) will rule and reign with Messiah forever in power (Revelation 3:21; 5:10). These are not believers of every age but identified as martyred saints—the faithful ones who remain loyal to God's commandments, even to the point of death. They are not stained-glass believers, but ordinary people sanctified by the Holy Spirit and committed to follow Jesus even under great persecution to live extraordinary lives in the face of severe trials.

14. What is Satan and the Evil One's ultimate sentence and punishment for their wrong-doings (Daniel 7:26; 2 Thessalonians 2:8; Revelation 19:19-20; 20:1-3)? _____

Their power will be totally broken. The Beast will be destroyed by King Messiah at His coming, and Satan will be imprisoned for 1,000 years.

Length Of The Court Proceedings

Daniel 8:11-12 describes the war in Heaven at the beginning of the end. The Little Horn power will grow in demonic strength, reaching all the way to Heaven through Satan and his vast army.

15. How does John depict Satan and his supremacy at the end of time in Revelation 12:3-4? _____
_____

John depicts Satan as a mammoth red dragon with seven heads, ten horns and seven crowns, representing human governments (New World Order). Note that three crowns are missing, indicating three nations on earth are destroyed around the time Satan reaches Heaven to battle Michael and His angels. Angels are often depicted as "stars" in the ancient Hebrew Scriptures. Satan is so powerful that his dragon tail symbolically sweeps away heaven's righteous stars and flings them to the ground in battle. Revelation 12 is a collage of complex images, which employs events of the past as though they are happening again; for, many past events are representative of episodes still to come.

16. Satan and his minions battle Heaven's angels, before he is hurled down (Revelation 12:7-9). How long does the symbolic woman run to hide from his anger, where she is taken care of (Revelation 12:13-14)?
_____

She is given protection for the same length of time that Antichrist rules—a "time, times and half a time"—1,260 days. It is also the same period the two witnesses will be ruling on earth.

Satan and his army will battle in Heaven, taking away the daily activities in Heaven's Sanctuary. Sometime after his defeat, the judgment will be set up to deal with his evil attack and deceptive actions on earth. Daniel heard a holy one speaking to another holy one (8:13); which is to say, one prophet questioned another—"how long?" Many others have asked the same probing question down through the centuries (Psalm 6:3; 80:4; 90:13; Isaiah 6:9-12; Habakkuk 2:6; Revelation 6:10).

17. The prophet asks (Daniel 8:13), "How long shall be the vision concerning the daily... and the transgression of desolation, to give both the sanctuary and the host to be trodden under foot?" In the margin of King James Version Reference Bibles, only One could offer the answer: Palmoni, the wonderful numberer of secrets. Messiah offered what period (Daniel 8:14)? _____

"It will take 2,300 evenings and mornings; then the Sanctuary will be reconsecrated"; which means to be returned to its rightful and holy use. In other words, when this time period is over the Court procedures in Heaven will close and Heaven's Sanctuary will return to its rightful purpose as the Kingdom's Temple of worship.

The question remains: what period does the 2,300 "evenings and mornings" represent? Some scholars, including those who collaborated on the King James Version of 1611, suggest the original language should be interpreted as 2,300 days; however, a sizeable group of theologians who understand the Hebrew and sanctuary context of Daniel's writing stand firm on the interpretation of 1,150 days.

Why? In the Hebrew Scriptures God ordained there should be evening עֶרֶב (erev) and morning בֹּקֶר (boker) sacrifices. Exodus 29:38-42 describes the burnt offerings made on the altar, twice a day. Therefore, if the judgment is to last "2,300" evening and morning sacrifices, the total period the judgment would be in session is 1,150 days. One day's sanctuary activities would include an evening sacrifice followed by a morning sacrifice. Likewise, 1,150 evenings, plus 1,150 mornings would equal "2,300 evenings and mornings," which would still equate to half the number—1,150 complete days. Remember, this number was supplied by Palmoni, the numbered of secrets; so, the true number would not be so obvious, rather... a mysterious number.

One last point; by the simple reading of Daniel, we know the judgment commences after the Papacy comes into world power, and we know he will rule for 1,260 days. Furthermore, the judgment will end just prior to Little Horn's downfall, for that is the verdict of the Court. The judgment must, of necessity, be a shorter duration than the 1,260 days of his reign. The 2,300 days interpretation would have to extend way beyond the other prophetic time periods of prophecy or would need to begin way before any other time line. The 1,150 days duration would allow the turmoil in Heaven and the Court of Law to begin and end during the Man of Sin's rule, which fits both Daniel and Revelation's prophecies.

The Distant Beginning Of The Courtroom Drama

Daniel was perplexed by the vision (8:15). Before him stood what looked to be a "man." Daniel heard a "man's voice" from the river Ulai demanding Gabriel tell Daniel the meaning of the vision of chapter 8. The Man, given a name later in vision as He who was *clothed in linen* (priestly garments) and standing above the river, is Michael (12:1, 7). Michael instructs Gabriel to explain the events.

**18. For the vision concerning the evenings and mornings, what does Gabriel tell Daniel (8:26)? _____
_____**

The vision concerns the distant future; it would occur well beyond Daniel's lifetime. So long in fact that Daniel was told he might as well "seal up the vision."

19. When would this vision and the perilous predictions of Daniel be unsealed and understood (Daniel 12:4)? _____

Only at the end of time would this vision of the Court and the 2,300 evenings and mornings truly be understood. Therefore, the beginning of the Courtroom events would come at the time of the end, and not before.

Ending Of The Judgment

One last time in Daniel's scroll, the Little Horn (little country—the Vatican leader) and his activities are described in lengthy detail that spans the second half of the final vision found in chapters 10-12. Just after describing his horrible crimes, the last and final element of the Courtroom proceeding is revealed in the prophecy in Daniel 11:45. The final Papal leader will set up his royal headquarters in Jerusalem for his last attempt to establish his religious rule from the Temple Mount. The masses will rejoice that God's two witnesses who opposed Antichrist's rule have finally been killed and silenced (Revelation 11:7-10). No doubt, with much pomp and ceremony, the Lawless One will parade onto the Temple Mount in Jerusalem to set up his abomination and to proclaim publicly his belief that he is God incarnate and is to be worshiped as the Divine (2 Thessalonians 2:1-4).

20. What is Michael's response to this abominable act, which brings the sentence and punishment of the Courtroom proclamation upon the False Shepherd (Daniel 12:1)? _____

Messiah will stand up from His throne, and then will begin the time of trouble so terrible it will never be repeated again in human history. Beginning at the House of God and spreading throughout Israel and then to the world, God's wrath will be unleashed upon sinful mankind.

21. Read Matthew 24:14-16, 20-22. How does it depict the final events? _____
_____

Once the abomination is set up as Daniel described, then God's elect must flee for their lives. God's judgment upon Jerusalem will be sure and swift. There will be no time for hesitation or delay. The elect, later identified as the 144,000 in the book of Revelation, must run for their lives.

22. What does Malachi disclose about Messiah's Day of Visitation to the Temple in Jerusalem once the abomination is set up (Malachi 4:5-6; 3:1)? _____
_____

Elijah, one of the two witnesses, will prophesy for 1,260 days (Revelation 11:3). He will be killed in Jerusalem, where Jesus said all God's prophets shed their blood (Luke 13:33) and will lie in the streets unburied for three and one-half days (Revelation 11:7-11) while the Man of Sin makes his way onto the Temple Mount. Shortly after, Michael, the Messenger of the Covenant, will stand and descend in the cloak of darkness with storm, thunder and lightning. Malachi asks, "But who can endure the day of His coming? Who can stand when He appears?" (3:2).

The Mystery Of The Sevens In Daniel's Prophecies

Daniel's prophecies were presented in an inspired order to reveal vital information concerning the last days. Seven sections describe the Little Horn Antichrist, and *immediately thereafter* seven sections describe

Insights In Prophecy
Unlock The Ancient Mysteries Of Daniel & Revelation
BIBLE DISCOVERY SERIES

the Court of Law. Although hidden for centuries in the scroll, each dual section is charted below to show the connection between each of the passages, as well as the progressive description of the Courtroom Judgment throughout Daniel—starting with the opening scene and concluding with the announcement of the Tribunal and the subsequent punishment. The Courtroom drama commences as Satan's/Antichrist's evil activities begin to unfold on the world scene and ends when Michael stands up to execute the punishment of the Court. This reveals the close connection between Antichrist's evil practices and Heaven's response through legal court processes and review of the evidence.

Seven Descriptions Of The Little Horn—Antichrist		Immediately Thereafter, *Seven* Descriptions Of The Courtroom Judgment	
1)	Daniel 7:7-8	9-10	Court Convenes: books open
2)	Daniel 7:11-12	13-14	Jurisdiction/Authority: all nations
3)	Daniel 7:19-21	22	Verdict: in favor of believers
4)	Daniel 7:23-25	26	Sentence: his power destroyed
5)	Daniel 8:9-13	14	Length: 2,300 e/m (1,150 days)
6)	Daniel 8:23-25	26	Time: at the unsealing of Daniel
7)	Daniel 11:21-45	12:1	Finale: Michael stands; Trib begins

Additional Study: Who Is "Palmoni"

"Palmoni" is found referenced in the King James Version of the Bible and is reported to have been a name noted in the original Hebrew during Daniel's second (2nd) vision. The Hebrew meaning, *"the numberer of secrets, or, the wonderful numberer"*. *"Pali"* means *"secret"* while *"pala"* means *"wonderful"*; and, *"mena"* means *"number"*. *"For to us a child is born, to us a son is given, and the government will be on His shoulders. And He will be called Wonderful [Hebrew "pele"],"* Isaiah 9:6.

The mysterious Palmoni of Daniel 8:13 points to the Messianic figure of the Old Covenant period--now known as the Son of God, the child born for our salvation—Yeshua, our Messiah. The assigned name Palmoni emphasizes that God through Christ is the source of all mysterious numbers—those of science, creation, the universe and finally the mysterious counting periods of the end-time prophecies.

Palmoni's identity is implied in a parallel event that occurs during Daniel's fourth (4th) vision found in Daniel 12:5-7. Daniel saw two witnesses on each bank of the Tigris river. One of the two witnesses asked the Man clothed in linen (Michael) another "how long" question: *" Then I, Daniel, looked, and there before me stood two others [two witnesses], one on this bank of the river and one on the opposite bank. One of them said to the Man clothed in linen [Michael/Messiah], who was above the waters of the river, "How long will it be before these astonishing things are fulfilled?" The Man clothed in linen, who was above the waters of the river, lifted His right hand and His left hand toward heaven, and I heard Him swear by Him who lives forever, saying, "It will be for a time, times and half a time [1,260 days]. When the power of the holy people has been finally broken, all these things will be completed."*

Note the similarity to the Palmoni message of Daniel 8:13-14: *"Then I heard a holy one [Palmoni/Messiah] speaking, and another holy one [one of the two witnesses] said to him, "How long will it take for the vision to be fulfilled—the vision concerning the daily... the rebellion that causes desolation, the surrender of the sanctuary and the trampling underfoot of the LORD's people?" He said to me, "It will take 2,300 evenings and mornings [1,150 days]; then the sanctuary will be reconsecrated."*

In Daniel's day the two witnesses, whom several Scriptural passages imply to be Moses and Elijah, knew that one day they would be personally involved in final events on earth, and wanted desperately to know how events would play out and how long the trial would last. Daniel had the high privilege to witness this interaction between the two notable prophets and Michael, as He disclosed the contents from the "Book of Truth" to His end-time witnesses rediscovered in Revelation 11. Gabriel told Daniel, *"I will tell you what is written in the Book of Truth. (No one supports me [Gabriel] against them except Michael, your prince)"* Daniel 10:21. The visions of Daniel and the book of Revelation relate to mankind the content found in a much older ancient book of Heaven, the *Book of Truth*.

The Daniel 12 vision is recapped in the prophecy John received and wrote about in the book of Revelation chapter 10, where he saw a scroll opened in the Angel's hand and His swearing to the truth of the matter: *"Then I [John] saw another Mighty Angel [Michael, after standing up; Daniel 12:1] coming down from heaven. He was robed in a cloud, with a rainbow above His head; His face was like the sun, and His legs were like fiery pillars. He was holding a little scroll ["Book of Truth"—Daniel 10:21], which lay open in His hand. He planted His right foot on the sea and His left foot on the land, and He gave a loud shout [of resurrection] like the roar of a lion. When He shouted, the voices of the seven thunders spoke. And when the seven thunders spoke, I was about to write; but I heard a voice from heaven say, "Seal up what the seven thunders have said and do not write it down." Then the Angel [Michael] I had seen standing on the sea and on the land raised His right hand to heaven. And He swore by Him who lives for ever and ever, who created the heavens and all that is in them, the earth and all that is in it, and the sea and all that is in it, and said, "There will be no more delay! But in the days when the Seventh Angel [Michael] is about to sound His trumpet [of resurrection], the mystery of God will be accomplished, just as He [Michael] announced to His servants the prophets"*—on the banks of the river a few hundred years earlier (Daniel 12).

It's insightful that after mentioning how Messiah's two *"servants the prophets"* (Revelation 10:7)—Moses and Elijah—had heard Michael's announcement that at the end of 1,260 days... "all these things will be completed" (Daniel 12:7), just a few verses later the 1,260 day end-time ministry the two witnesses is enlarged upon starting in Revelation 11:3-4, *"And I will appoint my two witnesses, and they will prophesy for 1,260 days, clothed in sackcloth."* They are *"the two olive trees"* and the two lampstands, and *"they stand before the LORD of the earth."* The connection is undeniable.

Noteworthy also is that the prophet Malachi subtly points out Jesus and His two witnesses in chapter 4 when he speaks of final events and the Day of the LORD. "Surely the Day is coming; it will burn like a furnace. All the arrogant and every evildoer will be stubble, and the Day that is coming will set them on fire," says the LORD Almighty. "Not a root or a branch will be left to them. But for you who revere My name, the sun of righteousness [Messiah] will rise with healing in its rays. And you will go out and frolic like well-fed calves. Then you will trample on the wicked; they will be ashes under the soles of your feet on the day when I act," says the LORD Almighty. "Remember the law of my servant **Moses**, the decrees and laws I gave him at Horeb for all Israel. "See, I will send the prophet **Elijah** to you before that great and dreadful day of the LORD comes. He will turn the hearts of the parents to their children, and the hearts of the children to their parents; or else I will come and strike the land [of Israel] with total destruction."

EL SHADDAI

אל שדי

Insights In Prophecy
Unlock The Ancient Mysteries Of Daniel & Revelation
BIBLE DISCOVERY SERIES

Lesson 8

LE**8**SON

THE GULF WAR CRISIS: THE BEGINNING OF SORROWS

Read Daniel 8:1-9; 11:1-4

- **Discover Which Gulf Crisis Leads Up To The Appointed Time Of The End**
- **Identify The Two Islamic Countries Involved In The Middle-East Turmoil**

In Daniel 7 we discovered the "four winds" (four angels) of Heaven stir up the great sea of peoples, and out of this divine movement emerges four governmental beasts: Lion with Eagle's Wings (United Kingdom/United States); Bear (Russian Federation); Leopard (China and Asian Countries); and Terrible Beast  with Ten Horns (Western European Union). From the Terrible Beast will emerge the "little horn" (Vatican) whose Pontiff will reign for a "time, times and dividing of time" (Daniel 7:25)—meaning, 1,260 days/3½ years.

In Daniel 8 we rediscover the four winds and the emergence of the little horn in verses 8-9. However, new events are now depicted, which were not found in Daniel's first vision (chapter 7). Two conflicts will ensue *before* the New World Order emerges and the Papal leader miraculously rises to power. Where are the battles located? These are some of the issues we will address in this study.

Daniel's second vision of the last days (chapter 8) comes to him a couple of years after the first one, recorded in Daniel 7. The prophecy was like the first one, he says. In the vision he finds himself beside the Ulai Canal or River, the region near the Persian Gulf in Old Babylon close to the border between Iraq and Iran, where the two great rivers meet—the Tigris and Euphrates.

Two-horned (Islamic) Ram

1. What kind of animal does Daniel see (8:1-4)? _____

The prophet saw a Ram with two horns and one horn was larger than the other and emerged last. The Ram charges to the west, north and south and becomes powerful. The Ram represents Islam and the two notable

horns of this prophecy depict two prominent Islamic countries. The horns are different sizes; a smaller horn sits next to the larger horn with the larger horn clearly representing the dominant of the two nations.

Daniel is in vision and finds himself at Susa. Modern Susa is about 100 miles north of the Persian Gulf in Iran, near the border of Iraq. Michael instructs Gabriel later in the chapter to explain the vision to Daniel (vs. 15-16). Animals represent significant geographical powers and horns in prophecy portray prominent nations in that alliance/area to which Heaven asks us to pay attention. Daniel is told the two on top of the Ram horns are two powers that would battle against Western powers, referred to in the prophecy as the Goat from the West.

2. At what point in human history is the vision going to be fulfilled (Daniel 8:7-19) according to Gabriel?
_____

Gabriel confirms twice, as an added form of emphasis, the confrontations conveyed in the vision concerns the "time of the end." However, as clear as Gabriel states this will occur during the last days, commentators have applied the vision to historical battles over 2,000 years ago, around 331 B.C. Clearly, this would be an application of the prophecy at best, but certainly not the fulfillment. We are nearing the end of time; and, for this reason, we will look at the world today and consider what nations might be represented in the vision.

3. According to Daniel 8:20, to whom does Gabriel associate the two-horned Ram? _____

Media and Persia.

As mentioned, the location of Daniel's ancient vision occurred near what would be today's Iraq and Iran border; therefore, by simple deduction we can conclude that Media refers to modern Iraq, and Persia to

modern Iran—a country whose name was changed from Persia to Iran less than 100 years ago in 1935. The dangerous Ram representing Islam is an animal representing a sizeable geographical area (nations in green map). The Islamic Ram of nations surrounds Israel and the Israel is Islam's primary foe. Islam is charging to the "the west and the north and the south" as it compresses upon Israel's borders from all sides, except the east Mediterranean. The two prophetically identified modern-day horns (Iraq and Iran) of the Islamic Ram sit in the same geographic area of Israel's historical enemies—ancient Babylon and Persia. It's as though the ancient conflicts are replaying again at the end of days; however, it's the larger horn that is given the lion's share of attention, prophetically speaking; and, Israel is assured her most zealous enemy—Iran will collapse under the military might of the West.

Another prophet—Jeremiah long predicted the massive downfall of Persia in the latter days, known in the Scriptures as Elam: "The word of the LORD that came to Jeremiah the prophet against Elam, in the beginning

of the reign of Zedekiah king of Judah, saying, "Thus says the LORD of hosts: 'Behold, I will break the bow of Elam, the foremost of their might. Against Elam I will bring the four winds from the four quarters of heaven and scatter them toward all those winds; There shall be no nations where the outcasts of Elam will not go. For I will cause Elam to be dismayed before their enemies and before those who seek their life. I will bring disaster upon them, My fierce anger,' says the LORD; 'And I will send the sword after them until I have consumed them. I will set My throne in Elam and will destroy from there the king and the princes,' says the LORD. 'But it shall come to pass in the latter days: I will bring back the captives of Elam,' says the LORD," (Jeremiah 49:34-39; NKJV).

Goat Coalition

4. Daniel 8:5 says a Goat with a prominent horn (country) comes from what direction to confront Iraq followed by Iran? _____

The Goat comes from the west from a great distance and at a remarkable speed to deal with the Islamic Ram with the two prominent horns—Iraq, followed by the larger Iran.

5. How successful is the Goat in dealing with these two countries (vs. 6-7)? _____

The two horns will be shattered. So strong is the Western Goat that he tramples the two-horned Ram with speed and power. First the smaller horn (Iraq), followed later by the larger horn (Iran).

Daniel 8:21 identifies the powerful Goat and the "horn" as the first king (first in standing—the most powerful). The translators identified the Goat as "Greece" which in Hebrew is actually "Yawan" ("Javan"). Javan was one of the sons of Japheth (Genesis 10:2), and at the writing of Daniel, Javan implied much more than one specific nation but massive powers from the west. Since the vision concerns the time of the end, it would be reasonable to identify the Goat as a coalition of western European powers and their military partners, including Greece (NATO), with the prominent horn as the first king in power.

Wikipedia says, "The North Atlantic Treaty Organization (NATO; also called the North Atlantic Alliance) is an intergovernmental military alliance based on the North Atlantic Treaty which was signed on 4 April 1949. The organization constitutes a system of collective defense whereby its member states agree to mutual defense in response to an attack by any external party. NATO's headquarters are in Brussels, Belgium, one of the 28 member states across North America and Europe, the newest of which, Albania and Croatia, joined in April 2009. An additional 22 countries participate in NATO's Partnership for Peace program, with 15 other countries involved in institutionalized dialogue programs."

For more info, visit http://en.wikipedia.org/wiki/NATO

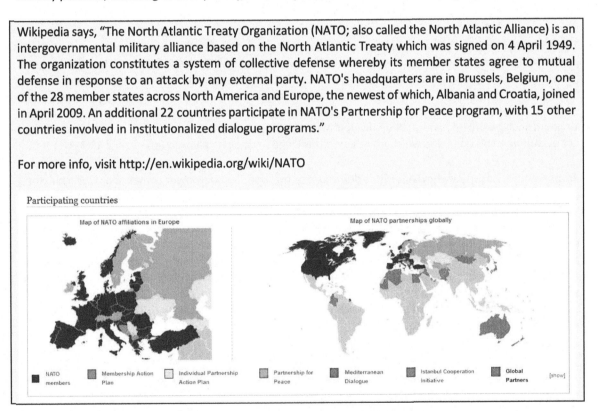

The First King—United States Of America

The large horn—the first king (first in power) and the most prominent in western strength in the NATO alliance—no doubt represents the United States. On March 19, 2003, President George W. Bush, 43rd President of the United States, along with other mainly western powers (the Multi-National Force—coalition forces) attacked Iraq. The bombardment began on Shushan Purim, the annual day of celebration in Jerusalem commemorating Israel's triumph over ancient Persia's attempt to annihilate God's people. Iraq was defeated in relative speed, just as the prophecy predicted, although skirmishes continued until the war's official end on December 18, 2011, just as Hanukkah celebrations were about to begin. The second and larger horn—Iran, will "come up last" (Daniel 8:3). The West will, as a continuation of this prophecy, confront the Persian Iran. And, we will likely see Iraq once again pulled back into the conflict when the West confronts Iran. In the end, we know both Iraq and Iran will fall victim to the power of the Western Goat coalition, with catastrophic consequences for the Islamic Ram in the Persian Gulf region.

We know this, because prophecy foretells the Western Goat with the notable horn (America) will furiously attack the Islamic Ram, striking the Ram and shattering his two horns. Daniel adds, "The Ram (Islam) was powerless to stand against him; the [Western] Goat knocked him to the ground and trampled on him, and none could rescue the Ram [Islam] from his power."

6. The West will successfully defeat the Islamic Ram with its two horns. However, after the victory what happens next (Daniel 8:8)? _____

When America and the NATO Coalition are basking in the glory of their decisive conquest, prophecy depicts the next major surprise: the prominent horn will be broken off.

The three following Daniel passages point to America's demise: "The first was like a lion [Britain], and had eagle's wings [U.S.]: I beheld till the wings thereof were plucked," Daniel 7:4. "Therefore the he goat [Western Coalition] waxed very great: and when he was strong, the great horn [America] was broken; and for it came up four notable ones toward the four winds of heaven," Daniel 8:8. "A mighty [U.S.] king shall stand up, that shall rule with great dominion, and do according to his will. And when he shall stand up, his kingdom shall be broken, and shall be divided toward the four winds of heaven; and not to his posterity, nor according to his dominion which he ruled: for his kingdom shall be plucked up," Daniel 11:3-4.

Prophecy does not specify how America's departure as the world's superpower comes about. Washington, D.C. edifices and/or New York financial district may be destroyed without warning, leaving the U.S. without political strength; global financial markets could be in a spiral. No doubt, social unrest will increase; and, unforeseen tragedies will explode upon the world scene. From the Iranian conflict forward, prophecy warns that natural disasters will also increase, including massive earthquakes. Tidal waves and high winds may buffet and destroy; America's vast military will endure great losses. Nuclear armaments may explode upon America's soil; if so, in a very short segment of time millions of lives could be destroyed. The American horn will be broken and her position of authority will diminish. When World War III erupts, it could be a very short but devastating period of global holocaust as America's power, along with many other nations, is broken and dispersed toward the four winds around the world.

Yeshua warned that these and other events will be just the "beginning" of sorrows and should not to be interpreted as the end of the world, according to Matthew 24:6-8: "You will hear of wars and rumors of wars, but see to it that you are not alarmed. Such things must happen, but the end is still to come. Nation will rise against nation, and kingdom against kingdom. There will be famines and earthquakes in various places. All these are the beginning of birth pains."

Satan, the ruler—the prince and power of the air (Ephesians 2:2), is much more formidable than our minds can envision. He will unleash his calculated and deadly plan, and demand his forces of evil march to war (Ephesians 6:12). Nations will erupt one against the other with military confrontations, sparking sorrow and social unrest. As global turmoil mushrooms, the population of Planet Earth will beg for a solution. Revelation 13 speaks of a false prophet given demonic power to perform miraculous signs involving fire (lightning?) from the sky. Added to the desolation of war, Satan could harness nature's elements and unleash environmental fury to bring the nations to his feet, humbled and ready for the Man of Sin—the false savior.

Devastation will increase on both land and sea; Revelation 12:12 warns, "Woe to the earth and the sea, because the devil has gone down to you! He is filled with fury, because he knows that his time is short."

7. Read Daniel 7:2-4. How does it describe the emergence of the four world power-bases and the demise of America's supremacy? _____

The four winds (four angels) of Heaven stir up earth's powers. The Lion (Great Britain) with Eagle's Wings (America) is one of the prominent four government coalitions. However, Daniel watched as the Eagle's Wings were "torn off." The United Kingdom/United States alliance will no longer fly free and swiftly. America will be humbled, so that the Man of Sin may come into view with strength and clarity. The world's mighty leader will emerge from the Western European Union, while the United State's dominion will be lost forever.

The Little Horn—The Mighty Ruler

8. Daniel 8:9 portrays the emergence of a "little horn," which will come out of one of the four larger power-bases that spread out in the four directions of the world—particularly the Western European Union. What is the smallest country in the world? _____

The Vatican sits on just 109 acres but will emerge as the leader of the world. Although the smallest of nations, the Holy See will rise to power, first taking control of nations to the east and south, then eventually the Beautiful Land, Israel (Daniel 8:9; 11:16).

The 50 Smallest Countries In The World

Rank	Country	Area (km²)
1	Vatican City	0.44
2	Monaco	2
3	Nauru	21
4	Tuvalu	26
5	San Marino	61
6	Liechtenstein	160

The southern and eastern directions of new power indicate that the countries in these two directions from Rome, Italy, may be the ones devastated by Russia when the Bear attacks the Western Europe Union (as covered in Lesson 4). The Bear will have "three ribs" in its mouth when it rises to devour much human flesh (Daniel 7:5), representative of the "three... horns" (three countries) uprooted and destroyed just as the little horn (Vatican) comes into power (Daniel 7:8). Of particular concern should be Italy, Spain, Portugal and Greece, although we do not know with absolute certainty which three countries the Bear will most shatter.

Insights In Prophecy
Unlock The Ancient Mysteries Of Daniel & Revelation
BIBLE DISCOVERY SERIES

Fourth Persian King & The Rise Of Donald Trump

Returning to the conflict that will ignite end-time events and World War III, Daniel's fourth and last vision provides even more details concerning the Persian Gulf confrontation with Persia (Iran). We find these details in Daniel 11:2, where we see the same powers and events as Daniel 8—Persia (Iran), Greece ("Javan"—western powers), a confrontation (Gulf War), and a mighty ruler and empire (United States), which will be broken and her power divided and parceled out to the "four winds".

Persia, whose name—as mentioned earlier in this lesson—was changed to Iran in 1935, was ruled by empires and dynasties. However, political revolution led to a major realignment of power and the *Islamic Republic* was established in Iran on April 1, 1979. A Constitution of the Islamic Republic was approved by national referendum in December, 1979. Iran transitioned to *elected* leadership, a clear change from the past. This ushered in the conditions for the end-time predictions of Daniel 11 to become reality. One key religious leader in the development of the Islamic Republic became the fourth and one of the most influential leaders in Iran—the wealthy Hojatolislam Ali Alvar Hashemi Rafsanjani.

9. In Daniel 11:2, the prophet wrote that in the "latter days" there will emerge in Persia (Iran) three kings; however, the fourth Muslim leader would be different in what way? _____

_____

The fourth shall be far richer than the previous three.

"Now then, I tell you the truth: Three more kings will appear [President Banisadr; President Rajar; and President Khamenei] in Persia [Iran, in the latter days], and then a fourth [President Rafsanjani], who will be far richer [much wealthier] than all the others. When he has gained power by his [personal] wealth, he will stir up everyone against the kingdom of Greece [Hebrew "Javan"—Greece; and the West]," Daniel 11:2. His influence and decisions in Iranian politics would change the course of Iranian history.

Persia's Presidents Since the Revolution
1st … Abolhassan Bani-Sadr. Ruled … 1980 - 1981
2nd … Mahammad Ali Raja'i   Ruled … 1981 - 1981
3rd … Sayed Ali Khamenei   Ruled … 1981 - 1989
4th … Akbar Hashemi Rafsanjani   Ruled 1989 – 1997
5th … Mohammad Khatami   Ruled … 1997 – 2005
6th … Mahmoud Ahmadinejad   Ruled … 2005 – 2013
7th … Hassan Rouhani   Ruled … 2013 – Present

Hassan Rouhani 2013-	Mahmoud Ahmadinejad 2005-2013	Mohammad Khatami 1997-2005	Akbar Hashemi R. 1989-1997	Ali Khamenei 1981-1989	Mohammad-Ali Rajai 1981-1981	Abolhassan Banisadr 1980-1981
7	6	5	(4)	3	2	1

Rafsanjani, the richest President in Iran's modern history, was President from 1989 to 1997, but did not fade into obscurity. His influence remained strong as one of the most powerful figures in Iranian politic, leading two top clerical bodies—the Assembly of Experts and the Expediency Council. In December 2001, Rafsanjani openly threatened Jews when he said a single atomic bomb has the power to completely destroy Israel, while an Israeli counterstrike can only cause partial damage to the Islamic world. Rafsanjani, the political father of Iran's nuclear energy program, ran again for the presidency in July 2005, but the man he lost to, Mahmoud Ahmadinejad, continued to ratchet up messianic rhetoric, calling into question the Holocaust and seeking the demise of Israel and America. However, the emphasis of prophecy falls on Rafsanjani, and his powerful, long-standing sway in Iranian politics will lead Islam to war, even in death. How?

Rafsanjani, through his wealth and decades of power, stirred up sentiment against the West. This "stirring" can be found in his involvement in the 1979 revolution, the ushering in of the radical mullah Ruhollah Khomeini, and his bellicose public statements against the West and Israel; but more importantly, his wealth and influence led to the initiation of Iran's nuclear weapons program in the 1980's. A recent January 16, 2017 article, *Nazarian: Rafsanjani, Father of Iran's Nuclear Program, Was No 'Man of Peace'* notes, "between birthing Iran's nuclear program, oppressing the freedom-craving Iranian people, and orchestrating international terrorist atrocities, Rafsanjani was anything but" peaceful.

Rafsanjani's nuclear program became the nucleus of Iran's power, posture and modern-day brazenness, which has played out time and again in the death of countless thousands. Iran has been involved in continuous state-sponsored terrorism against Israel and other Middle Eastern nations, and directly involved in the conflicts in Yemen and Syria.

Some considered Rafsanjani to be a front-runner to replace the supreme leader of Iran, Grand Ayatollah Ali Khamenei. Born in 1934, Rafsanjani turned 82, but then suddenly died of a heart attack on January 8, 2017, on the Biblical fast day of Asara B'Tevet—the fast of the tenth month found in Zechariah 8:19.

Wikipedia says, "Akbar Hashemi Rafsanjani (Persian: اکبر هاشمی رفسنجانی, translit. *Akbar Hāshemī Rafsanjānī* or Hashemi Bahramani; 25 August 1934 – 8 January 2017) was an influential Iranian politician, writer and one of the founding fathers of the Islamic Republic who was the fourth President of Iran from 3 August 1989 until 3 August 1997. He was the head of the Assembly of Experts from 2007 until 2011 when he decided not to nominate himself for the post. He was also the chairman of the Expediency Discernment Council. During the final years of Iran–Iraq War Rafsanjani was the *de facto* commander-in-chief of the Iranian military. Rafsanjani was elected chairman of the Iranian parliament in 1980 and served until 1989. He played an important role in the choice of Ali Khamenei as Supreme Leader... *Forbes* named him as one of the richest persons in Iran in 2003, with an exceeded $1 billion assets."

Daniel 11:3-4 continues: "Then a mighty king will arise [Donald Trump--his inauguration occurred ten days after Rafsanjani's burial on January 20, 2017], who will *rule with great power* and *do as he pleases* [President Trump, a man who is charting his own course and doing as he pleases, all against the norm]. After he has arisen [taken office], his empire [America] will be broken up [superpower destroyed; tragedies; war; economic collapse; social disorder] and parceled out toward the ***four winds of heaven***." Therefore, Donald Trump could be the last American President to rule, while the U.S. is a superpower; the sudden demise of America is foretold during his Presidency.

The prophecy ends, "It [American empire] will not go to his [America's] descendants [the normal election process may end; he could be the last President to be installed into office by American voters], nor will it have the power he exercised, because his [American] empire will be uprooted and given to others [the United Nations—New One World Order]."

So, here's what we've learned: The West will confront Iran in anger. This conflict could flair up due to an act of terrorism, a response to President Trump's decision to renegotiate or axe of the nuclear deal, or events surrounding the Temple Mount. And, when this conflict hits the world news (Daniel 8:1-7), we can be assured the appointed end-time crisis is at hand. Once ajar, the door of prophecy can never be shut. Mayhem will reign, and the world will never be the same.

The Hanukkah Connection To Overcoming Israel's Enemies
Parts if this Section Adapted from "Hanukkah Yes, But What About Kislev" Author Unknown

There are two prophetic watch periods that we should considered—Hanukkah and Purim. Hanukkah was not part of the original Festival celebrations Yahweh gave to the Israelites; nor is Purim, recorded in the book of Esther. However, God inspired their rehearsal celebrations for His divine purposes, in foretelling final events. In addition to the seven Festival events of Leviticus 23, both Hanukkah and Purim were instituted to commemorate God's mercy and His miraculous power and protection over Israel's enemies. Both remind Jews of victory over tyranny, and God's provision for His people—past, present and future, during the appointed time of the end, when bright hope will spring forth from the greatest of tragedies.

In the centuries before the birth of Jesus, the people of Israel and Jerusalem had been held under years of tribute to various conquering kings. One of these ruling monarchs was Antiochus, one of the Seleucid Kings who reigned in Syria. Resistance finally arose against him. Under the leadership of the Maccabees, the people of Jerusalem overthrew Antiochus and his pagan practices in 166 BC. The Syrians and their Greek religion were driven out, and the altar was rebuilt. The Temple was cleansed, restored, and rededicated to the service of Yahweh. The Festival of Hanukkah celebrates the re-dedication of the Temple following Judah Maccabee's victory over the Seleucids. According to Rabbinic tradition, the victorious Maccabees could only find a small jug of oil that had remained uncontaminated by virtue of a seal, and although it only contained enough oil to sustain the Menorah for one day, it miraculously lasted for eight days, by which time further oil could be procured. Therefore, it was decreed there should be eight days of celebration, with rejoicing and gladness, to mark the re-dedication of the altar, to remember the victory, and to recount the miracle of the supply of oil that lasted through this period. This occurred late in the year, connected to Haggai's Kislev 24th momentous prophecy.

Moses' first miracle was the *bush* that would *not burn* (Exodus 3:1-3); it was an amazing miracle that could not be missed. The miracle of Hanukkah was the *oil* that would *not burn*. However, it was a subtle miracle that unfolded over several days. Sometimes miracles are awe-inspiring, like the burning bush and parting of the Red Sea; at other times, they are slow and restrained, and take eyes of faith to see them. As the oil lasted eight days, so Jews too have survived the Diaspora, the pogroms, and the burning flames of Auschwitz; and, the state of Israel has been recognized and its prophetic role methodically reestablished through God's miraculous events starting with General Allenby's victory in 1917, the U.N. Mandate and Israel's Independence in 1947/48, the Six-Day War of 1967, and now events unfolding in 2017/18.

As in the past, Israel continues to be haunted by the Syrian and Iranian enemies on her northern border, along with foes such as Hezbollah, Hamas, Iran's Ayatollah, Iraq and Libya, all backed by anti-Semitism forged through UN votes cast by hostile international representatives. The prophet Haggai spoke prophetically of events in his day *and* trials of the last days—that God was about to exalt His chosen with blessings by overthrowing the nations and military might of Israel's enemies who hate them, including Damascus (Isaiah 17) and Iran (Daniel 8; Jeremiah 49); thereby, extolling Israel with miraculous victories and enlargement of its territory, as God promised long ago. Therefore, expect major military showdowns with Israel's enemies as the end-times begin.

Hanukkah begins each year at the end of 24th day of the ninth Hebrew month of Kislev, as the 25th day begins, which fluctuates on the Gregorian calendar each year (e.g., December 12, 2017 and December 2, 2018), and continues for eight days. Israel is surrounded by past and present enemies—Syria, Egypt, Jordon and Saudi Arabia, and distant foes such as Iran, Iraq, Libya and others. The prophet Haggai spoke prophetically of events in his day *and* trials of the last days—that God was about to bless Israel with eternal blessings by overthrowing the nations and military might of Israel's enemies who surrounded them, including Damascus (Isaiah 17); thereby, extoling Israel with miraculous victories and enlargement of their territory, as God promised long ago. There will no doubt be major military showdowns with Israel's enemies as the end-times begin. The enlargement of Israel's territory is a continuation of God's blessings that began 100 full years ago, with the Balfour Declaration on November 2, 1917. Forty days later the Turks surrendered Palestine to the British General Allenby during World War I, on the 24th day of Kislev (December 9, 1917). These historical events set in motion the restoration of Davidic sovereignty over the Holy Land that came to fruition through the United Nations Partition Plan for Palestine in late 1947, the events on May 14, 1948, and the War of Independence that ended in 1949, stirring the anger of Israel's enemies. This was followed by the Six-Day War in 1967, and the continued enlargement of Israel. Now, we are on the verge of Middle East war that will mushroom into immense tragedy, with unimaginable loss of life.

Still under the grip of King Darius and the Persia Empire in 520 BC, Haggai the prophet wrote, "Now *give careful thought* to this from this day on—consider how things were before one stone was laid on another in the LORD's temple... 'From this day on, from this *twenty-fourth day of the ninth month* [the eve of Hanukkah], *give careful thought to the day... Give careful thought... "'From this day on I will bless you.'"* The word of the LORD came to Haggai a second time on the *twenty-fourth day of the [ninth] month*: "Tell Zerubbabel governor of Judah that I am going to shake the heavens and the earth. I will overturn royal thrones and shatter the power of the foreign [Gentile] kingdoms. I will overthrow chariots and their drivers; horses and their riders will fall, each by the sword of his brother," (Haggai 2:15, 18-22).

As the sun fell across Israel, Europe, the United States and around the globe on December 12, 2017, millions of Jews and many Gentiles (Hebrew "goyim") prepared for and/or acknowledged the arrival of Hanukkah, also known as the Feast of Dedication and Festival of Lights (John 10:22-24). What might be lost is the modern ramifications of this ancient prophecy on the world stage, rooted in the historical grounding of the feast of Hanukkah itself, which is derived from the first evening of celebration—Kislev 24, the 24th day of the 9th month on the Jewish calendar. What follows is the Biblical backdrop and the timing of this annual festival, and what looks to have been at least a partial fulfillment of Haggai's 2,500-year-old prediction on December 12, 2017.

The book of the prophet Haggai comes to us from the 2nd year of the Persian King Darius, late summer, August, 520 BC. It is one of the most precisely dated books in the Hebrew Bible. Much like twins Zechariah and Malachi, all three were written during that crucial time of the "restoration" of Judah to the Promised Land following the Babylonian captivity. Collectively, they offered the last insights during the Old Covenant period in terms of how the Messianic redemption is to unfold. Both Haggai and Zechariah address their contemporary situation, as one would expect, and are concerned that the Temple be rebuilt and that the constitution of the new state of Judah be ordered according to the Torah. However, if read carefully, both clearly understand that this restoration of Judah is only a preliminary, even symbolic step in this "near and far" prophecy, to a coming great restoration of Judah and all Israel. Even though there is a Priest (Joshua), and a Governor (Zerubbabel) of the Davidic line, there is no anointing of the BRANCH (Messiah) figure of whom both Isaiah and Jeremiah had spoken. One way of putting this is to say that Haggai and Zechariah are working in the tall shadow of Jeremiah (see especially chapters 30-31), and they know, from his clear and powerful prophecies, that the final days have not come with this tiny little beachhead return of a portion of Judah to the land. But they do believe that this return of Judah is a "sign" of things to come, and a guarantee that the Plan of Yehovah, to fill the earth with justice and righteousness, through Abraham's seed, is not to fall to the ground.

And, this leads us to the curious and fascinating references to the 24th day of the 9th month—Kislev 24, now connected to the Hanukkah celebration. Notice, reading the book of Haggai is sequential, it takes you through the last months of the year during late summer and into the autumn period. It begins with the Rosh Chodesh of the 6th month (Haggai 1:1) corresponding in 2017 to August 23rd, the first day of the month of Elul—the annual month of repentance leading up to the High Holy Days; then, continues through the 21st day of the 7th month (2:1), which is the last day of Sukkot (corresponding to October 11, 2017), followed by the 24th day of the 9th month—December 12, 2017, connected to the first evening of the Hanukkah candle lighting. Haggai's third and fourth messages also come on this very day, emphasizing the date's significance. It is a short book, but if you skim through it you will see the building sequence.

Kislev 24 is highlighted four times in the second chapter of Haggai, verses 10, 15, 18 and 20. Twice it is emphasized that "from THIS DAY FORWARD I will bless you," and twice Haggai gets a special Word from Yehovah, on this very day. You must read the whole chapter to get the context. The message is basically that from that day forward Yehovah's final plans will begin with a BLESSING for Israel, which in turn will lead to God's plan to "SHAKE the heavens and the earth and ALL NATIONS," making Jerusalem the "cup of trembling" to surrounding nations foretold in Zechariah 12:2. And, in the end, Messiah will overturn world governments and shatter the power of all foreign powers on His Great Day.

This message is addressed to the two "messiahs," the "Priest" and the "King" or Governor, Joshua and Zerubbabel, respectively (2:4-5). They become "signifiers" of things to come. They are not the final two anointed ones, who in the last days point to Elijah the priest, and Moses the ruler, which two Zechariah picks up in his visions, especially chapters 4 and 6, and Malachi identifies by name. These two personalities, as well as the promised presence of the Holy Spirit (see 2:5 and Zechariah 4:6), are the guarantee that Yehovah will bring about these promises.

Notice, in correlation to Haggai, the prophet Zechariah begins getting his visions and messages in the 8th month (Cheshvan) of that same year (Zechariah 1:1), or mid-November (520 BC), followed by the 24th day of the 11th month (Shevat, typically in the January/February range; for example, January 30, 2019) the following year (Zechariah 1:7). He has eight, night visions, and they are all quite difficult to follow, but prophetically important in forecasting the redemptive future. There is much more detail in Zechariah, but as mentioned, the two, Haggai and Zechariah, should be read in tandem, as one explains the other. Now, note carefully, Kislev 24 is not specifically mentioned in Zechariah, but it is alluded to in chapter 4:8-10. It is the famous "day of small things," that nations, past and present, might dare "despise," because after all, this tiny little remnant of Judah in the petite land of Israel, beginning to lay the foundation of a nondescript temple, under the mighty thumb of the Persian empire, was hardly even worthy of the name of a city-state, much less a world kingdom, and yet had hopes and dreams and promises of dominion!

Chapters 7-14 of Zechariah, which he gets two years later, are quite different. They are straightforward, laying out, likely in some sequential order, both the preliminary events, and the detailed climax, of the "time of the end."

So, what about Kislev 24, which is now connected to the first night of Hanukkah? It seems to have a three-fold meaning. First, in the time of Haggai and Zechariah, it was the day marked for the promise that the redemption would ultimately come about, not by might, nor by power, but by the Spirit of Yehovah—and "in its time." Second, subsequently though history, this day seems to be one upon which key events take place, perhaps only a few of which have been recognized. And finally, it might well turn out that Kislev 24, and with it the Hanukkah celebration, will highlight what might seem a small but despised event, which will turn out to be a "countdown marker" for the soon unfolding mysterious 1260 days, 1290 days, 1335 days, 490 days and 2300 evenings/mornings (1150 days) of Daniel's visions displayed on *The Kingdom Calendar*; all of which, are intrinsically connected to the prophetic visions of Haggai, Zechariah, Malachi, Isaiah, Jeremiah, the Gospel accounts of end-time events (Matthew, Mark & Luke), and the book of Revelation.

Exactly seven days before Hanukkah on December 6, 2017, U.S. President Donald Trump was the first Gentile superpower leader to officially recognize by proclamation that Jerusalem is the capital of Israel, and  extolled plans for a new American Embassy in Jerusalem. This was timed, because the next day the President and First Lady Melania oversaw a small Hanukkah celebration at the White House, along with Vice-President Mike Pence and wife Karen, including Jewish Cabinet and Congressional members and other special guests. Donald Trump used the White House celebration to highlight his monumental decision to recognize Jerusalem as Israel's capital and seat of government. He entered the East Room then declared Hanukkah "especially special", because of his official edict. "There's a lot of happy people here. Jerusalem!" he spoke to a cheering crowd. He ended with these words, "God bless. May you all have a truly blessed and happy Hanukkah." Now, the world cannot ignore the fact that Jerusalem is indeed the undivided capital of the nation of Israel. President Trump Remarks at White House Hanukkah Reception

However, in contrast, the Muslim nations surrounding Israel and international bodies were "reeling" from the Jerusalem news, and condemnation and rioting began almost immediately. Then, on the seventh day of Hanukkah, Egypt and the UN Security Council advanced a resolution to reject America's recognition of Jerusalem; however, while 14 members voted in favor, the U.S. stood alone and vetoed it. It was the first veto cast by the United States in the Security Council in more than six years. Is this the beginning of the "blessings" for Israel, but also the "shaking of the nations," Haggai spoke of so many years ago, that would begin small, but grow in intensity?

If so, please give careful thought to this: December 12, 2017 was likely the fulfillment and beginning countdown for the Haggai prediction of Kislev 24, when the U.S. and Israel signed the secret pact to tackle the Iranian nuclear and missile threat. According to Israeli TV Channel 10, "Dramatic understandings" were agreed at the White House, and a deal was signed by the two countries' national security chiefs. The two nations secretly sealed a far-reaching joint memorandum of understanding providing for full cooperation to deal with Iran's nuclear drive, its missile programs and its other threatening activities. The document was signed on December 12 at the White House, culminating intensive talks between representatives of the major Israeli and American intelligence and defense hierarchies, headed by the US and Israeli national security advisers, H. R. McMaster and Meir Ben-Shabbat, respectively. Specifically, they agreed to set up joint teams to handle various aspects of the Iranian threat. The meeting confirmed that the U.S. and Israel "see eye to eye on the trends and processes in the region," and have now reached agreement on the strategy and policy required to deal with them. Israeli TV Channel 10 reporter Barak Ravid said, "With all due respect to President Trump's [December 6] declaration on Jerusalem [as the capital of Israel]", the December 12 "dramatic understandings" will have "a far greater impact on the security of Israel's citizens." What followed in 2018 was a series of Festival speeches and announcements in which President Trump, Secretary of State Mike Pompeo and National Security Advisor John Bolton forecasting the U.S. pressure on Iran would be increasing until a final confrontation, if need be. These occurred on Shavuot (May 21, 2018); Tisha B'Av (July 22, 2018); Sukkot (September 26, 2018); Simchat Torah (October 3, 2018), on the 100th Full Anniversary of the Balfour Declaration (November 2, 2018). All these were followed up on the 24th of Kislev (first evening of Hanukkah) with a reported U.S. bombing of the Iranian forces in Syria and Netanyahu's impromptu meeting with Mike Pompeo in Brussels concerning Iran and regional developments.

Consider The Haggai Prophecy Pattern: 2017-2018

The messages Haggai received on very specific dates set a pattern for modern last-day events as the appointed times of the end counting periods approach. His first encounter occurred on the "first day of the sixth month" (1:1)—the first day of the Jewish month of Elul, the annual period of repentance and serious reflection leading up to the High Holy Days, which in 2017 arrived on August 23rd, three days after the North American solar eclipse and darkening of the sun that crossed the United States on August 21st—a sky event that Jews consider to be a dire warning in the heavens for the nations of the world, but most specifically for America. Since that point, the U.S. has experienced several natural disasters and an ever-increasing concern over North Korea, Iran and Russia's intentions on the world stage.

Haggai's message was that God's people, not only in the United States but around the world, should "give careful thought to your ways" (1:5), because His people are lacking God's best. It's time to take care of spiritual matters above material/earthly pursuits, for the great shaking will soon overtake the planet and hardships will prevail. In this regard, God has offered ancient warnings for our modern times that global  shaking, and earth-shattering events and collapse are near, and it's time to focus on our relationship with our LORD and SAVIOR. The waves of prophetic events long ago foretold in Haggai, Daniel, Revelation, and the other prophetic scrolls, could overtake and bury us. Words cannot adequately portray the destructive episodes and magnitude of fear and turmoil just ahead. We must know Jesus—Yeshua as our personal Savior, and be spiritually prepared for the physical hardships, personal losses, and realities of a world gone mad.

Haggai's second encounter with the Heavenly Messenger occurred on the "twenty-first day of the seventh month" (2:1)—the last day of Sukkot—the Feast of Tabernacles, corresponding to October 11, 2017. The following day on Shmini Atzeret, the eighth day of celebration prescribed in Leviticus 23:36, President Donald Trump gave his notorious speech on Iran, decertifying the JCPOA deal—his first major step in leading the nations to the West's prophetic war against the Persians foretold in Jeremiah 49:34-39 and Daniel 8:1-8, to explode as "the time of the end," (vs. 17,19) begins.

This was followed by Trump's Hanukkah announcement to move of the US Embassy to Jerusalem and the secret pact signed at Hanukkah on December 12, 2017 at the White House to coordinate a united effort to deal with the Iranian threat. What followed in 2018 was US leadership speeches and actions to enforce ever increasing pressure on Iran, which always occurred on Biblical/Jewish holy days or historical dates of modern Israeli history to signal their prophetic significance.

The message of Haggai chapter 2 is particularly dedicated to those who are heeding the first message and have taken up the cause to work in building up the house of God. His words are "'Be strong, all you people of the land,' declares the LORD, 'and work. For I am with you... My Spirit remains. Do not fear,'" (2:4-5). Why the warning for His people to work, even while great turmoil is about to hit with unrelenting force? Because... "In a little while I will once more shake the heavens and the earth, the sea and the dry land. I will shake all nations" (2:6-7) in order that Heaven's Kingdom can be ushered in and "I [God] will fill this house [not made with human hands] with glory" when all the gathered nations enter the Bride's gates of pearl for the Sukkot wedding described in the Apocalypse of John to commence at the end of the counting periods (Revelation 7:9-17; 19:7-9).

"On the twenty-fourth day of the ninth month" (2:10) Haggai receives another message, which as mentioned is the date that leads up to the evening when the first Hanukkah candle is lit. The message the prophet receives relates to how a person is defiled. The warning is that the nation of Israel (but, also including believers of all nations who are grafted in) are defiled by sin and need to repent with sincere hearts. Tribulation sits at our doorsteps. Past economic troubles have already taught us that God's blessings can be extinguished in a single day, particularly as we embrace sin and remove God from the public square. However, we are to "give careful thought" to where we are in time, because from the "twenty-fourth day of the ninth month" and onward, God says "I will bless you" (2:18-19) by setting into motion God's final plan of redemption, which centers on Israel and Jerusalem. Nonetheless, the Trump blessing by the world's great superpower, by officially recognizing Jerusalem as the Jewish capital, *signifies* that soon believers of all nations—Jews and Gentiles alike—will inherit the New Jerusalem, as the eternal capital of Mashiach's Kingdom; but, it also *signals* global troubles and initiates a period of supernatural events foretold in the ancient Hebrew prophecies and illustrated through *The Kingdom Calendar*. Only through the birth pains, and the counting of the appointed times and purification through trials, can Messiah's eternal blessings be fully delivered to a chosen people ready to receive them.

Therefore, Haggai (2:20-22) is told, "I am going to shake the heavens and the earth. I will overthrow royal thrones and shatter the power of the foreign [Gentile] kingdoms. I will overthrow chariots and their drivers [military conquests]; horses and their riders will fall [both military machinery and fighters], each by the sword of his brother." The nations will turn on Israel and each other. The Haggai prophecy indicates fiery cosmic and seismic events will shake the planet, causing a major crisis-point in world affairs, and signaling death and turmoil that will eventually reach its climax a few years later at the Battle of Armageddon.

In Zechariah chapter 4, we find Zerubbabel mentioned again. Zechariah sees a Lampstand of seven lamps [representing Mashiach—the Menorah of the World], with *two olive trees*, one on each side of the Lampstand, which point to the two anointed witnesses—"these are the *two anointed* ones [Moses and Elijah], that *stand by the LORD of the whole earth*," (4:14 KJV). We find that *rulers, priests and prophets* are *anointed* throughout the ancient Scriptures. God's work is completed not by strength or military might, but by His miraculous intervention in the affairs of mankind: "Not by might nor by power, but by My Spirit,' says the LORD Almighty," (4:6). Revelation 11:4 adds a timeline of duty, connected to Zechariah's prophecy: *"And I will appoint my two witnesses, [Moses and Elijah] and they will prophesy for 1,260 days, clothed in sackcloth."* They are "the two olive trees" and the two lampstands, who "stand before the LORD of the earth."

In the book of Malachi, it is said of Elijah the prophet, "I will send My messenger, who will prepare the way before Me" for 1,260 days. "Then suddenly the LORD you are seeking will come to His temple; the Messenger of the Covenant, whom you desire, will come," says the LORD Almighty. But who can endure the Day of His coming?" And, "Remember the law of my servant *Moses*, the decrees and laws I gave him at

Horeb for all Israel. 'See, I will send the prophet *Elijah* to you before that Great and Dreadful Day of the LORD comes,'" (Malachi 3:1-2; 4:4-5).

The LORD continues in Zechariah 4:7 by describing a very important end-time event: "What are you, mighty mountain? You will become level ground." Only after the mighty mountain—the obstacle—is leveled can and will the last-day work begin, and the third Temple rebuilt. The obstacle shall give way, the difficulty must vanish, the opposition cease. Where is the mighty mountain, you ask? Where all the Temples have been built—Jerusalem, and specifically the TEMPLE MOUNT. Psalm 2:6 says, "I have installed My King on Zion, My holy mountain." And, "Great is the LORD, and most worthy of praise, in the City of our God, His holy mountain," (Psalm 48:1); followed by, "He has founded His City on the holy mountain," (Psalm 87:1). Soon, the Islamic structures on the Mount and Jordan's Islamic Waqf influence over the mountain will diminish, both in physical structures and overarching control. Following the Festival pattern, this great shaking of nations and Jerusalem will occur at some future Purim/Shushan Purim (next celebrated on March 1-2, 2018), eighty (80) days after the 24th day of Kislev—the first evening of Hanukkah. The destruction in Jerusalem will take away daily worship at the Western Wall and Temple Mount and start the 1,290 and 1,335 counting days of Daniel 12:11-12, followed by the 1,260 days.

So, what can we conclude from the Haggai and Zechariah prophecies, which are both filled with end-time predictions? The ancient visions and dates correlate to final events, that could well have already begun the last half of 2017 and continuing through 2018. At first, almost undistinguishable, slowly increasing after the solar eclipse with natural disasters of winds, fires, floods, growing plague concerns, and threats of Middle East turmoil; then, with the Trump "blessing" of Israel at Hanukkah on December 6, followed by his joint U.S.-Israeli pact against Iran--Israel's most prominent modern-day threat--exactly on December 12, 2017 (Kislev 24) the "twenty-fourth day of the ninth month."

Sukkot, the Feast of Tabernacles of early October 2017, offered us the opportunity to reflect upon where we are in prophetic time, and to be strong and to not fear what is to soon come as an overwhelming surprise to the nations. Now, we've reached the "twenty fourth day of the ninth month." The Hanukkah blessing to Israel could very well lead to the unfolding of final events that will build day by day towards natural and supernatural disasters, the Iranian confrontation and World War III, followed by the rise of the European Antichrist. However, no matter what global conflicts and unimaginable devastation occurs in the weeks, months or years ahead, we have the Light of the World to shine upon us. *The Kingdom Calendar* will guide us as we count Heaven's prophetic time, day by day; and, the Spirit will guide us, whether in life or death, as we depend upon Him. In the days of darkness, we may not always see God's hands, so we must trust above all in His heart of love, His Words of Truth, and His promise of an eternal Kingdom of peace, justice and happiness when tears are wiped away.

In conclusion, based on the official recognition of Jerusalem as Israel's capital, we may now consider the possibility that the Hanukkah celebration of 2017 "on our days and in our time," brought with it Haggai's "blessing" and soon "shaking" of nations. However, whether fulfilled now or in the future, every year, at this time, one's thoughts should go to this Festival date, given such an important emphasis by Haggai and Zechariah. On a personal level, it seems Hanukkah can always be a period of "renewal"; a time to be enlightened, considering God's past and future blessings as we anticipate our Messiah, the living Shamash—the Great Light.

The Purim Connection To Overcoming Israel's Enemies

As recorded in the Book of Esther, Haman, royal vizier to the Persian King Ahasuerus, planned to kill all the Jews in the empire, but his plans were foiled by Mordecai and his adopted daughter Queen Esther. This deliverance then became a day of feasting and rejoicing (Esther 9:1, 17). Purim's historical significance,

which originated in Iran in Esther's day (480 B.C.) when Jews won victory over their Persian foes, also foretells and forewarns of various conflicts Israel will have with modern-day Persia (Iran), which will initiate the appointed times counting periods and will continue during the final days.

"The cheerful heart has a continual feast," says Proverbs 15:15. Judaism teaches there are *two constants* that faithful Jews have longed for down through the centuries. First, "feasting continually," as illustrated in the Purim celebration; and second, the "continual," or *"tamid* offerings" offered twice daily at Jerusalem. Although Israel's arch rival Iran will be defeated, as will Syria and Israel's other surrounding enemies during the modern-day uprising foretold in Psalm 83, celebration over Israel's decisive victories will be transitory. As the counting periods begin, "daily" worship at Jerusalem's Western Wall will be taken away; as a result, Jews will long for the day when Jerusalem can be rebuilt, and worship can be restored at the Western Wall, and can begin anew in the rebuilt Temple on the Holy Mount after centuries of delay and expectation, finally putting to use the Temple Institute's restored sacred vessels.

Purim/Shushan Purim is preceded by *Taanit Esther*—the Fast of Esther. The Torah prescribes that whenever a Jewish army goes to war, the soldiers should spend the previous day fasting. This is in stark contrast to a secular army which spends the day preparing weapons and armaments. The Purim chorus is sung: "*Utzu etzah, vetufar; dabru davar, velo yakum; ki Immanuel,*" derived from the book of Isaiah. It is from the Hebrew text of God's warning to Israel's allied enemies, which are in partnership to wipe this people from the face of the earth: "*Devise your strategy, but it will be thwarted; propose your plan, but it will not stand, for God is with us,*" (Isaiah 8:10).

Once the Middle East erupts in a firestorm of conflict—the Persian Gulf conflict between the U.S. led coalition and Iran, along with Israel against her surrounding enemies, we can know with certainty the appointed end-time crisis is upon us. Israel's dominance will increase, eventually leading to the placement of the foundation stone for the Third Temple in Jerusalem. After the Middle East explodes, World War III will follow in quick succession. We will fear the end of civilization as we know it; but Jesus warned, "You will hear of wars and rumors of wars, but see to it that you are not alarmed. Such things must happen, but *the end is still to come*. Nation will rise against nation, and kingdom against kingdom. All these are *the beginning* of birth pains," (Matthew 24:6-8).

PROPHETIC NEWS EVENTS OF 2017 & 2018 LEADING UP TO WAR WITH IRAN IN EARLY 2019
(All Occurred On Biblical Days Or Significant Historical Dates)

Below are prophetic news events in the runup to the West's confrontation with Iran to begin in early 2019. We followed and realized that each time the Trump administration made significant public announcements related to confronting Iran, they occurred on Biblical Festivals or on significant historical dates of Israel's modern history over the last two years.

Shmini Torah (Eighth day celebration of Sukkot: Leviticus 23:39)—October 13, 2017
President Trump gives notorious speech on Iran, decertifying the JCPOA deal.
Related Article:

Trump de-certifies Iran nuclear deal, announces more sanctions against Iran; Trump decertifies Iran nuclear deal, slaps sanctions on IRGC in broadside at 'radical regime'

Hanukkah {Feast of Dedication: John 10:22)—December 12, 2017
The US and Israel sign a secret security pact. "*'Dramatic understandings' were agreed at the White House on December 12, and deal signed by the two countries' national security chiefs, says Channel 10"* in Israel.
Related Article:
Report: US, Israel sign secret pact to tackle Iran nuclear and missile threat

Shavuot (Pentecost)—May 21, 2018
Secretary of State Mike Pompeo gave a speech laying out 12 demands upon Iran
Related Article:
Pompeo's 12 Demands For Iran Read More Like A Declaration Of War Than A Path To Peace

Tisha B'AV (Fast of mourning of the fifth month: Zechariah 8:19)—July 22, 2018
President Donald Trump, Secretary Mike Pompeo and National Security Advisor John Bolton orchestrate concerted pressure against Iran with Tweets and speeches.
Related Articles:
No Walk-back This Time: National security advisor John Bolton doubles down on Trump's Iran threat; Trump issues rare all-caps tweet warning Iran of unprecedented consequences for threatening US; U.S. launches campaign to erode support for Iran's leaders; Secretary of State Mike Pompeo URGENT Speech on IRAN

Sukkot (Feast of Tabernacles)—September 26, 2018
President Trump's two UN speeches focused on Iran's aggressions--accusing Persia of sowing "chaos, death and destruction" across the Middle East. John Bolton also gave a speech with these words of warning to Iran. "There will be hell to pay" and "we will come after you." Furthermore, Mike Pompeo gave a speech related to Iran. The same day the US State Department issued a 48-page report called: A Chronicle of Iran's Destructive Activities. Last, but not least, Israel's Prime Minister Netanyahu gave a UN speech primarily about Iran's threat and secret nuclear sites.
Related Articles:
At UN, Netanyahu reveals Iranian nuclear warehouse, urges IAEA to go inspect it; US State Department Issues 48-page Report: Outlaw Regime: A Chronicle of Iran's Destructive Activities; President Trump SHOCKING Speech Chairs the UN Security Council Meeting; John Bolton: "There will be hell to pay" if Iran's Hassan Rouhani crosses the U.S.; President Trump's Address to the United Nations: Full Speech 9/25/2018; Pompeo accuses EU of 'solidifying Iran's ranking' as top state sponsor of terror

Simchat Torah (eighth day celebration of Sukkot: Leviticus 23:39)—October 3, 2018
President Trump's pressure on Iran increases once again. This time, Pompeo announced that the US is terminating the 1955 treaty, further severing ties with Iran, and Bolton warned Iran is not dismantling its nuclear program at the White House.
Related Articles:
Pompeo announces termination of 1955 bedrock US/Iran treaty in response to UN court ruling; US official: All signs indicate Iran increasingly pursuing nuclear weapons

Balfour Anniversary-- November 2, 2018
At the end of the 100th full year of the Balfour Declaration, President Trump made the official public announcement that the US is re-imposing all sanctions on Iran in three days.
Related Article:
US reimposes all sanctions on Iran lifted under nuclear deal

Hanukkah—December 2-10, 2018

President Trump gave a Hanukkah speech focused primarily on adding pressure on Iran, while Netanyahu and Pompeo make plans to meet. Also, DEBRAfile reported, "On Sunday, Dec. 2, US Marines opened artillery fire on Syrian and Iranian forces in the eastern Syrian Deir ez-Zour province" in an article called, "Netanyahu flies urgently to Brussels to discuss Iran's missile test with Pompeo.

Related Articles:

Netanyahu to meet US Secretary of State Pompeo in Brussels later Monday; World War 3: Iran says it's ready for offensive against US as navy ship enters Gulf—*"The USS John C. Stennis entered the Gulf on Friday as tensions continue to rise and reach unprecedented levels between Tehran and Washington.";* Hanukkah-President Trump INCREDIBLE Speech at Evening Hanukkah Reception at White House; U.S. Fears Iran Planning 'Massive Regional War' in Middle East; Netanyahu-Pompeo Brussels meeting is a warning to Lebanon—*"Netanyahu and Pompeo will likely discuss the quick establishment of Iran and Hezbollah's high-precision guided missile factories in Lebanon, as preparation for a possible Israeli action to thwart these efforts.";* Bolton: U.S. strongly supports Israel's efforts against Hezbollah – Arab-Israeli Conflict; Iran's Rouhani renews threat to blockade Gulf oil shipments; US urges Europe to impose sanctions on Iran over missiles – Israel Hayom; UN Security Council to meet on Iranian missile test; Iran EXPOSED: 'Uninspected' secret nuclear sites REVEALED, sparking World War 3 fears

---NOTES---

THE EXCELLENT ONE

אחד מצוין

Insights In Prophecy
Unlock The Ancient Mysteries Of Daniel & Revelation
BIBLE DISCOVERY SERIES

Lesson 9

SEVENTY WEEKS PROPHECY FOR ISRAEL & JERUSALEM

Read Daniel 9:20-27

- **Revisit the Vision, Times & Events Surrounding Israel's Last-Day Prophecy**
- **Explore The Future Of Our Most Favored Holy City—Jerusalem**

Thirteen years after Daniel received his vision in chapter 8 the Temple at Jerusalem still lay in ruins from Babylon's attack. With the time nearing for the end of their captivity, which the prophet Jeremiah predicted would last seventy years (Jeremiah 25:12), Daniel cried out in humble petition to God in a Day of Atonement (Yom Kippur) prayer of restoration. During this prayer the man Gabriel touched the prophet and said, "Daniel, I have now come to give you insight and understanding," Daniel 9:23. Gabriel then relayed time periods and events specific to Israel not for Daniel's day, but way into the future that would bring an end to sin and finalize the vision concerning Jerusalem. The messenger said, "Seventy (70) weeks are determined upon thy people [Israelites] and upon thy holy city [Jerusalem], to finish the transgression, and

to make an end of sins, and to make reconciliation for iniquity, and to bring in everlasting righteousness, and to seal up the vision and prophecy, and to anoint the most Holy. Know therefore and understand, that from the going forth of the commandment to restore and to build Jerusalem unto the Messiah the Prince shall be seven weeks, and threescore and two weeks: the street shall be built again, and the wall, even in troublous times," Daniel 9:24-25. It's interesting that the 70 Weeks happen to end on Yom Kippur, according to *The Kingdom Calendar* pattern.

As we study Daniel 9, we'll also discover the 70 Weeks are made up of three segments of time (49 days + 434 days + 7 days = 490 days). And, they are not relics of the past as is often taught; but instead, these time periods relate to modern-day events, which will soon come to pass during the appointed time of the end.

There are two common interpretations of the 70 Week prophecy found in prophecy circles. First, the "historicist" view which was introduced in the 13th century. This view promotes a 490 "year" interpretation of the prophecy based on a "day-for-a-year" theory. The 490 days turned into years are believed to be representative of historical events, which began with an Ezra decree to rebuild Jerusalem and ended at or near the time of the crucifixion.

There are two problems with this view. The day-for-a-year interpretation is borrowed from two other passages, and is not necessary to the prophecy, nor even implied in the text. One verse relied upon is in Ezekiel, a contemporary prophet to Daniel; he was told to lie on his side for 40 days, "each day for each year," (4:6). Notice that this opposes the concept; because, in this case Ezekiel's prophecy reduces the 40 years down to 40 days—the opposite effect. It cannot be applied to Daniel's 490 day prophecy. The second reference is in Numbers 14:34. The Israelites were told because of their disbelief they would have to spend 40 years in the desert—"one year for each of the forty days" the spies explored the land. At least this passage supports the theory. Applying Israel's day-for-a-year punishment, which occurred almost 1,000 years earlier, commentators arbitrarily turn the 490 *days* of Daniel 9:24 into *years*. However, we protest this as an unnecessary interpretation forced on the text that originated in the Dark Ages. Why? This view disregards the textual evidence, which simply relays a period of 490 days. By forcing this concept onto Daniel's end-time period (turning 490 days—1.3 years into 490 years—a monumental alteration to the text), the true meaning of the prophecy has been maligned. But, those who hold to the historicist view do not stop there; they also turn the 1,260 days, 1,290 days and other periods of days into century-spanning 1,260 years and 1,290 years; their whole prophetic view of Daniel and Revelation is based on this flawed hypothesis.

This interpretation disregards the Hebrew word "yom"—which means "days" and the end-of-the-world context of Daniel 9:24, and throws the altered timelines and predictions into the distant past. Every attempt should be made, first and foremost, to understand the prophecies in their original language; and, if this exegesis (critical explanation of Scripture text) does not blend with Daniel's other prophecies, Jesus' discourse in Matthew 24 and the book of Revelation, only then should other schemes be considered.

The second common interpretation of Daniel's 70 Weeks is the "futurist" view. Scholars of this view have also turned the 490 day prophecy into years, but instead of holding to a complete fulfillment in the past they recognize the end-of-the-world context of Daniel's vision. Therefore, the futurist interpretation places 69 weeks in the past, ending around the death of Christ. This is followed by a mysterious gap of time until Israel reaches the final events at the end of the age, where the prophecy picks back up again with one final week of years, promoting a seven year tribulation period.

There are two major errors with this view. First, like the historicist view, the day-for-a-year principle is forced upon the vision, which as mentioned is not needful or implied contextually. There is no support for turning the 490 days into 490 years, except conjecture (speculation; guesswork; theory). This view also disregards the simple reading of "seventy sevens" (490 days), in which every aspect of the prophecy will meet fulfillment. Second, there is no evidence for a nearly 2,000 year gap between the 69th week and 70th week. This is a contrived view imposed upon the text, which is not necessary at all. What we are really saying is "God, we know Gabriel told Daniel '70 weeks' but we want to turn the '70 weeks of days' into '490 years'". Let's stop second-guessing God. It's time for our generation to accept that Gabriel relayed the facts correctly, that God's prophets wrote what they heard, and Messiah meant what He said. In fact, the idea of a multi-century gap between verse 26 and 27 just doesn't hold up scripturally or exegetically; neither does widespread popularity make it so.

As noted in the introduction to our lesson series, the apostles, the prophets and early church held a literal view of Daniel—the belief that Daniel's prophecies would be fulfilled in a very short segment of time and Messiah would return in their lifetimes. It was not until the thirteenth century that a monk first took the liberty to change the prophetic "days" of Daniel into "years". This idea was picked up by Cardinal Nicholas Krebs (c. 1400-1464) whose work popularized the application of the day-for-a-year measurement of prophetic time. From these roots many scholars repeated the day-for-a-year view to the point it became elevated to undisputable dogma. It's an agreed reality that if a half-truth or an outright lie is repeated often enough and long enough, that people believe it as fact. We see this in all religions of the world.

All the same, in this lesson we are calling you back to a literal interpretation of Daniel 9, and its 70 weeks of 490 days. After reviewing the events that occur within this important time frame, then we'll merge it alongside the 1,335 days, 1,290 days, 1,260 days and 1,150 days of Daniel's visions as charted in *The Kingdom Calendar*. Since the 490 days parallel the other counting periods by having similar key points, then we must consider the entire Daniel 9 time period and its portrayed events to be part of the end-of-the-world prophecies, and not extended periods of historical time or relics of the past.

Insights In Prophecy
Unlock The Ancient Mysteries Of Daniel & Revelation
BIBLE DISCOVERY SERIES

1. For the benefit of what people and what city is the vision of Daniel 9:24 specifically given? _____
_____

Daniel's people—today's Jews, and Jerusalem.

2. How long is "seventy sevens," literally, "seventy weeks"? _____

70 X 7 = 490 / 70 weeks equal 490 days

3. What six events will bring the prophecy for Israel and Jerusalem to fulfillment (v. 24)? _____
_____
_____

1) to finish transgression
2) to put an end to sin
3) to atone for wickedness (Day of Atonement event)
4) to bring in everlasting righteousness (Kingdom of Righteousness)
5) to seal up vision and prophecy
6) to anoint the most holy (return the Most Holy to the proper state; only allowed once a year on the Day of Atonement)

All six predictions represent "Day of the LORD" fulfillments and are end-of-the-world in their context. These six elements blend alongside the predictions in the three other visions Daniel received about the appointed time of the end in chapters 7, 8 and 10-12. When the vision and its 490 day time frame meets fulfillment, it will finish transgression, put an end to sin, seal up the vision and return the sanctuary to its rightful state... events surrounding Israel and Jerusalem, which take us to the end of sinful activities and the dawning of God's eternal Kingdom.

In Chart I below the 490 days are charted in its most basic form with the six predictions meeting fulfillment at the Day of the LORD.

Chart I: Verse 24

/------------Prophecy For Israel & Jerusalem -------------/ DAY OF THE LORD
/---------------------------490 Days----------------------------/1) to finish [or, "restrain"] transgression
            2) to put an end to sin
            3) to atone for wickedness
            4) to bring in everlasting righteousness
            5) to seal up vision and prophecy
            6) to anoint the most holy

4. There are three segments of time which make up the 490 days—49 days, followed by 434 days, followed by 7 days. Verse 25 introduces two of the three divisions—"seven sevens [49 days] and sixty-two sevens [434 days]." There are several events also included. What are the three major events that will take place during these two periods, which are linked to one another in verse 25? _____
_____

1) issuing of the decree to restore and rebuild Jerusalem

2) anointed one, the ruler, comes [to Jerusalem]
3) rebuilding of [Jerusalem] streets and a trench in times of trouble

Gabriel states "from the issuing of the decree to restore and rebuild Jerusalem until the anointed one, the ruler, comes, there will be seven 'sevens' (49 days) and sixty-two 'sevens' (434 days)." It will be rebuilt with streets and a trench, but in times of trouble." The need to rebuild the city of Jerusalem implies devastation, possibly by a high magnitude earthquake. In Lesson One we learned that devastation will come suddenly early in the appointed time. In the aftermath, it will take some time for religious turmoil to subside before restoration can begin; then, the decree to "restore and rebuild" Jerusalem will be pronounced; and when it is made public, the 490 day counting period will commence.

We discover the 49 days (a tenth of the whole), which begin the 490 day counting period, are marked off from the 434 days. The 49 days represent a shorter preparation period to emphasize that we should consider where we are in prophetic time. There is also a similar 49 day counting period between Passover and Shavuot (Pentecost)—a time when believers are to count the days in preparation for spiritual renewal. The 490 days embody God's last call for Israel and Jerusalem, as a display of His continued patience and mercy that leads up to the Day of the LORD. However, the decree to rebuild a devastated Jerusalem that begins the 70 Week prophecy will only lead to greater sorrow and destruction upon the beloved City; because, despite prophecy's warnings, Israel's leaders will ultimately allow Antichrist into Jerusalem and onto the rebuilt Temple Mount to set up his abomination.

During the 2019-2022 Festival counting period, the first 49 days of the 490 day prophecy landed exactly between Tisha B'Av and Shabbat Nachuma on *The Kingdom Calendar*. Tisha B'Av is a sober annual fast that reminds Jews of the destruction of both Temples that occurred on this historic day. The first Sabbath after Tisha B'Av is Shabbat Nachuma—the "Sabbath of comforting." This Sabbath gets its name from the *haftarah* (a series of selections from the Hebrew Bible that is read publicly in the synagogue) from Isaiah 40:1-26 that speaks of "comforting" God's people for their suffering. It is the first of seven weekly haftarahs of consolation leading up to Rosh Hashanah, the Jewish New Year. During the future fulfillment period, God's people will experience tragedies throughout the 70 Weeks, but not without the hope of the Day of the LORD, the returning Messiah and His eternal Kingdom.

Chart II below maps the time line and events studied so far.

Chart II: Verses 24-25

/--------Prophecy for Israel & Jerusalem ------------Coming of an Anointed One--a Prophet
A ---49 Days---B------------------434 Days--------------C

A—decree will be given to rebuild and restore Jerusalem
A to C—Jerusalem will be rebuilt in times of trouble
B—no specific event is sited in the passage (represents a tenth of the whole—a counting time)
C—anointed one (prophet) comes to Jerusalem (no doubt, with an important final warning)

Continuing with our study, Daniel 9:26 says, "After the sixty-two 'sevens,' the Anointed One will be cut off and will have nothing." The New International Version (NIV) and the King James Version (KJV) scholars *interpreted* the "anointed one" to be Messiah and therefore capitalized the title; however, the original language does not demand the *anointed one* represent the Son of Man—the Messiah. In the Word of God an "anointed one" is a term most associated with *priests* (Exodus 28:41), *kings* (1 Samuel

16:13) and *prophets* such as Elijah and Elisha (1 Kings 19:16), and many versions are true to the original by pointing out in footnotes the language simply reads "an anointed one, the ruler"; which, could mean to say, an anointed king or a ruling prophet will arrive in Jerusalem.

Verse 26 says after sixty-two sevens or 434 days, the anointed one will be cut off. The New International Version footnote suggests the reading of the original text could be, *"the anointed one will be cut off but not for himself."* This verse has often been applied to the death of Jesus two thousand years ago; however, we are going to focus on the end-time context of the vision and how the events in Daniel 9 correspond to other prophecies about the last days.

5. Paul and the apostles believed they were living in the last days and on the verge of the imminent return of the LORD. In 2 Thessalonians 2:7 Paul taught the power of lawlessness was already at work and eventually the Man of Sin (Antichrist) would be "revealed" in the Temple in Jerusalem; however, he said the "[anointed] one who now holds it back will continue to do so" until what? _____

He is taken out of the way.

6. What will happen next, once "he" is taken out of the way (2 Thessalonians 2:8)? _____

The lawless one (Antichrist) will be revealed (as an impostor messiah: one who thinks himself to be God). Verse 4 states at the end of time "he sets himself up in God's [Jerusalem] Temple, proclaiming himself to be God." Here we find the connection between the two passages—their focus on Jerusalem and the Man of Sin's repulsive action—proclaiming himself to be God.

7. What is the outcome of his abominable act (v. 9)? _____

He will be overthrown and destroyed.

8. How does the language of Daniel 9:26, show similarity to 2 Thessalonians 2:7? _____
_____

Daniel is told the "anointed one", the prophet, will be cut off but not for himself, while Paul says the [anointed] one who now holds ["restrains" Antichrist] back will do so till He is taken out of the way.

The similarity is obvious between Daniel's *cutting off* and Paul's *taking out* of the way of a male figure, but the passage parallels go way beyond this one important aspect. In review of both texts, you'll discover both focus on the very end of time just before the Day of the LORD, and both passages spotlight Jerusalem and the Temple. Both Daniel 9:26 and 2 Thessalonians 2:7 expose the evil deeds of the Lawless One; which is to say, both passages focus the same end-time events. Amazing!

Therefore, these two texts in the Hebrew Scriptures are contextually connected. Both passages point to the death of the anointed one—Elijah, one of the two last-day heaven-sent prophets, who will rule by divine authority on earth as found in Revelation 11. Malachi 3:1-2 says, "See, I will send My messenger [Elijah], who will prepare the way [for My coming] before Me [for 1,260 days, then he will die a martyr's death in the streets of Jerusalem and lie unburied for 3½ days]. Then suddenly the LORD you are seeking will come to His [Jerusalem] Temple [to deal with the Man of Sin's evil act]; the Messenger [Hebrew "mal'akh"—angel; that is, Michael] of the Covenant [Ten Commandments], whom you desire, will come [to earth], says the LORD Almighty. But who can endure the Day of His coming? Who can stand when He appears?"

Revelation 11:3-13 reveals the ministry of two prophets during 1,260 days of the appointed time that runs parallel with the Lawless One's 1,260 day rule. Demonic deceptions that will overtake the world's population are to be countered by the work of these invincible messengers—Moses and Elijah—who will restrain Antichrist's abominable actions for a time, and will proclaim essential warnings during the last days, calling God's people to faithfulness.

As already mentioned, at the end of their 1,260 day ministry Revelation 11:7-8 predicts the two anointed ones will be murdered in the streets of the great city Jerusalem, where also our "LORD was crucified." That's why John, in the book of Revelation, speaks critically of Jerusalem's inhabitants, calling Jerusalem "Babylon" for "in her was found the blood of prophets and of the believers, and of all who have been killed on earth," (18:24).

When a true God-sent prophet speaks, it's as though God Himself has spoken. Hebrews 1:1 declares, "In the past God spoke to our forefathers through the prophets at many times and in various ways" and will do so again in the last days. When Elijah is killed, he will be *"cut off, but not for himself"*; he will be *"taken out of the way,"* and no one will be left to restrain the lawless Man of Sin from his evil act. With the two witnesses killed, the Man of Sin will step onto the Temple Mount and set up his abomination (Matthew 24:14-21), as also foretold by Daniel (12:11), and proclaim himself Master. **The Kingdom Calendar** shows the death of the two witnesses occur just before the Day of the LORD and the Great Tribulation, just as the 490 days prophecy predicts.

9. Consistent with Daniel 9:26, after the 434 days (sixty-two sevens) and the cutting off of the anointed one (Elijah), what will happen next to the rebuilt Temple and Jerusalem? _____

"The people of the [evil Papal] ruler who will come will destroy the city [Jerusalem] and the sanctuary [on the Temple Mount]. The end [of Jerusalem] will come like a flood: War will continue until the end [of prophetic time], and desolations have been decreed [in the prophecies]."

Jesus prophesied of Jerusalem, "Your house is left to you *desolate*," Matthew 23:38. Revelation agrees, "Come out of her [Jerusalem] My people so that you will not share in her sins, so that you will not receive any of her plagues; for her sins [of following after Antichrist, and killing the prophets, etc.] are piled up to Heaven, and God has remembered her crimes," (18:4-5). Paul recognized Jerusalem's sins even in his day; he wrote, "You suffered from your own countrymen... the Jews, who killed the LORD Jesus and the prophets and also drove us out," 1 Thessalonians 2:14-15. In the last days, apostate Christianity will join Islam and fallen Judaism in a triangle of sin against God's two prophets.

10. There is one seven (one week) time period which concludes the 490 days. What does Daniel 9:27 say the Lawless One will confirm for one week? _____

Antichrist will confirm a covenant for one week; in other words, he will make an agreement with Israel's leaders that will ultimately usher in death and destruction to Jerusalem, Israel, and then the world at large (Isaiah 28:17-19).

11. What will the wicked Ruler do in the middle of the week? _____

"In the middle of the 'seven' he will put an end to sacrifice and offering." He will stop the rituals so that he can use the Temple Mount for his own abominable act, 3 ½ days into the last 7 day week of Daniel 9.

12. After Elijah, the anointed one, is taken out of the way and the Papacy stops the Temple sacrifices, what is his next move? _____

"And on a wing of the [Jerusalem] Temple he will set up an abomination that causes desolation, until the end that is decreed [his punishment and death] is poured out on him." The abomination will be set up as spoken of in Daniel 12:11 and Matthew 24:15, but only for a moment until Michael stands and descends in the cloak of darkness to deal with his evil deed.

13. What is decreed in prophecy concerning the evil Ruler's future (9:27)? _____

His actions will lead to his demise, just as Daniel predicts in his three other visions: Daniel 7:26; 8:25; and 11:45.

"Therefore, this is what the Sovereign LORD says: 'Because you people [Israel] have brought to mind your guilt by your open rebellion [against the LORD], revealing your sins in all that you do—because you have done this, you will be taken captive. O profane and wicked Prince of Israel [Jewish Pope], whose day has come, whose time of punishment has reached its climax, this is what the Sovereign LORD says: Take off the turban [Hebrew: literally, "*mitre*"], remove the crown [kingship over Israel and the nations]. It will not be as it was: The lowly will be exalted, and the exalted will be brought low. A ruin! A ruin! I will make it a ruin! It will not be restored until He [Messiah] comes to whom it rightfully belongs; to Him I will give it,'" Ezekiel 21:24-27.

"Woe to the Worthless Shepherd [Papal Jew], who deserts the flock [leaves his Jewish roots and the Word of God]! May the sword strike his arm and his right eye! May his arm be completely withered, his right eye totally blinded!" Zechariah 11:16-17. From this passage we surmise this man, sometime before, during or at the end of his reign, will suffer a debilitating blow to his body.

Chart IV: 70 Weeks (490 days) Of Daniel 9
Verses 24-27

/-------------------Final Prophecy for Israel & Jerusalem -------------/ THE DAY OF THE LORD
                                                                                                    THE END
/--------49 Days -------/---------------434 Days----- / -----7 Days-----/ GREAT TRIBULATION
A   B   C 3½ D 3½ E

A—decree given to restore and rebuild Jerusalem (begins 49 day countdown)
B—no specific event given in the prophecy; mystery to be revealed at its fulfillment
C—anointed one, the prophet Elijah who rules, comes to Jerusalem to restrain Antichrist's abomination
D—anointed one, the prophet Elijah, is cut off and taken out of the way; meaning, he is killed
    Abomination is set up. He lies unburied in the streets of Jerusalem for 3½ days (Revelation 11:7-8)
E—the Day of the LORD; Elijah is resurrected back to life; prophecy is fulfilled: "to finish transgression, to put an end to sin, to atone for wickedness, to bring in everlasting righteousness, to seal up vision and prophecy and to anoint the most holy."

The true meaning of Daniel 9 has been veiled by many interpretations handed down to us through the centuries. However, the 70 Weeks will be understood in these last days as part of the Book of Truth unsealed (Daniel 10:21), for it need not stand alone independent of the other prophetic time periods of Daniel and Revelation or be relegated to the past. The 70 Week end-time predictions of Daniel 9 are relevant to the last days, and therefore merge alongside the episodes recorded in Daniel 12, Matthew 24 and Revelation 11. **The Kingdom Calendar** shows at the Day of the LORD the 490 day prophecy will come to an abrupt end, even if God has to intervene; for He "changes times and seasons" (Daniel 2:21) to meet the autumn Festival schedule for the Day of Atonement—the Day of the LORD.

Chart V: 70 Weeks (490 Days) Of Daniel 9:24-27

The Daniel 9 prophecy below has been connected with letter reference points to the 490 day time line, which will help clarify how the time lines and events will unfold in the future.

```
/----------------Final Prophecy For Israel & Jerusalem -----------------/ THE DAY OF THE LORD
                                                                            THE END
/--------49 Days -------/-------------434 Days---------- / ----7 Days------/ GREAT TRIBULATION
A                       B                                C 3½ D 3½ E
```

Vs 24 "Seventy `sevens' [70 weeks, or 490 days] are decreed for your people [Israel] and your holy city [Jerusalem] to finish [or "restrain"] transgression [E], to put an end to sin [E], to atone for wickedness [E], to bring in everlasting righteousness [E], to seal up vision and prophecy [E] and to anoint the most holy [E].

Vs 25 "Know and understand this: From the issuing of the decree to restore and rebuild Jerusalem [A] until the anointed one [prophet-Elijah], the ruler, comes [C], there will be seven `sevens,' and [then] sixty-two `sevens.' [434 days]. It [Jerusalem] will be rebuilt with streets and a trench, but in times of trouble [A to C].

Vs 26 After the sixty-two `sevens,' [434 days] [C] the anointed one [prophet Elijah] will be cut off [killed] and will have nothing [or, "but not for himself"]. [D]   The people [followers] of the ruler [Antichrist] who will come will destroy the city [Jerusalem] and the Sanctuary [E and beyond]. The end [E and beyond] will come like a flood: War will continue until the end [of the Great Tribulation] and desolations have been decreed.

Vs 27 He [Antichrist] will confirm a covenant with many for one `seven.' [7 days] [C] In the middle of the `seven' [days] [D] he will put an end to sacrifice and offering. And on a wing [of the Jerusalem Temple] he will set up an abomination that causes desolation [D], until the end that is decreed is poured out on him [E and beyond]."

The Abomination & The Temple Mount

About 40 years ago, by the third day of the Six Day War in 1967, God gave the armies of Israel clear and decisive victory over their surrounding enemies, as King David before them, restoring the fortunes of Jerusalem back to Israel. Although within their grasp, Israel's leaders decided against taking full control of the Temple Mount area amid fear of reprisal and conflict with the Muslims. However, the countdown of Israel's final days continued on their decisive march, which will not end until the final events of human history meet their fulfillment.

In the last days during **The Kingdom Calendar's** countdown, the Pope will make one last disastrous decision; he will step onto the epicenter of Bible prophecy—the sacred Temple Mount where he will not set up worship to the True God (as David did), but he will set up the idolatrous abomination (Pt. 17) that will bring desolation to Jerusalem. By doing so, he will, as King David years before him, trigger the last and shortest segment of time for Israel's punishment—the 40 days of Great Tribulation, known as the time of Jacob's trouble (Pt. 19). Jesus related the trouble this way, "So when you see standing in the holy place 'the abomination that causes desolation,' spoken of through the prophet Daniel—let the reader understand— then let those who are in Judea flee to the mountains," Matthew 24:15-16. Luke portrayed the great disaster to fall upon Israel and the City in this manner: "When you see Jerusalem being surrounded by armies, you will know that its desolation is near. Then let those who are in Judea flee to the mountains, let those in the city [of Jerusalem] get out, and let those in the country not enter the city [of Jerusalem]. For this is the *time of punishment in fulfillment of all that has been written*," Luke 21:20-22. In David's day, "When the Angel stretched out His hand to destroy Jerusalem, the LORD was grieved because of the calamity and said to the Angel who was afflicting the people, "Enough! Withdraw your hand. The Angel of the LORD was then at the threshing floor of Araunah the Jebusite [today's Temple Mount]," 2 Samuel 24:16. In contract, at that future day when the spurious King of Israel steps onto the Temple Mount, the destroying Angel's hand of destruction will not be stopped against Jerusalem. Punishment will begin at the Temple of God.

God's Last Call Of Grace

Our God has revealed His omniscient power time and again by predicting future rulers, decrees and dates. Only the God of Israel could have designed the numbered days thousands of years in advance of their fulfillment and set into motion His final plan of redemption. *The Kingdom Calendar*, revealing God's remarkable alignment of His prophetic counting timelines and the last Festival dates of human history, proves that we are nearing the end-of-the-world events. The great prophet Isaiah was instructed to go and warn stubborn Israel, "Be ever hearing, but never understanding; be ever seeing, but never perceiving. Make the heart of this people calloused; make their ears dull and close their eyes. Otherwise, they might see with their eyes, hear with their ears, understand with their hearts, and turn and be healed," Isaiah 6:9-10. The warning stands today. May the Holy Spirit open our eyes and ears to the path of righteousness during this period of the most convincing demonic deceptions to befall mankind! In the appointed days of the end, God will send his two prophets proclaiming last warnings and to offer direction. It is our duty to heed their message and to wait patiently by faith, even under duress, for the conquering Messiah at the end of His counting periods.

In this regard, the 70 Weeks (490 days) represent God's last call of mercy towards Israel and the city Jerusalem. Jesus warned the generation of His day, "Woe to you, teachers of the law and Pharisees, you hypocrites!... you say, If we had lived in the days of our forefathers, we would not have taken part with them in shedding the blood of the prophets... Therefore, I am sending you prophets and wise men and teachers. Some of them you will kill and crucify, others you will flog in your synagogues and pursue from town to town... O Jerusalem, Jerusalem, you who kill the prophets and stone those sent to you, how often I have longed to gather your children together, as a hen gathers her chicks under her wings, but you were not willing. Look, your house is left to you desolate. For I tell you, you will not see Me again until you say, Blessed is He who comes in the name of the LORD," Matthew 23:29-39. In fulfillment of His warning, within a few decades Jerusalem was ransacked and burned, and the Jews were scattered across the globe.

In the last 100 years, God has moved through world events and human affairs to bring the Jewish people back to the Holy Land for His closing work of redemption, just as Yahweh promised He would long ago (Deuteronomy 30:3; Zephaniah 3:20; Jeremiah 31:10; Ezekiel 11:17). The people of the Book have yet to learn just how precisely God's mysterious timelines have been slowly and methodically unfolding through the last few decades, signaled by Shemitah events (the counting of the seven-year cycles), the blood moon tetrads connected to the Festivals, and the Jubilee cycle. Yet, there is even more amazing accuracy just ahead as the Day of the LORD approaches. The day by day counting periods of Daniel and Revelation are not only linked to Israel's contemporary history, but last-day prophetic events are about to fall play out according to the Biblical/Jewish Festivals pattern, authenticating God's final call of repentance during the appointed times and seasons.

The Timeline Of Jewish History

Towards the end of World War I the *Balfour Declaration*—a letter from British Foreign Secretary Arthur James Balfour to LORD Rothschild dated November 2, 1917—made public British support for a Jewish homeland in Palestine, which was later recognized by the League of Nations. For close to 2,000 years, Jews had no country to call their own, but in the 1940s during World War II God heard the cries of Jacob from Hitler's prisons and gas chambers, and out of the holocaust He gave birth to the final generation. "Let this be written for a future generation, that a people not yet created may praise the LORD; The LORD looked down from His sanctuary on high, from Heaven He viewed the earth, to hear the groans of the prisoners and release those condemned to death," Psalm 102:19-20. One hundred full years later takes us to November 2, 2018. Two 70-day periods later take us to March 21/22, 2019 and Purim/Shushan Purim when the prophetic counting periods could begin with a Jerusalem disaster.

In November of 1947, the United Nations adopted the *Partition Plan for Palestine,* which soon thereafter led to the establishment of modern Israel when the

Rudi Weissenstein/Israel Ministry of Foreign AffairsDavid Ben-Gurion, the first Prime Minister of Israel, pronounces the Declaration of the State of Israel at the Tel Aviv Museum of Art on May 14, 1948. Above him is a portrait of Theodor Herzl, the father of modern political Zionism.

Declaration of the Establishment of the State of Israel was approved on May 14, 1948. Seventy full years hence from this prophetic event takes us to mid-May 2019, the Omer counting period, and the unfolding of final events. Just as Daniel waited seventy years for the restoration of Jerusalem in his day (Daniel 9:2), so the state of Israel will have waited for the final work of God as it relates to the Hebrew prophets, Jews and the beloved City.

Seven is the number of perfection and completion, and themes of sevens are found throughout the Scriptures. Peter asked Jesus "how many times shall I forgive my brother when he

sins against me? Up to seven times?" Matthew 18:21. Yeshua enlarged Peter's thinking when He responded that the brethren be forgiven "seventy times seven" [490 times] Matthew 18:22, (KJV). Messiah no doubt had the "seventy sevens" prophecy of Daniel 9:24-27 in mind. During the final 490 days God's forgiveness will be offered to Israel and the beloved City, while Israel's rebellion continues. Each day the Father pleads to not follow the Man of Sin; but, to turn to the true Messiah Yeshua while He may be found. Some will heed the invitation; others will not. May we be among those whose faith and abiding love stands the test of deception and many trials. Jesus said, "And many false prophets shall rise, and shall deceive many. And because iniquity shall abound, the love of many shall wax cold. But he that shall endure unto the end, the same shall be saved." Matthew 24:11-13.

PRINCE OF PEACE

פרינכע ופ פעאכע

Insights In Prophecy
Unlock The Ancient Mysteries Of Daniel & Revelation
BIBLE DISCOVERY SERIES

---- NOTES---

Insights In Prophecy

Unlock The Ancient Mysteries Of Daniel & Revelation

BIBLE DISCOVERY SERIES

Lesson 10

DETAILS OF THE MIDDLE EAST CONFLICT

LESSON 10

Read Daniel 10 & 11

- **Study About Egypt's Clash With The Northern Power**
- **Consider The King Of The North's Malicious Activities**

Chapter 10 introduces Daniel's final and lengthiest vision, spanning three full chapters (Daniel 10, 11 & 12). The end-time fulfillment of Daniel's vision is announced right in the passage itself: Daniel 10:14 says, "Now I am come to explain to you what will happen to your people [Israel] in the future, for the vision concerns a time yet to come." The King James reads, "What shall befall thy people in the latter days."

Daniel and his companions were standing on the bank of the Tigris River around 535 B.C. The prophet had been fasting for three weeks (vs. 1-4), then he saw the Man clothed in linen, whose majestic appearance caused Daniel to faint in fear. Chapter 10 then addresses the clashes between loyal and rebellious angels; encounters which increase during the last days. When Heaven's messengers under the guidance of Michael, the Prince of the Host, move in the affairs of men and travel throughout the earth, they encounter resistance from the demonic forces. Sometimes only the Prince, the Man dressed in priest's linen, can demand compliance and push on through the enemy's barriers.

The forty-five verses that comprise chapter 11 portray the ongoing struggle between the kings of the north and the south. Commentators have applied most of chapter 11 to historical events, jumping from century to century across the span of time to find possible fulfillments. The king of the north has been assigned to various powers—Syria, Turkey, Russia and Europe, to name a few. However, after many years of  consideration, this study will offer you a modern-day explanation of the vision. In the author's opinion, the entire chapter portrays events involving two adjoining nations—Egypt, the king(s) of the south and Israel, the king(s) of the north.

With this interpretation in mind, chapter 11 would be revealing several end-time clashes between Egypt (and likely other North African Islamic nations) and Israel, and the turmoil their leaders must face. The chapter implies there will be an internal power struggle in Egypt, and a turn-over of leadership; the reigning president of that day will be removed. What then follows is a series of clashes between Egypt and Israel during the counting periods of the appointed times.

Daniel 11 also notes a turn-over of power in Israel—at least three Israeli leaders rule during the appointed time of the end, starting with the current Israeli leader at the period the appointed times begin. He will be followed by a short-term Prime Minister—a raiser of taxes (v. 20), and finally by a contemptible outsider from Rome—the Jewish Papal Antichrist himself—he will become the king of the north (whose reign begins at Daniel 11:21). He will take control of Israel through intrigue and will gain the final foothold over Israel and Egypt with his vast European and international military forces. However, even his rule will be short-lived. Near the end of his evil reign, just before the Day of the LORD arrives... "the Man of Lawlessness [will be] revealed, the man doomed to destruction. He will oppose and will exalt himself over everything that is called God or is worshiped, so that he sets himself up in God's temple, proclaiming himself to be God," (2

Thessalonians 2:2-3). Daniel relays it this way: He will "plant his royal tents between the seas at the beautiful holy mountain [Jerusalem]. Yet he will come to his end, and no one will help him," (Daniel 11:45).

Michael, Daniel's Prince

1. What are the main features of the Man clothed in linen (vs. 5-6)? _____

2. How closely does this compare with the description of Jesus in Revelation 1:13-16? _____
_____

They are virtually the same.

3. What is the Man's name (Daniel 10:13, 21)? _____

Michael, Daniel's Prince. One of the many names for Jesus in the Scriptures.

Daniel was the only one to see the vision, while his companions were overwhelmed by fear and fled. He also grew weak in fear and dropped to the ground (vs. 7-9). John, the visionary author of the book of Revelation, also responded the same way when he encountered Messiah (Revelation 1:17). However, both prophets were touched by a steady hand and reassured.

4. Daniel was God's chosen servant (10:11-13). The messenger Gabriel told Daniel he was there to give him understanding. Although Gabriel was sent from the first day of Daniel's fast, why was he delayed from reaching the prophet (v. 13)? _____

The demon prince of Persia stopped Gabriel from reaching Daniel.

5. Ephesians 6:12 describes the evil forces in what terms? _____
_____

The evil angels are assigned territories and nations, and Gabriel encountered a powerful foe. However, Messiah, the leader of the heavenly forces (Revelation 12:7), took control of the situation and guaranteed Gabriel's safe passage.

Daniel is struck a second time by the overpowering encounter with Gabriel and he bowed in reverence with face to the ground. The messenger who looked like a man touched Daniel and gave him strength to continue. Gabriel tells the prophet he has arrived to help him understand the great conflict that will involve his people (Israel) at the end of time (10:14-21), as written in the Book of Truth. When his visit with Daniel was finished, Gabriel said he would continue to face future challenges by demonic forces. We may learn someday that Gabriel is the one who once before "prophesied of these, saying, Behold, the LORD cometh with ten thousands of his saints," (Jude 14); the one "translated that he should not see death; and was not found, because God had translated him: for before his translation he had this testimony, that he pleased God," Hebrew 11:5.

6. Michael, "your [Daniel's] prince" continued to help Gabriel. Why would Michael be called "Daniel's prince"? _____

Michael is simply another representative title for Messiah, Daniel's Savior and LORD, who was "with God," and "was God. He was with God in the beginning," (John 1:1-2).

Fourth Persian King

Daniel 11:1-3 offers a detailed explanation of last-day events starting with the conflict that was fostered by the fourth leader of Persia (Iran). This is a shortened version of events earlier portrayed in Daniel 8:1-8 between the Ram (Islam) with two horns (Iraq and Iran) and the western powers, led by a powerful U.S. President who rises up to initiate primary events of the last days. The details in these verses would help Daniel and future readers get their bearings as to the timing of the vision in relationship to the previous three chapters (7, 8 & 9). Once the U.S. President starts the modern-day Gulf War, and Iran is defeated, America—the primary leader of the Western coalition of nations—will be broken (as portrayed in Daniel 7:4 and 8:8) and U.S. dominance will be divided into four major regions of global power—"parceled out toward the four winds of heaven" (11:4), as also indicated in Daniel 7:2-3.

Prophecy foretells that in the "latter days" (10:14) there will emerge in Persia (Iran) "three kings" (or, rulers—11:2). However, the "fourth" ruler will stir up the Iranians against the "realm of Grecia". The same confrontation is spoken of in Daniel 8:21, and this vision identifies the powerful Western Goat and the "horn" as the first king (first in standing; the most powerful) as making war with a Ram (Islam) with two horns (Iraq and Iran). The translators identified the Goat as "Greece," which in the Hebrew text is "Yawan" or "Javan". Javan was one of the sons of Japheth (Genesis 10:2), and modern Javan implies more than just the nation of Greece, due to military protection agreements. Since the vision concerns the time of the end, it would be reasonable to identify the Goat as a coalition of western European NATO powers, including Greece, with the prominent horn as the first in power—the United States.

Persia, whose name was changed to Iran in 1935, was ruled by empires and dynasties. However, political revolution led to a major realignment of power and the *Islamic Republic* was established in Iran on April 1, 1979. A Constitution of the Islamic Republic was approved by national referendum in December 1979. Iran now had *elected* leadership, a clear transition from the past. This ushered in the conditions for the end-time predictions of Daniel 11 to become reality. One key religious leader in the development of the Islamic Republic became the fourth and one of the most influential leaders in Iran—the wealthy Hojatolislam Ali Alvar Hashemi Rafsanjani.

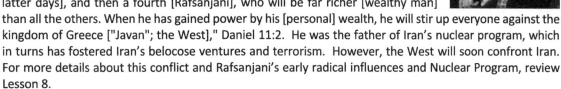

"Now then, I tell you the truth: Three more kings will appear in Persia [Iran, in the latter days], and then a fourth [Rafsanjani], who will be far richer [wealthy man] than all the others. When he has gained power by his [personal] wealth, he will stir up everyone against the kingdom of Greece ["Javan"; the West]," Daniel 11:2. He was the father of Iran's nuclear program, which in turns has fostered Iran's belocose ventures and terrorism. However, the West will soon confront Iran. For more details about this conflict and Rafsanjani's early radical influences and Nuclear Program, review Lesson 8.

Donald Trump: The Powerful U.S. President Of The Appointed Times

7. Daniel 11:4 predicts at or after Rafsanjani's reign, what kind of leader of the West will arise? _____

Donald Trump as a candidate was supported by many believers due to his plans to reduce abortions, to show American strength on the international stage, to support the nation of Israel, to fix or nix the Iran deal, and to support the traditional values America was founded on. However, because Trump's powerful presidency is identified in Bible prophecy, we must understand how his decisions will bring America to her knees. He is bound to fulfill the predictions of Daniel 8:1-8 and Daniel 11:3-4 to confront Iran, and thereby, defeat and overthrow the Persians; but also, forthwith to oversee the demise of America as the global superpower after Iran's decisive defeat, as a nuclear charged World War III kills untold millions and forever changes the power structures of the world. There is no human who can save an unrepentant nation that for decades has murdered over 500,000 babies every year in all 50 states, and today produces pornography, condones homosexuality and gay marriage, and is morally corrupt, in a world held under Satan's control. Only the King of kings, the LORD of lords is our hope.

Here's How the Daniel 11:1-4 Prophecies Have Already Been Fulfilled

On January 8, 2017 (on the Jewish/Biblical Asara B'Tevet Fast of the 10th Month—referred to in Zechariah 8:19), Iran's fourth President—Akbar Hashemi Rafsanjani, Persia's wealthiest leader of modern times whose rule was foretold in Bible prophecy (Daniel 11:2), died by heart attack at age 82. Why is this important? Because his rise to power in Iran would be a forerunner to another "mighty" leader who would then ascend to power and "do as he pleases."

Rafsanjani has, as prophecy foretold through his wealth and decades of power, stirred up sentiment against Western powers. This "stirring" can be found in his involvement in the Iranian revolution that would bring radical mullahs to power, and his public statements against the West and Israel; but most importantly, his wealth and influence led to the initiation of Iran's nuclear weapons program in the 1980's. The nuclear program is the nucleus of Iran's modern-day brazenness, which has played out time and again in Iran's continuous threats and involvement in state-sponsored terrorism against Israel and other Middle Eastern Sunni nations.

Akbar Hashemi R... 1989-1997 — (4)
Ali Khamenei 1981-1989 — 3
Mohammad-Ali Rajai 1981-1981 — 2
Abolhassan Banisadr 1980-1981 — 1

Biblical evidence, with commentary. Daniel "Now then, I tell you the truth: Three more Persia [modern-day Iran -- (1) President and (3) President Khamenei]; and, then a fourth [(4) President Akbar Hashemi Rafsanjani], who will be far richer than all the others [he was featured in the Forbes Magazine, because of his amazing wealth]. When he has gained power by his wealth, he will stir up everyone against the kingdom of Greece [Hebrew: "Javan"--Greece/the West]."

As stated, Rafsanjani did rise to power, being one of the wealthiest men in Persia. This religious mullah also stirred up Islam against the West by his revolutionary acts, his bold proclamations in support of Iranian ideology and his nuclear program. Rafsanjani died on January 8, 2017 and was buried on January 10, 2017. It's obvious now, Rafsanjani will not be personally involved in the upcoming Iran vs. West conflict, which war occurs just prior to America's demise. His national "stirrings" against the West have already been fulfilled during his lifetime of nefarious activities.

The Daniel 11 prophecy continues, with commentary: "Then a mighty king will arise [Donald Trump--his inauguration scheduled ten days after Rafsanjani's burial, on January 20,

2017], who will *rule with great power* and *do as he pleases."* President Trump is charting his own course and doing as he pleases, even against the norm. After he has arisen [taken office], his empire [America] will be broken up [superpower destroyed; likely due to war, tragedies, economic collapse, and social disorder] and parceled out toward the ***four winds of heaven."*** In other words, Trump is likely the last American President to rule while the U.S. is a superpower; the sudden demise of America will occur during his Presidency, which power will then be divided/dispersed to other nations... to the "four winds" around the globe by the New "One" World Order.

The prophecy ends, "It [American empire] will not go to his descendants [the normal election process may end; Trump could be the last President to be put in office by American voters], nor will it have the power he exercised, because his [American] empire will be uprooted and given to others [the United Nations--One World Order]."

What Other Prophecies Speak To America's Downfall?

Three distinct prophecies in the book of Daniel repeat this pattern of America's demise (Daniel 7:2-4; Daniel 8:5-8; Daniel 11:3-4). A "do as he pleases" political figure comes into power, angrily attacks Iran (likely, due to Iran's bad behavior); after which, his power is dispersed to the four corners of the earth... to the "***four winds***". It's important to note the "four winds" correlation repeated in the prophecies, which ties Daniel's three visions together.

The first reference we've covered above, pointing out the rise of Donald Trump after Rafsanjani's death and America's demise to follow; now, let's consider the second vision in Daniel 7:2-4: "In my vision at night I looked, and there before me were the ***four winds of heaven*** churning up the great sea [of nations]. Four great [political] beasts, each different from the others, came up out of the sea. The first was like a lion [Great Britain], and it had the wings of ***an eagle*** [America]. I watched ***until its wings were torn off*** [America's downfall as the world's superpower] and it was lifted from the ground so that it stood on two feet like a human being, and the mind of a human was given to it [indicating the rise of the False Prophet from the West]."

The third prophecy is found in Daniel 8:5-8; 17-22 and is clearly connected to the Daniel 11:3-4 vision, which points to Middle East conflicts involving Iraq, followed by Iran, and a notable horn— America/Trump who confronts Iran at the time of the end: "As I was thinking about this, suddenly a goat [Western powers] with a prominent horn [America/Trump] between its eyes came from the West, crossing the whole earth without touching the ground. It came toward the two-horned [Iraq & Iran, Islamic] ram I had seen standing beside the canal [in the province of Elam (v. 2)—modern-day Iran, at the Persian Gulf] and charged at it in great rage. I saw it [Western Powers] attack the [Islamic] ram furiously, striking the ram and shattering its two horns [destroying Iraq first, followed by Iran—the larger horn; Daniel 8:3]. The [Islamic] ram was powerless to stand against it; the [Western] goat knocked it to the ground and trampled on it, and none could rescue the [Islamic] ram from its power." As with Iraq, Iran's defeat is assured. The prophecy continues, "The [Western] goat became very great, but at the height of its power the ***large horn*** [America] was ***broken off***, and in its place four prominent horns grew up *toward the* ***four winds of heaven*** [America's power diminishes and is dispersed around the globe].

And, when does this vision meet its fulfillment? Daniel 8:17-18 clarifies, "I was terrified and fell prostrate. "Son of man," he said to me [Daniel], "understand that ***the vision concerns the time of the end."*** Again, he repeats, "I am going to tell you what will happen later in the time of wrath, because the ***vision concerns the appointed time of the end***. The two-horned [Islamic] ram that you saw represents the kings of Media [Iraq] and Persia [Iran--the "breast and its arms of silver" Daniel 2:32]. The shaggy goat is the king[dom] of Greece [Hebrew: "Javan"—Greece/Western powers--the "belly and its thighs of bronze"] and the large horn between its eyes is the first king [most powerful, Trump/America--"the head of fine gold"]. The ***four horns*** that replaced the one [Trump/America] that was broken off represent four kingdoms that will emerge from his nation [United Nations; New World Order--including the "legs of iron, its feet partly of iron and partly of clay"] but will not have the same power."

Kings Of The North & South

Once Iran is attacked and overcome by the American and Western coalition, the United States will fall from power in ways not specifically spelled out. Then, starting at Daniel 11:5, the chapter focuses back upon the Middle East and upon an ongoing engagement between two powers—the king of the north [possibly Israel, but this power will become clearer when final events begin], and Egypt, the king of the south—cloaked in the language of yesteryears. The Middle East has for centuries experienced mayhem and battles. Religious hatred and territorial control are nearly always the issue, with the land of Israel the prize. The following scenario is given as though Israel is the king of the north.

Verse 6 indicates internal strife in Egypt as end-time events begin. A military leader in a high position in the government will overtake the ruling Egyptian president (possibly a military coup), and will take over Egypt's leadership, probably due to the president's peaceful existence with Israel. The verse indicates Egypt may send a group in peaceful gestures to negotiate with Israel; however, Egypt's peace envoy will not be successful, and Egypt's leader will fall from power. By Verse 7 the prophecy suggests a powerful Egyptian commander will attack Israel with some success. Verse 8 emphasizes Egypt's victory, and also predicts that Egypt's new leader could indeed remain in power through the end of time, while Israel's Prime Minister will not (v. 19).

Verse 9 is more difficult, and there are several translations; however, the north's leader could try a somewhat unsuccessful military strike against Egypt. Verse 10 suggests another Israeli build-up for war and another attack against Egypt. In response (v. 11) Egypt will retaliate, slaughtering thousands, and yet Egypt will not be strengthened by this attack (v. 12). The northern leader will rebuild militarily, and "after certain years," literally, "at the end of the times, years," will plan new attacks (v. 13). Violent men in Egypt will rebel, but their attempts to overthrow the government will be unsuccessful (v. 14). Israel will attack a major city and will prevail against it, and Egypt will not be able to ward off the attacks (vs. 15-16). The northern leader will be firmly established in the "glorious land"—Israel and will exert great power.

Verse 17 indicates Middle East negotiations may once again be renewed. Israel's leader will offer covenantal concessions to manipulate the process. However, Israel will not succeed and these plans will not help his cause. The northern power will renew fighting and will focus on the coastlands of the Mediterranean, but a military commander will stop the onslaught by turning against the Israeli leader, who will die or be killed (vs. 18-19).

Verse 20 speaks of the new Israeli leader who will take control well into the appointed time of the end; albeit, within a short time he too will die, "yet not in anger or in battle." At verse 21 we notice a significant turning point. The last Israeli leader is introduced who will reign over the war-torn Middle East. He will divide the land, forsake the Holy Covenant, take away the daily sacrifice, set up the abomination and will persecute God's people until his death. By comparing the events of Daniel 11:21-45 with the actions of the evil leader of the end-times in Daniel's other visions, we are left with only one conclusion: the Papal leader obtains the title of "king of the north" and is given authority in the Middle East by promising lasting peace, with strong rule over Palestine and Israel. Jerusalem will be considered the International City of Peace.

The Last King Of The North—Antichrist

7. Daniel 11:21-24 predicts what kind of person will emerge to reign as the northern leader? _____
_____

A contemptible personality, not of natural royal linage, will seize power through schemes and secrecy.

He will talk of peace and negotiate his powerful takeover of the region, offering intriguing solutions to the continued fighting. All opposition will be swept away through military action, and under his counsel even the leader of the agreement will fall (v. 22).

The False Shepherd's promises will be worthless, as from the first his method will be deceit; with the help of influential supporters, he will become strong (v. 23). With Gentile coalition forces he will enter the richest area of Israel without warning and do something never done before: he will take the property and wealth of the rich and disperse it among the people. He will successfully besiege and capture powerful strongholds, but this will last for only a short while (v. 24).

8. What does the king of the north do next (Daniel 11:25-27)? _____

The dictator will see Islamic Egypt as a threat to his successes in the Middle East, and he will call for an attack.

Egypt will respond with military forces, but their plans will not succeed because there will be plots against the Egyptian leader (v. 25). Those in his own realm will eventually bring Egypt's leader down, his army will desert, and many will be killed (v. 26). Both the Man of Sin and Egypt's president will plot against each other during negotiations, attempting to deceive the other. But it will make little difference, because the end will still come at the appointed time (v. 27) and neither will prevail.

9. The Jewish leader will return from the negotiations with plans against what (v. 28)? _____

The Holy Covenant.

10. What does Deuteronomy 4:13 identify as the Holy Covenant? _____

The Ten Commandments, as permanently inscribed on the two tablets of stone by Yahweh's own hand.

11. At what time will Antichrist attack the south again (v. 29)? _____

At the "appointed time" of the end.

His assault will be very different from the first two battles, as written of earlier in the chapter. This time ships of the western coastlands of the Mediterranean will scare him off, and he will turn to vent his anger against the Holy Covenant. He will show favor to those in Israel who forsake the Ten Commandments as written by God's own hand (v. 30).

12. His armies will do what three terrible acts in Jerusalem (v. 31)? _____
_____

His Gentile forces will desecrate the Temple site and will abolish the daily sacrifices/worship at the Temple Mount. Then he will set up the abomination that causes a final and complete desolation upon Jerusalem.

13. What similar acts are found in Daniel 9:27? _____
_____

Once the sacrifices are stopped, his final act will be to set up his abomination on the Temple Mount, which will bring the fiery destruction of Jerusalem.

The Man of Sin will flatter with praise those Jewish leaders and teachers who forsake God's Law, but those who know their God will firmly resist him (v. 32). Those who are wise in the Word will instruct many, although many will be martyred. God's authentic followers will endure great trial for their faith and many others will join them who believe in the cause, but will not be truly sincere in faith. Others will be refined by trials, purified from sin and made spotless, while others will not endure to the end (vs. 33-35).

14. What will the king of the north do during the appointed time of the end (vs. 36-37)? _____
_____

He will do what he wants, magnifying and exalting himself above every other god. He will say unheard of things against God. His successes will continue until his time is up, for what prophecy has predicted will take place. He will show no regard for the gods of his fathers or for the one desired by women—the goddess of worship. He will exalt himself above them all.

15. What god is desired by women in Ezekiel 8:14? _____

Tammuz. The women wept for the Babylon god Tammuz, whose worship included that of his mother, Ishtar, with its mother-child myths.

16. What was Ishtar called in the Scriptures (Jeremiah 44:16-19)? _____

Queen of Heaven.

17. What goddess of today is a carry-over of the mother-child worship in Christianity? _____
_____

Virgin Mary, Queen of Heaven, goddess worship is very popular today, and will be multiplied by miracles, signs and wonders around the globe in the last days.

Daniel 11:38-39 tells us the masterful leader will regard no other god above himself, but instead will honor a god of fortresses. This may be a reference to Satan, the prince and power of the air, a demonic or military power which helps him gain territory and supremacy, or some god yet unknown. He will honor those who acknowledge his power, offering positions and even land.

18. When will the ruler of Egypt once again attack Israel (v. 40)? _____

At the time of the end, the last military conquest will continue all the way to Armageddon. With vast armies and military machinery, the Vatican will use the European forces to push southward into Israel, the Beautiful Land. He will overthrow the governments of Egypt and many other occupied lands, capturing the resources of Egypt, Libya and Ethiopia (vs. 41-43).

Daniel 11:44-45 takes us to the edge of time. News out of the north and east of Israel will alarm the global leader as he hears and sees vast armies marching towards the Armageddon confrontation, including Russia and Eastern Asian nations. He will set out in great rage to destroy and annihilate many.

19. Considering Revelation 9:16, how large are the forces that will advance towards Israel in the final moments of time? _____

200,000,000. A vast number of military forces, more than can be imagined.

20. Where does the king of the north pitch his royal tents (v. 45)? _____

His entourage sets up between the seas (Mediterranean Sea and Dead Sea) at the beautiful holy mountain—in Israel and Jerusalem. See also Isaiah 66:20; Daniel 9:16; and 2 Thessalonians 2:4.

21. What is his punishment for claiming Jerusalem as his after he steps onto the Temple Mount (2 Thessalonians 2:8-9)? _____

Read Daniel 7:26, Daniel 8:25, Daniel 9:27 and Daniel 11:45; each of Daniel's four visions foretell the demise of Antichrist, Satan's master leader of deception.

---- NOTES----

SON OF DAVID

סון ופ דאויד

Insights In Prophecy
Unlock The Ancient Mysteries Of Daniel & Revelation
BIBLE DISCOVERY SERIES

Lesson 11

INTRODUCTION TO THE BOOK OF REVELATION

LESSON 11

Read Revelation 1, 2 & 3

- Discover How The Visions of Revelation Relate To Daniel's Book Of Prophecy
- Investigate The Seven Promises For The Victorious Overcomers Of The Last Days

When we embark in the study of Revelation, we are projected into a different world. Here is something quite unlike the greater part of the Scriptures. Not only is the book unique, it can be difficult to understand. The book has stumped believers down through the centuries due to its complex nature; and therefore, its mysteries have been abandoned or have become the playground for bizarre explanations. However, the Greek word for revelation is *apocalypsis*, which means a "disclosure," or an "uncovering." So, what will its contents reveal, and when?

As we enter the final days, it is important that we study and understand the book of Revelation. In it are warnings we all must heed. And, this lesson series will prove that Revelation mirrors the prophecies of  Daniel and other ancient Biblical writings; this will not only add clarity to John's visions, but it will also allow us to draw out a clearer meaning of the two books. What is confusing in Daniel can be made clearer in Revelation, and vice versa.

Daniel is also a book specifically written for our day—the last days; and, we have attempted to prove it is much more than a book of historical events, which can be set aside as "no longer relevant". The evidence has been presented in Lessons 1 to 10, proving that Daniel exposes apocalyptic, last-day events to the same degree as the book of Revelation.

Now we will endeavor to examine the visions of Revelation in the context of the knowledge gained in our study of Daniel. The five major time periods of Daniel represent a roadmap through the appointed time of the end. One time period—the 1260 days (Daniel 7:25; 12:7)—is repeated in Revelation five more times (11:2; 11:3; 12:6; 12:14; 13:5) for a total of seven, as though to focus on this important time frame as the primary length of the end-time counting periods.

The lessons to follow will continue to prove that Daniel and Revelation are twin books; both represent the same events and counting periods of the appointed times. As we delve deeper into the apocalyptic mysteries, the various components of the prophecies will ultimately merge as a mosaic portrayal of chronological events that will soon rise from the ancient pages to confront us as headline news events.

1. Whose revelation testimony was given to John the prophet (Revelation 1:1)? _____

Jesus made the prophecies known by sending His angel to His servant John.

Gabriel, the angel (Greek-*aggelos*, meaning *messenger*), is most associated with the proclamation and delivery of prophecy (Daniel 8:16; 9:21), and he might have been the one sent to John to deliver the "testimony of Jesus Christ." The phrase "testimony of Jesus Christ" is repeated throughout Revelation (1:2; 1:9; 12:17). Revelation 19:10 clarifies, "the testimony of Jesus Christ is the *spirit of prophecy*"; in other words, the prophet's predictions of future trials and calamities, salvation and destruction, and the Kingdom of God soon to be established.

2. Deuteronomy 18:15, 18 promised that a "Prophet" would foretell things to come, and He would be from what race of people? _____

3. How long would the gift of prophecy be available, which proves a prophet may be called at anytime to serve God (Ephesians 4:11-13)? _____

Until we all come into the unity of the faith at Christ's revelation.

4. According to Revelation 1:3, blessed (happy) is the person who does what? _____

Reads, hears and takes to heart what is written in the book of Revelation.

Why? Because the end is near. Although written in Greek, the meaning of "hearing" and "keeping" in Hebrew gives deeper insight into what is implied here:

hearing – *shema,* to hear with understanding and obedience
keeping – *shamar,* to guard, protect, attend, take heed, observe, and preserve

The book of Revelation begins with a promised blessing to those who hear and obey. It ends with a curse (Revelation 22:18-19) to those who do not adhere to its teachings. Between these "bookends" is the message that those who hear and obey God's Word are the ones who will acquire life and the blessings of God, while those who disregard will die eternally. Consider the blessings of adhering to the prophecies from Yeshua found in Revelation 3:10, Revelation 14:12, Revelation 19:15 and Revelation 22:14. I plead with you, choose Jesus in faith and obedience, and receive His blessed life both now and for eternity.

Seven "spirits" are introduced in Revelation 1:4; they are before God's throne. These seven are mentioned several times in the book of Revelation (3:1; 4:5; 5:6). In the Scriptures seven represents perfection, so the perfect work of God is illustrated through the influencing work of the seven spirits. Hebrew 1:14 asks the question, "Are not all angels ministering *spirits* sent to serve those who will inherit salvation?" From this we learn the seven spirits represent seven angels/messengers who stand in the presence of God the Father (Isaiah 63:9; Zechariah 6:5; Luke 1:19).

5. What are the three titles assigned to Jesus (Revelation 1:5)? _____

The Faithful Witness signifies Christ's untiring work in representing God; the First Begotten of the Dead denotes His success over the grave; and, the Prince of the Kings of the Earth symbolizes God's sovereign control above the most powerful leaders of mankind—even over the Lawless One who is to come.

6. Faithful believers are already said to be "kings and priests." The original may be better stated, "a kingdom of priests" or "kingdom and priests." Review Revelation 5:10; 20:4, 6. What position will the overcomers have in God's kingdom? _____

7. Revelation 1:7-8 speaks of the "clouds of Heaven." What do the clouds represent (Matthew 16:27; 24:30-31; Jude 14-15)? _____

The angelic host—the armies of Heaven, and resurrected believers.

John says "every eye shall see Him." Christ's coming will be a spectacular worldwide event and will result in the destruction of all who are disobedient (Matthew 24:27-28). Those who crucified Jesus will also see Him (John 19:37; Zechariah 12:10). Daniel 12:1-2 predicts a special resurrection of both just and unjust. In this group raised from the dead are quite possibly those who put Jesus to death, who will see Messiah coming in the heavens to face His wrath. The whole earth will "wail" in fear when they see Christ returning to take vengeance on those who have lived defiantly.

The LORD's Day

Revelation 1:9-10 says the prophet John was on the Island of Patmos when He received the testimony of Jesus—the events recorded in the book of Revelation. John said he was being engaged by the Spirit on the LORD's Day. In the clear context of Revelation, John was taken forward in time to the Day Christ is exalted as Savior and LORD in His glorified body. The Revelator sees Messiah judging His people on that day as High Priest in the Holy Place ministering among the golden candlesticks and dressed in garments of a high priest.

Commentators have attempted to suggest John was promoting Sunday in this verse, a day which later in Christian history would be referred to as the LORD's Day. However, around 90 A.D. when John received the visions, the early church still observed of the seventh day Sabbath. This Jewish prophet is relaying a vision on a day the LORD Jesus claimed as His own; therefore, John is likely speaking about the Day of the LORD of which he had just written: "Look, He is coming with clouds, and every eye will see him" (v.7); that Day of "loud voice like a trumpet."

We want to remember two vital facts about the book of Revelation: First, it is a book of prophecy primarily concerning the time of Christ's return and the events that lead up to it (Revelation 1:1-3). Second, it is written by a Hebrew prophet who made many references to the language and expressions of the Old Testament. To him, the phrase *en teé kuriakeé heeméra* ("on the LORD's day")—and its Hebrew or Aramaic equivalent—would imply what is called in the Old Testament "the Day of the LORD," the time of the ultimate destruction that climaxes at the return of Messiah (Isaiah 13:6-9; Joel 1:15; 2:1; 2:11; Amos 5:18).

8. As for the day of worship, what is the LORD's Day according to the Word and the Word alone (Mark 2:28)? _____

The Son of Man is LORD even of the Sabbath.

If someone wants to insist that this text apply to a definite day of the week, he must look elsewhere to see which day the Scriptures call the LORD's Day. Jesus says in Mark 2:28 that He is LORD of the Sabbath; and therefore, as Master of that day, it belongs to Him. The day that belongs to Yeshua is the Sabbath, the seventh day of the week. Isaiah 58:13 calls the Sabbath "My [the LORD's!] holy day." The other six days are ours to fill with work and activities of life in general.

Finally, in the original commandment in Exodus 20:10, the LORD says, "*Remember* the Sabbath day by keeping it holy. Six days you shall labor and do all your work, but the seventh day is a Sabbath to the LORD your God." Therefore, if John's reference was to a day of the week—if he received the vision on the "LORD's day"—it was the seventh-day Sabbath, which God said to remember and not forget.

9. When was the Sabbath first instituted and given to all of mankind (Genesis 2:2-3)? _____

10. Does Jesus affirm it still relevant to the last days (Matthew 24:20)? _____ How? _____
_____

11. How do we know the Ten Commandments will be the measurement of end-of-time judgment (Revelation 11:18-19; 15:5-6)? _____

The Hebrew Scriptures give a clear connection between the revelation of the Ark of the Covenant and its contents—the Tablets of the Ten Commandments—at the moment of judgment for the sinners of this world.

Historical Background Of Sabbath & Sunday

The early church continued observance of the Sabbath by resting on the seventh day according to the God's Commandments, while Sunday grew in popularity as the day in commemoration of the resurrection of Jesus. For decades the two days were both held in esteem. In the first and second centuries, as Christianity's Jewish roots became more obscure and Gentiles gained leadership in the church, Sunday became the focal day of worship. It was the pagan day of sun worship and the day more common for worship to the Gentile converts.

The Sabbath became less important in the minds of religious leaders and converts so that by the fourth century, when the church had developed into an organized religion, the Sabbath was officially abandoned, and the organized church made Sunday the official day of rest. Only pockets of Christian believers and the Jews through the centuries believed it to be their obligation to "remember" the seventh day Sabbath, as God's command.

The Catholic Church officially transferred the command of Sabbath rest to Sunday, but there is no Biblical basis for this edict. Although men have attempted to change the Sabbath day of rest and to institute laws promoting rest on Sunday, God's Word stands the test of time. If God intended just one day of man's choice in seven to be a day of rest, He would have said so. However, God said to "*Remember* the seventh day," for it is easily forgotten in a secular world. The Gregorian calendar we use in modern times confirms the seventh day. Judaism maintained and confirmed the day for over 3,000 years, by their consistent observance each and every week from sundown Friday to sundown Saturday, proving Saturday is the seventh day Sabbath rest of the Scriptures.

Daniel 11:28-30 says the Papal leaders "heart will be set against the Holy Covenant... he will return and show favor to those who forsake the Holy Covenant." Yeshua said with undeniable candor: "*I tell you the truth, until heaven and earth disappear, not the smallest letter, not the least stroke of a pen, will by any means disappear from the Law until everything is accomplished.*" He linked the unchanging Law to the end of the age, and not until the disappearance of heaven and earth can the Commandments be modified or deleted. I don't know how Jesus could have made Himself any clearer on the matter.

Revelation distinguishes the authentic followers of Christ as those "who keep the Commandments of God" (Revelation 12:17), in contrast to those who will give their allegiance to Antichrist. He will forsake the Commandments for his own brand of Sabbath-keeping. Sunday will likely be both promoted and legislated as the law of the land. Idolatry and the worship of the Virgin Mary will be upheld, and God's commandment-keeping believers will face persecution, and even martyrdom, over these issues.

Insights In Prophecy
Unlock The Ancient Mysteries Of Daniel & Revelation
BIBLE DISCOVERY SERIES

Messiah's Future Glory

12. Revelation 1:13-17 describes the "Son of man." Compare this to Daniel 7:13. What title is found in both passages? _____

13. Jesus is claiming for Himself the title of *Son of Man* found in Daniel—a designation Judaism associates with Messiah. Compare the description of Michael—a title/name representing Messiah in the ancient book of Daniel before His human virgin birth—to Jesus in the book of Revelation. How are they similar?

Michael: Daniel 10:5-9	Jesus: Revelation 1:13-17
"eyes like flaming torches"	_____
"belt of the finest gold around his waist"	_____
"face like lightning"	_____
"arms and legs like the gleaming of burnished bronze"	_____
"voice like the sound of a multitude"	_____
Daniel "fell in to a deep sleep, my face to ground"	_____

14. In Revelation 1:18, Yeshua proclaims only He "hold[s] the keys of death and Hades [grave]." What happens when Michael stands at the end of the age (Daniel 12:1-2)? _____

There is a resurrection when the Archangel stands.

15. What does 1 Thessalonians 4:16 tell us about the return of the LORD Himself, and His voice that awakens the dead from the grave? _____

With Michael's loud voice, the "voice of the Archangel," the "dead in Christ will rise first." This is no ordinary messenger; it is the mighty life-giving earth-shaking voice of the Most High that raises the sleeping dead.

Sevens Of Revelation

The first chapter of Revelation ends with the messages of the sevens. John is told to write what he has seen in vision: what was then relevant to the Messianic congregations in his day, and events that will climax at the end of the age.

Heaven was intimately involved in the working of the seven congregations in Asia (today's Turkey), to whom the messages of Revelation were first sent. In the book of Revelation we'll discover seven churches (1:4) and seven golden lampstands (1:12). Seven stars (1:16, 20), the beast with seven heads (13:1), a dragon with seven crowned heads (12:3), and seven mountains (17:9) that represent seven kings (17:10). Major divisions of Revelation deal with seven seals (4:1 to 8:1), seven trumpets (8:2 to 11:19) and seven last plagues (chapters 15, 16). The six angels, plus the Son of Man, equal seven (chapter 14). Most important is the "Seventh Angel" who, when His voice begins to sound, will finish the mystery of God (10:7). With so many sevens in the book, we understand that "seven" represents fullness, completion and perfection—associated with and summed up by the returning King of kings, and the establishment of His Kingdom.

Today, we should also heed the seven messages to the seven churches of Asia. At the time of John's writing there were assemblies established in each of the seven cities named in chapters 2 and 3. John gave the seven churches distinct messages for their day, made up of compliments, rebukes and counsel for each local audience. However, within each message are found insights for the generations that would follow thereafter; but more importantly, we will find mysterious warnings for the overcomers of the last days.

Some assemblies were complemented on their good deeds and hard work, but Jesus told them they had lost their first love. They were counseled to listen to what the Spirit tells them, and to not shut out the voice that leads to repentance. The messages suggest that although these believers were dedicated and religious, still Christ was asking for more—for a life of victory.

16. In each of the seven messages, the subject of "overcoming" is repeated. Look up each verse and consider the results of a victorious life in Christ:

Revelation 2:7 _____
Revelation 2:11_____
Revelation 2:17_____
Revelation 2:26_____
Revelation 3:5 _____
Revelation 3:12_____
Revelation 3:21_____

Although the new birth defeat of sin and living in obedience is not a popular subject in Christendom today, Yeshua is our example of the ultimate overcomer (John 16:33). We cannot put our trust in any man's views, whether pope, priest, minister, president or king when it comes to spiritual matters. Maybe that's why there is an added emphasis in the book of Revelation: "Whoever has ears, let them hear what the Spirit says," (Revelation 2:7). God's Son is our Savior and the Mediator between God and man. When the masses will be trusting in religious leaders for spiritual and moral direction, wise believers must place their confidence ever more in Messiah and His Word. And, the test of a true messenger from God is whether he teaches the words of Christ and the "testimony" He gave to John in Revelation; if he does not, he is a false prophet.

16. The following are additional verses on living a victorious life. What can we learn from each verse?

1 John 5:4 _____
Romans 12:21 _____
1 John 4:4 _____
1 Corinthians 15:57 _____

Insights In Prophecy
Unlock The Ancient Mysteries Of Daniel & Revelation
BIBLE DISCOVERY SERIES

Lesson 12

LESSON 12

BEYOND THE OPENED DOOR: HEAVEN'S SANCTUARY

Read Revelation 4 & 5

- **Probe The Activities Within Heaven's Sanctuary**
- **Examine Who Is Involved In The Judgment**

John the Revelator was taken in vision beyond a door which opened into the Sanctuary. Chapters 4 and 5 describe the heavenly participants in events which John was privileged to experience firsthand. John saw a scroll having seven seals which locked away its top secrets. Only the Lamb was found worthy to unloose the seals. Once the seals were broken, terrifying events began to commence upon earth. The activities of Heaven's Sanctuary affect Planet Earth, and the impact is felt in the visible realm. The end of the age will be marked by profoundly troubling times. There will also be major disturbances and convulsions in the heavenly realms made visible in the skies above and upon the earth, as the transformation towards the

Kingdom of God begins to dawn upon civilization. The breaking of the seals begins the process of reunification between the seen and unseen worlds and is climaxed in the abolishing of evil throughout God's universe. The trumpet and bowl judgments continue this cleansing process until the eternal righteous Kingdom is ushered in and Messiah reigns supreme. Evil will and must cease to exist. Darkness will be banished when the Light of the World rises with healing in His wings.

Daniel's scroll, written five hundred years before the book of Revelation, was sealed by Messiah as noted in Daniel 12:4. Only He who had sealed the book centuries earlier was found worthy to open its contents. In so doing, John saw mirrored images of Daniel; and, in this lesson we will explore these places, persons and events. Only Messiah can choose the men, methods and timing through which His prophetic words will be unsealed in their fullest revelation to the last generation of believers at the time of the end, as He promised long ago in Daniel 12, verses 4 and 9. The book of Revelation is the key to unsealing Daniel, which together paints a detailed layout of end-time events and the appointed times counting periods.

Heaven's Temple & The Father On The Throne

Revelation 4 begins to relay events in Heaven, as John is taken upward in vision to the Temple and to events to unfold at the end of time. John saw a throne set in the Sanctuary, and the One who sat on the throne (Psalms 11:4)—the reigning Father. God looks like brilliant colorful stones of jasper and carnelian (Exodus 28:17-21). A rainbow of peace encircles the throne (Ezekiel 1:25-28). Before the throne is the sea of glass (Revelation 4:6) on which the redeemed of all nations, who have gotten the victory over the Beast, his idol, his mark and number of his name, will one day stand (Revelation 15:2) in triumphant glory.

In Revelation 4:1 the door was opened into a visionary scene, so John could see the proceedings in Heaven, and the prophet hears a loud voice; "And the voice I had first heard speaking to me like a trumpet said, "Come up here, and I will show you what must take place after this."

Insights In Prophecy
Unlock The Ancient Mysteries Of Daniel & Revelation
BIBLE DISCOVERY SERIES

1. What three names/titles are shown to be associated with a trumpet or similar loud sound (Daniel 10:6, 21; Revelation 1:13-15; Revelation 10:3, 7)? _____
In the book of Daniel the Archangel "Michael"—Daniel's Prince, and in Revelation "Son of Man" and the Mighty "Seventh Angel"; all three are identified as having loud voices like thunder, and all three represent Yeshua our Messiah.

2. Compare the following passages (Revelation 4:2-3; Revelation 5:6, 11-12; Daniel 7:9-10, 13-14). How are they similar? _____
_____

All depict a throne room in Heaven—God the Father sitting in power along with Christ who is standing and moving within the Temple ready to open the books of end-time judgment, accompanied by many angels— too many to number.

Twenty-Four Elders

While Daniel refers to most of the participates in the heavenly proceedings, Revelation 4:4, 10 and 5:8-10 introduces twenty-four elders dressed in white with crowns on their heads, sitting on twenty-four thrones surrounding God. They cast their crowns before Almighty in adoration and worship. The King James Version translates their new song of praise in adoration of the Lamb who had "redeemed us... out of every kindred, and tongue, and people and nation."

3. Who might these twenty-four be, and when did they arrive in Heaven (Matthew 27:51-53; Ephesians 4:8)? _____

At Yeshua's ascension, He led a multitude of captives to Heaven, raised to life in a special resurrection. These likely include prophets and leaders from Israel's past, and possibly Gentile converts to faith in the Sovereign LORD. The twenty-four elders are no doubt from this group of redeemed saints.

Some suggest these twenty-four represent the twelve patriarchs of the Old Covenant and the twelve disciples of the New Covenant, gathered from the nations from which they were scattered. On the other hand, they praise God in song because He has redeemed them from among a diverse group ("every tribe, language, people and nation"—K.J.V.), which would indicate a blend of both Jews and Gentiles.

Another less acceptable option is that the book of Revelation often depicts events in advance of their fulfillment as though already completed. In this light, this group of twenty-four may be a selected group from among the "great multitude" of "every nation, tribe, people and language standing before the throne and in front of the Lamb" having been taken out of the great tribulation at the end of time (Revelation 7:9). However, the twenty-four are intimately involved in the courtroom drama that occurs during the appointed time of the end, indicating their positions are current and active.

These twenty-four priestly elders are said to hold "golden bowls full of incense," (Revelation 5:8). As the priest for the people of God, Aaron was instructed to burn incense (Exodus 30:7-8). Psalms 141:2 says prayer is like incense before God, and Revelation 8:3-4 depicts a future moment when the censor of fiery incense along with the prayers of the persecuted will be thrown down to the earth, depicting the end of the judgment when all destinies will be sealed and judgment is to commence. The thrown censor portrays fiery retribution against the wicked in response to the prayers of the persecuted believers. The proclamation will be heard, *"Let the one who does wrong continue to do wrong; let the vile person continue to be vile; let the one who does right continue to do right; and let the holy person continue to be holy"* (Revelation 22:11-12), and Messiah will come quickly without delay to give every person according what they have done with their lives.

Three Portents & The Seventh Angel

Revelation 4:5 reveals the three awesome wonders—the "lightning, rumblings [voices-KJV] and peals of thunder," associated with God, His throne and His Son. We will discover additional Revelation references involving these three warning signs several times in the book.

4. Look up the following verses, and determine who is associated with the loud voice and stormy display of lightning (Revelation 10:1-3, 7; Revelation 11:15, 19; Revelation 16:17-18)? _____

_____

Many times in the ancient Hebrew Scriptures, Messiah was represented as "the Angel of the LORD"; compare Genesis 22:15-18 with Hebrews 6:13. Biblical evidence points to the fact that the Seventh Angel in Revelation represents (or is another name for) Michael of Daniel, and both represent Messiah, the Son of Man.

An angel, in the Hebrew Scriptures מַלְאָךְ, *"malach"* means "messenger". Jews hold that Michael is an archangel and one of the seven angels who surround God's throne. They believe Michael is the "Angel of the Presence" of God (Isaiah 63:9), and He intercedes in Israel's behalf before God. Unknown to our Jewish friends who have held Michael in such high esteem, they have been giving honor to Messiah, the Son of God, all these centuries.

Although a distortion by some religions, Michael is *not* a "created being." Yeshua, the Word, has been with the Father from the beginning (John 1:1-5), and He is our Creator. Just like our first names and business titles, they do not determine *who* we are; they only help describe us and set us apart from others. Jesus is also called a "Lion" and "Lamb" in Revelation 5:5-6, but these titles do not diminish His character, or cause us to believe Jesus is an animal. The use of the name Michael, the Archangel, the Lion and Lamb are employed to illustrate His multifaceted work and to teach His fulfillment of the Hebrew predictions (Daniel 12:1; Genesis 49:8-9; Isaiah 53:7).

Many scholars agree the title "Angel of the LORD" was often employed to represent Christ in the Hebrew Scriptures. Michael means "who is like God?" Why should we be surprised to find the "Seventh Angel" is another of Revelation's descriptive titles that represents the work of God's Son, since seven represents the "perfect" Messenger to mankind? This Messenger to our lost world was intimately and personally involved with the people of Israel, and now in these last days for the sake of all mankind to bring an end to the work of Satan and to offer redemption for all who trust in Him.

The book's return to the use of *Michael* and the *Seventh Angel* in Revelation is Heaven's attempt to show Messiah's identity, especially to Jewish readers who study the book of Revelation. When both disastrous and miraculous events come to pass in these last days, many individuals will dig into the prophecies and look to the Scriptures for understanding. Jews will discover the mysterious Archangel—Michael, whom they have held in high esteem, is none other than Yeshua—the very Messiah they have longed for all these centuries.

Insights In Prophecy
Unlock The Ancient Mysteries Of Daniel & Revelation
BIBLE DISCOVERY SERIES

Four Living Creatures

Revelation 4:6-11 depicts four unusual creatures that surround the throne of God. The Word illustrates their cleverness, strength, intelligence and swiftness by using descriptions like lion, ox, man and flying eagle. The prophet Ezekiel also saw these four living creatures (Ezekiel 1:5-24), as did Isaiah (6:2-3). John saw that each have six wings, which is one of their identifying characteristics in the Scriptures. These four creatures also introduce the four colored horses that emerge riding onto the world scene in the last days.

5. What do the prophets call these four other-world creatures (Ezekiel 1:5; 10:1-2; Isaiah 6:2; Revelation 7:1; Zechariah 4:2-5)? _____
_____

Daniel saw the four winds of Heaven (four living creatures) stirring up the four governmental powers of the end of time: Lion With Eagle's Wings, Bear, Leopard and Terrible Beast. The four angels represent Heaven's control over earth's powers (Daniel 2:21).

The Lion, The Lamb & Sealed Scroll

Revelation 5:1-10 explain events in Heaven involving the scroll in the hand of God sealed with seven seals. Whatever contents were within, they represented the mysteries of God. John heard the question asked "who is worthy to break the seals and open the scroll?" Its secret messages must be revealed. Like the scroll in Ezekiel 2:9-10, this scroll also contained "lament and mourning and woe," reflecting the catastrophic earth-shaking content in the book of Revelation. Unsealed messages do not mean the masses will read and heed the warnings; for, we are told, many are blinded because they honor God with their lips, but their hearts are far from Him (Isaiah 29:10-15). Still others do not care what the Word of God offers, although peace and hope in the comforting Savior are found within its ancient pages.

6. What scroll was sealed, having to do with final events of this world and the appointed time of the end (Daniel 12:4)? _____

Michael sealed the book centuries before, now Messiah is to break the seals and reveal the contents to John and to the world from the Book of Truth.

7. When was the scroll to be unsealed, and its contents understood? _____

John the Revelator wrote down the visionary events he witnessed about final troubles in symbolic characters and unusual descriptions around 90 A.D.; however, only at the end of time would his apocalyptic book be better understood. This would be accomplished through the blending of Daniel's predictions with those of Revelation, and Messiah's releasing of its sealed mysteries.

8. Why did John get so upset to the point of weeping (Revelation 5:2-4)? _____

At first it looked as though no one in Heaven or on earth was found worthy to open the scroll, and John wept because he wanted to look inside—to view its contents.

One of the twenty-four elders spoke up, "do not weep! See, the Lion of the tribe of Judah, the Root of David (Isaiah 11:10), has triumphed." He was worthy to open the scroll of seven seals. However, John did not see a magnificent Lion emerge in a display of power, but instead a meek Lamb, looking as though it had been slain. Jesus, the martyred sacrifice of God given as a Lamb to the slaughter, was found worthy to step up to the Father sitting on the throne and take the scroll from His right hand, for the Lamb had left His throne of power long ago and in humility arrived to take away the sin of the world (John 1:29).

Revelation 5:6 describes the Lamb as having seven horns and seven eyes (Zechariah 3:9; 4:10), representing the seven spirits of God sent out into the world. Earlier in Revelation 4:5, the seven spirits were portrayed as "seven lamps" blazing with fire. God has been working in the affairs of man since the beginning, but at the end of time there is a special work where God's messengers of His presence become intimately involved in the final appointed time of the end.

According to the Scriptures, the seven spirits described seven lamps to light the world, seven horns of powers and seven watchful eyes of judgment to illustrate the multifaceted role of the seven spirits. The "horns" represent power in prophecy, in the same way the four spirits (Zechariah 6:2-5; or, four winds) of Heaven—known as the four Living Creatures (Revelation 4:6-9), are involved with the seven horns of governmental power of the last days. The "lamps" represent light of knowledge, similar to the work of the "two candlesticks," and "olive trees" (two witnesses—Moses and Elijah: Zechariah 4:14; Revelation 11:3-4), and the "eyes" the work of Christ Himself, the Seventh, who sees all, knows all and judges all mankind.

John saw the four living creatures and twenty-four elders immediately dropped down to their faces before the Lamb in worship. Each one had a harp of musical praise and was holding golden bowls full of incense, which represent the prayers of the persecuted. They sing a new song of praise in adoration of the slain Lamb who is found worthy to open its seals and reveal its content.

Angels: Too Many To Count

Revelation 5:11-12 reveals the angelic host who witness the heavenly proceedings. John saw a retinue of angels, so many he could not begin to count them, who had gathered to play a vital role in the events of judgment and to give praise to the Lamb in the form of a sevenfold doxology.

9. In a loud voice they sang the Lamb was worthy to receive what seven (Revelation 5:12)? _____

_____

See also Revelation 7:11-12.

10. What does John hear next (Revelation 5:13)? _____

Creation sings out in honor to both the Father who sits on the throne and the standing Lamb. All of creation will sing of God's amazing grace and power.

To summarize, John wrote down his visual review of Heaven's participants and the proceedings in the Temple. This adds needed insight into the judgment that Daniel saw long ago, which will begin at the appointed time of the end in response to Satan's grand attempt to sway the whole world under his deceptive control (Daniel 7:9-10). However, the final verdict will declare that Satan (and Antichrist) must lose their dominion, which will be consumed in coals of fire and destroyed forever (Daniel 7:26; Psalms 11:6).

The Lamb of God, found worthy because of His humble sacrifice at Calvary, is intimately involved in events both in Heaven and on earth. The next lesson will begin with the breaking of the seven seals, which corresponds to Daniel's predictions given in his first vision in Daniel 7.

---NOTES---

Insights In Prophecy
Unlock The Ancient Mysteries Of Daniel & Revelation
BIBLE DISCOVERY SERIES

Lesson 13

THE COLORED HORSES & OPENING OF THE SEALS

Read Revelation 6

- **Determine The Meaning Of The Seven Seals**
- **Study What Is Represented By The Four Horsemen Of The Apocalypse**
- **Consider How The Sixth Seal Points To Total Desolation Of Planet Earth**

Daniel's book of prophecy was to be sealed until the end of time, according to the messenger (Daniel 12:4). In the Near East, the practice of sealing an important document was well-known. Royal seals were used for two reasons: First, to keep the contents safe and unaltered. Daniel's book of prophecy was certified to be an accurate transcript of what God had communicated to him. Second, to prove the scroll's authenticity and the contents were indeed true. Therefore, God was guaranteeing the preservation of

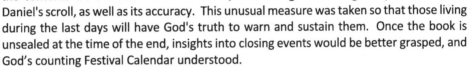

Daniel's scroll, as well as its accuracy. This unusual measure was taken so that those living during the last days will have God's truth to warn and sustain them. Once the book is unsealed at the time of the end, insights into closing events would be better grasped, and God's counting Festival Calendar understood.

It is common practice to lift a hand and swear to tell the truth, as in ancient times (Genesis 14:22; Exodus 6:8; Ezekiel 20:5); however, Michael raised both right and left hands towards Heaven swearing an oath of divine assurance. He promised the final troubles would last no longer than three and a half (or a "part") years—meaning 3-4 years—an intense period of persecution that will purify the wise who adhere to the contents of the scroll (Daniel 12:6-10). This sworn *limited* period of persecution will be found accurate as we continue to study John's Revelation visions.

The scroll in Revelation 5 contained seven royal seals, which could only be broken open by the Lamb having imperial authority earned by His sacrificial wounds. This lesson focuses on the contents of the first six seals. Chapter 7 is a parenthesis—an insertion for enhanced enlightenment of the seals; then the seventh seal is found in Revelation chapter 8. The Lamb (Jesus) was declared worthy to break open the seals and reveal their mysterious content. Therefore, the scroll represents the contents of the book of Daniel—itself part of Messiah's ancient Book of Truth (Daniel 10:21), which had been sealed earlier by Michael's proclamation (Daniel 12:4). Only Messiah could have both the authority to seal and unseal the book, in which are found the ageless mysteries of Almighty God.

When we begin to look for the meaning of the seals, we must remember what John saw was a revelation of Daniel's scroll being unsealed and rolled open to reveal its contents. How do we know? The first vision of the last days, which was given personally to Daniel (chapter 7), began with four animal creatures (governments) which will be overthrown by the conquering Messiah (v. 26). Revelation 6 also introduces four animals (governments) who, in turn, encounter the wrath of the conquering Lamb (vs. 15-16).

Various explanations have been offered over the course of time as to the identity of the four colored horses in the first four seals. Some sources believe they are representative of the history of the church between the time of Christ and the Second Coming. Others suggest end-time applications but leave little clue as to how they arrive at their conclusions. Comparing John and Daniel's prophecies help reveal the identity of the four horses. However, we recognize that these four horsemen are not men riding on flesh and blood horses but are *representative* of global powers that God will use to fulfill His divine plan at the end of the ages. There is a connection between the spiritual realm and natural world, both good and evil. Persecution from evil powers often provokes mankind to repent of their sins, to trust in a personal Savior and to follow

Him.

The prophet Zechariah first mentions the four colored horse symbolism. Zechariah is a prophetic book bursting with predictive last-day language. There we will begin our adventure for insight into the meaning of the four horsemen, as well as referring once again back to Daniel and other Biblical passages. Zechariah 6:1-5 says, "I looked up again, and there before me were four chariots coming out from between two mountains—mountains of bronze. The first chariot had red horses, the second black, the third white, and the fourth dappled—all of them powerful. I asked the angel who was speaking to me, "What are these, my LORD?" The angel answered me, "These are the four spirits [winds/angels] of heaven, going out from standing in the presence of the LORD of the whole world."

1. In Revelation 6:1 the Lamb of God breaks open the first seal. Who or what then summons the white horse to "come"? _____

The four living creatures have been identified as the four spirits or "seraphims" as found in Isaiah 6:2 and Revelation 4 (refer to Lesson 12). The first angelic creature demands the white horse and rider to gallop onto the world scene. This clearly illustrates Heaven's control over earth's governments.

2. What connection do the four horses have with the four angelic creatures (Zechariah 6:1-5)? _____
_____

The four "spirits" or "winds" go forth from standing before the LORD. We know the four angelic creatures of Revelation stand "around the throne" of God (Revelation 4:6).

3. What four stir up the four governmental animals in Daniel 7:2-3? _____

Heaven's four winds control events of this world, and political figures unknowingly "fulfill" God's will until His kingdom is ushered in (Revelation 17:17).

4. What do horses represent in prophecy (Revelation 9:16-18; Joel 2:1-5)? _____

Horses and horsemen represent the military might of nations. In Revelation 6 we see the symbolic horses of the end-time nations riding into action, but by verse 12 supernatural signs in the sky foretell the Day of the LORD and governments' destruction.

5. Joel 2:1-11 helps us understand Revelation 6. How? _____
_____

6. In Revelation 6:2 the first rider sits astride the White Horse. Who are represented by the counterpart animal—the first creature of Daniel 7:4—the Lion's With Eagle's Wings? _____

The British-American alliance; therefore, the White Horse likewise would represent the same power base. White represents military victory; the rider's bow might signify instruments of war; and the crown— the imperial leadership of these nations in modern world politics.

7. Revelation 6:3-4 introduces the Red Horse; what contemporary world power is known for their color red and symbolized as a Bear—the second animal in Daniel 7:5? _____

Daniel says the Russian Bear is told to "get up and eat your fill of [human] flesh." Likewise, the Red Horse of Revelation is given power to "take peace from the earth and to make men slay one another." While the White Horse's rider sports a "bow", the rider of the Red Horse is given a "large sword" of destruction by which he takes peace from the whole world. This sword is so breathtaking that fear overtakes the globe; the sword likely represents weapons of mass destruction.

Revelation 13:1-5 describes a massive beast of world governments created by combining Daniel's Leopard, Bear and Lion into a Beast—the New World Order. Although separate and distinct governments in Daniel's vision, in Revelation they are merged together as one ugly geo-political creature. As the last days begin, one of its heads will be hit with a deadly wound (nuclear attack), but the Beast will recover, and Antichrist will emerge from the ashes of war to rule for forty-two months—three and one-half years.

Revelation 13:14 forecasts a second figure of the end days—the False Prophet, who will make an image (statue) in honor of the world's united nations, which was "wounded by the sword and yet lived." The rider to wield a "sword" is the Red Horse's rider (6:4)—Russia, the Old Soviet Union. The Russian Federation will be the instigator of mass destruction, which in turn will usher in the Man of Sin (Antichrist) and renewed global unity for the survival of Planet Earth.

8. How many ribs does the Bear in Daniel 7:5 have in its mouth, as though having utterly devoured them? _____

Three ribs—Russia devours three countries to the bone.

9. How many crowns are discovered on the ten horns in Revelation 13:1, just before the 1260 day rule of Antichrist? _____

The Beast has ten horns and ten crowns in place.

10. Looking at Revelation 12:3, how many crowns are missing just before the 1260 day period of prophecy begins in 12:6 and 14? _____

Three crowns have vanished, signifying terrible destruction that has eliminated three nations/leaders.

11. We found in Daniel 7:7-8, in Lessons 4 and 5, the terrible Beast will be assaulted by the Bear. How many horns (countries) get torn out by the roots from this attack? _____

We believe the Terrible Beast represents the Western European Union of nations; here is where the Old Soviet Union will strike with a "large sword," devastating life and land in three countries in Europe.

12. Comparing Daniel 7 with Revelation 13, we notice governments of the world are working together sporting Seven Heads and Ten Horns in both books. Look up the creatures in Daniel 7:4-7 and count the number of heads and horns. Do they add up in the chart below to equal Revelation's count? _____

Insights In Prophecy
Unlock The Ancient Mysteries Of Daniel & Revelation
BIBLE DISCOVERY SERIES

WORLD GOVERNMENTS IN BOTH DANIEL AND REVELATION

The Daniel creatures—Lion, Bear, Leopard and Beast, show up in Revelation 13 as an amalgamated Beast comprised of Lion, Bear and Leopard; both have the equal number of heads and horns.

Daniel 7	Heads	Horns
Lion With Eagle's Wings (United Kingdom/United States)	___	___
Bear With Three Ribs (Russia)	___	___
Leopard With Four Heads (Eastern Asia)	___	___
Terrible Beast With Ten Horns (Western Europe)	___	___
Total of All—New World Order in Daniel	**7**	**10**

---

13. In Revelation 6:5-6 the third seal is broken, and the Black Horse is called upon by the third living creature to ride onto the scene. What was the third governmental power base paralleled in Daniel 7:6?

_____

Likely we see China and Eastern Asian countries, known for grain production.

14. What scourge is indicated by "a quart of wheat for a day's wages"? _____

Famine will plague the world during the last days, and food supplies will be limited and expensive. Yeshua also predicted scarcities, along with increased military battles and natural disasters, which would begin the sorrows of the last days (Matthew 24:4-8). Wheat and barley are used to make bread, a basic food in ancient times. The oil and wine represent the common liquids for cooking and drinking, which are not to be uselessly destroyed.

In the spiritual sense, there will also be a scarcity of sacred truth and teachings during the last days. Amos 8:11-12 projects, "The days are coming," declares the Sovereign LORD, "when I will send a famine through the land—not a famine of food or a thirst for water, but a famine of hearing the words of the LORD. Men will stagger from sea to sea and wander from north to east, searching for the word of the LORD, but they will not find it." God's truths will continue to the end of time, but certainly not in great abundance. Oil and wine are spiritual elements; for this reason, Heaven demands that these two ingredients should not be damaged in the course of unleashing the global heat wave and a parched planet. Even when the power of the holy people is being broken down by persecution, spiritual truths will not be totally extinguished for those who hunger and thirst after righteousness (Matthew 5:6).

15. Revelation 6:7-8 exposes the fourth seal. The fourth rider (named "Death") and the Pale Horse is most terrifying. Hades—the grave—follows close behind. This military machine is distinct in description, and rules over a "_____ of the earth." Again, this is evidence that these four horses represent the four global governmental power-bases of the end days.

16. How does the fourth Pale (Green) Horse compare to the fourth creature in Daniel 7:7, and what modern power might this symbolize? _____

138

Insights In Prophecy
Unlock The Ancient Mysteries Of Daniel & Revelation
BIBLE DISCOVERY SERIES

Western European Union seems to be noted here. This area is most closely associated with the Man of Sin, from which he emerges as the "little horn"—the smallest country in the world—the Vatican (just .2 square miles).

The Wicked One—a beast/man estranged from his Jewish roots and from the Covenant of his ancestors—and his followers will eventually destroy those who defy his decrees of idolatry; the believers who keep the Commandments of God. While the previous horses and riders use military might and food rationing to secure control, Antichrist is associated with the four Biblical woes: the "sword" (armed forces), "famine" (withholding food), "death" (executions), and "beasts of the earth" (hungry wild animals who will feast on the sick, exposed and vulnerable, and unburied corpses; also, may refer to Islamic terrorists and other religious crusaders)—all used to induce obedience to his commands.

17. Compare Revelation 6:8 to Ezekiel 14:21-23. What city is specifically named to receive these four disasters? _____ Why (Ezekiel 14:6)? _____

Jerusalem is named, because her religious and political leaders—despite the warnings of the Scriptures—will compromise with the Man of Sin during the last days and will allow this global ruler onto the Temple Mount to set up his abomination (idol) in the closing moments of time.

For this reason, at the end of the 70 weeks (Daniel 9:24-27) God will bring upon Israel the most terrible punishments—the "four sore judgments." Daniel 9:26 predicts the "people [armies] of the ruler [Antichrist] who will come will destroy the city [Jerusalem] and the [rebuilt] Sanctuary. The end will come like a flood: War will continue until the end [of time], and desolations [ruins] have been decreed."

This is why Jesus warned His followers of the end-days when they see "standing in the Holy Place the abomination that causes desolation, spoken of through the prophet Daniel" (Matthew 24:15), and when they see "Jerusalem surrounded by armies, you will know its desolation is near. Then let those who are in Judea flee to the mountains... for this is their time of punishment in fulfillment of all that has been written," (Luke 21:20-22) in the ancient prophecies—the Book of Truth.

18. Revelation 6:9-11 is the opening of the fifth seal. What does John see at its opening? _____
_____

The souls of men are seen under the altar.

In ages past, the altar was used for sacrifice. Clearly, this passage symbolizes those who will give their lives in martyrdom. Daniel also speaks of the overcomers' end-time persecution (Daniel 7:21, 22, 25; 11:33-35; 12:10). As the voice of Abel's blood cried to God from the ground (Genesis 4:10, 15) and God took vengeance upon Cain, so the martyrs cry out for Almighty to repay their enemies. This passage does not teach that naked souls are literally huddled under a physical altar. The symbolism teaches that white robes represent the righteous acts of the believers (Revelation 19:8), which is the promised attire at their resurrection. On the other hand, there will no doubt be mistreated believers huddled together on earth, crying out to God for His divine retribution against their persecutors; punishment the Scriptures promise Messiah will bring to pass in due time (Isaiah 63:1-6; Nahum 1:2).

19. How much longer will the martyrs wait for God's wrath to be poured out upon the rebellious world (Revelation 6:11)? _____

139

There will be a little period of waiting while a designated number of overcomers give their lives for the cause of Christ.

Persecution will be rampant, and the killing of God's people will be widespread around the globe. The church at Smyrna was warned about the final ten days when persecution will reach its zenith.

The Mysterious Ten Days Of Persecution

During the final moments just before the Day of the LORD, many believers will suffer martyrdom for their faith. Revelation 2:10 reveals a mysterious period that warns about this short but critical period of crisis: *"Do not be afraid of what you are about to suffer. I tell you, the devil will put some of you in prison to test you, and you will suffer persecution **ten days**. Be faithful, even to the point of death, and I will give you the crown of life."* Can you find the ten days just before the Day of the LORD on **The Kingdom Calendar**? Hint: there are exactly ten days between the Feast of Trumpets (Rosh Ha-Shanah) and the Day of Atonement (Yom Kippur). This is the "little season" spoken of in Revelation 6:11 (KJV)—the "Ten Days of Awe," as known in Judaism, in which the "number of their fellow servants and brothers who were to be killed as they had been was completed"; then the thunderous voice of the Archangel will raise the martyred saints, and the final end—the Great Tribulation will commence.

20. Revelation 6:12-17 opens the sixth seal. What supernatural cosmic disturbances occur as a result?
_____

This earthquake is not a localized shaking; it is worldwide, when the earth opens and mountain ranges will disappear and islands of people will slip into the sea. In its wake, tsunamis will rise up from the earth's shifting landmasses (Psalm 93:1-5) and walls of massive waves will pour over lands and peoples. A veil of complete darkness will encompass the globe as the sun, moon and stars are concealed. The stars falling to the earth may indicate a massive meteor shower and destructive fires that will plummet from the sky. And spiritually speaking, the falling stars portray the demise of fallen angels at the return of an avenging King.

21. When do these events occur, when comparing Matthew 24:29-31 and Joel 2:30-31? _____

The sixth seal events point to the Great Day of the LORD—what is referred to as Day 1335 (Daniel 12:12). The sky above will depart as a scroll to reveal the conquering King of kings.

22. Does Isaiah 34:2-4, 8-10 agree? _____ What is the result (Jeremiah 4:23-29)? _____
_____

The earth will be left totally desolate.

23. Who will rise up to shake terribly the earth (Isaiah 2:12, 17-21; Daniel 12:1; Hebrews 12:26; Joel 3:14-16)? _____

On the Great Day of the LORD, the Father "Him who sits on the throne" will accompany His reigning Son, the King of kings, to destroy all evil and conquer every foe. From world leaders, royalty, military generals, the rich and powerful—all the way down to the impoverished, absolutely every unbeliever will be destroyed.

Luke 21:25-28 says, "There will be signs in the sun, moon and stars. On the earth, nations will be in anguish and perplexity at the roaring and tossing of the sea [earthquakes and tsunamis]. Men will faint from terror, apprehensive of what is coming on the world, for the heavenly bodies will be shaken. At that time they will see the Son of Man coming in a cloud with power and great glory. When these things begin to take place, stand up and lift up your heads, because your redemption is drawing near."

The chapter ends with an all-important question in Revelation 6:17, "the great day of their wrath is come, and who can stand?" The destruction will reach around the world, in a stark reversal of Planet Earth back to its condition before the creation of beauty and light, back to global darkness. Who can stand? Chapter seven is about to answer this question by identify the group sealed for protection, so their lives may be spared during the 40 day Great Tribulation.

--- NOTES ---

KING OF ISRAEL

קינג ופ יסראעל

Lesson 14

THE 144,000 & GREAT MULTITUDE: THE FEAST OF TABERNACLES

Read Revelation 7

- **Identify The 144,000 Vs. The Great Multitude**
- **Search How & When The Great Multitude Escapes From The Great Tribulation**

Lesson 13 and Revelation 6 introduced six seals the Lamb of God opened to reveal their end-time content to the prophet John. Within the first four seals are found four colored horses, which signify four of the strongest political and military power alliances in our modern times.

The White and Red Horses—the United Kingdom/American Alliance followed by the Russian Federation—portray the military strength of the first two riders. The Black Horse—Eastern Asia points to a China and a confederation of powers, which hold sway due to their treasured commodities (cereals and grains) during a period of world famine. Most notable is the fourth Pale Horse—the Western Europe Union with the rider named "Death," who is none other than that Evil Prince, also referred to as Antichrist, who will rule supreme for 1,260 days during the appointed time of the end. Likewise, hundreds of years earlier the prophet Daniel was introduced to four animal creatures—the Lion, Bear, Leopard and Terrible Beast—from which the Man of Sin emerges from the fourth Beast to reign for 1,260 days. The four animal creatures of Daniel 7 relate directly to the four horses of Revelation chapter 6, although different symbolism was employed in each case.

The fifth seal points to the martyrs of the final conflict who are emblematically waiting for God's revenge, but who must be patient a short time longer before the wrath of Almighty God is released against the disobedience masses. The sixth seal then opens to reveal the scene of the Great Day of the LORD when the sun, moon and stars will be moved out of their places and the galaxy will split open revealing both Father and Son in swift flight to destroy those who are destroying the earth.

The question was asked in the last verse of Revelation 6, verse 17 (KJV), "For the Great Day of His wrath has come, and who shall be able to stand?" The answer to that question follows in Revelation 7, which is a *parenthesis—meaning "inserted as an explanation; an interlude"* between the 6th and 7th seal. This small 144,000 *numbered group* is identified as the survivors of the Great Day. These chosen and sealed individuals stand in sharp contrasted to the *great multitude* of every nation, tribe, people and language introduced later in the chapter; a group so massive that no number can be assigned, who escape the Great Tribulation to stand in God's presence.

Beginning with the first verse at Revelation 7:1, John sees four angels restraining the four winds, holding back the destructive power of God against the nations. The winds are not to yet harm the continents, the oceans, or the trees—a recognized food source (Leviticus 19:23). Spiritually speaking, it is about time for God to take down fruitless trees, and to save the trees that bear fruit. Jesus said, "By their fruit you will recognize them. Do people pick grapes from thorn bushes, or figs from thistles? Likewise, every good tree bears good fruit, but a bad tree bears bad fruit. A good tree cannot bear bad fruit, and a bad tree cannot bear good fruit. Every tree that does not bear good fruit is cut down and thrown into the fire. Thus, by their fruit you will recognize them," Matthew 7:16-20.

At this point in John's vision, the world's forces are agitated and posed to strike in a historic global confrontation, but God holds the nations back until the last of the righteous are secured. Revelation 7:2-3 introduces a Messenger who ascends from the east as the bright morning sun, having the protecting seal of God. He cries with a loud voice to hold back the angels of strife until He seals the 144,000 chosen ones with the Father's name in their foreheads (Revelation 14:1; Revelation 22:4).

1. Who is the Angel—Messenger from the east (Ezekiel 9:1-6; Daniel 12:1, 7)? _____
Isaiah 60:1-2 explains the identity of the rising Messenger and the time of the sealing. How? _____
_____

In the days of earth's cosmic disturbances, the sun will be darkened, the moon will not give its light, the stars will fall and there will be deep darkness. Michael, the Man clothed in linen, will descend with the light of His Shekinah glory to dispel the darkness and light the world.

The 144,000 Elect Chosen From The Twelve Tribes Of Israel

The Messenger will seal the 144,000 chosen for protection against the wrath to come at the final Exodus, as did the blood on the doorposts before the first Exodus. The Light of the World will be revealed, and God's wrath will begin to be released through His seven angels; at the same time earth's militaries head toward their final offensive. Jesus said, "But pray ye that your flight be not in the winter, neither on the Sabbath day: For then shall be *great tribulation*, such as was not since the beginning of the world to this time, no, nor ever shall be," Matthew 24:20-21. Daniel adds, "At that time Michael, the Great Prince who protects your people [Israel], will arise [from His throne]. There will be a *time of distress* such as has not happened from the beginning of nations until then. But at that time your people [Israel]—everyone whose name is found written in the book—will be delivered. Multitudes who sleep in the dust of the earth will awake" (12:1-2) in resurrection. John describes it this way, "The nations were angry, and your wrath has come. The time has come for judging the dead [for resurrection], and for rewarding your servants the prophets and your people who revere your name, both great and small—and for destroying those who destroy the earth," Revelation 11:18. But first... the sealing!

Sealing has two basic functions associated with it. In the Roman world, items were sealed to indicate ownership and to guarantee protection and deliverance. The sealing of the 144,000 in their foreheads indicate they belong to God (ownership) and will experience His security (protection). Their sealing will exempt them from God's wrath and the world's anger, which Revelation 7 announces is delayed temporarily until this smaller group of 144,000 is sealed, just as the lamb's blood on the doorposts in Egypt saved the Israelites from the destroying angel during the first Passover (Exodus 12:12-13).

2. According to Revelation 7:4-8, who are the 144,000? _____

This group is identified as from the lineage of Israel; so precisely branded that even their twelve tribal names have been listed. This is God's miracle. Jesus proclaimed, "With men this is impossible; but with God all things are possible," Matthew 19:26. The twelve tribes of Israel listed are unusual, because both Dan and Ephraim are missing. There's no reason given by John, but the most likely explanation likely implies the unfaithfulness of these two tribes noted in the Scriptures (Genesis 49:16-17; Hosea 7:1-16).

3. What did Paul say would happen once the full amount of Gentiles is brought into the fold (Romans 11:25-27; Revelation 6:11)? _____

"So all Israel [of all twelve tribes] will be saved."

God has not rejected His people—today's Jews (Romans 11:1-2), as many have suggested. Even though in the past they have persecuted and killed the prophets God sent to them (Romans 11:3-4), God has reserved a remnant (11:4-5). Because of their transgression, salvation has come to the Gentiles to make Israel envious (11:11). However, Jews have been given the promise that the "Deliverer will come from Zion; He will turn godlessness away from Jacob... and will take away their sins," Romans 11:26-27.

Revelation 7 is derived, in part, from events recorded in Ezekiel 9. In this passage, punishment of the idolaters in Jerusalem is the focus. Six men of judgment are called out, along with the Seventh—the Man clothed in linen. This Man in linen—in priestly robes (Leviticus 6:10; 16:32) is identified in Daniel 10 as Michael, and in the book of Revelation as the Seventh Angel. The righteous are identified and marked for protection: "Then the LORD called to the Man clothed in linen who had the writing kit at His side and said to Him, "Go throughout the city of Jerusalem and *put a mark on the foreheads of those who grieve and lament over all the detestable things that are done in it.*" He said to the others, "Follow Him through the city and kill, without showing pity or compassion. Slaughter the old men, the young men and women, the mothers and children, but *do not touch anyone who has the mark.* Begin at My sanctuary." So, they began with the old men who were in front of the temple," Ezekiel 9:2-6.

4. Why would God's judgment begin at the Temple Mount (Mathew 24:15-21; 1 Peter 4:17; Revelation 11:7-10)? _____

_____

This is the exact location where Israel's leaders will allow Antichrist to set up his defiling abomination, after the murderous killing of God's last two anointed voices of warning. Almighty God's wrath will no longer be held back; there has been enough warning through God's Word and His last-day prophets.

Then He said to them [God's seven], "Defile the temple and fill the courts with the slain. Go!" So, they went out and began killing throughout the city [of Jerusalem]. While they were killing and I was left alone, I [Ezekiel] fell facedown, crying out, "Alas, Sovereign LORD! Are you going to destroy the entire remnant of Israel in this outpouring of your wrath on Jerusalem?" He answered me, "The sin of the people of Israel and Judah is exceedingly great; the land is full of bloodshed and the city is full of injustice. They say, 'The LORD has forsaken the land; the LORD does not see.' So, I will not look on them with pity or spare them, but I will bring down on their own heads what they have done." Then the Man in linen with the writing kit at His side brought back word, saying, "I have done as You [the Father] commanded," Ezekiel 9:7-11.

Paul wrote, "For everything that was written in the past was written to teach us, so that through the endurance taught in the Scriptures and the encouragement they provide we might have hope," Romans 15:4. For example, we can link the sealing in Revelation 7 of the 144,000—12,000 from each tribe to historical events of Numbers 31. The question has been asked, "who shall be able to stand" in the Great Tribulation, and the Great Day of God's wrath against the nations? Armageddon represents the last great battle before the Promised Land of Heaven can be entered by His chosen people. Israel's past gives clues as to how this group is numbered and chosen.

5. How many men were chosen from each of the twelve tribes to go into battle against the Midianites, before their advancement into the Promised Land (Numbers 31:1-5)? _____

One thousand (1,000) from each of the twelve tribes were chosen for this battle against the vast armies arrayed against them. In Revelation 7, we discover the final number of chosen ones is twelve times the original group of 1,000—12,000 from each of the twelve tribes. You'll find the number 12 used in 187 places in the Bible, and there is significance to this number. The number twelve is very important to God and represents, in most cases, the number of perfection and authority. The number 12 shows up in the Book of Revelation 22 times, and particularly in the New Jerusalem.

6. How many of the fighting men who went into battle returned to enjoy the spoil from the war (Numbers 31:48-49)? _____

Not one was missing. God miraculously sealed each one by divine protection, and all survived the final battle before crossing the Jordon into the Promised Land.

During the Great Tribulation and Armageddon battle, not one of the sealed 144,000 will be killed; all miraculously survive this battle over the Gentile nations arrayed against the nation of Israel (Revelation 14:1). The survivors are called the remnant of Israel in Micah 2:12-13, who are carried through the trial by their King: "I will surely gather all of you, Jacob; I will surely bring together the remnant of Israel. I will bring them together like sheep in a pen, like a flock in its pasture; the place will throng with people. The One who breaks open the way will go up before them; they will break through the gate and go out. Their King will pass through before them, the LORD at their head."

This remnant will be spread across the globe and among the nations: "The remnant of Jacob will be in the midst of many peoples like dew from the LORD, like showers on the grass, which do not wait for anyone or depend on man. The remnant of Jacob will be among the nations, in the midst of many peoples, like a lion among the beasts of the forest, like a young lion among flocks of sheep, which mauls and mangles as it goes, and no one can rescue. Your hand will be lifted up in triumph over your enemies, and all your foes will be destroyed," Micah 5:7-9. "He will raise a banner for the nations and gather the exiles of Israel; He will assemble the scattered people of Judah from the four quarters of the earth. Ephraim's jealousy will vanish, and Judah's enemies will be destroyed," Isaiah 11:12-13.

7. What City is in the cross-hairs of the nations, that will be destroyed as the remnant is first scattered, then gathered, during the Great Tribulation (Ezekiel 14:12-23; Luke 21:20-24)? _____

Ezekiel wrote that if God were to send the four sore judgments upon Jerusalem and the people of Israel, only three righteous men alone—Noah, Daniel and Job—would survive. However, later in the chapter the prophet spoke of the 144,000 survivors in the Day of the LORD, including their sons and daughters, "For this is what the Sovereign LORD says: How much worse will it be when I send against Jerusalem my four dreadful judgments—sword and famine and wild beasts and plague—to kill its men and their animals! Yet there will be some survivors—sons and daughters who will be brought out of it. They will come to you, and when you see their conduct and their actions, you will be consoled regarding the disaster I have brought on Jerusalem—every disaster I have brought on it. You will be consoled when you see their conduct and their actions, for you will know that I have done nothing in it without cause, declares the Sovereign LORD," (14:21-23).

8. How does Isaiah describe the tender feelings God has towards Jerusalem despite her indulgence in sin and ongoing rebellion against the Creator (40:1-2)? _____

The Word says that when we see the conduct and actions of these 144,000 survivors in the Kingdom of God, we will find comfort in Jerusalem's tragedy that brought about this special group, whose arduous Exodus and ordeal will take them to the gates of the New Jerusalem.

9. How are the 144,000 of the twelve tribes eternally honored in the defensive structure of the New Jerusalem (Revelation 21:12; 15-17)? _____

The Great Multitude Of All Nations

10. Revelation 7:9-12 identifies a "great multitude." What is the size of this group? _____
How many nations and languages are represented, compared to the 144,000 from the twelve tribes of Israel? _____

This extremely large group, too massive to count, will be clothed in white robes of salvation as they stand before God at the great ingathering. The redeemed cry out in praise that their salvation has come from the Lamb and from God who sits on the throne.

It should be noted that this great multitude of overcomers do not receive the seal of protection; they will pay a heavy price for their faith. However, because of a special resurrection to call them home at the voice of God, they are found in Heaven's Temple just preceding the release of God's seven angels of judgment, who will soon exit with the trumpet and vial plagues.

11. Explore these passages to further clarify the identity of the great multitude:
Revelation 12:10-11 _____
Revelation 15:1-4 _____
Revelation 3:10 _____
Daniel 12:1-2 _____

As the texts above reveal, this group is not the saved of all the ages but are resurrected last-day victors who triumph over the Beast (Antichrist), over his image (idol), his mark and name. They show great "patience" and will not "shrink back," while enduring trial and persecution (James 5:7-11; Hebrews 10:35-38); and, they are willing to die as martyrs, if circumstances demand it. The end-times mandate patient endurance on the part of these tribulation champions of faith, because captivity and death are certain (Revelation 13:9-10). Those who obey God's Commandments and remain faithful to Yeshua are called upon for "patient endurance" throughout the book of Revelation (14:12).

12. What does the great multitude hold in their hands (Revelation 7:9b)? _____

The overcomers hold palm branches in their hands in praise to God.

13. When were palm branches used in celebration (Leviticus 23:33-35, 39-40)? _____

Sukkot (the Feast of Booths or Tabernacles) arrives five days after the Day of Atonement each year, and palm branches are waved before God during this Festival.

In Jerusalem long ago the children of Israel celebrated Messiah's Jerusalem arrival with palm branches shouting "hosanna" meaning, "save" (Matthew 21:8-9; John 12:13)—a quote directly from Psalms 118, and a song sung on the Feast of Tabernacles emphasizing ultimate deliverance. However, at the end of time a great multitude of all nations, along with the angels, 24 elders and four living creatures, will be gather in Heaven on this great prophetic Feast of Tabernacles, and will celebrate salvation praises of victory in the presence of both the Father and Son. All in Heaven will praise God with a sevenfold doxology, "praise and glory and wisdom and thanks and honor and power and strength to our God for ever and ever," Revelation 7:12.

Sukkot is the last of the fall Festivals, which takes place over seven days in Israel and eight days outside the land. These days of annual celebration, specifically the eighth day, are symbolic of eternity. The time cycle of sin is 6,000 years, followed by the 1,000-year Sabbath rest, which is then followed by the "Olam Haba"—the "eighth day" of eternity, which ushers in the new heaven and new earth.

In contrast, the 144,000 of all Israel will sing the song of Psalms 118 on earth during the "time of Jacob's trouble" (Jeremiah 30:7-11), while their enemies close in on them. God will scatter and chasten these chosen ones as they endure the Great Tribulation, but will not allow their martyrdom (Psalms 118:18). God seals them for protection against their enemies and the prevailing destruction of sea, land and trees.

The prophet Isaiah (4:1-6) tells of this future end-time prophetic Feast of Tabernacle celebration, and the 144,000 "in that Day" of the LORD. In this passage Messiah is fittingly named the palm "BRANCH of the LORD" along with the 144,000, the "survivors in Israel—those who are left [behind] in Zion," who are alive and "remain" to brave the 40 days—the Time of Jacob's Trouble. At this time "The LORD will wash away the filth of the women in Zion; He will cleanse the bloodstains [of the prophets and believers—Revelation 18:20, 24] from Jerusalem [the great city] by a spirit of judgment and a spirit of fire ["consumed by fire," Revelation 18:8]. Then the LORD will create over all of Mount Zion and those assembled there... a canopy [tabernacle]. It will be a shelter and shade from the heat of the day, and a refuge and hiding place from the storm and rain."

The following words of comfort often heard at funerals will hold significance for those living through the time of Jacob's trouble: "The LORD is my Shepherd, I shall lack nothing. He makes me to lie down in green pastures, He leads me beside quiet waters, He restores my soul. He guides me in paths of righteousness for His name sake. Even though I walk through the valley of the shadow of death, I will fear no evil, for You are with me; Your rod and Your staff, they comfort me. You prepare a table before me in the presence of my enemies. You anoint my head with oil; my cup overflows. Surely goodness and love will follow me all the days of my life, and I will dwell in the house of the LORD forever," Psalm 23.

14. Revelation 7:13-14 tells how one of the elders asked the prophet John "who are they [the great multitude of all nations], and where did they come from? John responded, "Sir, you know." What did the elder say? _____

The great multitude "have come out of the great tribulation"; or, as the original text reads, "have escaped from within the great tribulation." They have been raised to life (Revelation 3:10-11; 15:1-2) to stand before God, as the seven angels are sent out with God's final wrath. They endured with patience and overcome to the end (Matthew 24:13), so that they have earned the right to escape all those things that are coming upon the earth (Romans 5:9). "At that time Michael... will arise" in protection of His people (Daniel 12:1-3), and He "will descend and with the voice of the Archangel and loud trumpet, these dead in Christ are raised first." The 144,000 "who are alive and left behind" will a short time later at the end of Jacob's trouble "be caught up" with the great multitude whom "God will bring with Him... in the clouds," so that together they "meet the LORD in the air. And so, we will be with the LORD forever," 1 Thessalonians 4:13-18. The great multitude have "washed their robes and made them white in the blood of the Lamb." The Savior has "washed us from our sins by His own blood," Revelation 1:5, KJV. David cried out, "Wash away all my iniquity and cleanse me from my sin," Psalm 51:2. Humanly speaking, to wash with blood would not clean, but spiritually speaking, this is the only way to enter the Temple of God above. They are the invited guests to the wedding in Heaven between Messiah and the New Jerusalem during Sukkot.

Paul asked the followers at Corinth, "Do you not know that the wicked will not inherit the kingdom of God? Do not be deceived" (1 Corinthians 6:9-10) into thinking that one can wallow in sin and enter in the Kingdom. Paul continues, "But you were washed, you were sanctified, you were justified in the name of the LORD Jesus Christ and by the Spirit of our God," (v. 11). "Therefore, if any man be in Christ, he is a new creature: old things are passed away; behold, all things are become new," 1 Corinthians 5:17 (KJV).

The Word proclaims, "Come now, let us reason together," says the LORD. "Though your sins are like scarlet, they shall be as white as snow; though they are red as crimson, they shall be like wool. If you are willing and obedient, you will eat the best from the land; but if you resist and rebel, you will be devoured by the sword." For the mouth of the LORD has spoken," Isaiah 1:18-20.

15. In Revelation 7:15-17 the great multitude is promised a special position of service, which they will hold in God's throne room. What is it? _____

This faithful group will serve God day and night in His Temple, and God will spread His tent [canopy] of protection over them forever. Although they were kept from food and shelter and endured hunger, thirst and scorching heat, because they would not accept the mark of the beast God promises His eternal shepherding care. Springs of living water will be theirs, and God will wipe all tears of sorrow away.

In Biblical times, during the week of the Feast of Tabernacles, there was a ritual performed daily connected with the sacrificial ceremony. This was called *nisukh ha-mayim*—the liberation of water. The procession and celebration itself is called *simhat beit has-sho'eivah*—"the rejoicing at the place of the water-drawing."

Although we cannot be certain, it's possible Yeshua may have been born during Sukkot, which would account for all the rooms being filled in Bethlehem during the Feast of Tabernacles. It is written, "The Word became flesh and dwelt [literally "*tabernacled*" (KJV)] among us," John 1:14. Years later, Yeshua was baptized and immediately went into the wilderness for forty (40) days, lacking food and water, and was then tempted of the Devil. The watery immersion at or near Sukkot (Feast of Tabernacles) gave birth to Messiah's earthly ministry, which would eventually lead to Calvary three and one-half years later at Passover. Likewise, the 144,000 must also endure the forty (40) day tribulation during the Sukkot festival season. Moses and Elijah also have recorded events in their lives connected to 40 days of deprivation.

Jesus often used the Feasts to reveal His Messianic role and to teach spiritual lessons during His recorded ministry. Our LORD eloquently referred to the imagery of water on Sukkot: "the last and greatest day of the Feast [of tabernacles], Jesus stood and said in a loud voice, If a man is thirsty, let him come to Me and drink. Whosoever believes in Me, as the Scripture has said, streams of living water will flow from within him," John 7:37-38.

The Feast of Tabernacles, again... possibly marking the birth of Christ when He was delivered from Mary's water-filled womb, also points to the spiritual birth of the nation of Israel. The prophet Isaiah wrote about the judgment of the LORD against the disobedient souls in Israel, as well as the birth of Messiah followed by the emergence of a righteous nation (the 144,000) when he wrote, "Here that uproar from the city [Jerusalem], hear that noise from the Temple! It is the sound of the LORD repaying His enemies all they deserve. Before she [Israel] goes into labor ["birth pains"—Matthew 24:8], she gives birth [to a child]; before the pains come upon her, she delivers a Son [Yeshua]. Who has ever heard such a thing? Who has ever seen such things? Can a country be born in a day or a nation [of all twelve tribes] be brought forth in a moment [of time]? Yet no sooner is Zion in labor than she gives birth to her children [144,000]. Do I bring to the moment of birth and not give delivery [deliverance]? says the LORD. Do I close up the womb when I bring to delivery? says your God. Rejoice with Jerusalem and be glad for her, all you who love her; rejoice greatly with her all you who mourn over her [fiery chastisement]," Isaiah 66:6-10.

The 144,000 will emerge in a spiritual birth as a nation at or near the Feast of Tabernacles, baptized with the baptism of God's Spirit, scattered into the wilderness for forty (40) days of trial—the Time of Jacob's Trouble—to be tempted. However, the elect will not succumb to Satan's deceptions (Matthew 24:23-25), although tempted just as Christ was during His forty-day trial. Out of the excruciating pains of the Great Tribulation, as a woman experiencing childbirth, the children will be pushed through the channel of distress to be delivered healthy, pure and white into the hands of the Living God.

Twelve (12) The Number Of Government & Authority

As mentioned, there were 12 tribes in Israel, and this symbolizes the completeness of the nation Israel. Jacob had 12 sons, which were the heads or fathers of each of the 12 tribes of Israel. Here are other significances of the number 12 in the Word of God, and Israel's history.

- Jesus chose 12 disciples who later became the 12 apostles, which fit the context of the number 12 used elsewhere in the Bible as signifying governmental rule or authority.
- In Revelation, there are 24 elders sitting on 24 thrones (12 x 2) (Revelation 4:4).
- The New Jerusalem, which descends out of heaven, has 12 gates made of pearl which are manned by 12 angels. Each of the gates has been named after one of the 12 tribes of Israel.

- In Revelation 7, twelve thousand from each of the 12 tribes of Israel will be sealed and saved at the end of the present age.
- The walls of the New Jerusalem are measured at 144 cubits high, which is 12 multiplied by 12 (Revelation 21:16).
- The New City is also 12,000 furlongs squared (Revelation 21:16).
- There are 12 precious stones in the foundation of the New Jerusalem (Revelation 21:19-20).
- The wall of the City has 12 foundations with the 12 names of the apostles on each one (Revelation 21:14).
- The Tree of Life in the New Jerusalem will bear 12 types of fruit.
- Twelve thousand multiplied by 12 will be taken from the earth so that they may follow and serve the Lamb of God, wherever He goes (Revelation 14:1-5).
- The high priest's breastplate had 12 precious stones embedded in it.
- Jesus very first words were spoken at the age of 12 (Luke 2:42).
- There was a woman who had suffered from a blood hemorrhage for 12 years (Luke 8:40).
- There are 12 Minor Prophets in the Old Testament. They are called minor, not because they are less important than the Major Prophets, but due to their size being considerably smaller.
- There are 12 historical books in the Bible: Joshua, Judges, Ruth, 1 Samuel, 2 Samuel, 1 Kings, 2 Kings, 1 Chronicles, 2 Chronicles, Ezra, Nehemiah, and Esther.
- There were 12 loaves of permanent offerings on the golden table (Leviticus 24:5).
- There were 12 explorers or spies sent into the land of Canaan (Deuteronomy 1:23).
- Solomon had 12 administrators in his kingdom (1 Kings 4:7).
- There were 12 loaves of bread in the Temple (Leviticus 24:5).
- There were 12 men who laid 12 stones in building a monument to the LORD (Joshua 4:3).
- Elijah built an altar with 12 stones (1 Kings 18:31-32).
- Elisha was plowing with 12 yokes of oxen when Elijah called him (1 Kings 19:19).
- Nehemiah was appointed to be the governor in the land of Judah for 12 years (Nehemiah 5:14).
- The Book of Chronicles contained 12 great priests.
- When Yeshua was being arrested, He said He could call for more than "12 legions of angels" if He needed help (Matthew 26:53).
- The Bible is filled with multiples of the number of 12. For example, when the Temple was built, it's foundation was 60 cubits long (12 x 5) (2 Chronicles 3:3); the porch was 120 cubits high (12 x 10) (2 Chronicles 3:4); and, the Holy Place was overlaid with 600 talents of fine gold (12 x 50) (2 Chronicles 3:8). When the Ark was brought into it, 120 priests were "sounding with trumpets" (12 x 10) (2 Chronicles 5:12). When dedicating it, Solomon offered a sacrifice of 120,000 sheep (12 x 10,000) (2 Chronicles 7:5).
- There are 12 months in a year.
- There are 12 constellations of the zodiac.

LION OF JUDAH

ליון ופ חודאה

Insights In Prophecy
Unlock The Ancient Mysteries Of Daniel & Revelation
BIBLE DISCOVERY SERIES

Lesson 15

THE CLOSING JUDGMENT: THE DAY OF ATONEMENT

Read Revelation 8

- Learn Why The Seventh Seal Represents The Closing Judgment In Heaven
- Discovery Why There's Conflict Over God's Appointed "Times & Seasons"

God's courtroom judgment is evident in the books of Daniel and Revelation. In Revelation 8 we find the seventh seal opened, which describes the final opportunity to trust in Yeshua and His saving grace. This  just precedes the outpouring of God's wrath through the seven trumpet plagues. This seventh seal signals the closing judgment and end of probation (testing) for the entire civilization. Michael will stand for "the nations were angry, and Your wrath has come, and the time of the dead, that they should be judged, and that You should reward Your servants the prophets [Moses and Elijah] and the saints," (Revelation 11:18). God's mercy will end, as illustrated in the Day of Atonement Festival (Leviticus 23:26-29), when those who persist with an unrepentant heart will be cut off from among the people.

Revelation 21:11 also points to the closing judgment in Heaven and Court's decree just before Messiah returns in His brilliance to light the world: "Let him who does wrong continue to do wrong; let him who is vile continue to be vile; let him who does right continue to do right; and let him who is holy continue to be holy. Behold I am coming soon! My reward is with Me, and I will give to *everyone* according to what he has done." The focus of Lesson 15 and Revelation 8 takes us to that moment in time and this proclamation, which then leads to the release of God's wrath by the seven trumpeters.

As we have noted in the Insights in Prophecy Series, John wrote repeatedly about the events of the *sevens*. The *seventh seal* is opened to the *seven angels* who prepared to execute *seven trumpet* plagues; and, when the *Seventh Angel* sounds His trumpet Heaven declares the kingdom of this world is become the kingdom of our LORD and His Messiah Messenger, and He will reign.

In Lesson 12 we identified that Revelation 6:12-17 and the sixth seal opens at the visible and very dramatic Second Coming of the LORD with the armies of Heaven. We will also discover both the sixth trumpet (9:13-18) and sixth plague (16:12-16) also point to the stirring up of earth's military armies and the Armageddon confrontation at the visible return of Jesus. However, the seventh seal (8:1-6) and the seventh plague (16:17-21) are Sanctuary events, which release the Mighty Messenger to begin the Day of the LORD events at the seventh trumpet (10:1-7), all of which must occur before the Great Day of the LORD and the Armageddon confrontation—the Day when all enemies will be destroyed.

How do we know the events of the sevens precede the sixth seal, sixth trumpet and sixth plague? Both Father (He who sits upon the throne) and His Son will *leave* the throne room *together* and make their way to Planet Earth (Revelation 6:16; Luke 9:26) to finalize the plagues and to destroy all enemies of the Most High. Therefore, the seventh seal must be opened *prior to* the sixth seal, and the Seventh Angel must sound His trumpet and pour out His vial plague before the other six subordinate angels perform their duties. In the book of Revelation, the "sevens"—the 7th seal, 7th trumpet and 7th vial—all highlight Messiah's position of highest authority; and, all three point to the Festival day of greatest importance—the Day of Atonement

Insights In Prophecy
Unlock The Ancient Mysteries Of Daniel & Revelation
BIBLE DISCOVERY SERIES

(Yom Kippur), and not to a chronological count. In this case, the last (7th) trumpet and the last (7th) vial shall be first in this series of woes.

This challenges the commonly held view that the book of Revelation in it's entirely is a neatly arranged chronological presentation; in other words, the events of each chapter follow the one just before it. However, prophetic books are seldom neatly arranged in a sequential order. A review of the Hebrew Scriptures proves a theme is often repeated and scattered throughout the prophet's scroll using various symbols and idiomatic expressions.

So, it is with John's book of Revelation. Although the chapters lead us generally from beginning to end, within the prophecies there are "insertions" of passages that offer additional explanations; therefore, we often find overlapping events throughout the book. The student must look for commonalities between the various passages, much like a puzzle. For example, when an individual sees the *four worldwide portents*—"peals of thunder, rumblings [voices], flashes of lightning and an earthquake" we can be quite sure we have located a *specific point in time*; a *mile-marker*, we might say—the same *reference point*, like the matching pieces of a mysterious puzzle.

Therefore, the events of sevens—the 7th seal, 7th trumpet and 7th vial—all point to the same moment in time and are associated with perfection and completeness. Pt. 18 on *The Kingdom Calendar* features the pinnacle, or turning point, of the great controversy between good and evil—the Yom Kippur Day of Atonement, also known as the Day of the LORD (or, simply the "Day"), when Messiah descends in the stormy darkness to begin His triumphant reign, and when the mysteries of God will begin to be finished.

1. The Lamb opens the seventh seal in Revelation 8:1. What happens in Heaven that is so unique? _____
_____

The seventh seal event is so solemn that countless millions of Heaven's inhabitants hush in reverential silence. Time is slipping away, and eternity is at hand. The Day of the LORD is about to begin. The few minutes that remain indicates time is running out for every man, woman and child on Planet Earth.

Silence Precedes Judgment

We cannot overlook the Scriptural call for silence both in Heaven and on earth. All inhabitants of Heaven will halt in silence as an indicator that terrible events are about to erupt on Planet Earth, like the calm before a storm. Prophecy indicates that a day will come when the whole earth will be silenced just before the Day of the LORD begins, as the Judge makes the final decision between His wedding guests and those left in outer darkness (Matthew 8:11-12; 22:1-14; 25:30-34; note His wedding guests are gathered primarily from the "nations"—namely Gentiles). Zephaniah 1:7 says, "*Be silent* before the Sovereign LORD, for the *Day of the LORD is near*. The LORD has prepared a sacrifice; He has consecrated [set aside; distinguished] those [guests] He has invited."

The obedient believers are called to silence. Psalms 46:10 says, "*Be still*, and know that I am God; I will be exalted among the nations, I will be exalted in the earth." Lamentations 3:26, 28 adds, "It is good to *wait quietly* for the salvation of the LORD... Let him *sit alone in silence*." David writes, "*Search your hearts* and *be silent*," Psalm 4:4.

154

The whole world is called to reverence. "The LORD is in His holy Temple; let *all the earth be silent* before Him," Habakkuk 2:20. "*Be still* before the LORD, *all mankind*, because He has roused Himself [raised, or stood up] from His holy dwelling," Zechariah 2:13.

God will bring the whole world to an eerie silence by worldwide darkness: "In that day [of the LORD], declares the Sovereign LORD, I will make the sun go down at noon and darken the earth in broad daylight. I will turn your religious feasts into mourning and all your singing into weeping," Amos 8:8-9. "I will cover the sun with a cloud, and the moon will not give its light. All the shining lights in the heavens I will darken over you; I will bring darkness over the land, declares the Sovereign LORD," Ezekiel 32:7-8. "Blow the trumpet in Zion; sound the alarm on my holy hill [as on the Feast of Trumpets]. Let all who live in the land tremble, for the Day of the LORD is coming. It is close at hand—a day of darkness and gloom, a day of clouds and blackness," Joel 2:1-2. The Ten Days of Awe offer the last moments for repentant hearts as Yom Kippur nears.

How long does the darkness last? We don't know for sure but consider a similar plague at Israel's birth as a nation: "Stretch out your hand toward the sky so that darkness will spread over Egypt—darkness that can be felt... and total darkness covered all Egypt for *three days*. No one could see anyone else or leave his place for *three days*," Exodus 10:21-23.

Consider what is prophesied to happen after a three-day period in the future. "Come, let us [God's people] return to the LORD. He has torn us to pieces but He will heal us; He has injured us but He will bind up our wounds. After two days He will revive us ["bones came together, bone to bone... flesh appeared upon them... but there was no breath in them," Ezekiel 37:7-8]; and on the third day He will restore us ["and breath entered them; they came to life and stood up on their feet—a vast army," Ezekiel 37:10], that we may live in His presence," Hosea 6:1-2. "The Sovereign LORD says, I am going to open your graves and bring you up from them; I will bring you back to the land of Israel," Ezekiel 37:12.

Considering *The Kingdom Calendar*, the two witnesses will be killed just before God's mercy ends and heaven's lights are extinguished; then, "after the three and one-half days a breath of life from God entered them [in resurrection power], and they stood on their feet... then they heard a loud voice from heaven saying to them, Come up here. And they went up to heaven in a cloud [along with the raised tribulation saints], while their enemies looked on," Revelation 11:11-12.

"From Heaven you *pronounced judgment*, and the *land feared and was quiet*—when you, O God, rose up to judge [the wicked, and], to save all the afflicted of the land," Psalms 76:8-9. The prophet Isaiah adds, "Come near, you nations, and *listen; pay attention*, you peoples! Let the *earth hear*, and all that is in it, the world, and all that comes out of it! The *LORD is angry* with all nations; *His wrath is upon all* their armies. He will totally destroy them, He will give them over to slaughter... For the LORD has a *Day of Vengeance, and a [Eternal Jubilee] Year* of retribution, to uphold Zion's cause," (34:1-2, 8).

The Seven Angels With Trumpets

2. In Revelation 8:2 John saw seven messengers "stand before God." What were they about to be handed? _____

Each angel received one of the seven trumpets of judgment, which indicates they were about to blow the instruments of God's wrath.

There are non-canonical Jewish writings that did not become part of the Hebrew Scriptures, but these scrolls were noted in the Bible around 40 times (to name a few, Joshua 10:13; 2 Samuel 1:18; Numbers 21:14; 1 Kings 8:12–13; 1 Kings 14:19, 14:29; II Chronicles 9:29, 12:15, 13:22; and, 1 Samuel 10:25). There is a wealth of insight into Jewish thought and practices in these more obscure volumes. Two New Testament writers reference the *Book of Enoch* (Jude 4, 6, 13, 14–15; 2 Peter 2:4; 3:13). I Enoch 90:21 states there are "the seven... white ones." "The earliest reference to a system of seven... angels as a group appears to be in *Enoch I* (the Book of Enoch), which is not part of the Jewish Canon but is prevalent in the Judaic tradition, where they are named as Gabriel, Michael, Raphael, Uriel, Rague, Remiel and Saraqael," Wikipedia—Seven Archangels. The seven are also noted in Tobit 12:15, "I am Raphael, one of the seven angels who stand in the glorious presence of the LORD, ready to serve Him."

In the promise to Zechariah that he would have a son named John, one of the seven angels declared in Luke 1:19, "I am Gabriel, I *stand in the presence of God*." Isaiah 63:9 reveals, "In all their distress He too was distressed, and the *Angel of His Presence* saved them. In His love and mercy, He *redeemed* them; He lifted them up and carried them all the days of old." The only Angel who can *redeem* and *carry Israel all the days of old* is Michael, our Messiah—the Seventh Angel who stands in the presence of His Father—Almighty God.

Of course, the seven angels are also found throughout the book of Revelation. Jews who read the book would quickly understand the seven Revelation angels to represent the Angels (Messengers) of the Presence of God. Therefore, Michael would be one of the seven messengers who are intimately involved in the appointed time of the end. He is identified as the "Man clothed in linen"—the garment of a priest—and, it is He who cries out to hold the worldwide strife until His 144,000 is sealed.

Please never imagine that this teacher believes Michael to be just another of God's created beings; He is the Word and was with the Father from the beginning. "In the beginning was the Word, and the Word was with God, and the Word was God. He was with God in the beginning. Through Him all things were made; without Him nothing was made that has been made. In Him was life, and that life was the light of all mankind. The light shines in the darkness, and the darkness has not overcome it," John 1:1-5. The Angel of the LORD—Michael is another name for our Messiah; He is also called a *Lion* and a *Lamb* in the book of Revelation, but no one would suggest this implies He is a four-legged creature, or any less God. Yeshua is called inanimate objects—the Rock, Living Water, and Bread of Life; these describe but do not diminish the Creator of the Universe. These many names/titles in the Scriptures denote roles, which He has or will be fulfilling as He finalizes His plan of redemption.

This was a very common view until more recent times. Theologian and the Protestant reformation pastor **John Calvin** wrote, "As we stated yesterday, Michael may mean an angel; but I embrace the opinion of those who refer this to the person of Christ, because it suits the subject best to represent him as standing forward for the defense of his elect people." The great theologian, **John Wesley,** wrote in his commentary on Daniel 10:21, "Michael - Christ alone is the protector of his church, when all the princes of the earth desert or oppose it."

3. Trumpets will be distributed to the seven angels. To what special event in Israel's Holy Days do we hear trumpet blasts associated with the sevens (Leviticus 25:8-13)? _____

_____

Israel was to count off seven Sabbaths of years—seven times seven years, a total of forty-nine years. Then they were instructed to have the "trumpet sounded everywhere on the tenth day of the seventh month; on the Day of Atonement sound the trumpet throughout your land." Why? "Consecrate the fiftieth year and proclaim liberty throughout the land... it shall be a Jubilee for you... In this Year of Jubilee everyone is to return to his own property."

4. What event in Israel's history corresponds, in part, to the seven messengers and seven trumpets that will sound (Joshua 5:13-15; 6:4)? _____

The "Commander of the LORD's army" promised Joshua that Jericho would fall. Michael instructed the prophet to have seven priests carry seven trumpets, and for seven days to march around the city with the Ark of the Covenant and blow the trumpets. On the seventh day the army circled the city seven times, and on the seventh turn they blew their trumpets and gave a loud shout; the city immediately fell in ruins.

5. God warned Israel if the people do not obey, there would be consequences (Leviticus 26:18-46). How does this possibly relate to the seven trumpet woes? _____

Israel will be punished seven times, if the people refuse to listen to God's warnings from His prophets.

In Revelation 8:3 an angel steps up to the altar of incense in the Sanctuary having a golden censer, where he offers the prayers of the faithful as a sweet aroma before God. The incense represents many concerned prayers of the overcomers on earth during the appointed time of the end, asking for retribution for their sufferings.

The High Priest of Israel performed similar ceremonies on the Day of Atonement (Yom Kippur) once a year. He was to put on the sacred linen tunic, with linen undergarments along with a linen sash and turban. As part of the ritual, he would "take a censer full of burning coals from the altar before the LORD and... incense and take them behind the curtain" and into the Holy of Holies where the Ark of the Covenant resided (Leviticus 16:4; 16:12-13) and there make an atonement for the people.

6. In Revelation 8:5 what does the angel do with the censer and fire? _____

The filling of the censer with fire from the altar and hurling it to the earth would signify two important events: First, that God's mercy for mankind is now over. No further prayers of repentance will be entertained, because the cutting off time has arrived. Second, the believers' cries of retribution against their persecutors are being answered with fiery wrath direct from the Temple of God in Heaven (Revelation 6:9-10).

These requests of justice are reminiscent of Psalm 18 where David cried in his distress for God's response. The psalmist wrote Almighty will "come down" to bring judgment, in response to the prayers ascending to His throne: "In my distress I called to the LORD; I cried to my God for help. From His temple He heard my voice; my cry came before Him, into His ears. The earth trembled and quaked, and the foundations of the mountains shook; they trembled because He was angry. Smoke rose from His nostrils; consuming fire came from His mouth, burning coals blazed out of it. He parted the heavens and came down; dark clouds were under His feet. He mounted the cherubim and flew; He soared on the wings of the wind [four living creatures]. He made darkness His covering, His canopy around Him—the dark rain clouds  of the sky. Out of the brightness of His presence clouds advanced, with hailstones and bolts of lightning. The LORD thundered from heaven; the voice of the Most High resounded. He shot His arrows and scattered the enemies, great bolts of lightning and routed them. The valleys of the sea were exposed and the foundations of the earth laid bare at Your rebuke, O LORD, at the blast of breath from Your nostrils," Psalm 18:6-15. Messiah's *Day of Visitation* is His personal response to the prayers of the righteous, which visitation occurs at the Day of Atonement (Yom Kippur).

The prophet Ezekiel saw a similar vision concerning God's wrath against Israel for their practice of idolatry in the Jerusalem Temple (Ezekiel 9-10). The Shekinah glory left the Temple, which glory will return at the end of days to punish sinners and to clear out the Jerusalem Temple again. Ezekiel saw seven messengers: "six men" and "with them was a Man clothed in linen—a priest's robe—who had a writing kit at His side," (9:2). The seventh is no doubt Michael who is often described wearing Priest's clothing—the "man dressed in linen" (Daniel 10:5-6). Michael is admonished to "go throughout the city of Jerusalem and put a mark on the foreheads of those who grieve and lament over all the detestable things [idolatrous worship] that are done in it," (9:4).

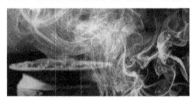

The "Man clothed in linen" was then to "go in among the wheels beneath the cherubim [four living creatures]. Fill your hands with burning coals... and scatter them [the fire of judgment] over the city" Jerusalem. So, He took "fire from among the wheels, from among the cherubim, the Man went in and stood before a wheel. Then one of the cherubim reached out his hand to the fire that was among them. He took up some of it and put it into the hands of the Man in linen, who took it and went out" (10:2-7).

7. With the throwing down of hailstone fire onto the earth in judgment, what four additional frightening portents jolt the planet (Revelation 8:5)? _____

Thunders, rumblings (voices-KJV), flashes of lightning and earthquake are added to the fiery hailstones. These four-spectacular portents are found also in Revelation 11:15, 18-19, and 16:17-21; and, they occur at the moment of the sevens (seventh trumpet; seventh bowl plague) in association with the Seventh Angel—Michael, when God's wrath is unleashed against the world; in other words, the beginning of the Day of the LORD.

The First Angel

8. According to Revelation 8:6-7, the first trumpet of God's wrath brings what upon the earth? _____
_____

Land masses are destroyed by hail and fire. In the trumpets, destruction is measured in the "third part," which is rooted in the Hebrew Scriptures.

9. To whom is the "thirds" associated (Ezekiel 5:2-5, 11-12; Revelation 16:18)? _____

The trumpet plagues are specifically against unbelieving Israel and the inhabitants of Jerusalem who have forsaken God to follow the Lawless One. Heaven cries out, "Come out of her [Babylon/Jerusalem] My people, so that you will not share in her sins, so that you will not receive any of her plagues; for her sins are piled up to Heaven, and God has remembered her crimes... therefore in one day her plagues will overtake her: death, mourning and famine. She will be consumed by fire, for mighty is the LORD God who judges her," Revelation 18:4-8. As Jesus said, "When you see Jerusalem surrounded by armies, you will know that its desolation is near. Then let those who are in Judea flee to the mountains... for it is the time of punishment in fulfillment of all that has been written," Luke 21:20-22.

10. What city will be split into "three parts" during the plague of the Seventh Angel, and the global earthquake (Revelation 16:19)? _____

The "great city" is identified as "where also their LORD was crucified," Revelation 11:8—Jerusalem. Yeshua said to the rebellious Jewish leaders of His day, "I must press on today and tomorrow and the next day—for surely no prophet can die outside Jerusalem! Jerusalem, Jerusalem, you who kill the prophets and stone those sent to you, how often I have longed to gather your children together, as a hen gathers her chicks under her wings, and you were not willing. Look, your house is left to you desolate," Luke 13:33-35.

The Second Angel

11. In Revelation 8:8-9 the second angel blows his trumpet. What falls from the sky into the sea? _____
_____

The burning mountain, which may plummet into the Mediterranean Sea, will destroy ocean life, cause shipwrecks, tidal waves and great loss of property and lives. Earth's life-sustaining geological system will be thrown into chaos as the end-of-the-world woes continue to unfold.

The Third Angel

12. The third angel sounds. The fresh water supply is contaminated by Wormwood. Jeremiah 9:11-16 describes this plague as against what city and its citizens? _____

Jeremiah prophesied, "I will make Jerusalem a heap of ruins, a haunt of jackals; and I will lay waster the towns of Judah so no one can live there... it is because they have forsaken My Law, which I set before them; they have not obeyed Me or followed My Law... see, I will make this people [Israelites] eat bitter food and drink poisoned water [wormwood-KJV]... I will pursue them with the sword until I have destroyed them." The fact is that humans can only survive a few days without fresh water, and the drinking water will go sour first in Israel then across the globe during the last 40 days of human history.

The Fourth Angel

Revelation 8:12-13 describes the fourth angel's trumpet. The galactic lights will be altered, and the days and nights will grow shorter. At the voice of the LORD, the "earth is broken up, the earth is split asunder, the earth is thoroughly shaken. The earth reels like a drunkard, it sways like a hut in the wind; so heavy upon it is the guilt of its rebellion that it falls—never to rise again," Isaiah 24:19-20. Job adds, "He moves mountains... and overturns them in His anger. He shakes the earth from its place and makes its pillars tremble. He speaks to the sun and it does not shine; he seals off the light of the stars," (9:5-7).

13. During the Great Tribulation, what will God do in order to cut short the persecution of His elect— those He has sealed for protection (Matthew 24:21-22)? _____

The forty (40) days of Jacob's trouble, as shown on *The Kingdom Calendar*, will be cut short when God shakes this planet out of its orbit. At Mount Sinai God's "voice shook the earth, but now He has promised, Once more I will shake not only the earth but also the heavens," Hebrews 12:26. The rotation of Planet Earth may well be sped up so that the days themselves are shorter, possibly by one-third of the day (Revelation 8:12). In this context, the day and hour of the Second Coming is beyond human knowledge. Matthew 24:36 proclaims, "no one knows about the day or hour, not even the angels in

Heaven, nor the Son, but only the Father." That is why Messiah waits in readiness for the Father's order to reap the harvest at the end of time (Revelation 14:14-15); only the Father knows that moment.

The Conflict Over God's Appointed "Times & Seasons"

In the book of Daniel, we discover two very interesting predictions about the final conflict of the ages. It involves God's "times and seasons," which are also called the "set times and the laws" of Almighty God. While Daniel prophesies our Creator can "change times and seasons" (Daniel 2:21), he also predicts the Man of Sin will, in contrast, attempt to "change the set times and the laws" (Daniel 7:25) of God. Therefore, prophecy is telling us to pay attention to these details, and to consider the opposing sides and what this means for the last-day overcomers. There are verses in the book of Daniel specifically connected to divine "secrets," which God promises to reveal to the wise and discerning at the appropriate time. Let's consider them now.

Concerning God, Daniel writes (2:20-22): "Praise be to the name of God for ever and ever; wisdom and power are His. *He changes times and seasons*; He deposes kings and raises up others. He gives wisdom to the wise and knowledge to the discerning. *He reveals deep and hidden things*" to the wise. We are reminded of a related promise in Daniel 12:9-12, where we are told the wise will understand two important timelines in the Hebrew prophecies when last-day events are about to begin: "Go your way, Daniel, because the words are rolled up and sealed until the time of the end. Many will be purified, made spotless and refined, but the wicked will continue to be wicked. None of the wicked will understand, but *those who are wise will understand*. "From the time that the daily [worship at the Western Wall/Temple Mount]... is abolished and the abomination that causes desolation is set up [on Temple Mount], there will be 1,290 days. Blessed is the one who waits for and reaches the end of the 1,335 days."

We want to learn about these details that have been hidden through the ages, which God promised He would reveal to the wise. It involves His prophetic timelines and His plans to change His "times and seasons". It also involves that evil actor who opposes truth and opposes God.

Regarding the evil Man of Lawlessness, Daniel writes (7:25): "He will speak against the Most High and oppress His holy people and *try to change the set times and the laws*. The holy people will be delivered into his hands for a time, times and half a time [3½ years; 1,260 days]." The New Living Translation says, "He will try to change their *sacred festivals* and laws"; and, the Wycliffe Bible says, "He shall think, that he can *change the times for the feasts*, and the laws."

Revelation 13:5-8 refers to the "Beast" and his evil practices, and the limited time he will rule over Planet Earth: "The beast was given a mouth to utter proud words and blasphemies and to exercise its authority for forty-two months [1,260 days]. It opened its mouth to blaspheme God, and to slander His name and His dwelling place and those who live in heaven. It was given power to wage war against God's holy people and to conquer them. And it was given authority over every tribe, people, language and nation. All inhabitants of the earth will worship the beast—all whose names have not been written in the Lamb's book of life, the Lamb who was slain from the creation of the world."

So, by the fact that Daniel predicts it, God can and certainly will change the "times and seasons" by His mighty voice; no matter what season Jerusalem is in, whether it be spring, summer or winter, Messiah's voice will rock this planet into the fall season to fulfill His autumn Festivals at the assigned moment in time.

On the other hand, the Beast, the demon-possessed man, will persecute God's people, and will attempt (although unsuccessfully) to change what Scriptures call God's "set times and the laws." The fact is, although men have often tried down through the centuries to alter the Word of God to fit their own inventions, no man—not even the pope—can change the declarations of Almighty God, whether the Sabbath, the Festival periods, or any other law of God.

The Festivals: Declaring The Past, Foretelling The Future

Long ago God established His seasonal Festivals, which He introduced to the Israelites in Leviticus 23. Passover (*Pesach*), the Feast of Unleavened Bread (*Hag HaMatzah*), the Feast of Firstfruits (*Bikkurim*) and the Festival of Weeks (*Shavuot*) represent the springtime Festivals, while the Feast of Trumpets *(Rosh Ha-Shanah)*, the Day of Atonement (*Yom Kippur*) and the Feast of Tabernacles (*Sukkot*) are celebrated in the autumn season. These sanctuary Feasts have celebrated Almighty God's leading of His people for many centuries, and also foretell events about the future. Many centuries after they were established, Yeshua fulfilled the spring Festivals at His death on the cross. Likewise, He is bound to fulfill the fall Festivals at His triumphant return. The autumn Festivals portray the unfolding of final events in Heaven and on earth and will be fulfilled by Messiah leading up to and during His

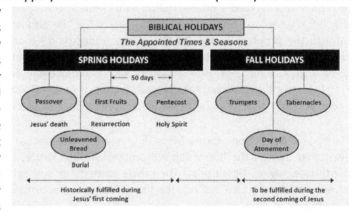

Day of the LORD climax of human history. Therefore, the Biblical Holidays offer the wise and discerning students of God's Word divine dates of end-time disaster and deliverance—the deep and hidden things that are in process of being revealed.

The apostle Paul also connected the "times and seasons" to the Day of the LORD—the coming of Jesus our Messiah and the fiery demise of sinners, when he wrote in 1 Thessalonians 5:1-6: "For you yourselves know perfectly well that the Day of the LORD so comes as a thief in the night. For when they say, "Peace and safety!" then sudden destruction comes upon them, as labor pains upon a pregnant woman. And they shall not escape. But you, brethren, are not in darkness, so that this Day should overtake you as a thief. You are all sons of light and sons of the day. We are not of the night, nor of darkness. Therefore, let us not sleep, as others do, but let us watch and be sober."

Paul shares that although sinners will not understand or acknowledge the times and seasons, those who are awake need not be in darkness that the Day should overtake God's people as a thief. As sons of light, we are not left in darkness like the world. We are to be sober and wise, knowing the times.

This leads to the big question. Why will the Lawless One attempt to change God's *set times and the laws*? He may do so attempting to preempt Messiah's final redemption plan that is promised to be completed during the fall Festival season, or in order to set himself up in the Temple, on the Temple Mount, and then proclaim himself "GOD"... at the time of his choosing. Once the Papal leader sets up the abomination, Messiah's visitation will surely come. Shrouded in darkness, the whole planet will quake in His fury, and it will be shaken off it's normal course so that even the "times and seasons" will be changed, which power Daniel wrote about long ago (2:20-22).

Paul continued to advise the watching believers on the disgraceful actions of Antichrist when he wrote in 2 Thessalonians 2:1-4: "Concerning the coming of our LORD Jesus Christ and our being gathered to him, we ask you, brothers and sisters, not to become easily unsettled or alarmed by the teaching allegedly from us—whether by a prophecy or by word of mouth or by letter—asserting that the Day of the LORD has already come. Don't let anyone deceive you in any way, for that Day will not come until the rebellion occurs and the Man of Lawlessness is revealed, the man doomed to destruction. He will oppose and will exalt himself over everything that is called God or is worshiped, so that he sets himself up in God's temple, proclaiming himself to be God."

Daniel wrote about that event (9:27): "He [the Man of Sin] will confirm a covenant with many for one 'seven' [one literal seven-day week]. In the middle of the 'seven he [the Man of Sin] will put an end to sacrifice and offering. And at the temple [Mount in Jerusalem] he will set up an abomination that causes desolation, until the end that is decreed is poured out on him." Jesus also warned the last-day believers living in the land of Israel, "So when you see standing in the holy place 'the abomination that causes desolation,' spoken of through the prophet Daniel—let the reader understand—then let those who are in Judea flee to the mountains. Let no one on the housetop go down to take anything out of the house. Let no one in the field go back to get their cloak. How dreadful it will be in those days for pregnant women and nursing mothers! Pray that your flight will not take place in winter or on the Sabbath. For then there will be great distress, unequaled from the beginning of the world until now—and never to be equaled again," Matthew 24:15-21.

The book of Revelation exposes Messiah's response to this act of defiance. It speaks of God's earth-moving event that changes the "times and seasons," when John wrote, "Out of the temple came a loud voice from the throne, saying, "It is done!" Then there came flashes of lightning, rumblings, peals of thunder and a severe earthquake. No earthquake like it has ever occurred since mankind has been on earth, so tremendous was the quake. The great city [Jerusalem] split into three parts, and the cities of the nations collapsed. God remembered Babylon the Great and gave her the cup filled with the wine of the fury of his wrath. Every island fled away and the mountains could not be found," (Revelation 16:17-20). How massive of an earthquake would cause islands to sink into the sea and mountains to collapse? The global quake Job wrote about long ago when God, "moves mountains... and overturns them in His anger. He shakes the earth from its place," (9:5-7) changing its orbit and position in the Milky Way Galaxy, and changing the times and seasons.

The primary period of the end-times during which the Papal leader is to reign, repeated seven times in the books of Daniel and Revelation, is 1,260 days (Daniel 7:25; Daniel 12:7; Revelation 11:2, Revelation 11:3, Revelation 12:6; Revelation 12:14; Revelation 13:5). At the end of his rule, God will unleash His wrath upon him and the disobedient crowds who followed him. Even though the punishments of the first four trumpeters of Revelation 8 are beyond the human mind to comprehend, the angel proclaims, "Woe! Woe! Woe to the inhabitants of the earth, because of the trumpet blasts about to be sounded by the other three angels," Revelation 8:13. Lesson 16 directs us to Revelation 9 and introduces us to two more frightening trumpet plagues.

LORD OF LORDS

לורד ופ לוורדס

Insights In Prophecy
Unlock The Ancient Mysteries Of Daniel & Revelation
BIBLE DISCOVERY SERIES

--NOTES---

Insights In Prophecy
Unlock The Ancient Mysteries Of Daniel & Revelation
BIBLE DISCOVERY SERIES

Lesson 16

LESSON 16

THE ABYSS: RELEASE OF THE DEMONS

Read Revelation 9

- **Explore The Woeful Activities Of Demonic Creatures**
- **Search How The Destruction Of Evil Angels Is Foretold**

Revelation 9 introduces the fifth and sixth trumpets, which are representative of God's wrath on the unrepentant leaders and residents of Israel that will succumb to the abominable idol worship. Paul wrote, "Concerning the coming of our LORD Jesus Christ and our being gathered to him, we ask you, brothers, not to become easily unsettled or alarmed by some prophecy, report or letter supposed to have come from us,

 saying that the Day of the LORD has already come. Don't let anyone deceive you in any way, for (that Day will not come) until the rebellion ["falling away" (KJV) from Biblical truths and warnings] occurs and the man of lawlessness is revealed, the man doomed to destruction. He will oppose and will exalt himself over everything that is called God or is worshiped, so that he sets himself up in God's temple, proclaiming himself to be God," 2 Thessalonians 2:1-4.

By the time the fifth and sixth trumpets are blown during the appointed time of the end, Heaven's judgment in review of the opened books (Daniel 7:9-10) will have concluded (Revelation 8:2-5), with the prayers of retribution being answered with a fiery punishment on the oppressors. As the port was shut on Noah's boat of escape to the antediluvian civilization just days before the great deluge of rain, so too the door of mercy be shut on the sinful just preceding the trumpet plagues. Noah prophesied about the downpour that was about to destroy the earth and his generation, but few listened. Likewise, Heaven's prophets and the wise will warn the nations of God's final judgments. They will be ridiculed; and, when the religious leaders and politicians proclaim "peace and safety; destruction will come on them suddenly, as labor pains on a pregnant woman, and they will not escape. But you brethren, are not in darkness so that this Day should surprise you like a thief," 1 Thessalonians 5:3-4.

"THE END" (Matthew 24:14)—the final days known as the Great Tribulation—will be a devastating time of mass destruction and annihilation. At the voice of God, the planet will be rocked and jolted, great cities will fall into heaps of rubble, and uncontrollable plagues and pestilences will sweep across continents; fires, storms and high winds, tidal waves, earthquakes, wars and bloodshed will overtake Planet Earth. Nearly as quickly as the earth was created with its beauty and splendor, the planet will be brought to desolation and ruin (Jeremiah 4:23-29).

Demonic activity is potent and real, although mostly unseen in this day and age. Many fallen angels still are free to move about within the boundaries that God has set: "For our struggle is not against flesh and blood but against the rulers, against the authorities, against the powers of this dark world and against the spiritual forces of evil in the heavenly realms," Ephesians 6:12.

The Word also speaks of the prison house of evil angels who are confined in a place called the "Abyss." Jesus confronted the demons who controlled the man of Gadarenes, and in fear they "begged Him repeatedly not to order them to go into the Abyss," Luke 8:28. Evidently, not all demons are allowed to run loose, but are confined in a deep prison; otherwise, there would likely be total mayhem.

Insights In Prophecy
Unlock The Ancient Mysteries Of Daniel & Revelation
BIBLE DISCOVERY SERIES

Peter wrote about a time before the ancient flood that evil angels were engaging in activities that were deplorable to God. Genesis 6:2-4 says "the sons of God saw that the daughters of men were beautiful and they married any of them they chose... the sons of God went to the daughters of men and had children by them. They were the heroes of old, men of renown." God decided to destroy the earth with a flood and to imprison these vile angels. Because of Messiah's death, resurrection and ultimate victory over Satan and these evil angels in prison are subject to his final authority (1 Peter 3:19-22). "The angels who did not keep their positions of authority but abandoned their own home—these He has kept in darkness, bound with everlasting chains for the judgment on the Great Day," Jude 6. "For if God did not spare angels when they sinned, but sent them to hell [Greek *Tartarus*], putting them into gloomy dungeons to be held for judgment... the LORD knows how to rescue godly from trials and to hold the unrighteous for the Day of judgment," 2 Peter 2:4-9. This indicates that their punishment is not additional jail time, but their ultimate fiery death.

Their final demise is foretold, but they are let loose for a short time by Almighty God's design to prove once again their evil ways: "In that Day the LORD will punish the powers in the heavens above [evil angels] and the kings on the earth below. They will be herded together like prisoners bound in a dungeon; they will be shut up in prison and be punished after many days," Isaiah 24:21-22. This is represented by the one thousand (1,000) year millennial delay found later in the book of Revelation.

Revelation 9 reveals there is a day of release, when the escape door will be opened, and all the imprisoned evil angels will be given freedom for a season to swarm from place to place and torture earth's inhabitants. This study will attempt to search out this terrible woe, and to bring some additional insights about the last moments of this beleaguered moaning planet.

The Fifth Angel

1. In Revelation 9:1 the fifth messenger of God sounds his trumpet of woe, and John saw a star fall to the earth. What does a "star" sometimes represent in the Word (Daniel 8:10)? _____

Stars can represent God's created beings or angels (both good and bad).

The fallen star came from Heaven, which would indicate a loss of position and a loss of light. Jesus relayed to His disciples how He had personally witnessed Satan "fall like lightning from Heaven," Luke 10:18, signifying he was destined to lose his power and dominion. Revelation 12:7-9 describes a battle in Heaven where Satan and his malicious army attempts to overthrow God's kingdom, but Michael and His army of angels push back and expel Satan to be "hurled to the earth, and his angels with him," Revelation 12:9. In contrast, the wise—"who lead many to righteousness"—are promised that in God's Kingdom they will "shine like the brightness of the heavens... like the stars for ever and ever," (Daniel 12:3).

2. What does Isaiah 14:12 add to what we've learned so far? _____

The fallen demon is given the key, by Heaven's authority, to unlock the shaft of the Abyss—the prison of evil angels (Luke 8:28). The earth will erupt like a volcano. So great was the smoke of the Abyss that the sky was darkened, and out of the smoke John saw locust with tails like scorpions that could hurt.

3. What areas are excluded from their destructive behavior (Revelation 9:4); and, who are to be the recipients of their wrath? _____

God's devastating plague of locust is recorded in Exodus 10, to try to convince Pharaoh to let God's chosen people leave Egypt on their way the Promised Land. The locust swarmed the land stripping all the crops. However, Revelation introduces us to swarm of demonic stinging locust. In this case, the evil angels are not to harm the crops, but to vent their anger on the immoral population of Planet Earth. We learn that they cannot harm those who are sealed; only those without the seal of God can be punished. By this we know that the fifth trumpet does not blow until after the sealing process takes place, based on the record of Revelation 7:1-4.

4. How important is the seal of God during the trumpets and plagues? _____

The seal is the only means of protection from the global turmoil at the climax of human history. All men and women without the seal are doomed.

5. What group specifically receives the seal of God, according to Revelation 7:2-4? _____

The 144,000 of the twelve tribes of Israel are the only ones said to be sealed.

6. By this point, the "great multitude" of all nations (overcomers) is safely located where, just before the seven angels with the seven last plagues are sent out (Revelation 15:1-2, 7-8)? _____
_____

7. The "great multitude" (in contrast to the 144,000 of Israel) comes out the midst of what (Revelation 7:9, 14)? _____

When Michael—the Seventh Angel trumpeter stands and with the loud voice of the Archangel and trumpet of God raises up the martyred tribulation believers (Daniel 12:1-2) along with the two witnesses (Revelation 11:11), He will take them to Heaven's safety. There, these victorious overcomers see all seven messengers preparing to emerge with God's wrath (Revelation 15:1-2). Only the 144,000 elect, who are alive and remain (1 Thessalonians 4:14-17)— but are sealed for protection (Revelation 7:4), endure the catastrophic days of the final judgment plagues, while the sinful inhabitants of earth are tortured and ultimately destroyed.

Revelation 9:5-6 says the horde of demonic locust is given limited power. Locusts are likely used to represent demons in that their life cycle involves a hatching and emerging from the ground; and, they travel in large groups. When the demons emerge, they could kill their human victims; however, God limits their punishment to painful stings like scorpions. The pain will be so intense that whoever is stung will long for death, but it will elude them. Why is death preferable? The pain of a typical insect sting goes away after a short period of time, but this scorpion-like attack will cause lengthy suffering. Their fiery throbbing sting is torturous, and men and women would rather die than continue day and night with no rest in such excruciating pain.

The *five months* may be a literal period; but more likely this symbolizes an important truth: five months is the longest possible life-span of a locust from conception, through the larva stage and to death. Therefore, the last generation of demonic locust that emerge from their prison will torture with a sting and will cause insanity for the period God assigns them, but afterwards their doom is certain. They will not live beyond their prescribed rampage; their final death is certain.

8. Ephesians 6:12 identifies the struggle we have today with demonic powers. How is it described?
_____

We struggle with demonic forces, powers in high or heavenly realms, against powers of darkness.

9. Revelation 9:7-10 depicts demons, and reveals several aspects about their abilities and nature. What does the following attributes portray about the demonic foes?

"like horses prepared for battle" — _____
"crowns of gold" — _____
"faces resemble human faces" — _____
"teeth were like lion's teeth" — _____
"breastplates of iron" — _____
"wings was like the thundering of many horses and chariots" — _____
"tails and stings like scorpions" — _____

These characteristics reveal the demons' war-like readiness and muscular build, their positions of authority, intelligence and beauty, immense danger to their prey, battle-worthiness and swiftness of flight in mass numbers, and the painful injury they will bring upon unrepentant men.

10. What name is assigned to the commander who rules over the locust in Revelation 9:11? _____

His name is Abaddon in Hebrew and Apollyon in Greek. These names mean "destruction" or "destroyer" in the original language.

The book of Joel, chapters 1 and 2, begins with many parallels to what we see in Revelation 9. The prophet, in speaking of the "Day of the LORD," mentions locusts bringing judgment on the land with "wine, oil, wheat and barley" being in short supply. They have teeth like lions. Notice the connection between the "locusts" and *"a nation"* that has overrun the land of Israel. Joel also speaks of the *"meal offering and the drink offering is cut off from the house of the LORD"* (relating to Daniel 9:27), with vines, trees and water streams drying up.

The Sixth Angel

In Revelation 9:12-15 the sixth angel blows his trumpet, and the four angels who were restrained at the river Euphrates are released. Land beyond the Euphrates signified heathen nations and demonic powers; therefore, at this moment in time events begin to transpire that lead up to the battle of Armageddon.

11. How many angels of Heaven are signified as controlling the earth's governments and militaries (Revelation 4:6-8; 7:1)? _____

Four angels; also known at the four living creatures. Now four angels are released to move great numbers of demonic and world militaries toward Armageddon.

12. How precise is Heaven's time-table for the final military battle, and the size of the army that will be positioned to enter the Middle East (Revelation 9:15-16)? _____

At the very hour on a specific day, month and year, 200,000,000 troops are to be released to complete their hostile engagements against Israel and the returning Messiah and His army.

In the language of days gone by, the prophet John sees horses and riders clad with red, blue and yellow breastplates, and horses spewing fire, smoke and sulfur. In the physical world, modern military machinery—tanks; helicopters, bombers, missiles, etc. will release their fiery and destructive artillery.

As seen earlier in verse 15, Revelation 9:18 states "a third" of mankind will be killed by the three plagues of fire, smoke and sulfur; the "third" symbolism points to events in the Middle East (Ezekiel 5:2, 12, 14; Revelation 16:19). This signifies the death of millions in this short but forceful period of the trumpet plagues.

13. The remaining people on earth will not repent of their evil deeds (Revelation 9:20-21). What are their sins and the spotlight of their wickedness at the very end of time? _____

Demonic worship in the last days will increase through worldwide visions and apparitions—miraculous signs and wonders (Matthew 24:24; 2 Thessalonians 2:9; Revelation 13:13); and, along with it the adoration of Marian idols. When one gives reverence to any kind of icon—even religious idols admired within Catholicism, that individual is truly worshiping Satan and the demons that are behind the idolatry, according to the Scriptures. That's why the Ten Commandments specifically warn against shaping idols of anything, or anyone, in Heaven or on earth (Exodus 20:4-6).

In 1 Samuel 15:22-23 it says, "To obey is better than sacrifice, and to heed is better than the fat of rams. For rebellion is like the sin of divination, and arrogance like the evil of idolatry. Because you have rejected the word of the LORD, He has rejected you." Ezekiel 23:48 warns, "You will suffer the penalty for your lewdness and bear the consequences of your sins of idolatry. Then you will know that I am the Sovereign LORD."

The Word of God says in times past the Israelites "did wicked things that aroused the LORD's anger. They worshiped idols, though the LORD had said, "You shall not do this." The LORD warned Israel and Judah through all His prophets and seers: Turn from your evil ways. Observe My commands and decrees, in accordance with the entire Law that I commanded your ancestors to obey and that I delivered to you through My servants the prophets." But they would not listen and were as stiff-necked as their ancestors, who did not trust in the LORD their God. They rejected His decrees and the covenant He had made with their ancestors and the statutes He had warned them to keep. They followed worthless idols and themselves became worthless. They imitated the nations around them although the LORD had ordered them, "Do not do as they do," 2 Kings 17:11-15.

The warning is clear. Do not get involved in worthless idols; lifeless images do not see, hear or walk. Therefore, if an idol ever bleeds, weeps or begins to animate and move, then know that a demon is working through the gold, silver, bronze, stone or wood (Revelation 13:14-15). In addition to demonic worship, the wicked will also be involved in murders, sorcery (magic arts by the use of drugs, spiritual incantations, and psychic powers), sexual immorality (spread by the proliferation of pornographic content through every form of sexual sin, including homosexuality, incest and bestiality) and robberies. If men and women want to worship idols and demons, and commit abominable acts, then God will open the Abyss and give mankind the desire of their heart.

---NOTES---

Insights In Prophecy

Unlock The Ancient Mysteries Of Daniel & Revelation

BIBLE DISCOVERY SERIES

Lesson 17

THE MIGHTY SEVENTH ANGEL ANNOUNCES THE DAY OF ATONEMENT

Read Revelation 10

- **Reaffirm The Identity Of The Seventh Angel**
- **Examine The Events At The Voice Of God**

The Cruden's Concordance of the Holy Scriptures defines *angel* as: *"A messenger, or bringer of tidings, and is applied, [1] To those intellectual and immaterial beings, whom God makes use of as His ministers to execute the orders of providence, Rev. 22:8. [2] To Christ, who is the Mediator and Head of the church, Zech. 1:12, Revelation 10:1."* Not surprising, Alexander Cruden and many commentators throughout the centuries have identified the "Angel of the LORD" and the "Mighty Angel" of Revelation 10 to be a description of none other than the Savior—Jesus our Messiah. As often mentioned in our lesson series, we are rediscovering was the common view in the church prior to the 19th century that today unlocks some of the ancient mysteries of Daniel and Revelation.

"Michael is specially designated in early Jewish writings and very frequently in the Book of Enoch as "the prince of Israel" (שרם של ישראל), and in later Jewish writings... as "the advocate of the Jews," according to the Jewish Encyclopedia. Our studies of apocalyptic passages, particularly Daniel chapters 10-12, have also shown that *Michael the Archangel* is called Daniel's *"Prince"* and is associated with resurrection. However, this is no ordinary "malak"; this is the very Son of God—the WORD who has been with the Father from the beginning, and who is God (John 1:1-3). Whether Christ is called *Michael*, the *Mighty Angel*, or as we will see in this lesson the *Seventh Angel*, these titles help us understand the many roles our Savior performs in the redemption of mankind. In fact, the Hebrew Scriptures are full of names and titles assigned to Messiah, including mammals—the *Lion* and *Lamb* in Revelation 5:5-6 (see The Names/Titles of God in the Scriptures at the end of this lesson).

Judaism also teaches there are seven "Angels of the Presence" of God. One of the seven is known as Michael, whom Jews believe to be their special protector. Many times in the Old Testament the "Angel of the LORD" appeared to Abraham and Moses, and led the children of Israel into the Promised Land (Genesis 22:15-18; Hebrews 6:13; Judges 10:16; Zechariah 2:8; Exodus 14:19, 24; 23:20-23; 32:34; 33:14-15; Deuteronomy 1:32, 33; Acts 7:35-38). Jews attribute these events to Michael. Believers now credit many of these events to the person of Jesus Christ, referred to as the Angel of the LORD in the ancient Hebrew Scriptures. The "Angel of His [the Father's] Presence" is none other than Yeshua, the Son of God, clothed in the linen garment—our great High Priest, who has ever been with His people, protecting them by night, and leading them on to the Promised Land against all enemy opposition.

The prophet Isaiah wrote of Israel's savior and redeemer: "Surely they are My people [Israel], sons who will not be false to Me; and so He became their Savior. In all their distress He too was distressed, and the *Angel of His Presence saved* them. In His love and mercy, He *redeemed* them; He lifted them up and carried them all the days of old," Isaiah 63:8-9. Messiah tenderly cared for His beloved people—the Israelites (Exodus

19:4; Deuteronomy 1:31; 32:11-12; 33:27; Isaiah 46:4). Revelation 8:2 mentions "seven angels who stand before God," who are given "seven trumpets" that are to be blown during the Great Tribulation. Revelation 10, the focus of this lesson study, describes the Mighty Seventh Angel's descent to earth and His tremendous loud voice and trumpet blast. Gabriel is also understood to be among the seven angel messengers who stand in the presence of Almighty God. Luke 1:19 reads, "I am Gabriel. I *stand in the presence of God*." A Jew who reads the book of Revelation would understand the seven angels standing before God, who are given seven trumpets and bowl plagues, to be the seven "angels of the presence" among whom Gabriel and Michael would be numbered.

Michael is simply another name representative of the Savior, the Angel of the Presence, the Redeemer of Isaiah (63:8-9). In fact, there are nearly forty or so Scriptural passages involving the Angel of the LORD, which we later associate with the Archangel Michael; His work of protection, redemption and resurrection, and His military role as Commander of Heaven's armies—the LORD of hosts. Considering the events associated with the work of the Mighty Angel of Revelation 10, a few verses later identified as the Seventh Angel, we are left with only one conclusion: Michael is another name for Messiah, and His identity has been shrouded, at least in part, until the time of the unrolling of the scroll—the final period for the redemption of Israel.

All through the centuries to our present day, Judaism has held Michael in high esteem; in so doing, they have unknowingly been giving honor and respect to the prophesied Savior and Redeemer. On the other hand, Christians in the last 150 years have lost the clear connection between Michael and the true Messiah, which the Protestant founders held; in part, because some religions, such as the Jehovah's Witnesses, have distorted this truth by *falsely teaching* that since Michael is an Archangel He must be *created*, like all other angels. This is not true. Although often referred to as the Angel of the LORD and Michael, the Son of God has been with the Father from the beginning. Before this distortion became a modern day phenomenon in Protestant America, reformers and many theologians of ages past understood Michael to represent Messiah. Now its taboo; but, that doesn't diminish the evidence and truth laid out in the Scriptures.

Comparing Identities

In Daniel 12:1, Michael is said to stand up from the throne to usher in the time of trouble; and, in Revelation 10:1, the Mighty Seventh Angel is said to descend with loud voice and trumpet blast to end any further the delay in judgment. Compare the following descriptions in the Word of God; let the comparative Scriptures define the truth, not the naysayers.

Michael—the Mighty Angel with other Scriptural references describing Jesus:

Mighty Seventh Angel—Rev. 10	**Yeshua (Messiah)—Matthew 17:5; Rev. 4:3; 1:15-16**
"robed in cloud"	"cloud enveloped them"
"rainbow above His head"	"rainbow... encircled the throne"
"face was like the sun"	"face was like the sun shining"
"legs were like fiery pillars"	"feet were like bronze glowing"
"shout like the roar of lion"	"voice was like... rushing waters"

Michael—Daniel 10:6	**Yeshua (Messiah)—Revelation 1:12-16**
"face like lightning"	"face was like the sun shining"
"eyes like flaming torches"	"eyes were like blazing fire"
"arms... legs like... burnished bronze"	"feet were like bronze glowing in furnace"
"voice like the sound of a multitude"	"voice was like the sound of rushing waters"

Insights In Prophecy
Unlock The Ancient Mysteries Of Daniel & Revelation
BIBLE DISCOVERY SERIES

From Another Scholar's Point Of View

Matthew Henry's Commentary On The Whole Bible (1706-1721)
Revelation 10

Here we have an account of another vision the apostle was favoured with, between the sounding of the sixth trumpet and that of the seventh. And we observe,

I. The person who was principally concerned in communicating this discovery to John—an angel from heaven, *another mighty angel,* who is so set forth as would induce one to think it could be no other than our LORD and Saviour Jesus Christ! 1. He was *clothed with a cloud:* he veils his glory, which is too great for mortality to behold; and he throws a veil upon his dispensations. *Clouds and darkness are round about him.* 2. *A rainbow was upon his head;* he is always mindful of his covenant, and, when his conduct is most mysterious, yet it is perfectly just and faithful. 3. *His face was as the sun,* all bright, and full of lustre and majesty, ch. 1:16. 4. *His feet were as pillars of fire;* all his ways, both of grace and providence, are pure and steady.

II. His station and posture: *He set his right foot upon the sea and his left foot upon the earth,* to show the absolute power and dominion he had over the world. *And he held in his hand a little book opened,* probably the same that was before sealed, but was now opened, and gradually fulfilled by him.

III. His awful voice: *He cried aloud, as when a lion roareth* (v. 3), and his awful voice was echoed by *seven thunders,* seven solemn and terrible ways of discovering the mind of God.

IV. The prohibition given to the apostle, that he should not publish, but conceal what he had learned from the seven thunders, v. 4. The apostle was for preserving and publishing every thing he saw and heard in these visions, but the time had not yet come.

V. The solemn oath taken by this mighty angel. 1. The manner of his swearing: *He lifted up his hand to heaven, and swore by him that liveth for ever,* by himself, as God often has done, or by God as God, to whom he, as LORD, Redeemer, and ruler of the world, now appeals. 2. The matter of the oath: that *there shall be time no longer;* either, (1.) That there shall be now no longer delay in fulfilling the predictions of this book than till the last angel should sound; then every thing should be put into speedy execution: *the mystery of God shall be finished,* v. 7. Or, (2.) That when this mystery of God is finished time itself shall be no more, as being the measure of things that are in a mutable changing state; but all things shall be at length for ever fixed, and so time itself swallowed up in eternity.

Henry, M. 1996, c1991. *Matthew Henry's Commentary on the whole Bible : Complete and unabridged in one volume* . Hendrickson: Peabody

Insights In Prophecy
Unlock The Ancient Mysteries Of Daniel & Revelation
BIBLE DISCOVERY SERIES

The Glory & Voice Of The Seventh Angel

Near the end of the appointed times counting periods, John indicates the Great Tribulation is about to commence, and the work of the seven is revealed: "Out of the Temple came the seven angels with the seven plagues. They were dressed in clean, shining linen and wore golden sashes around their chests." Revelation 15:6.

Revelation 10, the focus of our study lesson, reveals in detail the activity of one of the seven Angels of His Presence. This Mighty Angel, the Redeemer, will make His way quickly from Heaven to earth on one truly eventful day—the Day of Visitation. Setting foot on land and sea, He will raise His right hand in magnificent power, and with trumpet blast and loud voice He will utter seven thunderous messages. All nature will respond—lightning, voices, thunder and a global earthquake. Prophecy predicts, in the days when the Seventh Angel is about to sound His trumpet, the mystery of God will be accomplished," Revelation 10:7. Realizing the Seventh Angel's magnificent manifestations (lightning, voices, thunder and earthquake) and His control over nature, this must be understood to be Yeshua, our Messiah.

The Seventh Angel's face will glow "like the sun," Revelation 10:1. The sun, moon and stars will not give their light, and then Jesus will light up this dark world with His bright radiance. This will be a glorious day for believers and the Scriptures speak of this day: "Although the earth gives way and the mountains fall into the heart of the sea... God will help her at *break of day*. Nations are in uproar, kingdoms fall; *He lifts His voice*, the earth melts. God almighty is with us; the God of Jacob is our fortress," Psalms 46:2-7. "The

sun and moon will be darkened, and the stars no longer shine. The *LORD will roar from Zion* and *thunder* from Jerusalem; the earth and the sky will tremble. But the LORD will be a refuge for His people, a stronghold for the people of Israel," Joel 3:15-16. "The LORD roars from Zion and thunders from Jerusalem," says Amos 1:2. Messiah will not enter the New Jerusalem until He has entered the earthly Jerusalem to punish her for her sins. Messiah the Shekinah will shine forth with blinding brilliance, and Almighty God's final cleansing of the Holy of Holies and the whole universe will begin in earnest.

Upon the arrival of the Day of the LORD, it will be too late for repentance: "The Lion hath roared, who will not fear? The LORD God hath spoken, who can but prophesy?... in the Day that I shall visit the transgression of Israel upon him I will also visit the altars... and the horns of the altar shall be cut off, and fall to the ground," Amos 3:8, 14 (KJV). "Woe to you who long for the Day of the LORD! Why do you long for the Day of the LORD? That Day will be darkness, not light... Will not the Day of the LORD be darkness, not light—pitch-dark, without a ray of brightness? I hate, I despise your religious feasts... you have lifted up the shrine of your king [Antichrist], the pedestal of your idols, the star of your god—which you made for yourselves," Amos 5:18, 20-21, 26.

1. Revelation 10:1 tells of the Mighty Angel's descent to earth. Who is said to descend from Heaven to call forth the righteous from their graves (1 Thessalonians 4:16)? _____

The "LORD Himself" will "come down" with a "loud command, with the voice of the Archangel [Michael] and with the [seventh] trumpet call of God, and the dead in Christ will rise first."

It is Messiah's descent, His loud command, His voice as the Archangel, and His trumpet call that raises the dead. The Archangel's voice is not in addition to Messiah's voice, but rather is one and the same voice. Christ is the Archangel (Hebrew *arkˈeɪndʒəl*)—the Highest Messenger (*"Malak"*). The term "archangel" appears only twice in the Hebrew Scriptures: in Jude 9 at the resurrection of Moses, where it is applied to Michael, and in 1 Thessalonians 4:16, where the Archangel's loud voice raises the dead.

We see in Paul's description the same climax as is found in Revelation 10—the Mighty Angel, with loud voice and seventh trumpet. In addition, the identical event is also found in Daniel 12:1-3, 7, where Michael [Messiah] stands and descends to raise the dead. There He is found above the waters of the Tigris (Daniel 10:4-6), at the time when the Great Tribulation is about to commence (Daniel 12:1).   For further study: Psalms 17:13-15; 18:7-15; Job 19:25-27; 21:30.

2. How do we know it is Messiah's voice that calls the dead back to life at the resurrection (John 5:25-29)? _____

The dead will hear the voice of the Son of God, and they will be raised to live eternally.

3. Jesus has in His hand a "little scroll" opened in Revelation 10:2 as though ready to reveal its contents. What book's content is to be sealed until the end of time (Daniel 12:4)? _____

Daniel's book was sealed, but the good news is the book of Revelation—the testimony of Jesus Christ, was ordained and written to unlock Daniel's visions. Messiah's unfolding plan was first written in the Book of Truth before time began (Daniel 10:21; Psalm 139:16), and this gives us hope in Messiah's salvation as we pray for His return in our day and for the Holy Spirit to guide us moment by moment.

4. The fact that the scroll was "opened" in His hand says what? _____

The Book of Truth, revealed in Daniel's sealed visions and events, would finally be understood, for the mysterious events themselves are about to unfold. While the visions were sealed by Michael in Daniel 12:4, at the time of the end they are promised to be unsealed and revealed, with all the Book's mysteries completely fulfilled during the days of the voice of the Seventh Angel, when He begins to sound.

5. What is symbolized by the Mighty Angel planting securely His feet—the right on the sea and the left foot on the land? _____

The planting of both feet indicates complete control over all creation, seen and unseen, angelic and physical. Revelation 20:13 describes a future resurrection where the "sea gave up the dead that were in it, and death and Hades [the grave] gave up the dead that were in them." His people are gathered, whether in the earth or in the sea, as there is no hiding place where God cannot find the dead when He calls for them. The neutrons and atoms respond to His voice, and merge together once again to form the bodies of His saints.

6. The Mighty Seventh Angel will shout "like the roar of a lion," upon His arrival to earth (Revelation 10:3). How does this compare with the miracle of the Archangel's voice? _____

_____

1 Thessalonians 4:16 says the "voice of the Archangel" will call forth the "dead" to life.

7. Consider the following verses; how do they help identify the Mighty Messenger and the time of His powerful voice?

Amos 3:8 _____

Job 37:1-5 _____

Psalms 46 _____

Job 37:1-5 _____

Jeremiah 25:29-33 _____

Hosea 11:9-10 _____

Micah 1:3-5 _____

Amos wrote that the Sovereign LORD's voice is like "the lion has roared." Job wrote, "Listen to the roar of His voice... He unleashes lightning... and sends it to the ends of the earth... the sound of His roar; He thunders

with His majestic voice... God's voice thunders in marvelous ways." The song of Psalms speaks of a great earthquake, mountains falling into the sea causing it to "roar and foam... nations are in uproar, kingdoms fall; He lifts His voice, the earth melts."

The voice of God will shake Planet Earth and bring those on it to their knees, but it will be too late for repentance. Other prophets wrote of that time when God will stand up for battle and descend to earth with thunderous voice to visit the sins of the people. Revelation 10:3 says when the Seventh Angel shouts "the voices of seven thunders spoke," (NIV), or "seven thunders uttered their voices," (KJV).

8. Read Psalm 29 below. The seven voices of thunders that cause powerful events on earth are assigned to whom? _____

Verse

1   Psalm 29 A psalm of David.

1   Ascribe to the LORD, O mighty ones, ascribe to the LORD glory and strength.

2   Ascribe to the LORD the glory due His name; worship the LORD in the splendor of His holiness.

3   The **[1]** voice of the LORD is over the waters [sea]; the God of glory **thunders, the LORD thunders** over the mighty waters.

4   The **[2]** voice of the LORD is powerful [loud]; the **[3]** voice of the LORD is majestic.

5   The **[4]** voice of the LORD breaks the cedars [with mighty winds]; the LORD breaks in pieces the cedars of Lebanon.

6   He makes Lebanon skip like a calf [with mighty earthquake], Sirion like a young wild ox.

7   The **[5]** voice of the LORD strikes with *flashes of lightning*.

8   The **[6]** voice of the LORD shakes [with mighty earthquake] the desert; the LORD shakes the Desert of Kadesh.

9   The **[7]** voice of the LORD twists the oaks and strips the forests bare [with mighty winds]. And in His Temple all cry, "Glory!"

10   The LORD sits enthroned over the flood; the LORD is enthroned as King forever.

11   The LORD gives strength to His people; the LORD blesses His people with peace.

"The voice of the LORD is... 1) "over the waters; the God of glory thunders, the LORD thunders over the mighty waters"; 2)"powerful"; 3) "majestic"; 4) "breaks the cedars"; 5) "strikes with flashes of lightning"; 6)

"shakes the desert"; 7) and "twists the oaks and strips the forest bare." The "LORD is enthroned as King forever," after which the seven thunderous voices are heard, and all nature is moved at His cry.

In Revelation 10:4 the seven thunders represent *seven important messages from our Messiah King*, for John was about the write down the content when a voice from Heaven declared, "seal up what the seven thunders have said and do not write it down." Therefore, we know that when the Seventh Angel descends with the voice of God, the content of these seven secret messages will be made manifest.

Who will hear His voice? The dead in Christ will hear the voice of the Archangel, for they will be raised to life—a great multitude that no man can number. However, the seven messages are also for the 144,000 who are alive and will remain a short time longer to endure the Great Tribulation, but who have been sealed for protection. The wicked will hear deafening thunder but will not likely perceive the content of the announcements. Once before the voice of God was heard when the Son of Man was to be glorified, but the crowd did not understand the message. John 12:28-29 says, "Then came there a voice from heaven, saying, I have both glorified it, and will glorify it again. The people, therefore, that stood by, and heard it, said that it thundered: others said, An angel spake to Him."

Jesus blended the glorification of His death with His glorification at His visitation in Revelation 10, when He said: "Now is the time for judgment on this world; now the prince of this world [Satan] will be driven out. But I, when I am lifted up from the earth [both in crucifixion and glorification—Daniel 12:6-7], will draw all men to Myself," John 28:31-32; in other words, "receive you unto Myself; that where I am, there you may be also," John 14:3.

In Revelation 10:5 the Seventh Angel raised His *right hand* to Heaven and swore an oath. In Daniel 12:6 Michael raised His right and left hands to Heaven and swore that "It will be for a time, times and half a time [1,260 days]. When the power of the holy people has been finally broken, all these things [Daniel's prophetic events] will be *completed*."

9. According to Psalm 98:1-2, 9, when Jesus our Messiah begins to reign, how will victory be obtained, and when will He raise His arm in triumph, power and glory? _____

The Day of He raises His "right hand... His holy arm," marvelous things will be done and He will "reveal His righteousness to the nations" of the whole world. He will come to judge the earth. "He will judge the world in righteousness and the peoples with equity on that Day [of the LORD]."

10. The Seventh Angel vows no further delay, according to Revelation 10:6, in whose name? _____
_____

He raises His hand in sworn commitment to mankind that there will be no further delay in the fulfillment of prophecy when He descends to earth. He swears by the name of the Creator who fashioned Heaven, earth and sea and all that exists in them. He swears on His own good name, for there no one greater than Himself.

There is nothing that will remain outside the LORD's dominion, for it is He who "in six days... made the heavens and the earth, the sea, and all that is in them," Exodus 20:11.

11. To Whom does the Bible give credit for all of creation (John 1:1-4; Hebrews 1:2; Colossians 1:13-16; Ephesians 3:9)? _____

All things were made by the Son of God; He who spoke them into existence. By giving oath on His own authority, He swears the reunification of all creation into one—the eternal Kingdom of God.

12. Compare Genesis 22:15-18 to Hebrews 6:13 below. What can we learn? _____
_____

"The *Angel of the LORD* called to Abraham from heaven a second time and said, *"I swear by Myself, declares the LORD*, that because you have done this and have not withheld your son, your only son, I will surely bless you and make your descendants as numerous as the stars in the sky and as the sand on the seashore. Your descendants will take possession of the cities of their enemies, and through your offspring all nations on earth will be blessed, because you have obeyed Me," Genesis 22:15-18. The Hebrew writer states, "When *God* made His promise to Abraham, since there was no one greater for Him to swear by, *He swore by Himself,"* Hebrews 6:13. The Angel of the LORD, later identified as God, Messiah our Creator, made the sworn oath of promise to Abraham that he and his seed would be blessed.

13. Therefore, because He could swear by no one greater, who did He swear by? _____

He "swore by Himself."

God through Christ has a long history of swearing on His good Name. Consider the following texts: Genesis 24:7; 26:3; 50:24; Exodus 13:5; Numbers 32:10; Judges 2:1; Psalms 95:11; Jeremiah 22:5; Amos 6:8; Luke 1:73. Only God can swear, knowing what is promised will come to pass. In Revelation 10:6 the Mighty Angel vows that "there will be no more delay!" for the final fulfillment of prophecy and judgment of God. Michael, the *man* clothed in linen, swore similarly in Daniel 12:7 in a prophecy directed at the end of time and the Great Tribulation (vs. 1-2).

14. What time frame is involved in Daniel 12:7? _____

Michael, dressed in High Priest linen for the Day of Atonement (Yom Kippur) announcement, swears that when the "time, times and half a time" [1,260 days] are over "all these things [prophetic predictions] will be completed." Once the 1,260 days are finished, we can know assuredly that all prophetic mysteries will soon be over and Christ will finish His work in righteousness. Days and nights will be shortened and the celestial skies altered, so that the normal measurement of time is impossible (Isaiah 24:19-29; Daniel 2:21-22); therefore, man cannot know the day or hour of Messiah's climactic return, which is in the Father's hands.

15. What does the Angel promise in Revelation 10:7? _____

When the Seventh Angel is about to sound His trumpet, or as the King James reads, "in the days of the voice of the Seventh Angel," the mystery of God should be finished. In other words, when the Mighty Angel shouts with "a loud voice" as a lion roaring and "seven thunders" are heard around the globe, then mankind can know the end is upon them.

Revelation 10:7 notes this declaration of *"no more delay"* has already been *"announced to His servants the prophets."* We know the prophet Daniel both saw and heard Michael give a similar declaration in Daniel 12:7 hundreds of years earlier. Amos wrote of this day: "Surely the *Sovereign LORD does nothing without revealing His plan to His servants the prophets.* The Lion has roared who will not fear? The Sovereign LORD has spoken—who can but prophesy?" Amos 3:7-8.

16. Who does Daniel see standing on each side of the river, one of whom asked the question just *how long* before these astonishing events of Daniel are *fulfilled*? _____

Daniel saw "two others" who overheard Michael's vow of time (Daniel 12:5-7). Many have assumed these two to be angels, but prophecy is more specific. They are the two "servants the prophets," who in Revelation are always identified as the two witnesses—Moses and Elijah, whom Revelation 10:7 declares heard the sworn announcement of fulfillment hundreds of years earlier.

Matthew 17:2-3 relays an important event 2,000 years ago in the lives of Peter, James and John. Jesus took these three disciples aside and into a mountain. Although Yeshua looked like an ordinary Jewish man, He was about to show His closest companions a glimpse of His future glory. On the Mount of Transfiguration Christ displayed His Messianic glory and "His face shown like the sun." The Seventh Angel of Revelation 10, whom we know to be our Messiah, also comes down to earth in His future glory and "His face was like the sun," (v. 1). The three disciples were taken into the future to this very day spoken of in Revelation 10.

In the Transfiguration Moses and Elijah stood beside Jesus; in Revelation 11:4 these two are identified as the "two olive trees... that stand before the LORD of the earth." The two olive trees are first found in Zechariah 4:11-14 where the promise is made, "not by might, nor by power, but by My Spirit saith the LORD of hosts," (v. 6, KJV). The prophet Zechariah asked the Angel the identity of the "two olive trees" or "olive branches" on each side of the lampstand. He replied, "These are the two who are anointed to serve the LORD of all the earth" (NIV); or, "these are the two anointed ones, that stand by the LORD of the whole earth," (v. 14, KJV). These two were taken to Heaven early for a purpose: Elijah was transported directly to Heaven without experiencing death (2 Kings 2:11), and Moses was raised from the dead by Michael (Jude 9) and taken to Heaven, where each prophet stands as servant beside Christ in the Temple of God.

Because these two prophets are intimately involved in the final events through their personal ministry back on earth during the appointed time of the end, and because they will eventually give their lives in martyrdom (Revelation 11:3-12), they would personally witness the visions that Daniel received about the end of the age. That's why Daniel saw these two witnesses standing on each side of Michael on opposite banks of the river (Daniel 12:6-7). Noteworthy is the fact that the exact period which Michael gives as to the duration of the end-time events (time, times and half—1,260 days) is exactly the length of their earth-bound ministry during the last days—1,260 days (Revelation 11:3).

17. When the Seventh Angel sounds with a loud roaring voice and trumpet call, will His voice be heard on one day or during many "days"? _____

The verse says "in the days" when the voice of God is heard, then the mystery of God will be finished. His voice initiates the Day of the LORD and continues through the Great Tribulation, which will bring an end to all sin and usher in everlasting righteousness.

18. Once again, what specific event is associated with the descent of the Archangel from Heaven, His loud shout with trumpet call and the end of the age (1 Thessalonians 4:16)? _____

Paul reveals the LORD Himself will descend from Heaven with a "loud command" or "shout"—whose "voice [is] of the Archangel" Michael, and with His "trumpet" blast "the dead in Christ" will be raised to life. Daniel

12:1-2 connects Michael to this very resurrection as well, which leads to the Day of Visitation, the Great Tribulation and the end of the age. Moreover, He is specifically identified as the Life-giver in Jude 9, because it was "the Archangel Michael" who raised Moses to life centuries before, so that he, along with Elijah, might stand beside the LORD of the earth and complete the final warnings to mankind.

In Revelation 10:8-11 John was directed to take the little book of wrath and eat it up. Although sweet to his taste, it was bitter to his stomach. The prophet Ezekiel had a similar experience.

19. What does the scroll symbolize in Ezekiel 2:7-10? _____

Words of lament and mourning and woe, indicative of judgment.

Although the scroll tastes of sweet victory over evil, it did not set well with the prophet John. The scroll represents the unsealed judgments of Daniel signified in the trumpet and vials plagues of Revelation—the divine wrath of God against sinners. However, by eating the scroll the prophet's words were no longer his own, but the judgment call given by God to him. Jesus commissioned His seventy witnesses as He sent them out with this proclamation: "He who listens to you listens to Me; he who rejects you rejects Me; but he who rejects Me rejects Him [Father] who sent Me," Luke 10:16. Prophets are God's mouthpiece, and through them by God's Spirit "when He, the Spirit of truth, comes, He will guide you into all truth... He will tell you what is yet to come," John 16:13.

Peter announced the Day of the LORD with these words, "Repent, then and turn to God, so that your sins may be wiped out [of the books], that times of refreshing [rain—a storming downpour upon our parched planet] may come from the LORD, and that He may send the Christ [to earth on the Day of Visitation], Who has been appointed for you—even Jesus. He must remain in Heaven until the time comes for God to *restore everything* ["redeem" as in the Year of Jubilee—Leviticus 25:8-10, 23-30], as He promised long ago through His holy prophets. For Moses said, 'The LORD your God will raise up for you a Prophet [Yeshua] like me from among your own people [Israel]; you must listen to everything He tells you. Anyone who does not listen to Him will be completely *cut off* [as in the Day of Atonement and trumpet of Jubilee—Leviticus 23:27-29] from among His people," Acts 3:19-23.

Jesus said when you see Jerusalem surrounded by vast armies, then "stand up and lift up your heads, because your *redemption* is drawing near," Luke 21:28; the time of the "redemption of our bodies" to be transformed into glorified eternal stars (Romans 8:23; Daniel 12:3). However, for all the disturbing visions John the Revelator had seen so far, there were still more to come. He felt a sickening ill, but he "must prophesy again about many peoples, nations, languages and kings," Revelation 10:11; he couldn't pause or stop listening, for there was more revelations to come. In fact, he was promptly handed a measuring rod and was told to "go and measure the Temple of God," Revelation 11:1. The prophet Daniel had similar experiences; he was also troubled and became sick due to the visions he saw about the end of time (Daniel 7:15, 28; 8:27), but could not understand... to his dismay.

The prophet John had no idea just how far reaching his scroll of prophecies would travel in space and time. Written primarily to the seven churches, his ancient scroll of prophecies has been preserved throughout the centuries by God's divine hand, and its warnings read, studied, loved and contested. However, its dire warnings will spread around the globe, for it is the counsel from Messiah Himself to a troubled world—the testimony of Jesus Christ (Revelation 1:1-3). Along with the prophetic messages of Daniel and Revelation, the proclamation of God's Kingdom will "be preached in the whole world as a testimony to all nations, and then the end will come," Matthew 24:14; the mystery of God will be finished, just as He has promised so long ago. Today, we see but a poor reflection; but then, we will see Messiah face to face (1 Corinthians 13:12). We will know God personally and all questions will melt away. What a day!

Names/Titles for God in the Scriptures

Advocate (1 John 2:1)
Almighty (Rev. 1:8; Mt. 28:18)
Alpha and Omega (Rev. 1:8; 22:13)
Angel of the LORD (Judges 2:1-4)
Amen (Rev. 3:14)
Apostle of our Profession (Heb. 3:1)
Atoning Sacrifice for our Sins (1 John 2:2)
Author of Life (Acts 3:15)
Author and Perfecter of our Faith (Heb. 12:2)
Author of Salvation (Heb. 2:10)
Beginning and End (Rev. 22:13)
Blessed and only Ruler (1 Tim. 6:15)
Bread of God (John 6:33)
Bread of Life (John 6:35; 6:48)
Capstone (Acts 4:11; 1 Pet. 2:7)
Chief Cornerstone (Eph. 2:20)
Chief Shepherd (1 Pet. 5:4)
Christ (1 John 2:22)
Creator (John 1:3)
Deliverer (Rom. 11:26)
Eternal Life (1 John 1:2; 5:20)
Everlasting Father (Isa. 9:6)
Gate (John 10:9)
Faithful and True (Rev. 19:11)
Faithful Witness (Rev. 1:5)
Faith and True Witness (Rev. 3:14)
First and Last (Rev. 1:17; 2:8; 22:13)
Firstborn From the Dead (Rev. 1:5)
God (John 1:1; 20:28; Heb. 1:8; Rom. 9:5; 2 Pet. 1:1;1 John 5:20; etc.)
Good Shepherd (John 10:11,14)
Great Shepherd (Heb. 13:20)
Great High Priest (Heb. 4:14)
Head of the Church (Eph. 1:22; 4:15; 5:23)
Heir of all things (Heb. 1:2)
High Priest (Heb. 2:17)
Holy and True (Rev. 3:7)
Holy One (Acts 3:14)
Hope (1 Tim. 1:1)
Hope of Glory (Col. 1:27)
Horn of Salvation (Luke 1:69)
I Am (John 8:58)
Image of God (2 Cor. 4:4)
King Eternal (1 Tim. 1:17)
King of Israel (John 1:49)

Insights In Prophecy
Unlock The Ancient Mysteries Of Daniel & Revelation
BIBLE DISCOVERY SERIES

King of the Jews (Mt. 27:11)
King of kings (1 Tim 6:15; Rev. 19:16)
King of the Ages (Rev. 15:3)
Lamb (Rev. 13:8)
Lamb of God (John 1:29)
Lamb Without Blemish (1 Pet. 1:19)
Last Adam (1 Cor. 15:45)
Life (John 14:6; Col. 3:4)
Light of the World (John 8:12)
Lion of the Tribe of Judah (Rev. 5:5)
Living One (Rev. 1:18)
Living Stone (1 Pet. 2:4)
Lord (2 Pet. 2:20)
Lord of All (Acts 10:36)
Lord of Glory (1 Cor. 2:8)
Lord of lords (Rev. 19:16)
LORD [YHWH] our Righteousness (Jer. 23:6)
Man from Heaven (1 Cor. 15:48)
Mediator of the New Covenant (Heb. 9:15)
Messenger of the Covenant (Mal. 3:1)
Michael (Dan. 12:7; Jude 9)
Mighty Angel (Rev. 10:1)
Mighty God (Isa. 9:6)
Morning Star (Rev. 22:16)
Offspring of David (Rev. 22:16)
Only Begotten Son of God (John 1:18; 1 John 4:9)
Our Great God and Savior (Titus 2:13)
Our Holiness (1 Cor. 1:30)
Our Husband (2 Cor. 11:2)
Our Protection (2 Thess. 3:3)
Our Redemption (1 Cor. 1:30)
Our Righteousness (1 Cor. 1:30)
Our Sacrificed Passover Lamb (1 Cor. 5:7)
Power of God (1 Cor. 1:24)
Precious Cornerstone (1 Pet. 2:6)
Prince of Peace (Isa. 9:6)
Prophet (Acts 3:22)
Resurrection and Life (John 11:25)
Righteous Branch (Jer. 23:5)
Righteous One (Acts 7:52; 1 John 2:1)
Rock (1 Cor. 10:4)
Root of David (Rev. 5:5; 22:16)
Ruler of God's Creation (Rev. 3:14)
Ruler of the Kings of the Earth (Rev. 1:5)
Savior (Eph. 5:23; Titus 1:4; 3:6; 2 Pet. 2:20)
Seventh Angel (Rev. 10:7)
Son of David (Lk. 18:39)
Son of God (John 1:49; Heb. 4:14)
Son of Man (Mt. 8:20)
Son of the Most High God (Lk. 1:32)

Source of Eternal Salvation for all who obey him (Heb. 5:9)
The One Mediator (1 Tim. 2:5)
The Stone the builders rejected (Acts 4:11)
True Bread (John 6:32)
True Light (John 1:9)
True Vine (John 15:1)
Truth (John 1:14; 14:6)
Way (John 14:6)
Wisdom of God (1 Cor. 1:24)
Wonderful Counselor (Isa. 9:6)
Word (John 1:1)
Word of God (Rev. 19:13)

---- **NOTES**----

LORD OF HOSTS

לורד ופ הוסתס

Lesson 18

THE TWO WITNESSES: THEIR PASSOVER CONNECTION

Read Revelation 11:1-14

- Probe The Identity Of The Two Witnesses
- Consider Why Their Deaths Release Antichrist To Enter Jerusalem's Temple

The events portrayed in Revelation 11 are, in part, an unsealing and further clarification of Daniel 9:24-27, and the segment of time found there—the 70 Weeks (490 days). Revelation 11 relates to Jerusalem and the rebuilding of the end-time Temple (vs. 1-2), the appointed time (3½ year) counting period and testimony by the two witnesses, the cutting off in death of these two in the city streets (vs. 3-12), and the desolation of Jerusalem's holy site (v. 13) and the beloved city at large at the end of the age, as the Great Tribulation commences (vs. 15-19).

In similar manner, the 70 Weeks (490 days) prophecy of Daniel 9 reveals the appointed times and events surrounding Israel and Jerusalem (v. 24), the rebuilding of at least a partial Temple (v. 25), the cutting off of God's anointed (v. 26)—the death of one of the two witnesses (Elijah), and the desolation of Jerusalem and Temple Mount at the end of the age during the Great Tribulation (vs. 26-27).

Late in the counting periods, an official decree/declaration will be issued to rebuild an earthquake/war-torn Jerusalem, after the city is shaken by devastation as the end-time counting periods begin: "It [Jerusalem] will be rebuilt with streets and trench [water system], but in times of trouble," (Daniel 9:25) during the 70 Weeks prophecy. For "sixty-two 'sevens,' [434 days]" the construction will be underway; but in the middle of the last 7 days that end the 490 day prophecy, the "*anointed one* will be *cut off* and *but not for himself*," Daniel 9:26 (NIV f26).

Paul wrote about this very situation: "The [anointed] one who now holds it [lawlessness] back will continue to do so till he [anointed one—Elijah] is *taken out of the way* [martyred]. And then the lawless one [Antichrist] will be revealed [by stepping onto the Temple Mount in Jerusalem; and, declaring himself "God"], whom the LORD Jesus will overthrow... by the splendor of His coming," 2 Thessalonians 4:7-8.

As we learned in our last lesson, Revelation 10 depicts that future day of wrath when the Mighty Seventh Angel will "come down" from Heaven and will stand on both land and sea. All nature will respond when the Archangel's voice is heard, when His seven thunderous messages resound and shake Planet Earth. Revelation 11 is a continuation of the parenthesis (clarifying comments) that foretells events that lead up to the seventh trumpet and the Day of the LORD at verse 15, where we once again find the Seventh Angel at work with great voices and the momentous events that culminate with His loud cry.

Now we focus on Revelation 11. John had just eaten the sweet scroll of lamentations that left him with an upset stomach (10:11), now he was given a measuring device and was told to "go and measure the Temple of God and the altar, and count the worshipers there," (11:1). Measuring denotes building and/or measuring moral judgment, with special attention given to details and the assessment of the worshipers within the Temple.

Insights In Prophecy
Unlock The Ancient Mysteries Of Daniel & Revelation
BIBLE DISCOVERY SERIES

Measuring The Temple

1. What does measuring generally precede? _____

Measuring precedes construction. No doubt John understood the Temple, which lay in ruins in Jerusalem (around 90 A.D.), would one day be rebuilt, at least in part. Attention was to be given to the inner area of the Temple, while the outer court did not need to be measured for it will be trampled on by the Gentiles (outside the walls of the diagram below).

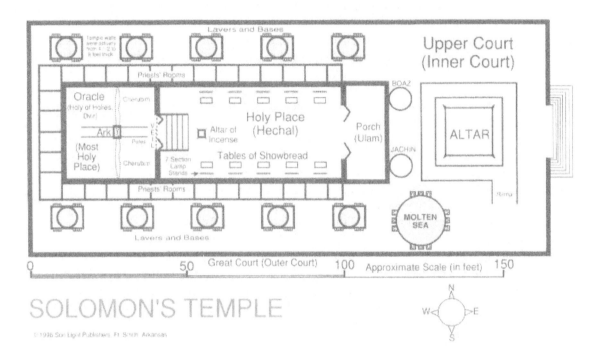

SOLOMON'S TEMPLE

After every meal many Jews pray the *amidah* with the petition added, "May it be Thy will that the Temple be rebuilt soon in our days." A rebuilt Temple is a sign in Judaism that the Messianic Age is at hand, as well as a signal to followers of Yeshua that the abominable event is about to take place.

2. Luke wrote, "Jerusalem will be trampled on by the Gentiles until the times of the Gentiles are fulfilled," (21:24). How long did the prophet John indicate the trampling of Jerusalem by the Gentile army would last (Revelation 11:2)? _____

The Gentile army will trample on the holy city for 42 months, equal to 1,260 days—about 3½ years.

The only way a modern-day Temple could be built on the Temple Mount is for the current status to change. This comes about by a devastating quake, which could happen anytime, whereby the current Temple Mount and structures drop into a pile of rubble. The political turmoil between Israelis and Muslims will escalate over this and will create the need for Gentile armies (3rd party) to surround the area for protection of the relics that remain in the debris in a long-term peace-keeping mission.

According to Luke 21:24-25, the *forty-two* (42) months lead eventually to the "signs in the sun, moon and stars and... men will faint from terror, apprehensive of what is coming on the world, for the heavenly bodies will be shaken." This number does not catch the attention of Gentile believers, but for Jews, *forty-two* is significant. Mystic (Kabbalah) Jews associate the "forty-two" (42) letter Name of God to the following: 1) God at creation, 2) the "visible" revelation of God at Mt. Sinai, 3) the eastern gate, 4) the arrival of the Messiah, and 5) the Shekinah coming to its final destination—the Tabernacle/Temple in the land of Jerusalem. In this regard, the *forty-two* (42) months mark off the prophetic time that Yeshua, the Creator, the Angel of the Covenant of Mt. Sinai, Messiah ben David, the Shekinah, will arrive from the east to His Temple in Jerusalem to deal with the evil foe who has entered onto the Temple Mount to proclaim himself "God".

John is told to measure the worshipers, implying protection from desecration during the trial. A spiritual aspect is also implied by the measurement of the inner Temple, where God dwells. How do worshipers express respect and show moral judgment? As we come into His presence, we need to address Yahweh with an attitude of awe. The twenty-four elders, representative of the redeemed, fall down with faces to the ground before Almighty. For us, bowing in this manner is certainly appropriate in showing honor to the Creator of the Universe, for He deserves our respect and prostrate humility in times of earnest prayer.

In addition, we need to consider the work of God in the Holy of Holies during the appointed time. In prophecy there are distinct activities noted that deserve our attention as well, as we evaluate the prophetic work in the inner Temple of God in Heaven. Therefore, we are to keep His commandments (John 14:15; 1 John 3:19-24), represented by the Ark of the Covenant and the Decalogue within, in the Most Holy Place beyond the veil; and, understand the sanctuary autumn Festival celebrations and their end-time fulfillment—the events that end *The Kingdom Calendar*.

3. In studying the events occurring in the Holy of Holies in Heaven and on earth during the last days, why is our sincere reverence and allegiance towards God especially merited at the end of time (Daniel 7: 9, 10, 13, 14, 21-22, 26-27)? _____

In Heaven, the Books of evidence are going to be opened and a very serious end-time courtroom drama will unfold. The Ancient of Days (Father) will sit upon His throne, a court of judgment will be called into session with books opened. The evidence will show that the Son of Man has the right to the Kingdom; but before the final judgment is rendered in favor of the overcomers, there will be many trials during the appointed times. During this period, the court will sit, the Beast's power will eventually be taken away and destroyed, and the Kingdom will be given to the saints of the Most High God.

Every individual must take one side or the other in the controversy: accepting the mark to buy and sell; thereby, trusting in men and not God; or, refusing the mark, and thereby, trust by faith in God's provision, whether that be feast or famine (see Revelation 13:16-17; 14:9, 11; 16:2; 19:20; 20:4). This culminates during the days of Heaven's judgment, and will determine each person's standing with God, for our actions will speak louder than our words. Will we trust God to care for us when we can't buy and sell? Yeshua said if we deny Him before men, He will deny us before the Father in Heaven. If we take the mark of the beast, we are openly admitting we don't have a personal faith-filled relationship with Jesus Christ, and do not trust Him as our Savior and LORD. When Messiah returns, the separation between saint and sinner will be complete: as John wrote, He will be "judging the dead [those worthy of resurrection]... and rewarding... your servants and those who reverence [His] name... and destroying those who destroy the earth," Revelation 11:18-19.

4. John was told to measure the altar (Revelation 11:1); what event will occur at the end of this courtroom drama that involves one of the altars (Revelation 8:3-5)? _____

Insights In Prophecy
Unlock The Ancient Mysteries Of Daniel & Revelation
BIBLE DISCOVERY SERIES

The two altars in the ancient Temple area provided means for 1) daily sacrifices, and 2) prayers represented by the altar of incense. These two symbolize that many believers will be sacrificed for their faith during the last days, as the final prayers of worship are being heard. Paul wrote, "Therefore, I urge you, brothers and

 sisters, in view of God's mercy, to offer your bodies as a living sacrifice, holy and pleasing to God—this is your true and proper worship," Romans 12:1. The end-time sacrifices may include our own necks, as lambs for the slaughter.

However, the guilty verdict will be pronounced against the Lawless One and his murderous gangs. Fire will be taken from the altar of incense in Heaven to be "hurled" to the earth. John saw "huge hailstones of about a hundred pounds each" piercing earth's atmosphere in a fiery plague upon mankind, when the verdict of the courtroom drama in Heaven becomes living reality on earth; then, the seven angels will be released

with God's trumpets and vial plagues.

5. The Word says the outer court and Jerusalem will be trampled upon by Gentiles for 42 months, meaning 1,260 days. To what evil leader does prophecy assign the 42 months or a "time [one year], times [two years] and half a time [one-half year]," (Daniel 7:25-26; Revelation 13:5-8)? _____

The "little horn" (prominent leader associated with a very small country), also known as the "beast" (a demonic force housed in human form) and commonly referred to as Antichrist, who will speak against and blaspheme the Most High, will persecute believers. He will try to change set times of spiritual rest and worship, along with religious Festivities—the very laws of God.

As already mentioned, *forty-two* (42) is a significant number in Jewish Mysticism, although the book of Revelation is dismissed as a fable and the true Messiah belied by this same group. Nonetheless, Kabbalists have taught that the number *forty-two* is associated with the timing of significant events, and there are *forty-two* segments of the Israelites journey in the wilderness, and this period leads to their arrival in the Promised Land. Thus, the final *forty-two* months of the end-times encompass events when the twelve tribes of Israel seek the true Yeshua—Messiah and His salvation. There are *forty-two* generations between Adam and Yeshua, as presented by Matthew's New Testament book. Again, with Messiah on earth delivered as a male child through the linage of Abraham, we have the symbolism of bringing unity from above to earth below though *forty-two* generations: "Thus there were fourteen generations in all from Abraham to David, fourteen from David to the exile to Babylon, and fourteen from the exile to the Christ," Matthew 1:17.

The number *forty-two* (42) also shows up in other Kabbalah mystical teachings. It's believed the "unifying of above and below" may be seen in the rod of Moses... This rod is said to have the name of *forty-two* letters engraved upon it: "And in the Egyptian's hand was a spear like a weaver's beam" (I Chr. XI, 23). This alludes to the divine rod which was in Moses' hand, and on which there was engraved the divine ineffable Name radiating in various combinations of letters. These same letters were in possession of Bezalel, who was called "weaver", and his school, as it is written: "Them hath he filled with wisdom of heart... of the craftsman and the skilled workman, and the weaver, etc." (Exod. XXXV, 35). So that rod had engraved on it the ineffable Name on every side, in *forty-two* various combinations, which were illumined in different colours," Soncino Zohar, Bereshith, Section 1, Page 9. This leads to our next segment—the two anointed witnesses of the last days.

The Two Anointed Ones

6. What is Heaven's response to Satan's overwhelming deceptions and the Beast's evil activities during the last 42 months (1,260 days) of human history? (Revelation 11:3)? _____

188

God will appoint power to His two witnesses, and they will prophesy for 1,260 days, clothed in garments of sackcloth—the attire of mourning and sadness (2 Samuel 3:31).

7. Who are the two anointed ones likely to be (Matthew 17:1-3, 11)? _____

Moses and Elijah are seen talking with Jesus at His future glorification, when His face will shine like the sun and His clothes will be white as brilliant light. At the transfiguration Elijah is promised once again to come and "restore all things." In addition, the two prophets' identities as Moses and Elijah are also confirmed by the witnesses' power to turn water into blood (Revelation 11:6), which Moses is known for (Exodus 7), and their power to destroy people with fire (Revelation 11:5), which Elijah is known for (2 Kings 1).

Jewish tradition also anticipates the arrival of both Moses and Elijah at the end of the age during Passover at the end of the Seder Festival meal?

Statements By Jewish Scholars Concerning...
PESACH (Passover) and ELIJAH

"After the blessing the wine is drunk. Before anyone drinks, however, some is spilled into a plate or tray. This gesture symbolizes sadness and loss; as *Shabbat* ends, so ends it glimpse of redemption, of a world made whole. *Havdalah* expresses a longing for a never-ending Shabbat, which for Jews is expressed in the image of the messiah and, because... Elijah will come after havdalah, it is traditional to sing "Eliyahu Hanavi" [which words are—Elijah the prophet, Elijah the Tishbite, Elijah from Gilad, Come to us soon in our days with Messiah child of David]." *Living A Jewish Life, 1991, by Anita Diamant and Howard Cooper, p. 63.*

"God promises: 'And I will take you to be My people, and I will be your God, And you shall know that I, the LORD, am your God who freed you from the burdens of the Egyptians' (Ex. 6:7). This covenantal relationship lies at the heart of the celebration of Passover. We rejoice for the past liberation from Egypt and for other redemptions by God since then. And because of the fulfillment of past promises, we anticipate at Passover the future final redemption. We create a special role for the prophet Elijah at the Seder as the symbol of our faith in the redemption soon to come." *The Jewish Holidays: A Guide & Commentary, 1985, by Michael Strassfeld, p. 7.*

 Revelation 11:4 describes the two as "the two olive trees and the two lampstands (menorahs) that stand before the LORD of the earth," as originally found in Zechariah 4—a prophetic book that points to the last days. Zechariah is given a vision of the heavenly Temple, and he sees the seven branch Candlestick which represents the *Light of the World*. He also notices "two olive trees" (4:3). Jewish commentators have understood that these olive trees on either side of the menorah would produce the oil that would feed the menorah's light. It was a self-sustained system of olive trees producing oil for the menorah that would stay lit from that very same oil.

8. What is said concerning their work in Zechariah 4:6? _____

"Not by might [of man's strength or position], nor by power [of government or armies], but by My [God's] Spirit, says the LORD Almighty." That's why in Revelation 11:3 it says God will "give power" (KVJ) to the two witnesses to testify of the truth, proclaim God's judgments, and perform miracles. They will come in the

power of Almighty. They represent the oil of the Spirit and light from Heaven—Menorahs to light our world during the darkest days of human history.

9. Zechariah asked the Angel in verse 11, "What are these two olive trees on the right and left of the Lampstand? What is His answer in verse 14? _____

These are the two who are anointed to serve the LORD of all the earth. The King James Version reads, "These are the two anointed ones, that stand by the LORD of the whole earth."

Anointing oil, mentioned 20 times in the Scriptures, was used in the Old Covenant period for pouring on (anointing) the head of the high priest and his descendants (to set them aside for holy use), for Israel's rulers (Saul—1 Samuel 10:1; David—16:13; Solomon—1 Kings 1:39), and sprinkling the tabernacle and its furnishings to mark them as holy and set apart to the LORD (Exodus 25:6; Leviticus 8:30; Numbers 4:16), and most importantly—Yeshua our Messiah's Spirit of anointing (Luke 4:18-19). Oil is often used as a symbol for the Holy Spirit in the Bible, as in the Parable of the Wise and Foolish Virgins (Matthew 25:1-13).

When did the two witnesses, Moses and Elijah, receive their positions in the Temple of God? Elijah was transported to Heaven without facing death to stand before God, because of His commitment to righteousness (2 Kings 2:11); and, Michael called forth from the grave the faithful prophet Moses (Jude 9), whom the LORD Himself had personally buried in secret, to stand before God, after being laid to rest just outside the Promised Land (Deuteronomy 34:1-12). Now these two faithful prophets, who have been standing before the throne of God in Heaven for centuries, will leave their glorious positions to return to a dark planet full of deception as oil of gladness, and lamps of light and truth for Almighty God.

10. What does the witness of two or three establish (Deuteronomy 17:6; 2 Corinthians 13:1; Matthew 18:16-20; Hebrews 10:28-29)? _____

In the mouth of two or three witnesses "every matter may be established"; even a death sentence can be secured by the testimony of two or three eye witnesses. If a man refuses to listen to the warnings, Jesus said treat them like a pagan because whatever is bound on earth by two or three together will be bound in Heaven. The two prophets—Moses and Elijah—are God's eyewitnesses to the unfolding of last-day events on earth. These two will pronounce judgment upon Jerusalem and the Lawless One just before their demise, because neither the religious leaders of Jerusalem or the Lawless One will heed their warnings.

11. What ancient prediction clearly proves that Elijah is a forerunner to Messiah (Malachi 4:5-6; 3:1-2)? _____

Elijah is promised to be sent by God before the great and dreadful Day of the LORD.

Malachi warns of a curse. In spite of the testimony of Elijah the majority will follow after the Beast, so the LORD will "strike the land with a curse." The Hebrew Scriptures say the curse is certain, because of disobedience (Deuteronomy 11:26-28).

12. What is the next event just after Elijah is finished with his counting 1,260 days of ministry, according to Malachi 3:1-2? _____

Malachi writes, "THEN SUDDENLY the LORD you are seeking will come to His Temple [in Jerusalem]… but who can endure the Day of His Coming?" His return will not be in defense of Jerusalem, but will lead to the destruction of the Temple and Jerusalem, because the leadership of the nation has remained stubborn with rebellious hearts.

13. What is the punishment for anyone attempting to kill the two prophets before their 1,260 days of ministry are complete (Revelation 11:5-6)? _____

The words of the prophets are like fire. If they proclaim death upon their attackers, fire will devour the aggressors. Jeremiah the prophet was told by God, "this is what the LORD God Almighty says: "Because the people have spoken these words, I will make My words in your mouth a fire and these people the wood it consumes," Jeremiah 5:14.

The two prophets will have power to affect nature, and will bind up the skies so famine will devour the nations for three and one-half (3½) years, just as Elijah once before held back the rain through prayer, calling on God's power to prevail for the same three and one-half 3½ year period of time (James 5:17). The earth will also be smitten by plagues during the appointed times counting periods, as Moses proclaimed in the land of Egypt thousands of years ago (Exodus 7:19).

Two primary reasons are given in the Scriptures for God withholding rain from His people: For serving other gods (Deuteronomy 11:16-17), and for forgetting the Holy Covenant—the Ten Commandments (Leviticus 26:15). For these reasons, the two witnesses will call forth plagues to bring to their knees those who are willing to humbly repent, and to move forward God's punishment and divine plan to completion against those who won't submit to the Creator.

Revelation 11:7 says when the two prophets have finished their 1,260-day mission the demonic power that ascends out of the Abyss will make war, overcome and kill them. Revelation 17:8 and Revelation 9:11 identify the ruler as coming out of the Abyss, who will soon thereafter go to his own destruction; Abaddon, or Apollyon in Greek, will silence God's last voices of warning.

Paul foretold this time. He wrote that before the Man of Lawlessness steps onto the Temple Mount in Jerusalem to set up his abominable idolatry—an act that will precipitate the Day of the LORD—the "one who now holds it back will continue to do so till he is taken out of the way," 2 Thessalonians 2:7. Speculation has flourished about this prediction over the centuries, identifying the "he" who would be "taken out of the way" with the Holy Spirit or the exit of the church in a secret rapture. However, the explanation is found within the Word of God.

Antichrist cannot enter the Temple as long as the two powerful anointed ones are alive to represent God's Spirit and restraining force against his evil activities. Paul had just told the confused church at Thessalonica that the Day of the LORD will not arrive *unless and until* the Man of Lawlessness is revealed in the Jerusalem Temple (2 Thessalonians 2:2-5). The Evil One is being held back so that he may be revealed at the proper time. The two prophets have a set period of 1,260 days to witness, and only after their prophetic work is completed will God allow their martyrdom. Once the anointed are "taken out of the way," the Papal leader will move onto the Temple Mount, set up his abomination and proclaim his false deity.

Death In The Great City

Revelation 11:8 identifies exactly where the two anointed ones lose their lives. After the deadly attack, the prophets will lie in the streets of the "great city." Revelation clearly identifies the "great city" in the Hebrew Scriptures; and therefore, we know with certainty that when the "great city" is noted in other passages in the Apocalypse prophecies we have the same location on the map.

John first associated the *great city* that's found in the book of Revelation with two other Middle East locations—a city and a nation—that are known for their rebellious history, according to the two prophets—Isaiah and Ezekiel. These two places were criticized in the Scriptures for their sinful past, and so the *great city* in Revelation has been called in scathing rebuke "Sodom" (Isaiah 1:10-11; Ezekiel 16:36-37, 48, 53) and "Egypt" (Isaiah 19:22, 25). Why? Sodom is known for *fornication* and Egypt for *idolatry*. As a further reprimand and reference to a specific location in Israel, the *great city* is identified in John's Apocalypse as "where also their [the two prophets'] LORD was crucified"—a particularly disparaging statement against the Holy City and her religious and political leaders, who long ago leaned on Rome to crucify Messiah on Golgotha.

John 19:16-20 says, "So the soldiers took charge of Jesus. Carrying His own cross, He went out to the place of the Skull (which in Aramaic is called Golgotha). There they crucified Him, and with Him two others —one on each side and Jesus in the middle. Pilate had a notice prepared and fastened to the cross. It read: JESUS OF NAZARETH, THE KING OF THE JEWS. Many of the Jews read this sign, for the place where Jesus was crucified was near the city [Jerusalem]." Before His death, Yeshua warned the city, "I must press on today and tomorrow and the next day—for *surely no prophet can die outside Jerusalem*! 'Jerusalem, Jerusalem, you who kill the prophets and stone those sent to you, how often I have longed to gather your children together, as a hen gathers her chicks under her wings, and you were not willing. Look, your house is left to you desolate'", Luke 13:33-35. Both Messiah and His message were despised and rejected, particularly by Jerusalem's religious leaders. The two lawbreakers crucified on each side of Jesus made a mockery of the two anointed ones—Moses and Elijah, whom Jesus revealed on the Mount of Transfiguration as the two who will accompany Messiah at His future glorification; the same two will *truly* give their lives as martyrs at the end of time.

14. What does this reveal about Jerusalem's apostasy in the last days (along with the other cities of the world; their churches, synagogues and mosques), and the evil state of affairs on Planet Earth? _____

_____

This fulfills the prediction Jesus made in Matthew 7:13-14, 21, that many go through the wide gate that leads to destruction while relatively few choose the narrow gate to life; and, not everyone that cries "LORD, LORD" will enter the kingdom of Heaven—only those who do the will of the Father.

In Jerusalem and across the globe, the false religious superiors in Judaism, Christianity and Islam will join in the joyous excitement when Messiah's two witnesses are killed in the city of Jerusalem and left unburied in open shame on the streets. This will expose their wretched evil minds, as well as their decision to follow after the world leader—the False Shepherd who will step onto the Temple Mount with celebration and fanfare. Later in the book of Revelation, God gives further rebuke to the *great city* Jerusalem with a third derogatory name. Jerusalem is also called "BABYLON THE GREAT" (Revelation 18:10, 18) for the drunken confusion she brings to the world. Why? She allows the leader of Roman Catholicism into the city, she rejects God's prophets and then rejoices when they are sacrificed in her streets. Jerusalem's leaders and the majority of the world's population will hate and despise God's two prophets (Revelation 11:9); and, because of their animosity, burial will be refused them and their dead bodies will lie in the streets of

Jerusalem for three and one-half (3½) days. The nations will gloat and celebrate their deaths (v. 10), because of the two prophets' punishments of earth's population with plagues for 1,260 days. Now, they think their troubles will soon be behind them.

Resurrection Of The Anointed Ones

15. What events occur at the end of the 3½ days (Revelation 11:11-12)? _____

The two prophets are resurrected to life; they stand to their feet and terror will strike those who see them. The two are called up to Heaven in a cloud with a loud voice saying, "Come up here," while their enemies watch in amazement.

16. What similar event occurs in Daniel 12:1-3, just after the king of the north (Man of Sin) plants his royal tents between the seas (Mediterranean and Dead Sea) in Jerusalem? _____

Michael will stand in protest and for the protection of His elect, and there will be both "resurrection" and the "sealing" of His elect (Revelation 7:1-4); then commences the "Great Tribulation".

17. Whose loud voice and trumpet blast raises the prophets and overcomers to life (Revelation 11:15)? _____

18. How does Paul identify the One who calls forth the dead (1 Thessalonians 4:16)? _____

The Archangel, known as Michael (Jude 9); and, in the book of Revelation known as the Seventh Angel, the Lamb and Lion, all of which are important titles representing the life and work of Yeshua our Messiah. He awakens the dead to life.

19. Who is the Life-giver, according to John 5:25? _____

Messiah's loud voice—the very Son of God, who has been with the Father from the beginning of time. As Daniel 12:1 says, "At that time Michael [Messiah]... will arise. Multitudes who sleep in the dust of the earth will awake: some to everlasting life, others to shame and everlasting contempt."

John 5:25, 29 points to the same resurrection event, but now Michael is called the Son of God: "The dead will hear the voice of the Son of God and those who hear will live... those who have done good will rise to live, and those who have done evil will rise to be condemned."

20. What does God give the Son authority to do at the time of resurrection (John 5:27)? _____

The authority to decide who He will resurrect for life and those destined for death, in order to reward the faithful and punish the unrighteous for their sins.

21. What disastrous event will occur in Jerusalem (Revelation 11:13-14)? _____
_____

22. The "tenth part" of the city will fall in the earthquake. What does a "tenth" indicate according to Leviticus 27:32? _____

The tenth is to be set apart for holy use. The tenth part of the city, set aside for holy use, is the Temple Mount—it will fall in final ruins from the severe global earthquake.

Matthew's account offers a historical event that parallels Revelation 11:13-19. In the Gospel we learn at Messiah's death the veil of the Temple was torn open to see into the Holy of Holies, along with an  earthquake and special resurrection (representing a limited number of saints—not all believers). In Revelation 11:13, we also read about an earthquake, a special resurrection (representing a limited number of saints—not all believers) in verse 18; and finally, the opening of Heaven's Holy of Holies to peer into the room of the Ark of the Covenant (verse 19).

Matthew 27:51-53 confirms at Yeshua's death, "At that moment the curtain of the temple was torn in two from top to bottom [exposing the inner place—the Holy of Holies]. The earth shook [earthquake] and the rocks split. The tombs broke open and the bodies of *many* holy people who had died were raised to life [resurrection]. They came out of the tombs, and after Jesus' resurrection they went into the holy city and appeared to many people."

23. Seven thousand are killed in the earthquake. Who are represented by the symbolism of the "seven thousand" (Romans 11:1-5)? _____

Long ago Elijah claimed the Israelites had "killed your prophets and torn down your altars," and he feared they were about to kill him too. God responded in confidence that "seven thousand" Israelites had not given up their faith to reverence Baal, although they were not known to the prophet. So too, at the end of time there will be an unknown remnant chosen by grace who will remain true to God and will not bow to Antichrist, but who will still die in the Jerusalem disaster. This group will rest from their labors, whether the number is literal or symbolic of the whole; it matters not.

24. Who are the survivors, or "remnant" (KJV), who are afraid but remain alive, who are left behind after the special resurrection, for the short but Great Tribulation (1 Thessalonians 4:13-18; Revelation 7:1-8)?

_____

While the martyred—the resurrected saints of the last days—are resurrected to life and taken to Heaven, the 144,000, sealed for protection, remain on earth alive to endure the Great Tribulation—the Time of Jacob's Trouble, which lies just ahead until the Great Day Messiah, with His army of saints and angels, come back to gather up the 144,000 to safety at the Armageddon event. They are called the "elect" in Matthew 24:20-31.

In Revelation 8:13, John describes an angel like an eagle flying through the sky proclaiming the fifth, sixth and seventh trumpet judgments as "woes" to earth's inhabitants; they warn of particularly harsh affliction, despair and misery for the masses. In Revelation 11:14 we are once again reminded of the special warning given in chapter 8, and now the third and final woe is coming quickly. This we will pick up in the next lesson, which will conclude our study of Revelation, chapter 11.

Insights In Prophecy
Unlock The Ancient Mysteries Of Daniel & Revelation
BIBLE DISCOVERY SERIES

Lesson 19

THE SEVENTH TRUMPET ANNOUNCES THE DAY OF ATONEMENT

Read Revelation 11:15-19

- **Investigate The Astounding Events Of The Sevens**
- **Review The Day Of Atonement (Yom Kippur) Events In The Book Of Revelation**

Revelation is a book of enlightenment into Daniel's predictions, as well as clarification of many prophetic passages throughout the entire Bible. Overall, the contents are presented in a chronological arrangement, meaning in the order of their future fulfillment. However, there are a whole string of events at the end of time that will occur in quick succession; therefore, sometimes a passage has been inserted to offer more details. It is known as a "parenthesis"—an insertion in the text to add clarity or details; but the parenthesis also can interrupt the chronological flow of the chapters.

For example, the angelic trumpet judgments one through six are found in chapters 8 and 9. However, chapter 10 and two-thirds of chapter 11 are inserted to offer more details that surround the trumpets. Then, you find the last judgment—seventh trumpet—at the end of Revelation 11.

Chapter 10 relayed the work of the Mighty Seventh Angel—the Lion & the Lamb, when He stands up from His seat of authority (Daniel 12:1) to leave Heaven to descend to earth to protect His people. He will set

foot upon earth and sea, at which time His powerful voice will be heard around the globe as the 40-day Great Tribulation begins; the days when the mystery of God will be finished.

The first two-thirds of Revelation 11 is a brief explanation of the 1,260 counting days of prophecy, which ends with the martyrdom of the two prophets (Moses and Elijah)—the days that just precede the sounding of the seventh trumpet. In the last third of Revelation 11 the seventh judgment is revealed, when the Seventh Angel blows His trumpet with earthshaking results. Verses 15 through 19 provide a wealth of information concerning the timing of the seventh trumpet and the Day it will fall on, as well as major events in Heaven and on earth that occur at its mighty blast. By close examination and diligent study of these verses, the wise can discover valuable insights into the future, which have long been hidden in the Book of Truth before the dawn of time.

1. In Revelation 11:15, the Seventh Angel sounds His trumpet. What do the voices in Heaven declare?

_____

The kingdom of the world has become the kingdom of our LORD [Father] and His Christ [Yeshua], and He will reign for ever and ever. Having been under Satan's influence for millenniums, the kingdom is taken back under Heaven's full control.

2. Who is given dominion according to Daniel 7:13-14? _____

The Son of Man—Jesus Christ is given full authority over all nations on earth when He steps before the Father at this crowning act.

3. What must take place before the coronation (Daniel 7:9-10)? _____

Long ago, Daniel connected the coronation of Messiah's full dominion and power with the opening of books and the Courtroom drama. There must be a Courtroom Judgment where the books of evidence are opened, and the facts revealed as to who should reign victorious—Messiah or the Accuser. This court will be called into session to deal with the evil coup, and to bring into judgment the work of the Devil and his Beast—the end-time world leader.

4. The outcome is already foretold. What is it (Daniel 7:26-27)? _____

Satan's domain will be stripped away, consumed and destroyed, while the Son of Man will be given full dominion over all the nations—a kingdom that will never end.

In Revelation 11:16-18 the twenty-four elders fall on their faces in humble adoration. They praise the LORD, God Almighty, who was and is, and is to come—the Eternal One, because He has taken back His great power to reign supreme. Their voices of praise reveal several truths that reveal the timing of the Seventh Angel and His trumpet blast.

5. What seven events follow the trumpet blast of the Seventh Angel (vs. 17-18)? _____
_____
_____

a) God begins to reign
b) the nations are angry
c) God's wrath has come
d) time for judging the dead
e) time for rewarding God's servants the prophets
f) time for rewarding God's saints and those who reverence His name
g) time for destroying those who destroy the earth

The Seventh Angel and His trumpet blast inaugurates the reign of Messiah fully over the earth. Because of this, the nations of the world are angry and ready for battle, because His reign begins with divine wrath and plagues.

6. The Seventh Angel inaugurates the judgment of the dead. What does it mean to judge the dead? ___
_____

According to 1 Peter 4:5, humans will have to give account to God, "who is ready to judge the living and the dead." Judgment means "to make a considered decision". Messiah decides who will be raised and who will not be raised; who will live and who will die.

Daniel 12:1-3 points to the same announcement of the trumpeting Seventh Angel (Pt. 18 *The Kingdom Calendar*) at Yom Kippur. Michael, the Archangel, will stand at the end of the "time, times and half of time" (v. 7) after the power of the holy people is broken, at the point when all things prophesied will be fully revealed. When He stands, He initiates the "time of distress such as has not happened before"—the Great

Tribulation. "But at that time your [Daniel's] people [Israel]—everyone whose name is found written in the book—will be delivered [sealed for protection—Revelation 7:2-4]. Multitudes who sleep in the dust of the earth will awake [in resurrection]: some [righteous] to everlasting life, others [sinners] to shame and everlasting contempt," (vs. 2-3).

This resurrection at the beginning of the Great Tribulation is not the general resurrection, but a special resurrection of a "great multitude that no man can count" (Revelation 7:9, 14)—a special group of "many" or "multitudes"—both saints and sinners, according to Daniel 12:2. Before their martyrdom, this great multitude of overcomers from all nations of the world will help proclaim the last-day gospel message before giving up their lives in service for God. "For this gospel will be preached in the whole world as a testimony to all nations, and then the end will come," (Matthew 24:14). These "eleventh hour" workers who have turned many to righteousness are rewarded along with Moses and Elijah—God's "servants the prophets," (Revelation 11:18).

Reward is given to the "saints and those who reverence" God's name. Daniel 12:3 says they will "shine like the brightness of the heavens, and those who lead many to righteousness, like the stars for ever and ever." Moses' face glowed with a reflective glory for some time after being with Messiah on Mt. Sinai (Exodus 34:29-30); so brilliantly, in fact, that the people were afraid to come near him. But on this Day of resurrection, the faithful workers for Yeshua will forever "shine as the stars," brighter than minds can fathom with beams of brilliance.

However, in addition to these overcomers, others will be raised at the seventh trumpet to "shame and everlasting contempt"—likely those who most opposed the work of God will be raised to experience the Great Tribulation period of plagues, and to see the King of kings returning in power and great glory. Even those who led Him to the cross and crucified Him may be brought back to life. Revelation 1:7 proclaims "Look, He is coming with clouds, and every eye will see Him, even those who pierced Him."

The Seventh Angel, the Archangel Michael, Yeshua our LORD and Savior—all One the same—will stand and "will come down from Heaven, with a loud command, with the voice of the Archangel and with the (seventh) trumpet call of God, and the dead in Christ will rise first," 1 Thessalonians 4:16. Once the resurrection occurs, then the "Great Tribulation" will begin as Revelation 11:18 identifies: "the time… for destroying those who destroy the earth."

7. Zechariah 9:14-17 and Joel 2:1-2 add what details? _____

_____

The Prophetic Yom Kippur (Day Of Atonement)

Revelation 11:19 is the last verse of our study, which reads… "Then God's Temple in Heaven was opened, and within His Temple was seen the Ark of His Covenant." At the time the Seventh Angel blows with loud trumpet, the Temple door(s) in Heaven are going to open wide. James 5:9 says, "You will be judged. The Judge is standing at the door!"

8. Which day is the only day of the Hebrew calendar when once a year the Most Holy Place can be opened to expose the Ark of the Covenant (Exodus 26:33-34; Leviticus 16:1-34)? _____

_____

Only on the Day of Atonement.

Once a year, the very special inner Holy of Holies compartment of the Sanctuary Temple—where the Ark of the Covenant dwells—is opened by the High Priest to make atonement for the sins of the people. On that day, he wore linen garments. On the future Day of Atonement Heaven's Temple—the Tabernacle of the Covenant Law—will be opened into the Most Holy Place and the Ark of the Decalogue will be exposed as the measurement of judgment for all mankind. May we each see the importance of God's Moral Law, and by faith follow Christ and His Law of Liberty as summed up in the Ten Commandments, which He wrote with His own finger and personal touch (Deuteronomy 4:13).

9. Revelation 15:5 also announces the opening of the Temple: "After this I looked, and I saw in Heaven the Temple – that is, the Tabernacle of the Covenant Law [Ten Commandments] – and it was opened." What group exits, and what does 15:5-8 tell us about the timing of the wrath of God? _____

_____

Immediately after the opening of the Temple and the Day of Atonement announcement, the seven angels (dressed in priestly linen) will be sent out to overtake the enemies of God and to destroy them.

10. What is nature's response when the Seventh Angel—Michael sounds His trumpet (Revelation 11:19)?

_____

The four global, breathtaking portents—powerful global storms of lightning, rumblings (voices), peals of thunder rumble throughout the earth, and the massive earthquake—plus, "a great hailstorm."

Daniel 2:20-22 speaks of this moment in time: "Praise be to the Name of God for ever and ever; wisdom and power are His. He changes times and seasons; He deposes kings and raises up others. He gives wisdom to the wise and knowledge to the discerning. He reveals deep and hidden things; He knows what lies in darkness, and light dwells with Him."

What does this mean? At the voice of Messiah, the whole planet will quake in massive convulsion and will be moved off its axis: "The earth shall reel to and fro like a drunkard, and shall be removed like a cottage; and the transgression thereof shall be heavy upon it; and it shall fall, and not rise again," Isaiah 24:20 (KJV). The seasons will be changed in a moment. It may be summer, but it turns to fall; or, spring and it turns to autumn. But this we know, God will complete His final acts at the fall Festival season, whether it comes naturally or by His mighty and powerful voice. Therefore, we must be ready at any moment to hear of the Jerusalem devastation that will take down the Temple Mount and Western Wall. This may come at Purim, or at any moment of any given year; but once this occurs, the counting periods of *The Kingdom Calendar* will begin. Day by day we can count the days, knowing that God has sworn on His own good name that once the 1,260 days are completed, His voice will be heard around the globe.

Wisdom and universal power are His. He can change the times and the seasons at the moment of His choosing, and Christ can take down kings in the destruction while raising up others. And, He gives wisdom to the wise, and knowledge to the discerning. The choice is yours if you will be among the wise and discerning on that Day. Whether on the right side or not, Jesus knows what is in your heart and hidden from others, and when the Light of the World shines on this dark planet, He will light up the world and reveal the deep and hidden mysteries to His saints, while destroying all remaining sinners during the Great Tribulation.

11. Along with the seventh trumpet, what other events in Heaven and on earth correspond to the Day of the LORD when God's supernatural display of global lightning, voices, thunder, earthquake and hailstorm hits Planet Earth according to the verses below?

Revelation 8:5-6 _____

Revelation 16:17-18 _____

The great global portents are always associated with the Seventh Angel, when He opens His seal, blows His trumpet and dispenses His vial of wrath. The verses point to that special Day—the opening of the seventh seal—when the seven angels exit the Temple and begin to pour out the seven vials of God's wrath.

Author: Isaac Watts

Isaac Watts was the son of a schoolmaster, and was born in Southampton, July 17, 1674. He is said to have shown remarkable precocity in childhood, beginning the study of Latin, in his fourth year, and writing respectable verses at the age of seven. His collected works, first published in 1720, embrace sermons, treatises, poems and hymns. His "Hymns" appeared in July, 1707. The first hymn he is said to have composed for religious worship, is "Behold the glories of the Lamb," written at the age of twenty. Some of his hymns were written to be sung after his sermons, giving expression to the meaning of the text upon which he had preached. Montgomery calls Watts "the greatest name among hymn-writers," and the honor can hardly be disputed.

305   The seventh angel sounded.   L. M.
             Rev. xi. 15.

Let the seventh angel sound on high,
Let shouts be heard through all the sky;
Kings of the earth, with glad accord,
Give up your kingdoms to the Lord.

Almighty God, thy power assume,
Who wast, and art, and art to come;
Jesus the Lamb, who once was slain,
Forever live, forever reign.

The holy ones in heaven, adore
The King who takes his royal power;
While angry nations dread their doom,
And quail because thy wrath has come.

Now must the rising dead appear,
Now the decisive sentence hear;
Now the dear martyrs of the Lord
Receive an infinite reward.

              Isaac Watts, 1709, ab.   v. 3, H., 1878.

---- **NOTES**----

Insights In Prophecy
Unlock The Ancient Mysteries Of Daniel & Revelation
BIBLE DISCOVERY SERIES

KING OF KINGS

קינג וף קינגס

Insights In Prophecy
Unlock The Ancient Mysteries Of Daniel & Revelation
BIBLE DISCOVERY SERIES

Lesson 20

THE WOMAN & THE RED DRAGON

Read Revelation 12:1-6

- **Examine Who Is Represented By The Woman**
- **Consider Why Satan Hates the Jews, And Why Anti-Semitism Is On The Rise**

Revelation 12 is a challenging chapter steeped in symbolism and analogy. This prophecy has the potential of polarizing people into two camps during the last days based on the way it is interpreted. Conviction over the proper meaning of this chapter is crucial, and understanding the *personification of the woman* will shield us from the myth, which will cover the globe, that the Virgin Mary is earth's saving force—a playback to the unifying feminine goddesses of the past.

Some leaders in Catholicism have viewed the woman of chapter 12 a representation of Mary, Mother of God; hence, paintings and idols depict her with the sun surrounding her head, often with moon and stars. Visions and apparitions of the supposed Mary, which thousands are said to have seen, have include signs in the sun, which as a circular disk is said to pulsate, twirl and shoot off colorful beams of red, orange, yellow, blue and so forth.

Is the woman of chapter 12 a depiction of the Virgin? As always, the Bible is its own best interpreter, and so we turn to its pages for insight into these all-important predictions of the last days.

When theologians and students of prophecy forget the Scriptures were written by Hebrew prophets, then private interpretations and traditions of men supersede the plainest teachings found in the Word of God. Revelation 12 depicts both historical and future end-time events as though occurring simultaneously. In this cross-over symbolism, the chapter reveals that the confrontation between Michael and Satan in times past will be repeated during the appointed time of the end.

Revelation 12:1 introduces a "great and wondrous sign" in Heaven—a woman clothed with galactic light. Does she portray a historical personality, a personality from Heaven, or a symbol of events to come? In Revelation there are *two prominent women*. Understanding this one fact alone is enough to guide us to the truth. The woman of Revelation chapters 12 and 21 represents the righteous city and people; whereas, the woman of Revelation 17 and 18 depicts a sinful city and people.

1. The virtuous woman is clothed in the beautiful bright sun, with the moon under her feet and a crown of twelve stars upon her head. What was the sun and moon made for, according to Genesis 1:14-16?

_____

The two great lights were made for "signs to mark seasons and days and years." While the world at large uses the sun to mark years, Israel uses a solar-lunar calendar to mark the seasonal Festivals of the LORD, along with days and years.

2. How did God use the symbolism of the stars, moon and sun to represent and set Israel apart from other nations (Genesis 37:9-11)? _____

Joseph had a dream in which the sun, moon and eleven stars—representing his eleven Hebrew brothers—would bow down to him, which eventually came to pass in Egypt during a time of severe famine. Comparing the Scriptural passage from which John the Revelator would have drawn this imagery, the stars surrounding the woman in Revelation 12 clearly represent the twelve patriarchs of Israel. Jacob blessed his twelve sons individually (Genesis 49:1), and the dozen blossomed into the twelve tribes of Israel (v. 28).

3. Acts 7:8 verifies this fact. How? _____

4. Twelve is nearly always associated with the people of Israel. Exodus 28:21 says what? _____
_____

The twelve stones in the priest's breastplate represented the twelve tribes.

There were *twelve* officers who ruled Israel (1 Kings 4:7); *twelve* Hebrew apostles perpetuated the lineage of the dozen (Matthew 10:2); according to Revelation 21 and 22, the foundation walls of the New Jerusalem will display the *twelve* names of the apostles (Revelation 21:14); the city will be comprised of the *twelve* gates, *twelve* guardian angels, *twelve* names of the *twelve* tribes, *twelve* foundations, *twelve* fruits and *twelve* thousand furlongs of the four-sided city.

The *moon* and *sun*, which adorn the woman of Revelation 12:1, symbolizes a truth much greater than these solar system spheres might at first evoke. As noted, Genesis 1:14-16 tells us that our Messiah Creator called

into existence the sun and moon "*as signs* to *mark seasons and days and years*." God, in turn, used these massive sky lights to institute His spring and fall Festivals based on their daily, yearly and seasonal movements—the relationship between the moon cycle and the rotation of the earth around the sun. Leviticus 23:4 reads, "these are the LORD's appointed feasts, the sacred assemblies you are to proclaim at their *appointed times*," (NIV); or, "*in their seasons*," (KJV).

Therefore, the *"wondrous sign"* of the sun and moon depicted in Revelation 12 symbolizes the seasonal Feasts, which come and go each year according to the planetary movements. This fact, in turn, further establishes that the woman of Revelation 12 represents the *nation of Israel*. By instituting the Festivals over 3,000 years ago, the Holy One of Israel would weave a thread through the fabric of time that would connect Israel's conception to her birth as a "holy" nation, while helping to maintain the woman's unique identity as a chosen people throughout the centuries until the Kingdom of God was permanently established. The woman of Revelation 12, therefore, represents a protected Israel.

The Virtuous Woman & The Immoral Woman

Throughout the Hebrew Scriptures, the people of Israel and the beloved city Jerusalem are often symbolized as either a virtuous or adulterous woman, depending on her response to God's leading through His prophets.

5. How do the references below symbolize Israel's spiritual condition?

Jeremiah 2:2-3 _____

Jeremiah 3:8-9 _____

Jeremiah 3:20 _____

Jeremiah 6:1-8 _____

Ezekiel 23:1-4 _____

Lamentations 1 _____

Revelation 17:1-6 _____

Revelation 21:2, 9-10 _____

In multiple passages, Israel and Jerusalem are identified as the adulterer, the unfaithful and the prostitute slated for destruction, because of her rejection of truth and breaking of her Covenant with God.

The Hebrew prophets of old who delivered the messages of warning to Israel about her impending destruction for lack of obedience were often hated and killed. No one likes bad news; but when a prophet warns that God's people, city and land are subject to Divine discipline it seems far-fetched. Yet today, the cost of disobedience remains unlearned, despite all the historical lessons of the past and the prophetic portents foretold to come during the end days.

In the last days, God will send His two anointed ones to warn, but they will be rejected and killed in Jerusalem's streets. There will be a price to pay. Most devotees in the three Abrahamic religions—Judaism, Christianity and Islam—cannot comprehend that today's twenty-first century Jerusalem could be subject to complete ruin; however, the Scriptural evidence is abundantly clear on this matter. Jerusalem's first devastation may be due to a seismic earthquake early in the appointed times; but, the second will come about due to God's judgment. May we be among those who "grieve and lament over the detestable things that are done" on the Temple Mount in Jerusalem in the last days (Ezekiel 9:4), for destruction will begin with the people who claim to know God (Matthew 7:21; 1 Peter 4:17-18) and will quickly spread to the whole world (Ezekiel 9:6).

Yeshua cried out before His sham trial, "O Jerusalem, Jerusalem, you who kill the prophets and stone those sent to you, how often I have longed to gather your children together, as a hen gathers her chicks under her wings, but you were not willing. Look, your house is left to you desolate," Matthew 23:37-38. Israel's rabbinic leadership, with the help of the Roman judicial system, made sure that Jesus was crucified and killed.

6. The "great city" in the book of Revelation is first identified as the location where what happened (Revelation 11:8)? _____

Where our LORD was crucified; there's no dispute—Jesus was crucified at Jerusalem. The Great City is also called derogatory names—Egypt and Sodom, for what the Hebrew Scriptures called the sins of idolatry and adultery; her leadership and inhabitants' compromise with other religions.

Covenant-breaking residents of Jerusalem are given a third insulting name in the book of Revelation. The rebellious woman is said to sit on the end-time world governments as though on display—the focus of the whole world. She is decked with the riches of the nations, but sadly she has on her forehead "MYSTERY BABYLON THE GREAT THE MOTHER OF PROSTITUTES AND OF THE ABOMINATIONS OF THE EARTH," Revelation 18:3-5.

7. How is her final desolation described in Revelation 18:2-8? _____

The Virtuous Woman

In contrast, now we want to return to the honorable woman of Revelation 12. This woman is pregnant and in her last moments before birth. She is in birth pains and pushing to bring to completion her child/children. In Matthew 24:8 Jesus revealed, concerning the final destruction of the fallen city Jerusalem—which He had just declared would be left desolate, when wars, famines, pestilences and earthquakes suddenly escalate they are signs that "all these things are the beginning of *birth pains*" for Israel, Jerusalem and the Jewish people. Birth pains ultimately lead to the birth of a child; and, in the larger context—a kingdom and people for God.

8. Revelation 12 is derived, in part, from Isaiah 66:6-10, which symbolizes parallel births. What two origins are depicted in these verses? _____

_____

She delivers a "Son," which, in turn, leads to the birth of a virtuous "nation."

The birth of Messiah, and in the final moments of time the birth of a nation, is revealed in Isaiah's analogy of the woman, just as in the book of Revelation. A new and virtuous nation (144,000—Revelation 7:1; 7:4; 14:1-3) will emerge when Jerusalem is in intense sorrow and pain; and, when the voice of the LORD is heard from the Temple. For "suddenly the LORD... will come to His Temple... but who can endure the day of His coming?" Malachi 3:1-2.

In contrast, most adherents in Judaism and Christianity will be Covenant-breakers. They will see in the self-exalting pope the long-awaited savior and consider him the son foretold to come to birth in Revelation 12. Many in synagogues and churches will consider themselves the righteous woman in travail, believing that God miraculously rose up a religious man to save the planet and to offer them protection. Nevertheless, the true virtuous woman symbolized and depicted in Revelation 12 will be *persecuted* by Satan, instead of sheltered; they will have to *run* into the wilderness for protection. From this larger group, the 144,000 elect (12,000 from each tribe) will emerge in that spiritual birth foretold long ago.

9. In Revelation 12:3 another sign appears in Heaven—an enormous red dragon. Who is represented by the dragon (Revelation 12:9)? _____

10. The dragon has "seven heads and ten horns." What do these symbolize (see Lesson 5, if need be)?

_____

Earth's governments and military powers are carried by the supremacy of Satan during the final conflict; the political beast is Lucifer's heads and mouthpieces of destruction that will hurt and destroy the remnant of God's people. In truth, Satan is synonymous with governments, and the governments are Satan's means to his end—full control of Planet Earth. The Devil will even reach God's throne room, as depicted in this vision of the ferocious red dragon beast, and he will bring great turmoil upon Heaven and to the nations here on earth—war, bloodshed and mass destruction. The seven heads and ten horns (7X10) represent 70 nations of the world, indicating Satan's worldwide control of the planet during the last days. To Jews, the number 70 symbolizes the world. They believe there are 70 nations in the world, 70 languages, and 70 princely angels. It is said the Greek translation of the Bible, the first to make it available to the Gentile, was done by 70 Jewish scholars, who, though working separately, produced 70 identical translations.

11. In Revelation 13:1 the ten horns (countries) are adorned with *ten crowns* (rulers); however, in Revelation 12:3 there are only *seven crowns*. Why (Daniel 7:7-8)? _____

Three nations of the Western Europe Union will collapse from attacks launched by the Old Soviet Bear (Daniel 7:5), that holds the three ribs (or tusks) in its mouth. Out of massive holocaust Satan will exalt a new, previously obscure, religious leader who will emerge from the ashes of war, accompanied by demonic apparitions and deceptions. In the middle of great tragedies of nuclear conflict, calamities by wind, fire, massive earthquakes, tsunamis, and widespread pestilence and disease, Satan will unleash his great supernatural trickery on humanity. And, shortly after Lucifer and the fallen angels, who once enjoyed Heaven's prestige, will make their final attempt to takeover the throne of God.

The Beast will take captive Planet Earth, while Satan marches with his campaign of destruction to Heaven's doors (Revelation 12:3). He is angry that his time is short. In past history, Satan used the heathen King Herod in an attempt to stamp out the promised Messiah (Matthew 2:12-16) at a young age. Later he exploited Rome's crucifixion cross (Luke 23:33), but the child who was to rule with a rod of iron (Revelation 2:27) rose again and was caught up to God and to His throne. At the appointed time, Satan will make one last attempt to stamp out the Kingdom of God in an attempted overthrow of Heaven, but to no avail. Then he will turn his attention back on the virtuous woman.

In spite of the battles that will rage in Heaven and on earth during the appointed time of the end, the woman—the twelve tribes of Israel—will receive divine protection for 1,260 days (42 months of 30 days). Yeshua the King, whom she gave birth to nearly 2,000 years ago, will soon after His coronation in Heaven, come down and visit the sins of the wicked woman. At the Day of Visitation, He will provide the divine sealing of the elect; however, He will once again be taken "up to God and to His throne." The righteous elect—the 144,000—of "all Israel" (Romans 11:26), promised from the time of Abraham (Genesis 22:15-18) to become a great spiritual nation, will be brought to birth in the final moments of time into the hands of the Living God.

As mentioned in other lessons, forty-two (42) holds special significance in Judaism. During the 42 months (1,260 days), the woman will flee into the wilderness where Israel will take refuge—both literally and symbolically. Jews associate the "forty-two" letter Name of God to the following: God at creation (Yeshua), the "visible" revelation of God (Angel of the Covenant) at Mt. Sinai, the eastern gate, the arrival of the Messiah, and the Shekinah coming to its destination—the Temple in the land of Jerusalem. Therefore, the 1,260 days of the appointed times, divided into 42 segments of time, represents the prophetic period through which Israel and this world must travel until the Visitation of Messiah, the Creator, the Angel of the Covenant, Messiah ben David, who will arrive at the eastern gate—when the Name of God will be proclaimed in all of His redemptive glory, and when all Israel will be sealed and saved (***The Kingdom Calendar*** Pt. 18).

As the appointed time of the end begins, Lucifer and his army will ascend to Heaven and take up battle regiment. A war will break out, and according to John, the Dragon's (Satan's) tail is so powerful that "a third of the stars" will be flung to the earth. The seer has made direct reference to Daniel's vision concerning the "little horn"—the little country—from which Antichrist will emerge. Satan, through the efforts of the Beast and his united forces, will quickly grow in power on earth, and then Lucifer's powerful forces will reach up to the "host [angels] of the Heavens."

Insights In Prophecy
Unlock The Ancient Mysteries Of Daniel & Revelation
BIBLE DISCOVERY SERIES

Daniel was the first to see the conflict that will reach to the courts of Heaven in the last days in Daniel 8:9-12: "Out of one of them came another horn [Antichrist/Satan's military powers]... It grew until it reached the host [angels] of the heavens, and it threw some of the starry host [angels] down to the earth and trampled on them [in battle]. It set itself up to be as great as the Prince of the host [Michael]; it took away the daily [worship in Heaven] ~~sacrifice~~ (not in original text) from Him, and the place of His Sanctuary [in Heaven] was brought low. Because of rebellion [by Satan/Antichrist], the host of the believers and the daily [worship in Heaven] ~~sacrifice~~ was given over to it. It prospered in everything it did and truth was thrown to the ground."

Although Michael and His angels will be victorious in routing Satan and his fallen foe out of Heaven, on earth the angelic host will be drawn into the conflict to defend the Covenant-keepers here on earth. The battle will rage about us, both seen and unseen, during the appointed time of the end. Many virtuous angels will struggle with the forces of evil in high places, until Michael stands and unleashes His mighty wrath (Daniel 12:1-2) to finalize the defeat of Satan and his army. Both Daniel and John relay that the end-time governments, ruled by the Wicked One in triune power with the False Prophet and Satan the Dragon (Revelation 16:13-14), will grow ever stronger in power with supernatural demonic strength. In response, the general assembly in Heaven will bring the Court of Law into session (Daniel 7:8-10) for 2,300 evenings and mornings, meaning 1,150 days (8:14), to deal with the evil coup. The cast down thrones will be set up after the battle and the Books of evidence will be opened for review; however, the outcome in favor of Messiah and the overcomers has already been foretold (7:26).

12. Revelation 12:5 says Israel gave birth to a Son, a male child, who will rule all nations with an iron scepter. What does Isaiah 9:6 say of His birth and rule? _____

"For to us a Child is born, and to us a Son is given, and the government will be on His shoulders. And He will be called Wonderful Counselor, Mighty God, Everlasting Father, Prince of Peace." Additional references: Luke 2:11; Matthew 28:18.

13. Genesis 49:10 identifies the Savior and scepter of iron will come from what tribe? _____

Messiah was to come through Judah; Matthew 1:1-16 offers the genealogy of Yeshua.

According to Revelation 12:5, Messiah was snatched up to God and to His throne. Acts 1:9 says the disciples saw Jesus "was taken up before their very eyes, and a cloud hid Him from their sight."

**14. What position has Christ been given in relation to the Father (Ephesians 1:20-22)? _____
_____**

15. Revelation 12:6 indicates Satan will pursue the woman to destroy her—those of Israel who will not break the Covenant Commandments of God. However, she will flee "into the desert to a place prepared for her by God, where she might be taken care of for how many days? _____

She will be protected for 1,260 days, or three and one-half years—the same time period the two witnesses will be on earth as their divinely appointed guardians, during the appointed time of the end (Revelation 11:3-6).

Lesson 21

SATAN WARS AGAINST HEAVEN & EARTH

Read Revelation 12:7-17

- **Discover When & Why Michael Fights Satan Head-On**
- **Identify Why Lucifer Is So Angry With The Commandment-Keepers**

As noted in Lesson 20, the symbolism of Revelation 12 seems to depict both historical episodes of the past and events at the appointed time of the end, as though occurring simultaneously to indicate their connectivity. This chapter points out the conflict between the forces of good and evil, and ultimately Satan's demise. However, as humans we are not entirely sheltered from the raging battle, and in this sense we must be ready to unite our efforts with Jesus our Messiah, and to respond to the battle cry.

Revelation repeats the call for personal victory: "To him who overcomes, I will give the right to eat from the tree of life" and "he who overcomes will not be hurt at all by the second death," 2:7, 11. The conqueror

recognizes the reward beyond the struggle and by hope and faith never gives up. The last-day saints will face difficult trials during a hard and tiresome journey; but, God is not surprised. He knows every trial we face, and if we continue to trust in Him moment by moment He will guide us through the appointed time of the end and deliver us into His eternal kingdom. Jesus promised salvation and rewards to His champions of faith: "He who stands firm to the end will be saved," Matthew 24:13. Paul wrote that our best efforts to imagine the future prepared for the faithful falls short of the reality of Heaven's unseen and mysterious opportunities, "Eye hath not seen, nor ear heard, neither have entered into the heart of man, the things which God hath prepared for them that love Him," 1 Corinthians 2:9 (KJV).

Life is full of decisions, but none more important than on whose side we will take our stand in the final conflict of the ages. Before us are two powerful rulers—Satan, the Prince of this world (John 14:30; 16:10) and Messiah, the Prince of the host (Daniel 8:11; 11:1). The choice is ours; to whom will our loyalty be given? Will our decisions under persecution prove our faith to be authentic, or a shallow pretense?

We think of Heaven as a safe haven where no misery ever interrupts the ageless tranquility, but long ago pride entered the heart of Lucifer, and a sinful rebellion raised its ugly head. At the end of time, Heaven's harmony will be interrupted once again. Revelation 12:5 spoke of the male child who governs, and who was snatched up to God and His throne. Verse 7 continues, "Then war broke out in heaven. Michael and His angels fought against the dragon, and the dragon and his angels fought back." The prophet John saw an intense battle rage; Michael and with His military forces battle Satan and his trained bandits. This is no ethereal conflict, nor child's play. It is real and horrific. We don't know how this conflict is fought, whether hand to hand combat, the clashing of swords or larger instruments of war; but, it is deadly, with dire consequences to those involved on both sides. Who says angels cannot die? Only our preconceived notions.

Lucifer began his career of deception in Heaven; and then, in the Garden of Eden cloaked as a lone serpent. Now, he has grown into a monster of sorts—a violent and hideous dragon backed by his evil forces. He will take Planet Earth captive through first instigating worldwide tragedy of war and bloodshed through his human proxies. Natural disasters of earthquakes, forces of winds and waves, raging fires, mass holocaust, ruin and distress in untold forms will spike creating fear and global pandemonium; then, demonic miracles of peace will offer a false sense of hope in the risen man—the Man of Sin. The world will take Lucifer's bated hook, but with it he will drag this planet into his net of deception, death and further annihilation. The ancient Biblical prediction warns that God allows the deception to occur for the many haters of the truth who reject Messiah's merciful salvation: *"Even him, whose coming is after the working of Satan with all power and signs"* including Satanic miracles on a mass scale *"and lying wonders"–apparitions telling lies. "And with all deceivableness of unrighteousness in them that perish; because they received not the love of the truth, that they might be saved. And for this cause God shall send them strong delusion"* which God allows, *"that they should believe a lie,"* 2 Thessalonians 2:9-11 (KJV).

1. In the vision of Revelation 12:3-4, where does this end-time battle take place? _____

Having brought Planet Earth under his powerful sway, he will march with armies to Heaven's gates to claim victory and to exalt his throne above the stars of God. Satan will attempt to overthrow Heaven's Temple and God Himself that he might achieve his ultimate dream—to sit on the mount of the congregation, in the sides of the North (Isaiah 14:12-14). He wants desperately to reign in power and majesty by deposing "the Most High."

Lucifer's arrival in Heaven is symbolized as a dominant geopolitical dragon with "seven heads and ten horns and *seven (7) crowns* on his heads," (12:3). However, Revelation 13:1 (KJV) describes the same dragon with "seven heads and ten horns, and upon his horns *ten (10) crowns*." The loss of *three crowns* from earth's governments is because "one of the heads of the beast seemed to have had a fatal wound"—a terrible tragedy of great magnitude—the national fatalities of World War III. In this fatal blow to one of the governmental heads, three "kings" or "leaders" are killed/deposed, so that only seven remain—plus, the emerging eighth, the Man of Sin.

This harps back to Daniel 7:7-8: "After this I saw in the night visions, and behold a fourth beast, dreadful and terrible, and strong exceedingly; and it had great iron teeth: it devoured and brake in pieces, and stamped the residue with the feet of it: and it was diverse from all the beasts that were before it; and it had *ten horns*. I considered the horns, and, behold, there came up among them another little horn, before whom there were *three of the first horns plucked up by the roots*: and, behold, in this horn were eyes like the eyes of man, and a mouth speaking great things," denoting Antichrist's authoritative rule. Daniel continues, "And he shall speak great words against the Most High, and shall wear out the saints of the Most High, and think to change times and laws: and they shall be given into his hand until a time and times and the dividing of time," (v. 25)—meaning, 3½ years; or, 1,260 days.

These passages prove there will be pronounced global upheaval on earth—World War III *just before* the 1,260 counting days begin; so, what does this expose? Satan must arrive in Heaven for battle *after* the great blow to the worldwide governmental dragon, which leads to a "forty-two month" (13:5)—1,260 days of rule by the demon Beast (Antichrist) over Planet Earth (Revelation 13:5). Ephesians 6:12 advises, "For our struggle is not against flesh and blood, but against the rulers, against the authorities, against the powers of this dark world and against the spiritual forces of evil in the heavenly realms."

2. According to Daniel, which creature's head will be hit by mass destruction symbolized by the loss of *three horns* or countries (7:7-8)? _____

The fourth Beast—Western Europe Union made up of ten prominent countries will be attacked by the Russian Bear (7:5) with mass destruction and a fatal blow. The wounded Bear will rise up and "eat [his] fill of [human] flesh," as symbolized in the three ribs in its mouth. Mass annihilation, on a scale beyond human consciousness lies before us with tragic loss of countless lives. Of particular concern are the southern European countries (Italy, Greece, Portugal and Spain), but only when this holocaust occurs can be know with certainty the three devastated countries. Prophecy has foretold the attack in vivid detail.

Revelation 12:8 indicates that throughout history and up to the end-of-days conflict, Lucifer lost his position in Heaven, but still has a "place in Heaven." So, although sin has been prevalent God did not totally shut the door upon Satan's entrance before God—the relentless Accuser of the brethren.

3. How do we know Lucifer has had access to God's throne room even after sin entered his heart (Job 1:6-7)? _____

4. What does Revelation 12:10 promise about the Accuser of our brethren? _____

His demise is certain. The Adversary has gone before God relentlessly "day and night" to accuse and dispute. Knowing his downfall and imprisonment in only a short time away, he will rise up in anger to battle Michael and His faithful angels. However, Satan's repeated attempts to usurp God's authority and take the warfare to the throne of God will lead to his imprisonment; and finally, to his ultimate demise.

5. What is said of the Satan's upcoming imprisonment (Revelation 20:2)? _____

Cruden's Concordance says it was believed in ages past that "dragons" were "old serpents grown with age to a prodigious size." Therefore, it's not surprising to see the serpent/dragon symbolism in the book of Revelation, since the Devil presented himself as a beguiling serpent in the Garden of Eden (Genesis 3:3. So, by the end of the recorded Scriptures in the book of Revelation, Satan has grown into a grotesque multi-head dragon amalgamated with world governance symbolizing excessive dominance to persecute and kill any and all who opposes him.

6. What does Isaiah prophesy about Leviathan—the sea monster's punishment on the Day of the LORD (27:1)? _____

7. Satan was also symbolized as the king of Tyre in Ezekiel 28:11-19. What type of punishment and final death is prophesied by the holy prophet, and where will it occur (18-19)? _____
_____

A fire will come out from within Satan himself, and it will consume him and reduce him to ashes on the earth. He will come to a horrible end, and will exist no more.

8. Isaiah 24:21-22 describes the punishment of the "powers in the heavens"; or, as the King James Version reads, the "host of the high ones on high." What is it? _____
_____

9. The brother of Jesus also described the fate of the fallen angels. What does he say concerning their imprisonment and future judgment of eternal fire, like that which reduced Sodom and Gomorrah to ashes (Jude 6-7)? _____
_____

Peter also spoke of fallen angels who were cast down to hades, to a dungeon to be held for judgment. He wrote of God's judgment upon Sodom and Gomorrah—how He burned the cities and their inhabitants to ashes, "making them an example of what is going to happen to the ungodly," (2 Peter 2:4-6).

10. Where will the fire blaze, according to 2 Peter 3:7? _____

The skies above and the Planet Earth are "reserved for fire, being kept for the Day of Judgment and destruction [annihilation] of ungodly men."

11. Just how complete will the fiery destruction of sin and sinners be (2 Peter 3:10-13; Malachi 4:3)? ___
_____

The original Greek literally reads, "The earth and everything in it will be burned up." What we know as Planet Earth will be completely destroyed, along with Satan, all sinners and the rebellious host.

12. Once the Great White Throne judgment is over how does Revelation 20:9 describe the consuming fire that God calls from above upon Satan and all sinners? _____

The fire "devours" them.

13. What is said about our God in Hebrews 12:29? _____

God is a "consuming fire."

14. For whom was the judgment fire originally planned for (Matthew 25:41)? _____

15. Revelation 12:10 says a loud voice is heard, when Satan's rule will be totally broken. Salvation, power and kingdom of God, and authority of Christ, are declared. When does this transpire according to Revelation 11:15? _____

At the voice of the Seventh Angel (Michael), on the Day of the LORD, Messiah is given rule and Satan's demise will be sealed. For millennia the Devil has had access to God and has brought accusations against the saints, but the Day will arrive when no further arguments or charges will be entertained. At the same time, all destinies will be sealed and the door of mercy will be forever shut for all who rejected Christ.

16. What follows the proclamation, according to the prophet (Revelation 11:18-19)? _____
_____
_____

The nations of the world are stirred up in anger because God's wrath is beginning; the hour for judging the dead has arrived—who will be raised to life at the first resurrection; the hour for rewarding God's two servants the prophet and the overcomers who reverence God's name is come; and, the time to destroy those who destroy the earth.

17. Whom does John identify with this hour of proclamation (Revelation 12:11)? _____

The victorious martyrs for Yeshua are identified—specifically, those who overcame during the final conflict, the individuals Satan most opposed and accused before God. They conquered in three ways: 1) by the blood of the Lamb sacrificed for them, 2) by the word of their testimony, and 3) by their willingness to die for the Lamb.

 These faithful prisoners of persecution placed their trust in the Lamb of God, who takes away the sin of the world. Their words testify of their commitment to God's Commandments (Revelation 12:17), and to their keeping of the spirit of prophecy warnings (Revelation 19:10) found in the book of Revelation (1:2-3). Finally, these persecuted multitudes of all nations who will give their lives in loyalty to God, remaining faithful at the point of death and personal loss, will be resurrected to life at the seventh trumpet (Revelation 2:10; 6:11; 7:9; 13:10; 15:2—Pt. 18 on *The Kingdom Calendar*). This large group of martyrs, too many to count, will be victorious in faith over the Beast, his image and his mark; they "came to life and reigned with Christ a thousand years. (The rest of the dead did not come to life until the thousand years were ended.)" Revelation 20:4-5.

18. Although there will be great rejoicing in Heaven, including this great multitude resurrected and transported before the throne and the Lamb (Revelation 7:8-17) at the seventh trumpet, to whom is the warning given concerning Satan's fury (Revelation 12:12)? _____

Satan has only a short time left—the brief but dreadful 40-day Great Tribulation—also known as the Time of Jacob's (Israel's) Trouble. He will explode in anger against anyone left on earth who opposes him—namely the 144,000 elect of the twelve tribes sealed for protection, but who will still be subject to Satanic resentment and trickery (Matthew 24:15-26).

19. Revelation 12:13-14 begs the question: why is Satan so angry with the woman (Israel) who had given birth to Messiah Jesus? _____

Yeshua, the Son of Man is the Adversary's arch enemy. Christ receives dominion and glory which Satan wants above all else. Since he cannot defeat Messiah and His angels, he will turn his attention to the beloved woman. Satan knows there is no better way to injure God than through hurting those He loves.

However, the woman (Israel) will be given "two wings of a great eagle" so that she might "fly to a place of safety where she can be taken care of for a time, times and half a time, out of the serpent's reach." In the last days, there will be a land of refuge and safety for Covenant-keeping Israel that only Heaven knows, but Almighty God will provide the means of safety—a land of freedom, and a home for these brave souls. The prophet John made direct reference to Isaiah 40:28-31, a passage of hope particularly for Israel. Elohim will give strength to the weary and power to the weak. The enemies who pursue the believers will grow tired and weary, even the young men of valor will stumble and fall, "but those who hope in the LORD will renew their strength. They will soar on wings like eagles; they will run and not grow weary, they will walk and not be faint" as they outrun the wrath of Satan and enemies of God.

20. How long will Israel be under the divine care and protection (Revelation 12:14)? _____

Three and one-half years, the same period as the Beast's rule (Revelation 13:5; Daniel 7:25). The two anointed witnesses will guide and protect them (Revelation 11:3-6); otherwise, Satan would crush them all.

21. According to Revelation 12:15-17 Lucifer sends an overwhelming disaster to destroy Israel with a flood, but what does the earth do? _____ What does the flood waters represent (Revelation 17:15? _____

A tsunami of Gentile enemies tries to wash away and destroy the chosen ones, but the earth opens up and miraculously swallows the pursuing flood of military armies—saved against all odds. The woman, represented by the twelve tribes of Israel, is saved.

22. The woman will be safe for 1,260 days, protected by Heaven's two ambassadors and supernatural intervention. The remnant of saints to whom Satan then turns his attention is identified by what two distinguishing remarks? _____

Lucifer understands that any attempt to destroy the twelve tribes of the chosen elect will be impossible, so he turns his attention to make war against her offspring—[1] "those who obey God's commandments and [2] hold to the testimony of Jesus."

23. What do these two characteristics mentioned above signify (Revelation 22:14; 1:2-3; 19:10)? _____
_____
_____

The remnant of saints, both Jew and Gentile alike, obey God's commandments, and follow the counsel of the book of Revelation.

24. What does Satan through the Antichrist Beast attempt to destroy during the appointed time of *the* end (Daniel 11:28; 30-36)? The Holy _____

25. What is the Holy Covenant (Deuteronomy 4:13)? _____

Satan desires to stamp out the Commandment-keepers for they are the light and salt of the earth, and they most oppose the idolatrous worship that will be made popular during the appointed time of the end.

26. By what will the world be judged on the Day of the LORD (Revelation 11:19)? _____
_____

At the seventh trumpet, the Ark of His Covenant will be revealed, and between the Cherubim is the throne of God. Encased below in the golden box are the Ten Commandments as inscribed and given to mankind long ago by the finger of Yahweh, which still remain today as God's Moral Law. All ten are valid and based on the immutable character of Almighty God, including the seventh-day Sabbath; this day of rest was first given to all of mankind at creation (Genesis 2:2-3) and reaffirmed in stone with the command to "Remember"... although forgotten by even those who claim to exalt the Word of God. The commandment against idolatry and the worship of images remain as well, as do all the other commandments; because, "not the smallest letter, not the least stroke of a pen, will by any means disappear from the Law until everything is accomplished" and "heaven and earth disappear," Matthew 5:17-18.

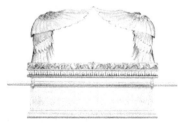

Insights In Prophecy
Unlock The Ancient Mysteries Of Daniel & Revelation
BIBLE DISCOVERY SERIES

Lesson 22

THE BEASTS: GOVERNMENTS & RULERS OF THE APPOINTED TIMES

Read Revelation 13

- **Explore What Nations Likely Comprise The Two Government Beasts**
- **Search The Power & Deceptive Tactics Of The Beast & False Prophet**

We are ready to examine Revelation 13 closely to determine if it is the unsealing (further enlightenment) of Daniel's first vision several hundred years earlier, recorded in Daniel 7. Revelation 13 is divided into two sections. The first ten verses describe the nations of the world combined as a united front, identified as the first "Beast"; and, a great global calamity out of which the newly recognized world leader will emerge to rule for 42 months, or 1,260 days.

The second half, verses 11-18, describes the second "Beast" animal, or governments, that will garner support of the first Beast (Antichrist) through the miracles of the False Prophet—another key figure in final events. This political-religious union will be instrumental in forcing worship of the image, the international icon of false worship, and will create the economic protocol that will ultimately mark individuals and control business transactions around the globe.

FIRST BEAST

Daniel 7 and Revelation 13 locate geographically the two key characters of the appointed times, the Beast and the False Prophet, who will control and influence the New World Order. We know both chapters cover similar periods, because both passages depict a dreadful Beast with seven heads and ten horns, made up of Lion, Bear and Leopard, which give way to a blasphemous leader who will rule for three and one-half years. And, each

SECOND BEAST

chapter foretells of the overcomers' persecution during last prophetic counting days of human history.

Beast From The Sea

1. Revelation 13:1 says the prophet John saw in vision the dragon (Satan) sitting on the shore. A gruesome governmental creature emerges from where? _____

2. Read Daniel 7:3. Where do his visionary creatures rise from? _____

3. What does water represent in prophecy (Revelation 17:15)? _____

The water/sea represents many nations and peoples worldwide, meaning an amalgamation of many Gentile nations.

A natural animal would have just one head with one or two horns; but, this grotesque Beast—representing the nations of the world is malformed with "seven heads and ten horns," which is noted several times in

213

prophecy (Revelation 12:3; 13:1; 17:3; Daniel 7:1-7). The symbolism teaches through its size and abnormal characteristics the ugly realities of a diverse and massive world government by which the demonic Man of Sin will be carried along. To add insult to injury, on each prominent head is written a blasphemous name. Blasphemous means profane, sacrilegious, offensive and ungodly. Evidently the action taken by the rulers and governments involve religious edicts and laws against Almighty God and His servant followers.

4. In Revelation 13:2, what three animals are added to the fourth deformed creature to make up this disfigured multi-headed Beast? _____

The Beast is comprised of leopard, with feet of a bear and mouth of a lion. By employing the same leopard, bear and lion creatures of Daniel 7, the prophet John is connecting the two prophetic visions. He is confirming the Revelation 13 vision depicts similar events, as found in the Daniel 7 vision. Satan the Dragon gives the Leviathan sea creature its power, throne and great authority (Revelation 12:9); this will be a time when governments will not be friendly to God's true followers, but rather antagonistic and hateful. Satan will employ the geopolitical union of the New World Order to stamp out the opposition, and to further his plans for global dominion.

The following chart illustrates the connection between Revelation 13 and Daniel 7, where both symbolize the end-time governments of the world.

The New World Order
Seven Heads---Ten Horns in Revelation and Daniel

Revelation 13:1-2
One Monstrous Beast Out of the Sea
Beast With Characteristics of Leopard, Feet of a Bear, Mouth of a Lion
Seven Heads and Ten Horns ....7 Heads....10 Horns
Total: New World Order...7 Heads...10 Horns

- -

Daniel 7:1-7
Four Monstrous Beasts Out of the Sea
Lion With Eagle's Wings ....1 Head.......0 Horns
Bear With Three Ribs ....1 Head.......0 Horns
Leopard With Four Heads/Four Wings ....4 Heads.....0 Horns
Terrible Beast With Ten Horns ....1 Head.....10 Horns
Total: New World Order ....7 Heads...10 Horns

- -

Lion With Eagle's Wings represents ....Great Britain/ United States
Bear With Three Ribs represents ....Russian Federation—Old Soviet Union
Leopard With Four Heads/ 4 Wings ....China and Eastern Asia Nations
Terrible Beast With Ten Horns ....Western European Union of Nations

While Daniel describes the four end-time powers as separate and distinct beasts, John now sees them combined and working as one. In Daniel 7, the fourth and most dreadful beast is the European Union sporting ten of the most prominent horn nations; however, in Revelation the sea monster only has just hints of the Lion, Leopard and Bear—again signifying the European Union's overwhelming authority over human affairs as it emerges the dominate power of the final days.

This is the New World Order, or Grand Design, described in the Scriptures. In both Daniel and Revelation, the emergence of the beasts from the sea heralds the world leader who will rise up from Europe out of the global upheaval and the New World Order to rule for a very specific 1,260 counting days.

The United Nations continues to advance global peace and unity; however, Revelation 13:3 introduces a catastrophic calamity. One of the following seven heads (either the head of Great Britain/United States; the head of Russia; one of the four heads of Eastern Asian Nations; or the head of the Western European Union with 10 Prominent Horn Nations) will receive a fatal blow. The attack looks as though it could bring quick demise of the mighty Beast from the sea; nevertheless, the grotesque political creature will recover with even greater power and strength after the attack. We will determine which head is injured next.

5. Revelation 12:3 describes the Dragon sporting seven heads and ten horns; however, John relays something quite unusual. By the time the Red Dragon reaches Heaven, three crowns are lost—from 10 to seven (7). The question must be asked, why are the three crowns missing (Daniel 7:7-8)? _____

_____

The Russian Bear is said to have three ribs in its mouth and is told to devour much human flesh. In this regard, the Bear will attack the Western European Union. Three horns (countries) will be quickly uprooted and destroyed in this World War III event, just as Antichrist (the little horn) rises to power to rule for three and one-half years.

Likewise, in the book of Revelation, a great calamity occurs whereby three crowns (rulers) will be remove just before the three and one-half year rule of the Beast (Revelation 13:3-5). A man from the "little horn" or "little country"—the Holy See of Rome—will rise to supremacy out of Russia's fatal attack on the European head. So, after the great annihilation of three European countries, Antichrist will rise up from the ashes as world leader; however, the astonished masses will unknowingly be worshiping a demonic power. Many will acknowledge, "Who is like the Beast? Who can wage war against it?" Revelation 13:4.

6. What does Luke indicate will propel the world leader to global dominance (21:9-11)? _____

_____

Fearful events and great signs from heaven.

It is written the Man of Lawlessness will rise to power and be held in high regard because of the "work of Satan displayed in all kinds of counterfeit miracles, signs and wonders," 2 Thessalonians 2:9. Revelation 16:14 declares that Satan, the Beast and the False Prophet are instruments of evil—"the spirits of demons performing miraculous signs."

Matthew 24:24 adds that false prophets and messiahs will "perform great signs and miracles" hoping to deceive God's chosen. The human mind cannot comprehend the magnitude of the nearly overwhelming deceptions that are about to take the world captive. Demonic apparitions disguised as much-loved religious figures will speak with flattery to hide their tenacious lies, for Satan himself "masquerades as an angel of light," 2 Corinthians 11:14. Through the mouths of false prophets and messiahs, Satan will distort Scriptures and prophecies to further his evil ploy.

It is possible that these deceptions and miraculous signs may be seen in public view in the skies and around the planet, with the sun becoming the circumambient glory of a false Virgin, about to give birth to the child—the Beast—who thinks he is chosen to rule all nations with a scepter of iron. Should we not be surprised that demons would cover themselves with the cloak of one so precious as Mary, the mother of Jesus?

The planet will be embroiled in nuclear holocaust and global upheaval; and, fear will grip mankind thinking WWIII will usher in the annihilation of all mankind and the end of the Planet Earth. Then, the multitudes will see a great sign and will hear words of comfort, unity and peace. "Follow the chosen one," it will be heard, "the designated vessel of peace in the midst of calamity, and all will be well." Consciences of men and women, ignorant of Scriptures' warnings, will cry out that this is from God—but they will be wrong, dead wrong.

"Mankind has abandoned God and religion," it will likely be heard, and "God is calling the world to Himself." "Now that God has intervened, the ministry of the Papacy to all men must begin." Masses of people will bow in reverence; sadly, the world be taken captive by Satan's masquerade. Jesus warned, "A wicked and adulterous generation looks for a miraculous sign," Matthew 16:4.

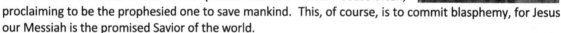

Revelation 13:5 notes the world leader, a demon cloaked in the body of a highly intelligent man gifted in language and of Jewish descent, will articulate the call of all mankind to follow his spiritual counsel. He will boast often, proclaiming to be the prophesied one to save mankind. This, of course, is to commit blasphemy, for Jesus our Messiah is the promised Savior of the world.

7. How does the following passages (Daniel 7:8; 7:25; 8:25; 11:23; 11:32) describe the evil ruler's ability to use his intellect to boast and rise to global fame? _____
_____
_____

Daniel saw in vision a man pontificating boastful words. He will take to himself position, rule and power not given him by God, but by Satan.

8. How long will Antichrist exercise his authority? _____

42 months of 30 days, or 1,260 counting days. See Daniel 7:25; 12:7; Revelation 11:2; 11:3; 12:6; 12:14 for other people and events associated with the same counting period.

In Revelation 13:6-8 the Beast opens his mouth to slander the Holy One of Israel, Heaven and those who live above. He will elevate himself as mediator between God and man, and demand that all spiritual decisions come through him. He will take to himself the glory and honor due God, His Name and His Tabernacle. Furthermore, he and his followers will persecute true believers and put many to death for their witness against him during the appointed time of the end. Believers who reject him to follow the book of Revelation's warnings will be considered law-breakers and criminals. However, committed followers of Yeshua will not give up their faith during the course of the conflict, even at the threat of livelihood and even death.

The omnipotent all-knowing Almighty God knows all and foreknew the course of human history before Satan's rebellion. The Holy One also looked through the portals of time to see who by faith would trust in Him and overcome to stand victorious on the other side of the battle—those who would remain faithful throughout the Ages to Come; and, God said it is good, and preordained that those individuals He saw victorious would indeed be called and glorified. Indeed, our salvation is not related to our merits, but only on the calling and grace of God.

"For those God foreknew He also *predestined* to be conformed to the likeness of His Son, that He might be the firstborn among many brothers," Romans 8:29. "And those He *predestined*, He also called; those He called, He also justified; those He justified, He also glorified," Romans 8:30. "He *predestined* us to be adopted as His sons through Jesus Christ, in accordance with His pleasure and will," Ephesians 1:5. "In Him we were also chosen, having been *predestined* according to the plan of Him who works out everything in conformity with the purpose of His will," Ephesians 1:11.

"Salvation is found in no one else, for there is no other name under Heaven given to men by which we must be saved," Acts 4:12. Salvation can be found in no other name at all. His Name is above every name in Heaven and on earth; above rabbi, priest, pastor and pope. A great multitude of all nations—faithful followers around the globe—will continue to trust in His promises and will not deny Messiah and His testimony in the face of persecution and martyrdom.

9. According to Daniel 7:9-10; 13-14; 22; 26, after the Little Horn Ruler comes onto the world scene, what opens up in Heaven? _____

A Court of Judgment will be brought into session for investigation of the books of record. Heaven will deal severely with Satan's malicious rebellion against Heaven, and the Lawless One's persecution of the saints.

**10. What two attributes does God ask of overcomers during the final conflict in Revelation 13:9-10? __
_____**

Jeremiah 15:2 says, "Those destined for death, to death; those for the sword, to the sword; those for starvation, to starvation; those for captivity, to captivity." Even the overcomer's destined persecution on earth is in God's hand, but their dreadful experiences will end in eternal reward.

Whether by poverty, imprisonment or death, believers named in the Book of Life must endure with both patience and faithfulness. Do not be surprised if you face great trials at the hands of former acquaintances, friends or relatives. Jesus said, "Remember the words I spoke to you: 'No servant is greater than his master.' If they persecuted Me, they will persecute you also," John 15:20.

The response of committed followers of Messiah in the face of tyranny must be one of nonresistance and no retaliation: first, because armed resistance will be futile; and second—and more importantly— because the Lamb has already guaranteed our victory. The overcomers will conquer this spiritual battle not with the sword, but with "the blood of the Lamb" and "the word of their testimony," Revelation 12:11. Therefore, until the Beast's forty-two months are over (v. 5), those destined for imprisonment will go to prison and those destined for death will be killed. Our sole responsibility is to be faithful and endure the counting days of the storm. The Father and the Lamb will intervene in due time.

John's point is not unlike Paul's in Romans 12:19-21: Do not take revenge, my friends, but leave room for God's wrath, for it is written, "It is mine to avenge; I will repay," says the LORD. Instead, "If your enemy is hungry, feed him; if he is thirsty, give him something to drink. In doing this, you will heap burning coals on his head. Do not be overcome by evil, but overcome evil with good."

Second Beast From The Earth

Revelation 13:11 introduces a second beast, a nondescript creature that sports two horns—which in prophecy represent nations. This creature rises from the earth. If the sea represents multitudes of nations and diverse languages (Revelation 17:15), the earth likely signifies the emergence of the beast with one common language.

11. How many horns, or countries, protrude from the beast? _____

Two countries are illustrated by the two horns.

12. The counties are known for their gentle lamb-like disposition, but at the appointed time of the end what does the beast begin to sound like? _____

A dragon—a clear reference to satanic cruelty and deceptions (Revelation 12:9). The creature, once well-known for its peaceful freedom-loving governance, will begin to speak in angry intolerance.

13. Daniel 7:4 also describes a two-nation power alliance. What is said of the Lion (Great Britain) with Eagle Wings (United States) that would suggest a *key personality* emerges from one of these countries?
_____

*Once the wings are torn off and America falls from superpower status, the Lion will be lifted up and "it stood on two **feet like a man**, and a **heart of a man** was given to it."*

The creature takes on human qualities, and prophecy is shouting "watch for a man" who will travel (feet) as an ambassador and give life (heart) to Antichrist's deceptions. Daniel is introducing the powerful end-time personality—the False Prophet—who will merge his efforts with the Man of Sin.

Of course, Daniel uses equivalent symbolism when he introduces the primary personality, the Antichrist. The prophet wrote that he will surface in connection with a little country—the "little horn" Vatican—illustrated by the animal's horn procuring human qualities: "eyes like the **eyes of a man** and a **mouth that spoke** boastfully," (7:8). The ruler visualizes (eyes) world dominion, and because of his miraculous comeback and ascent to power, and his academic credentials and skilled language, all ears will be turned to listen to his counsel (mouth). He is not afraid to speak highly of himself and what he thinks he can accomplish, and the global population will reverence and obey his commands.

The first beast of Revelation 13:1-10 is made up of many nations and led by the Man of Sin. The second beast sports just two horns (two nations) in 13:11, but will produce a personality—the False Prophet who lends support to the first prominent world leader—the Papal Antichrist.

14. According to Revelation 16:13-14, what three personalities are most instrumental in the worldwide deceptions of the last days? _____

The three are: the Dragon—Satan (Revelation 12:9); the Beast—Man of Lawlessness (Revelation 13:1-10); and, the False Prophet (Revelation 13:11-17); these three comprise the evil triumvirate.

15. How much power is the False Prophet given (Revelation 13:12)? _____

He is given great authority, alongside Antichrist.

This malicious dual, through whom Satan works, materializes when the first global-wide beast—made up of the most powerful United Nations members—emerges unified after the WW III events. The False Prophet from the British-American alliance will clasp hands with Rome. The once peaceful, freedom-loving leaders will begin to speak like the "dragon". Religious freedom will be suppressed as countries unite in their persecution of God's people—those who follow the testimony of Jesus Christ and keep God's unchangeable commandments.

Antichrist (of European roots) and the False Prophet (from British-American roots) will promise world peace through false religion, and Planet Earth will be taken captive. What makes the wine of delusion so intoxicating is the drink will combine Christian principles with pagan practices and Mother/child idolatry, topped with hints of Judaism, with emphasis on the beloved city—Jerusalem. In this way, Christians, Jews and Muslins will succumb to spiritual drunkenness and stupor.

16. Like the great prophet Elijah, the False Prophet will perform many miracles in order to capture the adoration of the masses (Revelation 13:13). What is his nearly overwhelming miracle? _____

_____

As Jesus calmed the winds that troubled the sea (Mark 4:39), Satan will, through his proxy, use nature's forces to amaze the people and to gather support for demonic delusions.

Whether wind, waves, earthquakes, fires, storms, volcanic activity or other catastrophes, there's nothing beyond Satan's unbridled power he won't use to terrorize the planet into following him and his partners in crime. We are warned not to allow even miracles of nature itself—even the call of lightning from the sky—to sway us away from Revelation's warnings. The great calamities of nuclear war, fears of growing war, famines and earthquakes which begin the sorrows of the end times (Matthew 24:6-8) are used by Satan to deceive and united the nations under his control for the sake of saving the planet.

Miracles are associated with both the Beast and the False Prophet who are Satan's counterfeit to Heaven's two last-day prophets—Moses and Elijah. There's a lesson to be learned. No miracle, great or small, can be a measurement of truth. Voices and the sights and sounds of our senses are emotionally driven, and can be very deceiving. Only God and His Word and the warnings contained within its pages can be trusted.

17. Revelation 13:14 states that the geopolitical beast will receive the fatal blow from the sword and yet the united global beast lived on. What horse is said to hold the "large sword" (Revelation 6:3-4)?

_____

Russia, the Old Soviet Union, corresponds to the "red horse"; Russia will take peace from the earth with its large nuclear sword.

18. The False Prophet can perform great miracles and signs. What does he set up in honor of the great religion, in view of the united nations? _____

Once under his spell, the False Prophet demands the nations to set up an image in honor of the beast.

The statue of honor will be erected. Most religious teachers will join in this commandment-breaking practice. Even some in Judaism, a stronghold against the building and worshipping of idols will break their Covenant with God in worship to this image. Protestants and Catholics, Muslims and other religions the world over will succumb to the prevailing influences of that day and will pay respect to this unholy abomination.

The idolatry in question is also defined as adoration of the state. The state, with the help of religious institutions, will attempt to make itself the object of worship and to claim allegiance that belongs to God alone. As long as the state is simply the state, an institution created by God (as it was for Paul in Romans 13:1-7), or at least tolerated by God (as it was for Peter in 1 Peter 2:13-17), it's possible for believers to be good and loyal citizens. But when the state oversteps its bounds in breaking the Laws of God, compliant citizenship is no longer an option. The battle lines will be drawn, if forced to go against the Law of God—we must obey God rather than man. "Hear the words of this Covenant, and speak to the men of Judah and to the inhabitants of Jerusalem; and say to them, 'Thus says the LORD God of Israel: "Cursed *is* the man who does not obey the words of this Covenant which I commanded your fathers in the day I brought them out of the land of Egypt, from the iron furnace, saying, 'Obey My voice, and do according to all that I command you; so shall you be My people, and I will be your God," Jeremiah 11:2-4. However, our role in the battle is a passive one governed by the counsel of verse 10: "if anyone is to go into captivity, into captivity he will go," and "if anyone is to be killed with the sword, with the sword he will be killed."

19. Which commandment of God is broken when images are worshiped (Exodus 20:1-17)? _____
_____

20. Once the idol is erected, what is the False Prophet empowered by Satan going to do (Revelation 13:15)? _____

The manmade image will seemingly come to life.

One Catholic author, Michael H. Brown, in his book, The Final Hour, extols the many visions of the Virgin Mary enshrined around the world. On page 276 he writes about a supernatural event in 1985 concerning a statue of Mary erected in Ireland: "The statue movements were pronounced, continuous, and at times nearly violent. Even disbelievers saw the statue quaking... This time it wasn't movements or superimpositions. This time it was a full-fledged, speaking apparition... The Virgin was suddenly a moving, breathing person—not a stone monument... The Virgin identified herself as the "Queen of Peace" and requested families to pray the Rosary together... [She said] I want your prayers continuously."

God warns about end-time events through His prophet Habakkuk: "Write down the revelation and make it plain on tablets so that a herald may run with it. For the revelation awaits an appointed time; it speaks of the end and will not prove false. Though it lingers, wait for it; it will certainly come and will not delay... Of what value is an idol, since a man has carved it? Or an image that teaches lies? For he who makes it trusts in his own creation; he makes idols that cannot speak. *Woe to him who says to wood, 'Come to life!' Or to lifeless stone, 'Wake up!'* Can it give guidance? It is covered with gold and silver; there is no breath in it," (Habakkuk 2:2-3, 18-19).

"All who make *idols are nothing,* and the things they treasure are worthless. *Those who would speak up for them are blind; they are ignorant,* to their own shame," Isaiah 44:9. "Like a scarecrow in a melon patch, their idols cannot speak; they must be carried because they cannot walk. Do not fear them; they can do no harm nor can they do any good," Jeremiah 10:5. "The *idols speak deceit,* diviners see visions that lie; they tell dreams that are false, they give comfort in vain. Therefore, the people wander like sheep oppressed for lack of a shepherd," Zechariah 10:2.

In reality, those who bow will be worshiping the demons who make the idols speak: "The rest of mankind that were not killed by these plagues still did not repent of the work of their hands; they did not stop *worshiping demons,* and idols of gold, silver, bronze, stone and wood– idols that cannot see or hear or walk," Revelation 9:20.

21. What will the corrupt statue announce (Revelation 13:15)? _____

All who do not worship the image should be killed, no exceptions.

Shadrach, Meshach and Abednego once faced a similar test. The demand was given to bow down before the golden image, but they said "we will not serve your gods or worship the image of gold you have set up," Daniel 3:18. The faithful three were put to a fiery test but were ultimately saved. May this be a lesson to those of us who face the test of the appointed times and seasons. In unwavering faith, we may live or die; but if death, we will be ultimately saved, and raised to life eternal.

22. The False Prophet forces everyone, from the lowest to the highest social status, to receive a mark on their right hand or forehead. This mark sets up the system for what? _____

The identification allows for control over the populace. Food and shelter will be given only upon acceptance of the false religion, and society's system of buying and selling tied to the identifying mark needed in order to obtain the necessities of survival. By so doing, Satan will force worship of himself and a false religion, even if it means death for his opponents. The mark and how it will be put into operation has not been spelled out in prophecy; however, the details will become very apparent at the unrolling of the scroll.

The Beast & His Number 666

The Beast has a mysterious number associated with him (Revelation 13:18). The Living Bible paraphrases the verse: "Here is a puzzle that calls for careful thought to solve it. Let those who are able, interpret this code: the numerical values of the letters of his name add to 666!"

If there has been one mysterious verse in the prophecies that has captured the minds and imaginations of thousands of Bible students, scholars and teachers throughout the centuries, it is Revelation 13:18—the prediction of Antichrist and his number 666! When God hides the meaning no man can know it, but when His hand is removed all men can see it, if they desire.

God has revealed a dire warning through His prophet John for these last days, for God knows the future and is "declaring the end from the beginning, and from ancient times the things that are not yet done," Isaiah 46:10. When Antichrist is revealed, the wise will be able to count the letter values of his name, and thereby know that he is the Evil One foretold in the prophecies. There will be no mistaking; the overcomers will know he is the prophesied one by his numbered name, words and actions.

Insights In Prophecy
Unlock The Ancient Mysteries Of Daniel & Revelation
BIBLE DISCOVERY SERIES

23. How do we know that individuals having wisdom will "understand" foretold rulers and events, while the wicked are deceived (Daniel 12:4, 10)? _____

The wise will understand the unsealed book of Daniel and the unfolding of his predictions in the book of Revelation. Solomon wrote, "Better a poor but wise youth than an old but foolish king who no longer knows how to take warning," Ecclesiastes 4:13.

Wisdom is not bestowed to the lazy or neglectful. "The fear of the LORD is the beginning of knowledge, but fools despise wisdom and discipline. If you call out for insight and cry aloud for understanding, and if you look for it as for silver and search for it as for hidden treasure, then you will understand the fear of the LORD and find the knowledge of God. For the LORD gives wisdom, and from His mouth come knowledge and understanding," Proverbs 1:7; 2:3-6. Having the Spirit's wisdom, you can know God's will and way. You will be able to stand; to even stand alone if need be, during the appointed time counting periods of the end.

Today, the English language is one of the most widely used tongues around the globe. However, at the writing of Revelation the English dialect and its alphabetic symbols were yet to be created. God could look through the portals of time to the 21st century, knowing full details including the Beast's name and the letter values that would add to 666. By God's design, more Scriptures have been printed and distributed in English than any other language, and by this tongue His prophetic warnings in the book of Revelation—"the testimony of Jesus Christ," Revelation 1:1-2—and the gospel of the kingdom have and will continue to reach around the globe, then the end would come (Matthew 24:14).

The cryptogram seems to be skillfully woven into the verse itself, and the mysterious code is found in the final number: 666. What do we find? The repeating multiples of 6 offer the clue to the alphabetical values, which can be used to decipher this ancient code. We assign to the 26 letters in the English alphabet accumulative values in multiples of 6 starting with A: 1X6, then B: 2X6, then C: 3X6, etc.). Here's how the values are designated:

1	A = 6		14	N = 84
2	B = 12		15	O = 90
3	C = 18		16	P = 96
4	D = 24		17	Q = 102
5	E = 30		18	R = 108
6	F = 36		19	S = 114
7	G = 42		20	T = 120
8	H = 48		21	U = 126
9	I = 54		22	V = 132
10	J = 60		23	W = 138
11	K = 66		24	X = 144
12	L = 72		25	Y = 150
13	M = 78		26	Z = 156

The following name LUSTIGER is given as an example. The letters of this last name add up to 666.

L	72
U	126
S	114
T	120
I	54
G	42
E	30
R	108
	666

The Papal Antichrist must also fulfill the ethnic, political and religious criteria found in the prophecies, along with the numerical value of the letters of his name. Antichrist (meaning, "opposing-messiah") has not yet taken his role. When this man/demon rises from the ashes of war by miraculous displays of Satanic power, clothed in human form and religious robes, we must point out his evil role and practices that will threaten the lives of countless individuals like the Jewish holocaust and pogroms of centuries past. Nonetheless, we must highlight his evil ways in humility and love. Paul wrote, "And though I have the gift of prophecy, and understand all mysteries, and all knowledge; and though I have all faith... and have not love, I am nothing," 1 Corinthians 13:2. Love for others must be the motivation for sharing insights into prophecy; to build up the body of Christ, not to destroy. The Ancient of Days will judge the demonic Beast clothed in human flesh. Vengeance is God's alone. "Do not take revenge, my dear friends, but leave room for God's wrath, for it is written: "It is mine to avenge; I will repay," says the LORD," Romans 12:19.

---- NOTES----

MOST HIGH GOD

האל הגבוה ביותר

Lesson 23

SEVEN PERSONALITIES AT WORK DURING THE APPOINTED TIMES

Read Revelation 14

- **Investigate The Work Of The Six Messengers & The Son Of Man**
- **Learn How God's Warnings Reach Around the Globe**

The first five verses of Revelation 14 propel us into the future to Day 1335, when the gathered 144,000 "firstfruits" harvest will stand on Mount Zion before God's throne singing victorious hymns of praise. The fifteen verses that follow describe events leading up to this joyous celebration.

Much like the sixth seal (Revelation 6:12-17) and the sixth trumpet (9:13-21), these verses take the reader to the very end of the conflict when the 144,000 are translated; but, before this happy reunion, the elect must first endure the last forty days in earthly turmoil—the Time of Jacob's Trouble. *Seven messengers* are seen at work in this chapter, and are intimately involved in the counting days of prophecy as deliverers of God's final warnings and ultimate destruction, which returns the planet back to its desolate condition prior to creation: "The earth was without form, and void; and darkness was on the face of the deep," Genesis 1:2. Jeremiah wrote about the Day of the LORD, "I looked at the earth, and it was formless and empty; and at the heavens, and their light was gone. I looked at the mountains, and they were quaking; all the hills were swaying. I looked, and there were no people; every bird in the sky had flown away. I looked, and the fruitful land was a desert; all its towns lay in ruins before the LORD, before His fierce anger," Jeremiah 4:23-26.

This colorful painting—*seven angels* with seven tongues of fire above their heads as portrayed in this Jewish work called *A Light to Jerusalem*, not only depict the *seven messengers* (five across the top, and two on each side with shofars), but seven flames are painted at the bottom of the artwork; six smaller flames, and in the middle is the seventh, with the seventh larger than the other six. "Is not *My word like fire*," declares the LORD?" Jeremiah 23:29.

This painting could easily represent Revelation 14 and appears in the 5760 Jewish Art Calendar provided by the Orthodox Lubavitch. It is placed on the page related to the months of Elul and Tishrei, the sixth and seventh months of the Biblical calendar (the months of August-September-October on the Gregorian calendar) when the High Holy Days are celebrated—Rosh Hashanah, Yom Kippur and Sukkot. It is this Festival season when the seven angels will, no doubt, begin to unleash their trumpet and vial plagues of vengeance.

John's book of Revelation has held its secrets for nearly two thousand years; but now by the grace of God, the mysteries can be unlocked as Daniel is merged alongside Revelation as complimentary books. Jesus once said, "Many prophets and righteous men have desired to see those things which ye see, and have not seen them; and to hear those things which ye hear, and have not heard them," Matthew 13:17 (KJV).

The final generation will have the privilege to comprehend the ancient mysteries that prophets yearned to comprehend but could not. We are nearing the events foretold by the Jewish prophets, and we must understand how governments and powerful leaders in our contemporary world will match with accuracy the divine prophecies. Otherwise, we may be taken captive by the overwhelming desire to follow the delusions and dictates of these men, and not God.

The Kingdom Calendar offers insight into the counting periods and pattern of end-time events. Only when the portentous episodes begin to unfold will we truly appreciate the precise details God has given us; its accuracy will encourage believers to hold on by faith to the "testimony of Jesus" given to John on the Island of Patmos.

Revelation 14 holds obscure, but vital, communication from Heaven, which we will review in this study. Previous lessons have described the work of the seven angels who blow the seven trumpets (chapters 8-10)—the same seven messengers who also pour out the seven plagues against the unrepentant world (chapters 15-16). This lesson series have demonstrated repeatedly how the designations *Seventh Angel* and *Michael* represent Yeshua, the Son of Man. Revelation 14 adds to this claim, as the lay out of the seven personalities of Revelation 14 are visually illustrated in this simple chart.

REVELATION 14

SON OF MAN #7

	Angel #3		Angel #4			
Angel #2				Angel #5		
Angel #1					Angel #6	
vs. 6-7	v. 8	vs. 9-12	vs. 14, 16	v. 15	v. 17	v. 18

Revelation 14 describes six angels at work, three on each side of the seventh—identified as the Son of Man. The seven represent the symbolism of the living Menorah of Heaven's Temple. Messiah is the middle messenger posed and ready to offer spiritual light: "God is light, and in Him is no darkness at all," 1 John 1:5. The middle flame signifies Christ, and is called *Ner Elohim*; also referred to as the *shamash*, or "servant lamp," since it is the source from which the others are kindled after their oil supply is renewed. And, when evil must be extinguished, the flame of the Menorah turns into the fire of judgment.

The duties of the seven are revealed in their order of delivery, according to how the events will transpire on earth. The first three proclaim life-saving counsel to the world before the Day of the LORD and show that these chosen messengers will personally proclaim last-day warnings to ensure that they circle the globe. The first messenger warns the Judgment is in session in Heaven, and that worship must be given to the Creator, and Him only, for the sentence of the Court is forthcoming (vs. 6-7). The second announces that Babylon is fallen, and to be aware—the whole world is intoxicated by Israel's acceptance of false Christianity (v. 8). And, the third cautions no man should worship the Beast or his idol or accept the false messiah's mark of allegiance (vs. 9-12).

The last three announce salvation and destruction. The fourth angel exits from the Temple Court in Heaven with the Father's announcement it is time to reap the good harvest from the ground, raised in resurrection (v. 15). The fifth announces the time has come to cut down and gather the wicked (v. 17). And, the sixth angel gathers the harvest of sinners to cast them into fiery destruction (v. 18). In the middle of the six angels you find the conquering Messiah—the Seventh Messenger—the announced King sitting upon the white cloud of glory with a harvesting tool in hand, and adorned with a crown of gold.

1. The Lamb is standing in Revelation 14:1. Who is represented by the Lamb (Revelation 5:5-6)? _____
_____

2. Mount Zion referred to in verse 1 is located where, as also described by Paul in Hebrews 12:22 and Galatians 4:26? _____

3. The 144,000 are identified as what ethnic group in Revelation 7:4? _____

The Father's name in their foreheads seals the twelve tribes of Israel from the torment and destruction of the plagues. Likewise, the mark of the beast, which the rebels receive in their foreheads, is closely associated with Antichrist's name (Revelation 13:16-17), while the seal of the Father and Son is associated with the Divine name and salvation. This proves that the sheep (saved) are being separated from the goats (lost), through decisions made during our lifetime, starting with a living faith in the Son of God (Matthew 25:32-33).

In ancient times, a royal seal signified ownership, the territory and authenticity of the document when affixed by the ruling king. The Ten Commandments hold a divine seal; it is found in the fourth commandment. There we discover both the name of King—"LORD" Creator, and His domain—"earth, sea and all therein." In this sense, the Sabbath signifies the seal of the Divine decree, and the 144,000 are keepers of the Covenant commandments of God. However, this seal is more than a conscientious observer of God's commandments; it represents the faithful heart of an obedient and submissive servant.

A Hebrew servant could voluntarily decide to serve his master by declaring, "'I love my master... and do not want to go free; then, his master must take him before the judges. He shall take him to the door or the doorpost and pierce his ear with an awl. Then he will be his servant for life," Exodus 21:5-6. This mark was a visible sign of his allegiance to his master, just as the 144,000 receive the seal of God as the sign of allegiance and voluntary service to their Messiah for the rest of their lives.

The 144,000 are chosen and sealed by their Owner for divine protection, just as the blood of the slain lamb was painted over the doorposts of Israel in Egypt so the death angel would pass by. John saw the virtuous 12,000 from each tribe, who will one day stand on Mount Zion in the New Jerusalem triumphant over the beast and his image, eternally secure from any further conflict.

4. In Revelation 14:2-3, John hears a loud roar like rushing waters and loud thunder. Whose voices are represented (Revelation 1:15; 10:1-3; 15:1-3; 19:1)? _____

The loud thunderous roar of praise is likely from three sources: First, Messiah's loud voice. Second, John hears harps playing and countless singing voices in Heaven. Chapters 15 and 19 identifies the musical players and singers as the great multitude of all nations (Jews and Gentiles)—"those who had been victorious over the beast and his image and over the number of his name," (v. 2). Finally, the 144,000 are singing with roaring praise a new song of victory. Who knows, maybe the innumerable angels are celebrating too!

5. The prophet writes that only the 144,000 can learn a special new melody, and with Messiah sing its lyrics. Why? _____

Surely John associated this end-time vision to the words of Psalm 149:1-3, which admonishes "Sing to the LORD a new song, His praise in the assembly of the saints. Let Israel rejoice in their Maker; let the people of Zion be glad in their King. Let them praise His Name with dancing and make music to Him with tambourine and harp. For the LORD takes delight in His people; He crowns the humble with salvation."

The 144,000 will have just endured the 40 days of Jacob's trouble—a time of Great Tribulation when the plagues are striking fear, terrible calamities annihilate mass populations of cities and towns, food and shelter are scarce, and the enemy is pursuing the righteous ones. Only Moses, Elijah and Jesus endured similar 40-day wilderness experiences without food, water, shelter and comfort.

As part of the annual Festival celebrations, immediately after Yom Kippur (Day of Atonement) the people of Israel are to begin building outdoor lean-tos for Sukkot—the Feast of Tabernacles. Five days later, observers step out of the comfort of their familiar surroundings to stay in their temporary huts (*sukkahs*), which God commanded to be built (Leviticus 23:34-44). Jewish scholars associate living in makeshift shelter as a remembrance of the *forty years* the children of Israel wandered in the wilderness, living in tents on their way to the Promised Land.

After over 3,000 years of rehearsing this Festival, Sukkot will meet its fulfillment both in Heaven and on earth; on earth by the last generation of celebrates— the 144,000 of the twelve tribes. They will scatter into the wilderness to live in makeshift shelters from God's proclaimed Yom Kippur until the end of time, enduring hardship for 40 days—each day for a year (Numbers 14:33-34)—on their way to Mount Zion (*The Kingdom Calendar*—Pts. 18, 19, 20 and 21).

6. Revelation 14:4-5 identifies the 144,000 as chosen, not having been defiled with women, so they are called what? _____

Virginity signifies purity; because of their spotlessness, the 144,000 members of the twelve tribes of Israel will have the unique privilege of following the Lamb wherever His travels in the Kingdom to come. In contrast, the "great multitude" of all nations who give their lives in faithful service during the last appointed time counting periods will serve God the Father "day and night in His Temple," Revelation 7:9, 15.

7. The 144,000 are also called "firstfruits." What does this designation portray (Jeremiah 2:1-3; Deuteronomy 15:19; 1 Corinthians 15:20)? _____
_____

Firstfruits focus on setting apart as holy to God; the first of all who are blessed, who follow later.

Israel was set apart and consecrated, in that these chosen were the first to be led through the wilderness to the Promised Land—Canaan. The firstborn and harvest of the *firstfruits* were to be distinguished as holy unto God in the family and daily agricultural duties. Messiah was called the *firstfruits* of those who will be raised from the dead. In this regard, the *firstfruits* indicate the first of a larger harvest; meaning, the holy harvest that will later emerge at the end of the 1,000-year millennial delay at the general resurrection.

The 144,000 have been "redeemed" and "purchased" by the blood of the Lamb. Messiah gave His life that He might surround Himself with faithful followers of His own choosing, who know from experience the depth of His love. He will single out for Himself only those who are found without lying tongues and with blameless hearts.

8. Read Zephaniah 3:13. How does it describe this remnant? _____

"The remnant of Israel will do no wrong; they will speak no lies" or deceit. Only by their calling and Divine help do they stand the test of trial. Jude 24 says, "To Him who is able to keep you from falling and to present you before His glorious presence without fault and with great joy."

Malakh & Angellos: Messengers Of Hope & Warning

After describing the 144,000 redeemed, along with their victorious arrival and celebration on Mt. Zion in Heaven, the 14th chapter of Revelation shifts to events leading up to the firstfruits harvest and how their salvation came about. As a point of clarification, the Western view of an angel is typically always a supernatural messenger from God, conveying news from God to men. However, the Hebrew word for angel מַלְאָךְ—"*malakh*" and the Greek term ἄγγελος, ου, ὁ--"*angellos*" are misunderstood by most Bible students. Strong's Concordance teaches angellos is "an angel, messenger. Properly, a *messenger* or *delegate*—either human (see the following verses where angellos is used to describe a human messenger: Matthew 11:10; Luke 7:24, 9:52; Galatians 4:14; and Philippians 2:25) or heavenly (a celestial *angel*); someone *sent* (by God) to proclaim His message." In other words, we need to be careful in our assumption an angellos, conveyed in English as either a messenger or angel, has to always be a supernatural being with wings; in many cases, the malakh and angellos of the Scriptures have been assigned to human messengers.

Messiah Jesus is also called *The Angel of the LORD* in the Hebrew Bible, for example in Zechariah 12:8: "On that Day the LORD will shield those [144,000], so that the feeblest among them will be like David, and the house of David will be like God, like the Angel of the LORD going before them." Wikipedia states, "In the Hebrew Bible the noun *malakh* "messenger" is used 214 times, of which approximately (according to translations in the King James Version) 103 times concern human messengers and 111 times concern heavenly messengers.

The term "מַלְאָךְ יהוה" (*malakh YHWH*), Hebrew for "Messenger of Yahweh", in the King James Version "Angel of the LORD", occurs 65 times and always in the singular. In the English translation it is usually accompanied with the definite article. The first reference is found in Genesis 16:7-12 where it says that "the Angel of the LORD" appeared to Hagar as she was fleeing in the wilderness from the rage of Abraham's wife. The Angel told her to go back home, and then He revealed to her that she was pregnant with a son whose name would be called Ishmael. A study of the subsequent appearances of the Angel of the LORD makes it very clear that they were pre-incarnate appearances of Yeshua. A good example is found in Exodus 3. There we are told that the Angel of the LORD appeared to Moses in the burning bush (verse 2). Then we are later told that the Angel spoke to Moses and said, "I am the God of your father, the God of Abraham, the God of Isaac, and the God of Jacob" (verse 6). In Exodus 23 we are told that God the Father spoke to Moses and said He would send an Angel to guide and protect the Children of Israel in the Wilderness. He refers to this Angel as "My angel" and states that "My Name is in Him" (Exodus 23:20-23). This is obviously no ordinary angel; this is the Most Holy One, later revealed in the person of Yeshua our Messiah.

The First Angel Messenger

9. What is the primary message of the first emissary (Revelation 14:6-7)? _____
How widespread will his message reach? _____

The eternal gospel will be proclaimed around the globe—to every nation. The message includes the loud cry, "Fear God and give Him glory because the hour of His Judgment has come. Worship Him who made the heavens, the earth, the sea and the springs of water."

10. Why would this global proclamation to "fear and worship the Creator" of the universe represent one of the three last messages to mankind? _____

The appointed time of the end will herald the hour of Judgment for all of mankind—the final division between the righteous and unrighteous.

11. In Revelation 22:11-12, what is Messiah's decree just before He returns that proves this point? ____
_____

"Let the one who does wrong continue to do wrong; let the vile person continue to be vile; let the one who does right continue to do right; and let the holy person continue to be holy. Look, I am coming soon! My reward is with Me, and I will give to each person according to what they have done."

12. Daniel 7:9-10 depicts the Judgment Court in Heaven. How? _____
_____

The Sanctuary in Heaven will be rearranged, with many gathered around to witness the proceedings and hear the evidence.

Before the Courtroom Judgment begins, war will shatter Heaven's peace and rout the Sanctuary in Heaven (Revelation 12:7; Daniel 8:10-11); but, after Michael's victory over Satan and his army, thrones will be moved into place (Daniel 7:9-10) and God the Father will take His place upon the Seat of Judgment; then, for 1,150 days the Books of Evidence will be opened. Decisions will be made that will influence the outcome. On earth, it is a time of solemn reflection when we must decide either to follow Jesus and His testimony, or Antichrist and his decrees. What destiny will we decide upon? Will we live by faith in worship of our Creator, or compromise in fear with the world's leader and the majority around us? Who we trust will determine either life or death. In the last days, our faith cannot be secreted away in quiet worship. Like Shadrach, Meshach and Abednego, our actions will expose our hearts—whether we are living by faith in the Son of God, or not. Authentic faith does not allow us to deny Christ by either words or actions. Jesus warned, "Whoever denies Me before men, him I will also deny before My Father," Matthew 10:33.

13. What commandments will be the basis of this Judgment (Revelation 11:19; 15:5)? _____

The Ten Commandments, as written on tablets of stone and protected in the Ark of the Testimony, will be the basis of the judgment hour decisions.

14. How does John tie worship of God with our response to His Law (1 John 2:3-4; 3:3-4; 3:22; 5:2-4)? __

_____

15. John the prophet conveys that an intrinsic part of the eternal gospel is the worship of the Creator. What commandment is intimately tied to the creation of God (Genesis 2:1-3; Exodus 20:8-11), as noted earlier in our lesson? _____

The Second Angel Messenger

The second angel gives a clear warning, "Fallen! Fallen is Babylon the Great, which made all the nations drink of the maddening wine of her adulteries," Revelation 14:8.

16. Read Revelation 17:18 and 11:7. What great city is identified as Babylon? _____

Jerusalem, the city of three religions—Judaism, Christianity and Islam—should refuse the arrival of the Wicked One, but instead will allow him, through Jerusalem's political and religious leaders, onto the reconstructed Temple Mount and into her rebuilt Temple. Babylon promotes the erroneous worship of idols and the fraudulent Man of Sin. Nations will be intoxicated with this wine of mystery and deception.

17. God has allowed enemies to destroy Jerusalem in times past because of her sin. What did Jesus say about Jerusalem in Matthew 24:2-3, and the necessity to leave quickly in the last moments of time (Matthew 24:15-21; Luke 21:20)? _____

_____

18. Why would it be necessary for Jerusalem's identity to be masked in secrecy in Revelation's prophecies, cloaked behind the Babylon name until the appointed time of the end? _____

_____

That the eyes of the willful and obstinately ignorant might be blinded from the truth (Isaiah 42:18-25; Matthew 15:14; 23:16; Romans 2:17-24; 11:7-9, 25-27; 2 Corinthians 4:3-4; 1 John 2:11; Revelation 3:17).

God has hidden His mysteries through the ages. Even today, we do not fully comprehend all future events; but if our hearts are willing we will not despise His counsel. Not until Michael, the Seventh Angel, begins to speak loudly His thunderous commands at Yom Kippur will all the mysteries of God be finished (Revelation 10:7). However, prior to this Daniel 12:4 declares that many end-time prophecies will be understood in a new light by those who are wise, when the "time of the end" is about to begin. Even then, followers of God must live through trials by faith and with unanswered questions; nonetheless, the wicked will not perceive the events unfolding around them, because of their unbelief.

The Third Angel Messenger

The third messenger of global influence declares with a loud cry, "If anyone worships the Beast and his image and receives his mark on the forehead or on the hand, he too, will drink of the wine of God's fury," Revelation 14:9-10. Here is the ominous warning against anyone following the Beast's profane counsel against God, worshiping his idol or receiving his mark that allows for buying and selling.

19. What type of punishment comes with conformity to his decrees? _____

231

A fiery demise—the smoke of their torment rises forever and ever.

The original idiomatic expression "smoke will rise forever" comes from Edom's fall in Isaiah 34:8-10, and denotes a complete and thorough destruction. The smoke does not literally raise forever as proven by the Isaiah chapters; but rather, relays the fact that Edom would not be rebuilt again after the Day of the LORD. In fact, "from generation to generation it will lie desolate." However, the day will arrive when "desert and parched land will be glad; the wilderness will rejoice and blossom," Isaiah 35:1. Sodom and Gomorrah, as examples of the wrath of God in the last days, "*suffered the vengeance of eternal fire*" (Jude 7), yet the flames do not continue today. The destruction is eternal, but not the flames.

Revelation 14:11-12 testifies, "There is no rest day or night for those who worship the beast and his image, or for anyone who receives the mark of his name. This calls for patient endurance on the part of the saints who obey God's commandments and remain faithful to Jesus."

20. Why do the wicked suffer constant turmoil with restless days and nights? _____
_____

The righteous keep God's commandments and carry on with an unwavering faith in Jesus. In contrast, the wicked may be supplied with food and shelter in the closing moments of time, but they will have no peace because of their sinful lives and uncertain future. "There is no soundness in my flesh because of thine anger; neither is there any rest in my bones because of my sin," Psalm 38:3. "But the wicked are like the tossing sea, which cannot rest, whose waves cast up mire and mud," Isaiah 57:20.

20. As the Day of the LORD draws near, the three messengers will complete their warnings in concerted effort with human laborers in Christ; but, what will happen to many faithful workers in the last moments of time (Revelation 14:13)? _____

Many saints will be laid to rest during the closing moments of time. Their good deeds will follow them with rewards of service at their resurrection.

The SON OF MAN: The Seventh Personality

The three messengers have completed their worldwide ministry. Now John sees a white cloud, and seated on the cloud was one "like a *son of man*" with a crown of gold on His head and a sharp sickle in His hand," Revelation 14:14.

John is connecting Daniel's prediction concerning "one like the *son of man*, coming with the clouds of Heaven" (7:13-14), who will step before the Ancient of Days to receive His kingdom. The future virgin birth and deity of One called Yeshua had not yet been fully revealed in Daniel's day. The prophet simply stated he saw what looked to be a human—a son of a man—in the middle of angelic beings approaching the Father. Now in Revelation 14, John sees "one like a son of man" seated in authority, wearing His awarded crown and posed to harvest the precious grain at the end of time; however, He waits for the final word from the Sanctuary.

The Fourth Angel Messenger

The fourth angel emerges from the Temple in Heaven with demands from the Father to His Son—the High Priest, "Take your sickle and reap, because the time to reap has come, for the grain harvest of the earth is ripe," Revelation 14:15-16. The resurrection harvest is fully mature, and the overcomers are ready to be gathered up from the ground.

22. Read 1 Corinthians 15:35-49. How does Paul describe in agricultural terms the death of the old body, which then springs forth as a new imperishable one? How is the grain harvest of Revelation 14 described earlier by Paul (15:51-54)? Who is identified as worthy of the resurrection (15:58)? _____

_____

Paul speaks of the resurrection in terms of sowing and harvest.

That seed which is planted and dies eventually breaks through the soil and springs up to new life. The earth-bound body will give way to the eternal; the natural body will be raised as spiritual; the perishable body we now possess will one day be imperishable. Paul continues by saying "we will not all sleep" in death, "but we will all be changed—in a flash, in the twinkling of an eye, at the last [seventh] trumpet. For the trumpet will sound, the dead will be raised imperishable." He finalizes his thoughts with this admonition: "Stand firm. Let nothing move you. Always give yourselves fully to the work of the LORD, because you know that your labor in the LORD is not in vain." Laborers for Christ who endure to the end, even in the face of death, will be saved (Matthew 24:13). Yeshua also said that "unless a kernel of wheat falls into the ground and dies [in death], it remains only a single seed. But if it dies, it produces many seeds [a great harvest]. The man who loves his life will lose it, while the man who hates his life in this world [willing to die to self and/or die in martyrdom] will keep it for eternal life," John 12:23-26.

23. Why does Messiah await the announcement from His Father (Matthew 24:36; Acts 1:7)? _____

_____

Jesus has always been attentive to His Father's will (John 4:34; 5:30; 6:38). The appointed hour of Messiah's revelation is known only by the Father, and it is His decision when final permission is given through the announcing fourth angel for Yeshua to reap. The Son of Man takes His symbolic sickle and gathers in the fall harvest.

The Fifth & Sixth Angel Messengers

The fifth angel emerges from the Temple in Revelation 14:17. His work follows just after the completion of the righteous harvest; however, this messenger carries a tool of doom. The sixth angel—the angel in charge of the altar of fire in Heaven—called out in a loud voice to the fifth angel, "take your sickle and gather the clusters of grapes from the earth's vine, because its grapes are ripe," (14:18).

24. What type of harvest is spoken of here (Revelation 14:19-20; Matthew 13:37-43)? _____

_____

25. The chapter concludes with the symbolism of a winepress, where the sinners of violence are trampled underfoot in God's anger. Joel 3:13 and Isaiah 63:1-6 describe the same event. How? _____

_____

Insights In Prophecy
Unlock The Ancient Mysteries Of Daniel & Revelation
BIBLE DISCOVERY SERIES

The Word of God takes us to that future Day of wrath when Messiah will rise up to tread the winepress and do "His work, His strange work, and perform His task, His alien task," Isaiah 28:21.

So great is the magnitude of the slaughter outside the city of Jerusalem that prophecy represents the bloodshed as bridle high, and the length as about 180 miles (or 300 kilometers) long—the approximate north and south span of Israel from Mt. Hermon to Masada in the days of John's revelations.

The prophet Isaiah wrote about the Messiah Warrior in chapter 59, "He saw that there was no one, He was appalled that there was no one to intervene; so, His own arm achieved salvation for him, and His own righteousness sustained him. He put on righteousness as His breastplate, and the helmet of salvation on His head; He put on the garments of vengeance and wrapped Himself in zeal as in a cloak. According to what they have done, so will He repay wrath to His enemies and retribution to His foes; He will repay the islands their due," (vs. 16-18). David wrote, "Why do the nations conspire and the peoples plot in vain? The kings of the earth rise up and the rulers band together against the LORD and against His anointed, saying, "Let us break their chains and throw off their shackles. "The One enthroned in Heaven laughs; the LORD scoffs at them. He rebukes them in His anger and terrifies them in His wrath, saying, "I have installed My King on Zion, My holy mountain," Psalm 2:1-6.

The prophet Zephaniah writes in the first chapter of his scroll (1:2-18) about the Day of the LORD, and in very clear terms describes the fate of all the wicked and the destitution of Planet Earth when Almighty God is done with the wrath of His fury, including those who remain in in the rebellious city of Jerusalem. Whether you believe the disturbing finality of a desolate earth at the Armageddon battle is up to you: "I will sweep away everything from the face of the earth," declares the LORD. "I will sweep away both man and beast; I will sweep away the birds in the sky and the fish in the sea—and the idols that cause the wicked to stumble." "When I destroy all mankind on the face of the earth,"  declares the LORD, "I will stretch out My hand against Judah and against all who live in Jerusalem. I will destroy every remnant of Baal worship in this place, the very names of the idolatrous priests— those who bow down on the roofs to worship the starry host, those who bow down and swear by the LORD and who also swear by Molek, those who turn back from following the LORD and neither seek the LORD nor inquire of Him." Be silent before the Sovereign LORD, for the Day of the LORD is near. The LORD has prepared a sacrifice; He has consecrated those He has invited."

The prophet continues, "On the Day of the LORD's sacrifice I will punish the officials and the king's sons and all those clad in foreign clothes. On that Day I will punish all who avoid stepping on the threshold, who fill the temple of their gods with violence and deceit. "On that Day," declares the LORD, "a cry will go up from the Fish Gate, wailing from the New Quarter, and a loud crash from the hills. Wail, you who live in the market district all your merchants will be wiped out, all who trade with silver will be destroyed. At that time I will search Jerusalem with lamps and punish those who are complacent, who are like wine left on its dregs, who think, 'The LORD will do nothing, either good or bad.' Their wealth will be plundered, their houses demolished. Though they build houses, they will not live in them; though they plant vineyards, they will not drink the wine." The Great Day of the LORD is near—near and coming quickly. The cry on the Day of the LORD is bitter; the Mighty Warrior shouts His battle cry."

Zephaniah finalizes his prophecy with these words, "That Day will be a day of wrath—a day of distress and anguish, a day of trouble and ruin, a day of darkness and gloom, a day of clouds and blackness—a day of

234

trumpet and battle cry against the fortified cities and against the corner towers. "I will bring such distress on all people that they will grope about like those who are blind, because they have sinned against the LORD. Their blood will be poured out like dust and their entrails like dung. Neither their silver nor their gold will be able to save them on the Day of the LORD's wrath." In the fire of his jealousy the whole earth will be consumed, for he will make a sudden end of all who live on the earth."

Again, Yeshua warns the beloved city of Judaism, Christianity and Islam, "When you see Jerusalem being surrounded by armies, you will know that its desolation is near. Then let those who are in Judea flee to the mountains, let those in the city get out, and let those in the country not enter the city. For this is the time of punishment in fulfillment of all that has been written," Luke 21:20-22.

---- NOTES----

THE MAJESTY
ON HIGH

העונש על הגובה

Insights In Prophecy
Unlock The Ancient Mysteries Of Daniel & Revelation
BIBLE DISCOVERY SERIES

Lesson 24

THE OPENED TEMPLE: ARK OF THE COVENANT REVEALED

Read Revelation 15

- Discover Why The Opened Temple Declares The Day of Atonement As The Day Of The LORD
- Explore Why The Ark Is Revealed Just Before God's Wrath Is Poured Out

John's attention is turned to a "great and marvelous sign: seven angels with the seven last plagues." The seven angels stand prepared with vessels of God's wrath, ready to emerge from the Temple to pour out their fiery contents upon earth's rebellious inhabitants.

What the prophet sees is preparation for the onslaught of apocalyptic catastrophes from the throne room of God that will raze the ecological system of Planet Earth—the plants, animals and all living creatures; and, the chaos will grow more dreadful day by day as time marches on towards the Armageddon battle at Day 1335.

At this point, God's patience with sin and sinners has expired. The length and culmination of the appointed times and seasons counting periods have already been predetermined by the Ancient of Days and recorded in the Book of Truth. The 1,150 counting days of the Courtroom Judgment will close (Pt. 18) and all prayers will cease to be heard, when the destiny of every living man, woman and child will be sealed.

The prophet John recorded the concluding proclamation heard at the end of the 1,150 counting days of Judgment, when Messiah will end probation and divide the saved from the lost with His Courtroom decree: "He that is unjust, let him be unjust still: and he which is filthy, let him be filthy still: and he that is righteous, let him be righteous still: and he that is holy, let him be holy still. And, behold, I come quickly; and My reward is with Me, to give every man according as his work shall be," Revelation 22:11-12 (KJV).

1. Where is the location of the great and marvelous sign (Revelation 15:1)? _____

Heaven's seven angels with vials in hand signal calamity is forthcoming and represent mystical events and global portents direct from God Himself through His assigned messengers of doom. When all seven angels have poured out their vials against sinful humanity, God's wrath will be finished.

2. God's anger is unleashed during the *Great Tribulation*. Review *The Kingdom Calendar*; how many days will the final plagues last? _____

There are 40 days between Yom Kippur and Day 1,335, during which the last plagues will be delivered; however, these days will be cut short, so no man can know the day or hour of Messiah's visible return.

3. John saw the sea of glass mixed with fire (Revelation 15:2). Where is it located (Revelation 4:6)? ___

_____

4. A large group of victorious saints are identified safe and secure in Heaven's Temple *before* the outpouring of God's wrath. How is this diverse group of overcomers described, who have endured Antichrist's 1,260 days of rule? _____

They are identified as having first overcome the beast, his image and his number; they are not the saints of all the ages, but rather end-time victors. They will endure harsh treatment, but will not yield to idolatry, accept the mark to buy or sell, or honor the Beast's name.

5. What work must be performed before the final wrath is unleashed (Revelation 7:2-4)? _____ _____

The 144,000 elect must be sealed for protection to withstand the dangers of the Great Tribulation until the visible return of Christ. They are the only saved ones who are "alive and will remain" after the resurrection of the great multitude that no man can number; and therefore, the only ones to be sealed for divine safety against the onslaught of evil forces and God's trumpet and vial woes.

6. What multitude of countless believers arrive in Heaven to stand before the throne in the Temple (Revelation 7:9), identical to the group of Revelation 15? _____

In contrast to the 144,000 from the twelve tribes of Israel, the "great multitude" of every nation, tribe, people and language are seen standing before the throne in Heaven on the sea of glass. This great number of saints "come out of [escape from the midst of] the Great Tribulation," just as it is about to begin.

7. Revelation 3:10 and Luke 21:36 speak about the escape of these last-day victors from the Great Tribulation testing, where they will stand safe and secure before the Son of Man. How are they described? _____

"Since you have kept My command to endure patiently, I will also keep you from the hour of trial that is going to come upon the whole world to test those who live on the earth." And, "Be always on the watch, and pray that you may be able to escape all that is about to happen [on earth], and that you may be able to stand before the Son of Man [in Heaven]."

8. When their salvation comes, how is the group praised (Revelation 12:11)? _____

They are overcomers who did not shrink from the threat of death or deny Christ, because they loved the Savior more than their own lives.

9. Where will these victorious saints serve for all eternity (Revelation 7:15)? _____

These martyrs will serve before and in the presence of God forever. They will never worry about food, water or heat of day. Sadness and sorrow will not afflict them anymore.

The Song Of Moses

Revelation 15:3-4 identifies these end-time victors—the kingdom rulers—who will receive musical instruments distributed by God and sing the song of Moses and the Lamb. Gifted with the ability to play without having learned the instruments beforehand, and as though they had played a lifetime, the singers praise Yahweh for His marvelous deeds, proclaiming that His acts of punishment are just. The multitude, so large that no one could count, declares in praise, "all nations [of every nation, tribe, people and language]... come and worship before you, for your righteous acts [of judgment] have been revealed" to the whole world by Heaven's seven destroyers.

The entire Song of Moses is found in Deuteronomy 32:1-43. The hymn was sung just before the prophet's death as guidance for the people of Israel so "that you may command your children to obey carefully all the words of this law," (32:46).

However, Moses rightly predicted that in spite of his dire warnings after his death "you will utterly corrupt yourselves, and turn aside from the way which I have commanded you; and evil will befall you in *the latter days*; because you will do evil in the sight of the LORD, to provoke Him to anger through the work of your hands [idolatry]," (31:29 KJV).

The song speaks of the Rock, and of His righteous judgments. Although Israel was the "apple of His eye," she is warned not to forget her heritage and forsake Hashem to follow strange gods and idols. Otherwise, God's wrath will be kindled and it will "devour the earth and its harvests and set afire the foundations of the mountains," (32:22). God proclaims, "I will send wasting famine against them, consuming pestilence and deadly plague," (32:24).

Adonai continues in Deuteronomy 32:40-41, "I will lift My hand to Heaven and declare: As surely as I live forever... I will take vengeance on My adversaries and repay those who hate Me." "Rejoice, O nations, with His people, for He will avenge the blood of His servants [the martyred]; He will take vengeance on His enemies and make atonement for His land and people," (32:43).

Earlier in the life of Moses, he and the children of Israel sang a song of deliverance after crossing the Red Sea, which also honored the strong arm and powerful hand of the LORD. He wrote, "Your right hand, O LORD, was majestic in power. Your right hand, O LORD, shattered the enemy," Exodus 15:6.

At the time when the Lawless One pitches his royal tents in Jerusalem and sets up the abomination, he will reach the apex of God's wrath. He will come to a swift end. Michael will stand and the "time of distress such as has not happened" before will commence. Israel will be delivered, and the Archangel's voice and trumpet blast of resurrection will be heard. He will raise His hands and "swear by Him who lives forever... all these things [prophecies of Daniel] will be completed," Daniel 11:45; 12:1-3, 7. The resurrected are gathered to Heaven and sing with Moses the song of victory... for they endured to the end.

The Opened Temple: Yom Kippur—The Day Of Atonement

10. At Revelation 15:5 John's attention turns once again to the Temple in Heaven. The Sanctuary is described as housing what? _____

He sees the Tabernacle of Testimony; in other words, the Ark that resides within the Holy of Holies in the Temple. The primary purpose of the earth tent Temple that Moses built was to house the Ark of the Covenant (1 Kings 8:20-21), and between the cherubim the blazing glory of God dwelled (Exodus 40:34-35; Exodus 9:3). God set aside the inner chamber of the Ark as residence for the most revered of all religious artifacts—the Ten Commandments of God. The tablets of stone, written by God's own finger, were to be honored and preserved by His people. Exodus 25:10-22 describes the making of the Ark of the Testimony for this purpose.

The Holy of Holies was so sacred that it was off limits even for the High Priest, except one day a year. Only on the Day of Atonement was the High Priest allowed to open the veil, and cautiously enter in with much trepidation. Yom Kippur is the most solemn and holiest day of the Festival year, and it finalizes the ten Days of Awe—of reflection, repentance and Divine judgment—from the Feast of Trumpets to the Day of Atonement. Yom Kippur is spent in prayer, fasting and seeking God's grace and mercy.

The Day is also considered to be a day of announcement. God's sacred Name YHWH (Yahweh) was pronounced by the High Priest before the general assembled masses in the Temple courtyard. The ultimate

יהוה

Yahweh

fulfillment of the Day of Atonement will occur at the end of the appointed time when Messiah Himself will suddenly come to the Jerusalem Temple in the darkness of storms to pronounce with loud thunderous voice His authority as King over all the earth (Malachi 3:1-2).

The three and one-half years of global famine will be broken. "He bowed the heavens also, and came down; and darkness was under His feet. And He rode upon a cherub, and did fly: and He was seen upon the wings of the wind. And He made darkness pavilions round about Him, dark waters, and thick clouds of the skies. Through the brightness before Him were coals of fire kindled. The LORD thundered from heaven, and the Most High uttered His voice. And He sent out arrows, and scattered them; lightning, and discomfited them. And the channels of the sea appeared, the foundations of the world were discovered, at the rebuking of the LORD, at the blast of the breath of His nostrils," 2 Samuel 22:10-16.

Judaism teaches the whole world is suspended in judgment—who shall live and who shall die—at Yom Kippur. One author wrote, "The concluding service of Yom Kippur takes its name and imagery from the symbol of the closing of the gates of Heaven. Originally it may have referred to the closing of the Temple gates. This imagery of time running out recurs throughout the service. For example, the liturgy is changed from *zakhreinu le-hayyim* to *hotmeinu le-hayyim*—from "remember us" to "seal us"—in the Book of Life," page 117, The Jewish Holidays: A Guide and Commentary, by Michael Strassfeld.

In times past, as the priest would enter and exit the Holy of Holies, the Ark of the Testimony and the glory of God would be exposed briefly as a reminder of God's Holy Law and sacred standard. So too, on the final Day of Atonement the Temple will be opened to expose the Ark of the Covenant and the blazing glory of God (Psalms 19:10; Revelation 15:8), who will come by way of the east (Ezekiel 43:2; 7). On this Day, the whole world will distinguish the Law and the glory of the One they have despised (Numbers 14:21; Isaiah 40:5). And, when Messiah shines forth and His loud voice is heard, He will gather to Almighty those who have made a sacrifice in life and death to Him (Psalm 50:1-6; Psalm 96:13; Psalm 98:9).

11. God in the person of Messiah descended to reveal His Law to the people at Mt. Sinai. Read Exodus 19 and 20. This historical event foreshadowed the future Day of the LORD and gives us a glimpse into the last Day of Atonement at the end of time.

    a. What prophet declared the coming of Messiah (19:9-10)? _____

    b. The LORD descended in a thick [dark] what (19: 9)? _____

    c. How many days of preparation did the LORD give the people to meet Him (19:10-11)? _____

    d. What sound would call the people to meet God (19:13)? _____

    e. When the third day arrived, what time of the day was it (19:14-16)? _____

At the dawning of a new day, as the light broke the darkness.

   f. What supernatural phenomenon accompanied the coming of the LORD (19:16)? _____
   Voice as a trumpet, thunderings, lightning, thick cloud, fire and earthquake.
   g. Who was called up to meet God (19:20)? _____
   h. What did God reveal at His visitation (Exodus 20:1-17)? _____

The Moral Law of God—the Ten Commandments—are revealed. Just as Messiah came down from Heaven to declare His righteous Law at Mt. Sinai, so too at the end of time Yeshua will come down again in similar fashion to exalt His Law of liberty (James 2:8-13).

12. Read the seven passages below. How do other prophets connect the events of the Day of the LORD with the Mt. Sinai experience? _____
_____
_____

~ Joel 2:1-2, 10-11: _"Blow the trumpet in Zion; sound the alarm on My holy hill. Let all who live in the land tremble, for the Day of the LORD is coming. It is close at hand—day of darkness and gloom, a day of clouds and blackness. Like dawn spreading across the mountains a large and mighty army comes, such as never was of old nor ever will be in ages to come… Before them the earth shakes, the sky trembles, the sun and moon are darkened, and the stars no longer shine. The LORD thunders at the head of His army; His forces are beyond number, and mighty are those who obey His command. The Day of the LORD is great; it is dreadful. Who can endure it?"_

~ Joel 3:14-16: _"Multitudes, multitudes in the valley of decision [ten days of Awe between Rosh Ha-Shanah and Yom Kippur]! For the Day of the LORD is near in the valley of decision. The sun and moon will be darkened, and the stars no longer shine. The LORD will roar from Zion and thunder from Jerusalem; the earth and the sky will tremble. But the LORD will be a refuge for His people [144,000 elect], a stronghold for the people of Israel."_

~ Amos 1:2: _"He said: "The LORD roars from Zion and thunders from Jerusalem; the pastures of the shepherds dry up, and the top of Carmel withers."_

~ Amos 5:18-21: _"Woe to you who long for the Day of the LORD! Why do you long for the Day of the LORD? That day will be darkness, not light. It will be as though a man fled from a lion only to meet a bear, as though he entered his house and rested his hand on the wall only to have a snake bite him. Will not the Day of the LORD be darkness, not light—pitch-dark, without a ray of brightness? I hate, I despise your religious feasts; I cannot stand your assemblies [for that is when the end will come]."_

~ Micah 1:3-7: _"Look! The LORD is coming from His dwelling place; He comes down and treads the high places of the earth. The mountains melt beneath Him and the valleys split apart, like wax before the fire, like water rushing down a slope. All this is because of Jacob's transgression, because of the sins of the house of Israel. What is Jacob's transgression? Is it not Samaria? What is Judah's high place? Is it not Jerusalem? Therefore I will make Samaria a heap of rubble, a place for planting vineyards. I will pour her stones into the valley and lay bare her foundations. All her idols will be broken to pieces; all her temple gifts will be burned with fire; I will destroy all her images. Since she gathered her gifts from the wages of prostitutes, as the wages of prostitutes they will again be used._

~ Micah 3:2-12: *"You who hate good and love evil; who tear the skin from My people and the flesh from their bones; who eat My people's flesh, strip off their skin and break their bones in pieces; who chop them up like meat for the pan, like flesh for the pot? Then they will cry out to the LORD, but He will not answer them. At that time, He will hide His face from them because of the evil they have done. This is what the LORD says: As for the prophets who lead My people astray, if one feeds them, they proclaim `peace'; if he does not, they prepare to wage war against him. Therefore, night will come over you, without visions, and darkness, without divination. The sun will set for the prophets, and the day will go dark for them. The seers will be ashamed and the diviners disgraced. They will all cover their faces because there is no answer from God. But as for Me, I am filled with power, with the Spirit of the LORD, and with justice and might, to declare to Jacob his transgression, to Israel his sin. Hear this, you leaders of the house of Jacob, you rulers of the house of Israel, who despise justice and distort all that is right; who build Zion with bloodshed, and Jerusalem with wickedness. Her leaders judge for a bribe, her priests teach for a price, and her prophets tell fortunes for money. Yet they lean upon the LORD and say, Is not the LORD among us? No disaster will come upon us. Therefore because of you, Zion will be plowed like a field, Jerusalem will become a heap of rubble, the Temple hill a mound overgrown with thickets."*

~ Zephaniah 1:14-18: *"The Great Day of the LORD is near—near and coming quickly. Listen! The cry on the Day of the LORD will be bitter, the shouting of the warrior there. That day will be a day of wrath, a day of distress and anguish, a day of trouble and ruin, a day of darkness and gloom, a day of clouds and blackness, a day of trumpet and battle cry against the fortified cities and against the corner towers. I will bring distress on the people and they will walk like blind men, because they have sinned against the LORD. Their blood will be poured out like dust and their entrails like filth. Neither their silver nor their gold will be able to save them on the Day of the LORD's wrath. In the fire of His jealousy the whole world will be consumed, for He will make a sudden end of all who live in the earth."*

13. Only one other time in the book of Revelation is the Temple said to be "opened," (11:19). What global phenomena accompany this swinging door? _____

14. What events are about to begin once the door on the Temple is opened (11:15-18)? _____
_____
_____

15. When Messiah exits the Temple, what corresponding events occur on earth that parallel Mt. Sinai, according to the three passages below? _____
_____
_____
_____

~ Isaiah 24:18-23: *"Whoever flees at the sound of terror will fall into a pit; whoever climbs out of the pit will be caught in a snare. The floodgates of the heavens are opened [in thunderous downpour], the foundations of the earth shake [in powerful worldwide earthquake]. The earth is broken up, the earth is split asunder, the earth is thoroughly shaken. The earth reels like a drunkard [off its axis], it sways like a hut in the wind; so heavy upon it is the guilt of its rebellion that it falls—never to rise again. In that Day the LORD will punish the powers in the heavens above ["prince and powers of the air"] and the kings on the earth below. They will be herded together like prisoners bound in a dungeon; they will be shut up in prison and be punished after many days [1,000 years]. The moon will be abashed, the sun ashamed; for the LORD Almighty will reign on Mount Zion and in Jerusalem, and before its elders, gloriously."*

~ Isaiah 26:17-21: "*As a woman with child and about to give birth writhes and cries out in her pain, so were we [Israel] in your presence, O LORD. We were with child, we writhed in pain, but we gave birth to wind. We [Jews] have not brought salvation to the earth; we have not given birth to people of the world. But [in spite of Israel's failure] Your dead will live; their bodies will rise [in resurrection]. You who dwell in the dust, wake up and shout for joy. Your dew is like the dew of the morning; the earth will give birth to her dead. [Now that the dead are raised] Go, My people [144,000], enter your rooms and shut the doors behind you; hide yourselves for a little while [40 days of Jacob's Trouble] until His wrath has passed by. See, the LORD is coming out of His dwelling to punish the people of the earth for their sins. The earth will disclose the blood shed upon her; she will conceal her slain no longer.*"

~ Hebrews 12:18-29: "*You have not come to a mountain [Mt. Sinai] that can be touched and that is burning with fire; to darkness, gloom and storm; to a trumpet blast or to such a voice speaking words that those who heard it begged that no further word be spoken to them, because they could not bear what was commanded: If even an animal touches the mountain, it must be stoned. The sight was so terrifying that Moses said, I am trembling with fear. But you have come to Mount Zion, to the heavenly Jerusalem, the city of the living God. You have come to thousands upon thousands of angels in joyful assembly, to the church of the firstborn, whose names are written [in the Book of Life] in Heaven. You have come to God, the Judge of all men, to the spirits of righteous men made perfect, to Jesus the mediator of a new covenant, and to the sprinkled blood that speaks a better word than the blood of Abel. See to it that you do not refuse Him who speaks. If they did not escape when they refused Him who warned them on earth, how much less will we, if we turn away from Him who warns us from Heaven? At that time [at Mt. Sinai] His voice shook the earth, but now He has promised, Once more I will shake not only the earth but also the heavens. The words "once more" indicate the removing of what can be shaken—that is, created things—so that what cannot be shaken may remain. Therefore, since we are receiving a kingdom that cannot be shaken, let us be thankful, and so worship God acceptably with reverence and awe, for our God is a consuming fire.*"

16. What is said concerning the Judge and His declaration that separates saints and sinners in the four passages below? _____

_____

_____

~ James 5:9: "*Don't grumble against each other, brothers, or you will be judged. The Judge is standing at the door!*"

~ 1 Peter 4:5: "*But they will have to give account to Him who is ready to judge the living and the dead.*"

~ 2 Timothy 4:1: "*In the presence of God and of Christ Jesus, Who will judge the living and the dead, and in view of His appearing and His kingdom, I give you this charge,*"

~ Revelation 22:11-12: *Jesus declares at the end of the 1,150 days of Judgment,* "*Let him who does wrong continue to do wrong; let him who is vile continue to be vile; let him who does right continue to do right; and let him who is holy continue to be holy. Behold, I am coming soon! My reward is with Me, and I will give to everyone according to what he has done.*

The Seven Angels

Revelation 15:6 identifies the carriers of doom—the seven Angels of the Presence of God—who emerge with bowls of God's plagues.

17. How are they dressed? _____

In clean, shining linen with golden sashes around their chests.

18. Christ is clothed and described similarly in Revelation 1:13-16. Why? _____
_____

19. Daniel also describes Michael in Daniel 10:5-6. How close is it to the likeness John saw of Christ in Revelation? _____

20. The linen garments signify what (Exodus 28:40-43)? _____

Revelation 15:7-8 concludes this short chapter. John describes how one of the living creatures hands the seven bowls to the seven messengers filled with fire from the altar, representing the wrath of God. Smoke ascends from the glory of God and from His power. So dreadful is the wrath to come that no one dare enter the Temple until the seven angels have completed pouring out the seven plagues, for fear they will die also.

21. Study the three passages below and determine how the future Day of Atonement in Heaven's Sanctuary corresponds to Temple events here on earth in the past. What can we learn? _____
_____
_____

~ Exodus 40:33-35: *"Then Moses set up the courtyard around the Tabernacle and altar and put up the curtain at the entrance to the courtyard. And so Moses finished the work. Then the cloud covered the Tent of Meeting, and the glory of the LORD filled the Tabernacle. Moses could not enter the Tent of Meeting because the cloud had settled upon it, and the glory of the LORD filled the Tabernacle."*

~ Leviticus 16:2, 4, 12-13: *"The LORD said to Moses: "Tell your brother Aaron not to come whenever he chooses into the Most Holy Place behind the curtain in front of the atonement cover on the Ark, or else he will die, because I appear in the cloud over the atonement cover... He is to put on the sacred linen tunic, with linen undergarments next to his body; he is to tie the linen sash around him and put on the linen turban. These are sacred garments; so he must bathe himself with water before he puts them on... He is to take a censer full of burning coals from the altar before the LORD and two handfuls of finely ground fragrant incense and take them behind the curtain. He is to put the incense on the fire before the LORD, and the smoke of the incense will conceal the atonement cover above the Testimony, so that he will not die."*

~ 1 Kings 8:9-12: *"There was nothing in the Ark except the two stone tablets that Moses had placed in it at Horeb [Mt. Sinai], where the LORD made a covenant with the Israelites after they came out of Egypt. When the priests withdrew from the Holy Place, the cloud filled the Temple of the LORD. And the priests could not perform their service because of the cloud, for the glory of the LORD filled His Temple. Then Solomon said, "The LORD has said that He would dwell in a dark cloud.*

Insights In Prophecy
Unlock The Ancient Mysteries Of Daniel & Revelation
BIBLE DISCOVERY SERIES

Lesson 25

THE END: SEVEN ANGELS WITH PLAGUES OF DEVASTATION

Read Revelation 16

- **Consider How Earth's Ecological System Will Collapse**
- **The Splitting Of Jerusalem's Three Religions—Judaism, Christianity & Islam**

Individuals who give their alliance to the Beast and his image during the counting days will have protection by the government and will have improved access to food and shelter. In contrast, the faithful—consider rebellious and a threat to world peace will endure deprivation, persecution and derision, whose hope will remain in the soon-returning King.

The book of Revelation makes it clear that the Global Leader will enjoy worldwide adoration. His cohort, the False Prophet, will make the image (idol) in honor of the world religion, which will speak as though alive,

and cause all who will not worship the image to be threatened with death (Revelation 13:14-15).

Near the end of the appointed times, the "abomination that makes desolate"—the detestable act that will demand God's holy wrath and desolation on Jerusalem, and then the world at large—will be set up on the rebuilt Temple Mount. The Man of Sin will announce he is more than mere human—he is God in the flesh (2 Thessalonians 2:4). At that time, Michael will stand up and then "there will be a time of distress such as has not happened from the beginning of nations until then," (Daniel 12:1, Matthew 24:15-16, 21).

Revelation 15 exposes the moment when Heaven's Temple is opened on Yom Kippur—the Day of Atonement just after the close of the 1,290, 1,260, 1,150 and 490 counting days. The seven angels of wrath will then emerge with seven deadly plagues that will destroy Planet Earth. Jesus said, "If those days had not been cut short, no one would survive, but for the sake of the elect [144,000] those days will be shortened," Matthew 24:22.

In Revelation 16, the focus of this lesson study, the seven angels are posed and ready; then the command from the Temple is heard, "go, pour out the seven bowls of God's wrath on earth." The seven plagues closely parallel the seven trumpets in many regards. However, the trumpets are limited geographically and in severity, while the seven last plagues plunge the world into global chaos and destruction.

1. How did Jesus identify the event that will set in motion the Great Tribulation of the world (Pt. 19; Matthew 24:12-22)? _____

_____

After the gospel goes to the whole world and all have had the opportunity to decide for or against Christ and the mark of the Beast, the final confrontation between good and evil will commence. The setting up of the abomination in the Temple, predicted by Daniel (9:27; 11:31; 12:11), and confirmed by Jesus (Matthew 24:15-22), is the atrocity that results in the ruin of all who have worshiped the Man of Sin and those who joined in Jerusalem's idolatry. Paul sustained the teaching that the Lawless One would enter the Jerusalem Temple where he proclaims himself God, resulting in his speedy demise (2 Thessalonians 2:3-10).

2. How many days are there between the two periods found in Daniel 12:11-12? _____

At the end of the 1,290 days, the abomination that is to be set up in Jerusalem will result in mass desolation. Daniel is then told there is a blessing for those who attain Day 1,335. Therefore, the seven last plagues will be poured out during those final days. Jesus warned of great danger, and advised the elect that when they see the abomination being set in place on the Temple Mount to run for their lives away from Jerusalem and Judea, because a short but deadly Great Tribulation is about to commence (Luke 21:20-22; Matthew 24:15-22).

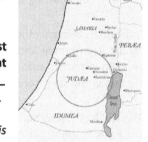

3. What did Yeshua say about the speed in which He will take revenge against those who are pursuing the 144,000 elect who will be crying out day and night for deliverance during the Great Tribulation (Luke 18:7-8)? _____
_____

Jesus said that His chosen ones would be crying out for deliverance, but His vengeance would come quickly; and, that so few would remain alive who believe in Him that faith would be very rare and hard to find just before the Great Day of the LORD.

The parable of the persistent widow and the judge portrays the importance of the relentless prayers of the 144,000 who are alive and will remain on earth until the climactic return of Messiah (1 Thessalonians 4:17) at the Armageddon battle. Once the full count of overcoming Jews and Gentiles from the nations have been martyred (Revelation 7:9), resurrected and taken to Heaven to stand before God, the remaining elect of all Israel—of all twelve tribes—are promised deliverance (Romans 11:25-26). However, God will use the Great Tribulation as a tool to "turn godlessness away from Jacob." Although the seven angels emerge from His Sanctuary to destroy all the nations, Messiah says to Israel... "I will not completely destroy you" Israel. "I will discipline you [during the Time of Jacob's Trouble—Jeremiah 30:7] but only with justice; I will not let you go entirely unpunished," Jeremiah 46:28.

4. Revelation 16:1 says John heard a voice from the Temple telling to the seven angels to do what? _____
_____

The First Angel Messenger

5. According to Revelation 16:2, God's divine judgment begins to fall upon the wicked because they have done what? _____

The decision to accept the mark and worship the idol brings upon mankind a terrible series of disasters, beginning with ugly and painful sores from which they cannot find rest, day or night. This disease in whatever form it takes will be devastating to body and soul. It is just the beginning of several life-altering, fearful events that hit one after the other.

The Second Angel Messenger

The oceans are next to be targeted (Revelation 16:3). The second angel pours out his fiery bowl on the sea. It is said that water makes up about 70% of the Earth's surface, while the other 30% consists of continents and islands. To break the numbers down, 96.5% of all the Earth's water is contained within the oceans as salt water, while the remaining 3.5% is freshwater lakes and frozen water locked up in glaciers and the polar ice caps. Of that fresh water, almost all of it takes the form of ice: 69% of it, to be exact.

6. What becomes of the fish and all ocean creatures? _____ What is the likely outcome for Planet Earth? _____

The oceans will cough up every imaginable creature, and the stench will grow unbearable. Ships will be halted from the putrid and poisoning dangers. Beaches will be lined with decaying carcasses, and as the winds and waves increase the contamination will be poured even further inland. Words cannot truly describe the oceans of death that will cover the globe, as the once predictable ecological system spirals out of control.

7. How did Jesus describe the fear and anguish at the roaring and tossing of the sea during the Great Tribulation (Luke 21:25-26)? _____

The Third Angel Messenger

Revelation 16:4-7 exposes the work of the third angel of destruction. He pours out his bowl on the rivers and fresh water sources around the planet.

8. Why is drinkable water so important for survival? _____

At least 60% of the adult body is made of water and every living cell in the body needs it to keep functioning. Water acts as a lubricant for our joints, regulates our body temperature through sweating and respiration, and helps to flush waste. The maximum time an individual can go without water is about one week—an estimate that would certainly be shorter in difficult conditions, like broiling heat.

Water is the primary source that sustains life. We can live without food for an extended time, but drinkable water is a necessity. Life can be measured in mere days without it. Water will be more valuable than gold (James 5:1-9) during the days of the Great Tribulation.

9. With water scarce and survival utmost, what will individual attitudes be towards one another (Matthew 10:34-36; 24:10)? _____

There will no doubt be fights to death over a few sips of water in those days, as gangs will rule the day.

10. The angel over water gives glory to God, because He judges mankind righteously. In light of the terrible devastation upon the planet and mankind, how can God stand justified by His decision to act (v. 6)? _____

God will judge mankind for the martyrdom of His believers and prophets. He sent His messengers to forewarn and teach truths through His Word. In the last days, many believers will take hold of the testimony of Jesus and God's prophetic warnings, and the gospel of the Kingdom will be shared. A "great multitude" of victors from all nations will stand firm until the end, even to death. Those who despise the counsel of the prophets must pay for their hatred and slaughter of God's faithful; they spill the blood of the victorious saints, so they will then be given blood to drink.

11. What city has been foremost in killing God's messengers through the centuries, and during the last days (Matthew 23:34-38), whose desolation is prophesied? _____

12. In Revelation 6:9-11 the martyrs who gave their lives at the altar of sacrifice cried, "How long... until You judge the inhabitants of the earth and avenge our blood?" What are the martyrs' words upon seeing the work of the third angel (Revelation 16:7)? _____

The Fourth Angel Messenger

13. The fourth angel will pour his fiery coals upon earth's source of heat and light (Revelation 16:8-9). What is the result? _____

Earth's temperature will rise as the population is scorched from the suffocating heat. Solar blasts of radiation cause burnt skin to welt into painful blisters, as the wicked taste of the fiery demise soon to overtake all of them. In agony they blaspheme God, but there is no repentance. Their hearts have been hardened, as they continued a long time unresponsive to the prophets' counsel, the Word of God and the Son's light and grace.

The Fifth Angel Messenger

14. Revelation 16:10-11 describes the fifth angel's attack on the seat of the Beast in what way? _____

Daniel 7:11-12 also describes the destruction of the Western European beast power prior to the other nations. Volcanic blasts may cause this darkness, we don't know; but, ash and raging fires would certainly cause people to "gnaw their tongues in agony" when we think how suffocating volcanic ash could be, in addition to the other plagues they will be enduring. The fifth plague plunges the enemy's realm into darkness, "because men loved darkness rather than light," (John 3:19). Yet, the rebellious population will not repent of their evil deeds against God's people, and their rejection of the Creator of the Universe. Their doom is written in the book of records.

The Sixth Angel Messenger

In Revelation 16:12-16, the sixth angel dries up the river Euphrates with his fiery bowl of wrath, so that the kings of the east can make their way westward. The sixth trumpet also mentions the angels at the river Euphrates, who will lead millions of soldiers into battle.

15. What nations are east of Israel that will likely be part of the last remnant of the world's governments?

_____

Waters in prophecy signify peoples and nations of the earth. The drying of the Euphrates may indicate an opening for military troops and hardware from the East through the removal of opposing forces in the Iraq/Iran region. Many Eastern Asian countries including China, Japan and a host of other countries will emerge from the east marching to battle. Russia, a northeastern country, and her allies, will also be part of the masses of armies racing to the Middle East for the great and final battle of the ages.

16. Why will they be gathering to Israel, according to Revelation 16:16? _____
_____

17. How will the King of the North (Antichrist) respond to the menaces from the east and north, which threatens his newly established royal site in Jerusalem, just before his demise (Daniel 11:44-45)? _____
_____

The Evil Triumvirate

Revelation 16:13-14 foretells a time when evil spirits come out of the mouth of the Dragon (Satan), the Beast (Antichrist) and the False Prophet. "Then I saw three impure spirits that looked like frogs; they came out of the mouth of the dragon, out of the mouth of the beast and out of the mouth of the false prophet.

They are demonic spirits that perform signs, and they go out to the kings of the whole world, to gather them for the battle on the Great Day of God Almighty." These three evil leaders in partnership during the end-times could be referred to as the ***Evil Triumvirate***. Triumvirate means "*government by triumvirs; an association or group of three.*" Why three? Satan often counterfeits what is holy, so that he might deceive the masses; therefore, he attempts to fabricate the ***Holy Trio*** revealed at the Mount of Transfiguration in Christ's future glory, composed of Jesus, Moses and Elijah (Matthew 17:2-3).

In reference to the confusion that will abound during the Great Tribulation, Jesus gave a well-defined warning about false messiahs and false prophets (Matthew 24:23-26). Satan, along with the demonic Antichrist and the False Prophet, will attempt to take the place of Messiah and the two witnesses. Lucifer will surely speak words of comfort and hope, like those of Yeshua. The three may offer healing and perform miracles to gather to themselves a worldwide military alliance. They will likely declare that weapons must be mobilized against the massive stone (Daniel 2:34-35, 44-45), which is heading towards Planet Earth. The politicians comply around the globe, and the battle of the Great Day of God Almighty is made ready.

Revelation 16:15 affirms that even though this period in prophecy is distinguished by the prophetic time-line of 40 days, still Jesus proclaims, "I come like a thief!" Matthew 24:36-44 tells us the no man knows about that day or hour when the final destructive events of the Great Day of the LORD will begin, not even the angels in Heaven. "Blessed is the one who stays awake and remains clothed, so as not to go naked and be shamefully exposed," (v. 15).

Jesus said that if the owner of the house had known at what time of night the thief was coming, he would have kept watch and would not have let his house be broken into and destroyed. Then he tells His elect, "so you also must be ready, because the Son of Man will come at an hour when you do not expect Him"; because, despite many warnings the Great Day of the LORD will still arrive unexpectedly upon the earth-dwellers, and they will not escape God's wrath. For further study, see Luke 12:39-40; 1 Thessalonians 5:2; 2 Peter 3:10; and, Revelation 3:3. *The expression "I come like a thief" is always associated with the Day of the LORD and divine wrath, not a secret rapture.*

18. Revelation 16:15 confirms there will be believers on earth awaiting the Great Day of the LORD—the Day of blessing. How do we know? _____

The 144,000 sealed elect must not deny Christ in the face of death or lose faith, but stay awake to prophetic warnings and keep their clothes of righteousness, so they will not be found naked at the return of the LORD; and, they most certainly will.

19. What day does Daniel 12:12 identify as the Day of blessing for those who *wait* for their salvation? _____

Day 1,335—"Blessed is the one who waits for and reaches the end of the 1,335 days," some 40 days or so after the abomination is set up in the Jerusalem Temple. However, even the days will be cut shorter than 24 hours, and with the upheaval of the trumpet and plagues, with days and nights difficult to distinguish, it will be impossible to know the day and hour of Messiah's triumphant revelation in the sky.

20. What will those who have not worshiped the Beast, but *waited* for their Redeemer, proclaim (Isaiah 25:9 KJV)? _____

21. Revelation 14:14-16 tells us the Son of Man will *wait* for the Father's word, for what? _____
_____

Messiah waits for word from the Temple to reap the harvest of souls.

22. Acts 1:6-7 validates the Father's control over this moment in time. How? _____

23. Matthew 24:21-22 clarifies the pointlessness of trying to predict the very day or hour of the Great Day of the LORD. What confirms this? _____

Armageddon

Revelation 16:16 testifies about the gathering of kings and militaries together to battle and identifies the location as "Armageddon." Revelation 19:19 also speaks about this gathering of politicians and their armies to war against the King and His army that is traveling towards earth. Megiddo, in Old Testament times, was identified as a place of battle where Israel fought with Gentiles armies; for example, in Judges 5:19. Both Ahaziah and Josiah died at Megiddo (1 Kings 9:27; 23:29-30). Armageddon is in Israel (see the map below); King Solomon enlisted slaves "to build the LORD's Temple, his own palace, the supporting terraces, the wall of Jerusalem and Hazor, Megiddo and Gezer," 1 Kings 9:15.

The prophet Zechariah (12:10-11) tells of the day Israel sees the returning Messiah; they "will mourn" and "grieve bitterly for Him." On that day "the weeping in Jerusalem [Israel] will be great, like the weeping of Hadad Rimmon in the plain of Megiddo," when King Josiah died.

In the days leading up to Armageddon, God will "gather all the nations to Jerusalem to fight against it; the city will be captured, the houses ransacked, and the women raped," (Zechariah 14:2). Then, the Great Day of the LORD will commence when the conquering King and His armies come down to battle earth's military powers that destroyed Jerusalem. Almighty declares, "I will set out to destroy all the nations that attack Jerusalem" (12:9) at the battle of Armageddon.

24. How does John describe the Armageddon events at the opening of the sixth seal (Revelation 6:12-17)? _____

_____

A massive earthquake will rock Planet Earth; and, global turmoil will escalate. The sun will be blackened, the moon will turn to red blood, and fiery sky debris will begin to fall to earth. The heavens above will part like a scroll at the return of the King of the Universe, as an opened door. The kings, princes, generals, the rich, the once mighty in power, along with the slave and free (in other words, every single man and woman) will fear for their lives. However, their greatest horror is facing God Almighty who they eventually see sitting on the throne and heading towards earth, and from the wrath of the conquering Lamb! Why? Because the Great Day of wrath is come and who can remain alive? The sixth seal and sixth bowl take us to the very edge of eternity and the completion of the Day of the LORD, when all enemies will be conquered.

The Seventh Angel Messenger

Revelation 16:17 introduces the Seventh Angel. Michael pours out his fiery bowl of coals into the air after having snatched them from the burning altar in Heaven's Temple. Elohim responds from the Temple, "It is done!" The question remains, "What is done?" The events of the seventh seal and the seventh trumpet parallel the seventh bowl. We know this with certainty, because at the breaking of the seventh seal (8:1-5), the sounding of the seventh trumpet (11:15-19) and the pouring out of the seventh bowl (16:17-21) the great worldwide portents—lightning, rumblings (voices), peals of thunder and a severe earthquake—occur as signposts for this monumental moment. In other words, the events of the seventh seal, trumpet and bowl are synchronized actions, and all occur at a specific point on Heaven's Festival Calendar—pinpointed to a specific day on *The Kingdom Calendar* Pt. 18—the Yom Kippur Day of Atonement, which at the voice of God He brings to pass (no matter what time of the year or calendar day it may be).

Therefore, the seventh seal, trumpet and bowl take us back in time from Day 1,335 and the Great Day of the LORD to the very beginning of the Day of the LORD, at Yom Kippur. This Day ushers in that moment in time when the prayers of retribution from all the believers are turned against the wicked (8:4-5); when the kingdom of the world will just have been awarded to the Son of Man and He will begin to reign; and, when the nations will become enraged. It is the time for judging between those who will live and who will die, and the Day for rewarding the dead in Christ in the first resurrection.

This Day, the final and prophetic Day of Atonement, transports us to the opening of the Holy of Holies in the Temple by the High Priest—as in the Old Testament imagery—when the door of the Temple in Heaven opens to expose the Ark of the Covenant, wherein are found the Ten Commandments, so the world may see the Law by which they all must be judged (11:15-19).

25. The question remains concerning the proclamation from the Temple, "It is done." What has been accomplished in Heaven? _____

_____

Insights In Prophecy
Unlock The Ancient Mysteries Of Daniel & Revelation
BIBLE DISCOVERY SERIES

The work of the Judgment Court in the Sanctuary will be completed at the voice of the Seventh Angel.

During the 1,150 day counting period the Judgment Court will be in session, which will end just before the Day of the LORD. According to Daniel, Heaven's daily activities will be interrupted and taken away by Satan's attack on God's Sanctuary, and the Man of Sin's evil practices on earth. The heavenly Sanctuary will be trampled underfoot during the court proceedings (8:11-12); for 2300 evenings and mornings (1150 days) the judgment will continue (8:13-14); thrones will be set up and books of evidence opened (Daniel 7:9-10). Near the end of this period, the Son of Man will enter before the Ancient of Days to receive His just Kingship (7:13-14); the Father will pronounce a decision in favor of the righteous believers (7:21-22); the Little Horn's domain will be officially stripped from him and given to the believers (7:26-27); and, in the end Michael will stand to execute the sentence of death upon Antichrist and all the wicked who have followed him (11:45; 12:1). It is at this moment the words are heard, "It is done"; Satan's demise is certain, and Messiah's reign inaugurated. Judgment then begins at the house of God in Jerusalem, where truth was to have been proclaimed, but instead was extinguished so Antichrist might reign from Jerusalem.

26. How does the words of Messiah "It is finished" in times past portray similar events that will be repeated at the end of time, when the declaration is made once again (Matthew 27:51-52)? _____

_____

At the crucifixion, the veil at the Jerusalem Temple was torn open exposing the Holy of Holies where the Ark and Mercy Seat of God once resided. There was an earthquake in Jerusalem and a special resurrection, where a small number of saints rose to life. In similar manner, at the end of time when God's voice is heard throughout the earth, Heaven's Temple door will be opened and the world will see the Ark of the Covenant—the golden fixture holding the Ten Commandments, and Jerusalem and the whole earth will quake with immense commotion. Graves will be opened, and a great multitude of tribulation victors will be resurrected and taken to safety inside Heaven's Temple (Daniel 12:1-3) for the Feast of Tabernacle celebration.

27. How massive will the earthquake be, according to Revelation 16:18? _____

28. Hebrews 12:26-27 describes the magnitude of seismic activity, even to the point that the sun, moon and stars above are moved out of place. What is written? _____

At the Voice of God, the earth will be moved from its very foundations.

Daniel writes of this moment: "Praise be to the Name of God for ever and ever; wisdom and power are His. He changes times and seasons [with massive earthquake]; He deposes kings and raises up others. He gives wisdom to the wise and knowledge to the discerning. He reveals deep and hidden things; He knows what lies in darkness, and light dwells with Him," Daniel 2:20-22.

29. How does the following verses add to this picture of volcanic activity and galactic upheaval that will cause this planet to sway from its axis, even changing rotational intervals and the seasons, at the voice of God (Job 9:5-8; Isaiah 13:13; 24:20)? _____

_____

The whole earth will heave and swell, and the waves of the sea will flow over the land. Seaports will be swallowed up by the angry waters. Earth's surface will break up, and the very foundations will give way. Large mountain ranges will sink, and islands and peoples will disappear into the dark watery deep. The global-wide earthquake will turn Jerusalem--the united city into a divided city, as major cities of the world tumble into ruins with unimaginable loss of life. From New York to Los Angeles, Beijing to Moscow, Paris to Berlin, Cape Town to Cairo, Rio de Janeiro to Caracas... the great cities with their skyscrapers will collapse one after the other, as 100-pound fireballs will fall from the heavens to destroy and burn what remains. Imagine the worst of all global events, and our minds cannot comprehend all that is to come during the 40 days of the Great Tribulation. Luke 21:22, 25-28 sums up the Tribulation events this way, "For this is the time of punishment in fulfillment of all that has been written... There will be great distress in the land and wrath against this people...There will be signs in the sun, moon and stars. On the earth, nations will be in anguish and perplexity at the roaring and tossing of the sea. People will faint from terror, apprehensive of what is coming on the world, for the heavenly bodies will be shaken. At that time, they will see the Son of Man coming in a cloud with power and great glory. When these things begin to take place, stand up and lift up your heads, because your redemption is drawing near."

The 144,000 elect of the twelve tribes of Israel will be saved and gathered out of the final turmoil when the Son of Man appears in power and great glory: Jeremiah 30:7 reminds us, "Alas! for that Day is great, so that none is like it: it is even the Time of Jacob's trouble; but he shall be saved out of it." "No weapon forged against you will prevail, and you will refute every tongue that accuses you. This is the heritage of the servants of the LORD, and this is their vindication from Me," declares the LORD," Isaiah 54:17.

Jerusalem: Three Religions, One City

Revelation 16:19-20 declares that cities around the globe will fall into heaps of ruin, and the united Great City Jerusalem itself will be split into three parts. Why? The city is known for her three religions—*Judaism, Islam and Christianity.* These three merges in the last days under the banner of the Evil One. However, this unity is short-lived for at the great earthquake, during the pouring out of the seventh bowl of God's wrath, the city will be split into three parts—physically and symbolically tearing apart the three religions that  united under one voice during the counting days of the end.

30. Why is Jerusalem judged, and what is the meaning of Babylon's great divide (Ezekiel 5:2; 5-6; 12-13)?

_____

Jerusalem's leaders will rebel against God's Law to follow the false Shepherd, even more than the nations around her. Therefore, a third will be burned with fire, a third killed with military action, and a third (144,000) will be scattered to the wind to be pursued.

31. How does the prophet Zechariah describe this event (13:8-9)? _____
_____

32. What is said about the massive earthquake in the land of Israel in Ezekiel 38:19-23? _____
_____

Revelation 16:20 exposes the magnitude of the earthquake upon the whole planet, even to the point that "every island" will break apart and will sink into the sea, and "the mountains" ranges will dissolve away.

33. What rains down upon mankind that adds to the horror of this moment in time (Revelation 16:21)?
_____
_____

34. Luke 17:25-26 supports this fact. How? _____

35. Daniel predicts Jerusalem will be rebuilt during the last days (9:25-26), even though her final demise is certain. Ezekiel prophesies destruction against her hastily built walls in what way (13:10-16)? _____
_____

Elijah's Warnings Go Unheeded

Malachi 3:1-2 prophesies, "I will send My messenger [Elijah] who will prepare the way before Me" for 1,260 days—Pt. 9 to Pt. 17. "Then... the LORD... will suddenly come to His Temple" in Jerusalem; "the Messenger of the Covenant"—Michael, "whom you desire, will come... but who can endure the day of His coming?"

Jeremiah adds significant details into this "time of visitation," (Pt 18) when Messiah will suddenly descend in the darkness of the stormy night to His Temple to destroy and cleanse it from the abomination that will be set up in it. The false prophets will promise Jerusalem's safety and world peace, but they will be wrong: "For they have healed the hurt of the daughter of My people slightly, saying, Peace, peace; when there is no peace. Were they ashamed when they had committed abomination? Nay, they were not at all ashamed, neither could they blush: therefore shall they fall among them that fall: in the *time of their visitation* they shall be cast down, saith the LORD," (8:11-12; KJV).

Jeremiah 9:9-11 warns, "Shall I not *visit them* for these things? saith the LORD: shall not My soul be avenged on such a nation as this? For the mountains will I take up a weeping and wailing, and for the habitations of the wilderness a lamentation, because they are burned up, so that none can pass through... And I will make Jerusalem heaps, and a den of dragons; and I will make the cities of Judah desolate, without an inhabitant," (KJV).

---NOTES---

Insights In Prophecy
Unlock The Ancient Mysteries Of Daniel & Revelation
BIBLE DISCOVERY SERIES

Lesson 26

MYSTERY BABYLON & THE SEVEN POLITICAL LEADERS

Read Revelation 17

- **Focus On The Identity Of Mystery Babylon The Great**
- **Identify The Seven Rulers Of The End-times**

Revelation chapters 17 and 18 have been a source of speculation of sometimes bizarre reasoning over the centuries; and rightfully so, for this has been God's mystery held secret through the ages. The Reformers assigned MYSTERY BABYLON THE GREAT to Catholicism, but this idea has been either dismissed or down-played by many Protestants today. Rome is thought to be the great city Babylon, and still others have written that Iraq's modern-day rebuilding constitutes Babylon of prophecy, or New York City fits the bill; but, future events will prove all these ideas wrong.

Added to the mysterious Babylon are the seven kings of Revelation 17, who are considered historical personalities by most commentaries. However, the chapter's true intent must be understood by first considering the source of the visions: Jesus—*a Jewish-born Messiah* (Revelation 1:1-3), and the author of the book of Revelation: John—*a Jewish prophet writing primarily about events affecting Israel and Jerusalem, to be delivered to seven churches made up primarily of Jewish converts to Yeshua*. In addition, the primary context of the book concerns future *last-day events*, including this all-important chapter.

The *end-time* context of the prophecies of Revelation is self-evident, so why would we apply chapter 17 to long-dead historical political leaders? Prophetic views, widely taught in theological training centers today, are rehashed interpretations of scholars and teachers who lived hundreds of years ago. These people are dead and gone; but God's Spirit is alive and well! Let God speak and let His Holy Word bear witness to the final unsealing that can enlighten believers, who must endure this final conflict and global upheaval.

The Two Cities Of Revelation Represent Two Women—One A Prostitute, The Other Messiah's Bride

Revelation 17 exposes the condition of the woman—the *great whore*—and the political landscape around the globe during the *final 40 days* known as the Great Tribulation, as the conflict of the ages nears its climax. Chapter 16 has just described the terrible global punishments of the seven bowls of God's wrath. Therefore, the seven kings of chapter 17, five of which are fallen, represent *end-time last-day world leaders* who have been killed in the plague disasters of the previous chapters, poured out against the nations. They are not, as has often been published in commentaries and books of prophecy, historical

political personalities of ages past.

John provides a unique contrast between the two cities of Revelation, one wicked and one virtuous, and both are introduced by one of the seven angels. Revelation 17:1 communicates that *"One of the seven angels who had the seven bowls"* come to John inviting him to a desolate location to witness the judgment of the adulterous wife—the woman who left her first love to find wealth, protection and splendor from the Beast of nations. The Angel said, *"Come, I will show you the punishment of the great prostitute"* who sits on many waters" of the nations. The first woman turns from Heaven's favor and from God's husbandry to become a prostitute, and by doing so has enticed the whole world into her sin of rejecting Messiah and welcoming Antichrist. In symbolism she sits atop the Dragon of the sea, which signifies her global adoration and embrace particularly by the three Abrahamic religions—Judaism, Christianity and Islam—found throughout the "peoples, multitudes, nations and languages" of the world (v. 15).

Consider this in contrast to the description of the second woman later in Revelation 21:9; where, no doubt, the same Seventh Angel is introducing a virtuous woman: *"One of the seven angels who had the seven bowls"* came to John inviting him to a high mountain to see the honorable lady. The Angel said, *"Come, I will show you the Bride, the Wife of the Lamb."* He continued, "And He carried me away in the Spirit to a mountain great and high, and showed me the *Holy City, Jerusalem*, coming down out of heaven from God," (v. 10).

1. What is the first woman's Biblical reputation (Revelation 17:2)? _____

There is great disappointment in Heaven, because of the prostitute's behavior. She was once the bride of Messiah, but now she will turn to the Man of Sin and the political leaders around the world to support and protect her. By doing so, she proves that she has forgotten her Covenant with God. Although loved by Almighty God, she has had a checkered background from the beginning. Historically, God's people honored Elohim with their lips, but their hearts were often far from Him. Yahweh freed the Israelites from Egyptian slavery, and they began their love affair with a Covenant relationship at Mt. Sinai, described as a marriage in the Scriptures. However, as Moses soon discovered, she often departed from her relationship with the Living God to prostitute with other religions of her day, and to worship images of wood and stone.

"Go and proclaim in the hearing of Jerusalem: "This is what the LORD says: "'I remember the devotion of your youth, how as a bride you loved Me and followed Me through the wilderness, through a land not sown. Israel was holy to the LORD, the firstfruits of His harvest; all who devoured her were held guilty, and disaster overtook them,'" declares the LORD," HOWEVER, "on your clothes is found the lifeblood of the innocent poor, though you did not catch them breaking in. Yet in spite of all this you say, 'I am innocent; He is not angry with me.' But I will pass judgment on you because you say, 'I have not sinned," Jeremiah 2:2-3; 34-35.

On a similar path, the early church began her walk with Christ, but she too departed from the way. In the centuries to follow Christianity's love for pagan idols and sun worship was so deeply rooted, that the Ten Commandments could not be accepted as they read. The religious hierarchy erased the second commandment against idolatry from her creeds and split the tenth commandment on covetousness into two, to maintain the count of ten. Nevertheless, revision of God' Holy Word is strictly forbidden (Matthew 5:17-19; Revelation 22:18-19).

The commands of the Decalogue have been cunningly altered and shortened to downplay the Law of God. The fourth commandment demands that we "Remember the seventh day" to keep it holy. Now the command has been tainted to read, "Remember to keep holy the LORD's Day." No priest, pope, theologian, church or religious organization has the right to change the ten precepts of Elohim, written in stone by His own hand. Still, it is man's obstinate nature to challenge God's Word, and to skirt around His clear commands for the sake of convenience and tradition.

2. Revelation 17:2 says, "The kings of the earth committed adultery and the inhabitants of the earth were intoxicated with the wine of her adulteries." What does spiritual adultery imply, according to Jeremiah 3:8-9? _____

As noted, Judaism and Christianity turned from the living God to fall down before idols and icons made of wood and stone, popes and false prophets. In the last days, Catholic and Protestant Christians, Jews, Muslims and the whole world will be taken into idolatry through deceptive signs and miracles. Both liberal and Evangelical Christians, who should know better, will lose their good senses when they drink the wine of delusion. The long history of God's people defecting to the other side, who once followed His divine precepts, will continue during the counting periods of the appointed time of the end.

3. Jeremiah 7:17-20 parallels events at the end of time. How? _____
_____

Long ago in Judah and in Jerusalem, the prophet Jeremiah reprimanded the Israelites for worshiping the ancient goddess Ishtar, the Queen of Heaven—known as the merciful mother who intercedes for her worshipers. During the appointed time of the end, the demonic goddess figure of the Virgin Mary, the Queen of Heaven, will once again be worshiped in Jerusalem's streets.

4. Why does God's judgment come against Jerusalem/Israel for her sins, according to Jeremiah 51:5-8?
_____

Jerusalem will offer her cup of delusion to the whole world with joy and excitement, and the masses will be intoxicated to the point of losing their good judgment (Revelation 11:10). Her end will come along with those who join in her licentious and abominable activities. For a Biblical description of Israel's/Jerusalem's past failures illustrated as an adulterous wife, read Ezekiel chapter 16 at the end of this lesson.

5. The Seventh Angel moves John in vision to a desolate location. There he sees a symbolic scarlet beast covered with blasphemous names. Where does John find Babylon in Revelation 17:3? _____

She is found in the barren wilderness, where Israel long ago was lost in rebellion against God and Moses.

Exodus 16:1 tells of Israel's travel in the "Wilderness of Sin" on their way to Mount Sinai long ago, and about their constant complaints against Moses and God. The dry desert signifies a lack of Heaven's blessings—a spiritually desolate condition. In Revelation, the woman—fallen Jerusalem/Israel—is sitting on top and being carried along by the seven head and ten horn political Beast. The scarlet color signifies spiritual rebellion (Isaiah 1:16-18), and the blasphemy against the Holy One of Israel because of her outspoken and deceptive statements. The whole world focuses on Jerusalem as the hope of the nations—the International City of Peace. The "great city" is the pinnacle city of the globe, and the geopolitical Beast carries her, giving her constant attention and recognition.

6. The faithless woman of the last days is dressed how (Revelation 17:4)?
_____

As we enter the end-times, she will be shaken and in shambles, but the nations will take her from the dirt and dismay to give her royal treatment; she will be dressed with purple and scarlet, and decked with jewels—the best her lovers can give her. She will be enticed by wealth, extravagance and luxury; all eyes will be on her;

but, in her symbolic hand will be the golden cup with the intoxicating wine of abominations (idolatries) and adulteries, which she bids the nations to drink with her in honor of Antichrist.

7. How does she contrast the New Jerusalem—the beautiful woman who will replace her on the new earth (Revelation 21:2, 10-11)? _____

8. What is stamped in the harlot's forehead, as her title (Revelation 17:5)? _____
_____

MYSTERY BABYLON THE GREAT THE MOTHER OF PROSTITUTES AND OF THE ABOMINATIONS OF THE EARTH.

9. Why has her Revelation identity, "Mystery Babylon" been, for the most part, hidden through the centuries until the end of time? _____

Jerusalem is the beloved city of the three Abrahamic religions of the world. She has been trampled upon through the centuries; how much more if the nations had known that she would displease God at the end? She is a loved city by all; such ill, we do not desire to fall on her. We "pray for the peace of Jerusalem" Psalm 122:6. Yet, our hearts ache for her final ruin, according to the Scriptures. Therefore, God has hidden her identity behind the mask of Mystery Babylon, Sodom and Egypt (Revelation 11:8); then, when the time of her greatest sin arrives, she would be exposed for her decisions along with those who climb into bed with her. How sad that the beloved city, through the actions of her leaders and citizens, will forsake Almighty God in adoration of Antichrist and his dumb idols—and the demons behind them; and, furthermore, will celebrate the deaths of God's last prophets, while inviting the robed Antichrist into her and onto her Temple Mount with his abomination.

The small nation of Israel and the great city Jerusalem will remain the focus of the world to the very end. She is the hope of the nations, the City of Peace. But, as the "mother" of prostitutes, she will have daughters who will follow in her foot-steps. The cities around the globe will celebrate her centrality to world events, and the world's religions will join her in their love for the Papal leader.

Revelation 17:6 records the woman is drunk with the blood of the saints and martyrs. She persecuted and killed many Hebrew prophets (Jeremiah 38:4; Matthew 23:35-38; I Thessalonians 2:14-15; Acts 7:52) who in their day bravely offered dire warnings about the city's pending desolation. The leaders hated the greatest prophet of all—Yeshua, who warned of the same sad end. The citizens were cautioned about Jerusalem's demise of 586 BC and 70 AD; and now, the last-day saints and prophets who by resolve give final notice of Jerusalem's desolation during the Great Tribulation will do so at their own peril.

10. What does Revelation 18:24 say of the women—the great city Babylon? _____

In her is found the blood of the prophets (of old, along with Jesus; and, finally, Moses and Elijah), and of the victors, and all killed on the earth. She carries much blame for the martyrdom of the faithful through the centuries, and now at the end of time as well.

11. Consider the passage Luke 13:33-35. What insight does this offer? _____

Because of Jerusalem's killing of God's prophets down through the centuries, including the true Messiah—Jesus, she is warned that fiery "desolation" is her final judgment.

12. Lamentations 4:11-13 also supports this truth. How? _____

The Seven Head & Ten Horn Monstrous Beast

Revelation 17:6-7 points out how the prophet John was amazed by the splendor of the woman being carried on top of the seven head, ten horned horrific Beast (the symbolism noted: 7 heads X 10 horns = 70; the number 70 in Judaism represents the Gentile nations that originally came from Noah). Even John sensed the lure of the beautiful woman, and felt her entrapment, for he also loved the city; but, the Angel brought the prophet back to his senses by asking pointedly, "Why are you astonished?" John was then promised a disclosure of events, which would seem to focus less on the woman and more on the Beast that will carry her, and the satanic power that lifts the seductive woman to her position of honor.

Our studies have shown the *seven head-ten horned Beast* represents modern nations, as found in both Daniel and Revelation. The following chart of the New World Order visually illustrates the nations involved from the symbolic creatures of prophecy, and the harmony between the two books written hundreds of years apart. Revelation is a commentary on Daniel, and both reveal modern governments.

The Last-Days New World Order
The Seven Heads—Ten Horns in Revelation and Daniel

Revelation 13:1-2
One Monstrous Beast Out of the Sea
With Smaller Characteristics of Leopard, Feet of a Bear, Mouth of a Lion
Seven Heads and Ten Horns ....7 Heads...10 Horns
Total: New World Order..**7 Heads...10 Horns**

Daniel 7:1-7
Four Monstrous Beasts Out of the Sea
Lion With Eagle's Wings ....1 Head......0 Horns
Bear With Three Ribs ....1 Head......0 Horns
Leopard With Four Heads/Four Wings ....4 Heads.....0 Horns
Terrible Beast With Ten Horns ....1 Head.....10 Horns
Total: New World Order ....**7 Heads....10 Horns**

Lion With Eagle's Wings represents ....Great Britain/ United States
Bear With Three Ribs represents ....Russian Federation—Old Soviet Union
Leopard With Four Heads/Four Wings ....China & Eastern Asia Nations
Terrible Beast With Ten Horns ....European Union of Nations

While Daniel describes the four regions of power as separate and distinct beasts, John later saw them combined and working as one. In Daniel 7 the fourth and most dreadful beast is the European Union; however, in Revelation the sea monster only hints of the Lion, Leopard and Bear—again signifying the European Union's overwhelming power as it emerges the dominate player of the final days. This is the New World Order, or Grand Design described in the prophetic books. In both Daniel and Revelation, the emergence of the Beast(s) from the sea heralds the deceptive world leader who will rise out of the New World Order to rule for 1260 days.

Seven Secret Kings & The Eighth Ruler

The remainder of Revelation 17, verses 8-18, adds even more to the mystery of the global political Beast. The chapter shifts from the seven political heads, illustrated in the chart above, to the seven crowned leaders of those power bases. In Revelation 12:3 we find the same structure. First, the passage introduces the Dragon with the "seven heads and ten horns, and seven crowns upon his head." By verse 9, we learn the Dragon is Satan, the demonic leader behind the monstrous Dragon. In Revelation 13:1-7 we again see the same structure. First, introducing the Beast with "seven heads and ten horns"; then, the message shifts to the leader himself who is also referred to as the "Beast"—the Lawless One. Likewise, here in Revelation 17:8 we notice the same framework—a shift from the politically allied Beast with "seven heads and ten horns" to the Beast leader, and the seven crowned leaders who rule over the seven political heads of the sea monster.

The chapter continues by focusing on the defeat of the Beast—the world's religious leader and his global religiosity, and the demise of the seven crowned political leaders. Again, we must remember the context of the chapter, which is concentrating on "end-time" catastrophes, not on historical leaders of the past.

The seven bowls of God's wrath have already been revealed (chapters 15-16), and have begun to be poured out. By this time in the visionary scenes, nations have fallen along with some of their political leaders. The world's Papal leader is struck dead after he sets up the abomination, for "the Beast [Antichrist], which you saw [earlier], once was [alive], now is not [alive], and will come out of the Abyss and go to his destruction." In fact, John is told the whole world will be astonished at the Beast's reappearance after having been struck down, for "he once was [alive], now is not [alive], and yet will come [alive, once again]," verse 8.

The people are warned to "come out of her [Jerusalem], My people, so that you will not share in her sins, so that you will not receive any of her plagues," Revelation 18:4. Why? The Beast has entered onto the Temple Mount to set up his abomination (Matthew 24:15). This horrific sin will bring Heaven's wrath. Without delay Messiah will "suddenly... come to His Temple; the Messenger [Michael, the Great Archangel] of the Covenant [deliverer of the Ten Commandments at Mount Sinai] ... but who can endure [remain alive at] the Day of His coming?" Malachi 3:1-2. John sees the judgment of the great city Jerusalem, and the massive ruin that befalls her. The prophet notices the Beast is not alive; yet, he is still to be found once again breathing and standing erect! This sounds like one final grand deception is about to be played upon the population again—the Beast who will not die.

"This calls for a mind with wisdom," John is told (vs. 9-11). "The seven heads are seven hills on which the woman sits. They are also seven kings [of the last days]. Five have fallen [in ruin; war; plagues.], one is [still alive], the other [the eighth] has not yet come; but when he does come, he must remain for a little while. The Beast who once was [alive], and now is not [alive], is an eighth king. He belongs to the seven and is going to his destruction." The number eight (8) is the recognized symbol in prophecy for both resurrection and a new beginning. Prophecy is therefore leading us to understand that the last and eighth ruler to arrive on the world scene is nothing less than a demonic power from the abyss, masquerading as the Messenger of light—displaying miraculous powers in one last stand against the true Messiah.

"Here is the mind which has wisdom," says Revelation 17:9; surely, we want to be wise in our assessment of this chapter. The seven heads of the political beast are seven hills (mountains, or national alliances) on which the woman sits atop. In other words, the governmental monster is identified by the seven global powers listed above in the New World Order chart, and the adulterous woman (Jerusalem), who sits atop the Beast, is identified as the supreme city of the nations. The seven hills are not representative of Rome as many surmises, for the seven hills boast of seven kings. There are not seven kings reigning from the seven rolling hills of Rome; this is much bigger.

The Ten Regions Of The World

From here, the text shifts to another set of political rulers in verse 12. Daniel 2:21 says there will come a day when God "changes the [appointed] times and the seasons" at the same time "He removes kings and raises up kings; He gives wisdom to the wise and knowledge to those who have understanding." Wisdom is a *gift* from God, so that we might gain the correct understanding about the rise and fall of political leaders in our day. The ten horns are ten kings who will have not yet ruled as the group of ten up to this point. However, in the closing moments of time, the global governments create a united front.

In the United Nations Annual Report: ***The Millennium Development Goals Report 2015,*** we find the world has already been mapped into ten regions (see below); and, the following map and paragraph are found on page 71 of the report: *"This report presents data on progress towards the Millennium Development Goals for the world as a whole and for various country groupings. These are classified as "developing" regions and "developed" regions.* The developing regions are further broken down into the subregions shown on the map. These regional groupings are based on United Nations geographical divisions, with some modifications necessary to create, to the extent possible, groups of countries for which a meaningful analysis can be carried out. A complete list of countries included in each region and subregion is available at mdgs.un.org."* Source: http://mdgs.un.org/unsd/mdg/Resources/Static/Products/Progress2015/English2015.pdf

Regional groupings

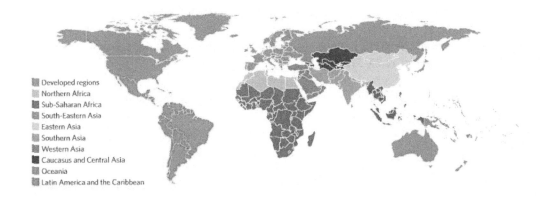

- Developed regions
- Northern Africa
- Sub-Saharan Africa
- South-Eastern Asia
- Eastern Asia
- Southern Asia
- Western Asia
- Caucasus and Central Asia
- Oceania
- Latin America and the Caribbean

Although we do not yet know the how the final division of ten will look, we know the ten regions will be assigned and represented in prophecy by the ten kings at the very end of days.

The Evil Triumvirate—Satan, the Beast, and the False Prophet will unite the kings through a series of miraculous signs; and together, they will make plans to conquer the threat from the sky—the large mass that is heading towards Planet Earth—the Rock of disaster, which threatens mankind with global extinction. However, they will in truth be confronting the returning King of kings and His massive army.

14. How long will the ten kings rule with Satan and give their allegiance to the Beast (v. 12)? _____

In symbolic language, noting the futile shortness of time left for Planet Earth, they are said to rule only "one hour" together.

15. According to verse 14, what is the last purpose for their united front? _____

Satan and his cohorts will deceive the nations; the world's militaries will turn their weapons upon the returning Messiah and His army, likely believing it is a massive asteroid or aliens heading towards Planet Earth.

16. When Messiah returns to conquer all remaining sin and sinners, what group is coming with Him in the sky? _____

Those who are "called, chosen and faithful" victors, overcomers of the Beast, his number and name.

17. The following passages further identify this group, which returns with Messiah on the Great Day of the LORD—Day 1335 (1 Thessalonians 3:13; 4:14; Jude 14). Who are they? _____
_____

"God [the Father] will bring [along] with Jesus those who have fallen asleep in Him [but who are raised to life on Yom Kippur]." Jude adds, "the LORD is coming with thousands upon thousands of his holy ones [a great multitude that no man could count—Revelation 7:9] to judge... all the ungodly of all the ungodly acts they have done." Also, Michael's angels return to gather God's scattered elect (Matthew 24:30-31).

Revelation 17:15-16 identifies the "waters... where the prostitute sits, are peoples, multitudes, nations and languages." Jerusalem will be known as the pinnacle city—the great city of the earth, carried by the world's political powers, as the whole world marvels at her and gives her a great deal of attention.

18. However, what will the attitude of all the nations eventually be towards Jerusalem, and what will the armies of the earth do to her (Ezekiel 16:37-39)? _____

After having used her, the prostitute's lovers will despise her and will turn on her, leaving her naked.

19. Why does the Beast and nations turn against Jerusalem (Revelation 17:16-17)? _____
_____

20. What is John's footnote to the whole chapter in Revelation 17:18 that points to the prostitute, Mystery Babylon, in a negative light? _____

The "great city" is openly and unequivocally identified in Revelation 11:8 as, "where also their [the two witnesses'] LORD was crucified." The message is clear; the city (although she was to be holy and a lighthouse of truth), that long ago rejoiced at the death of Yeshua, will one day in the future celebrate the death of His two last-day witnesses—Moses and Elijah. The "great city" will reject the two prophets, just as her religious leaders despised the greatest Prophet two thousand years ago; and, what was the result of Israel's/Jerusalem's rejection? The desolation of 70 A.D. is a reflection of the final ruin, which will fall speedily upon Jerusalem in the closing hours of time—by earthquake, destruction and fire.

In Daniel 2, King Nebuchadnezzar had a dream about a statue. No one could tell the monarch his dream, so Daniel asked his three friends to pray that God in His mercy would reveal the dream to him. Daniel 2:19-23 says, "During the night the mystery was revealed to Daniel in a vision. Then Daniel praised the God of heaven and said: "Praise be to the Name of God for ever and ever; wisdom and power are His. He changes times and seasons; He deposes kings and raises up others. He gives wisdom to the wise and knowledge to the discerning. He reveals deep and hidden things; He knows what lies in darkness, and light dwells with Him. I thank and praise you, God of my ancestors: You have given me wisdom and power, You have made known to me what we asked of You, You have made known to us the dream of the king."

Daniel goes to the king and relays the dream as follows, "Your Majesty looked, and there before you stood a large statue—an enormous, dazzling statue, awesome in appearance. The head of the statue was made of pure gold, its chest and arms of silver, its belly and thighs of bronze, its legs of iron, its feet partly of iron and partly of baked clay. While you were watching, a rock was cut out, but not by human hands. It struck the statue on its feet of iron and clay and smashed them. Then the iron, the clay, the bronze, the silver and the gold were all broken to pieces and became like chaff on a threshing floor in the summer. The wind swept them away without leaving a trace. But the rock that struck the statue became a huge mountain and filled the whole earth," Daniel 2:31-35.

The prophet finishes with these details: "After you, another kingdom will arise, inferior to yours. Next, a third kingdom, one of bronze... Finally, there will be a fourth kingdom, strong as iron—for iron breaks and

smashes everything—and as iron breaks things to pieces, so it will crush and break all the others. Just as you saw that the feet and toes were partly of baked clay and partly of iron, so this will be a divided kingdom; yet it will have some of the strength of iron in it, even as you saw iron mixed with clay. As the toes were partly iron and partly clay, so this kingdom will be partly strong and partly brittle. And just as you saw the iron mixed with baked clay, so the people will be a mixture and will not remain united, any more than iron mixes with clay. In the time of those kings, the God of heaven will set up a kingdom that will never be destroyed, nor will it be left to another people. It will crush all those kingdoms and bring them to an end, but it will itself endure forever. This is the meaning of the vision of the rock cut out of a mountain, but not by human hands—a rock that broke the iron, the bronze, the clay, the silver and the gold to pieces," (39-45).

Here we see a statue representing historical powers, Babylon, followed by the Medes and Persian, swallowed up by the Alexander the Great's Greece and followed by the Roman armies. All these powers were enemies and held sway over the people of Israel; however, we also notice the statue vision has contemporary fulfillment, because the final demise of the ten toes is a direct result of the returning King—the conquering Messiah in our day. Therefore, this statue has meaning for our modern times, because the whole statue crumbles upon the returning defeat of the Rock—King of kings.

So, what meaning does the statue have today? The chart above demonstrates the last-day fulfillment of the vision of Daniel 2. First, the head of gold is Babylon, which is modern-day Iraq. This country has, for the most part, now been defeated (2003-2011). The chest of silver—Medes and Persians, is today's Iran. Modern Iran will soon be defeated; Greece will then fall (either financially, or from a Russian attack); followed by the final defeat of Rome at the end of the appointed times, indicated by the Daniel 7:11-12 prediction: "Then I continued to watch because of the boastful words the [Vatican] horn was speaking. I kept looking until the [European] beast was slain and its body destroyed and thrown into the blazing fire. (The other beasts [governmental powers] had been stripped of their authority, but were allowed to live for a period of time.)" After Europe's fiery demise, attention turns to the ten toes of iron and clay (10 Regions of the World) that rule only one hour just before the return of Messiah.

After the demise of all human governments and all sinners, along with all evil angels, and after the imprisonment of Satan, the earth will be left in darkness, without form, and void of all life. Messiah will establish His Eternal Kingdom in Heaven, where He has gone to prepare a place for us and will come again and receive us unto Himself that where He is we may be also (John 14:1-4). After 1,000 years in the New Jerusalem in Heaven, His Kingdom will be transferred to this earth at the end of the millennial delay, when the New Jerusalem descends to a renewed Planet Earth after the Great White throne judgment and fiery demise of the old planet and all sinners.

The apostle Peter wrote, "Dear friends, this is now my second letter to you. I have written both of them as reminders to stimulate you to wholesome thinking. I want you to recall the words spoken in the past by the holy prophets and the command given by our LORD and Savior through your apostles. Above all, you must understand that in the last days scoffers will come, scoffing and following their own evil desires. They will say, "Where is this 'coming' He promised? Ever since our ancestors died, everything goes on as it has since the beginning of creation." But they deliberately forget that long ago by God's word the heavens came into

being and the earth was formed out of water and by water. By these waters also the world of that time was deluged and destroyed. By the same word *the present heavens and earth are reserved for fire, being kept for the Day of Judgment and destruction of the ungodly*."

He continues, "But do not forget this one thing, dear friends: With the LORD a day is like a thousand years, and a thousand years are like a day. The LORD is not slow in keeping His promise, as some understand slowness. Instead He is patient with you, not wanting anyone to perish, but everyone to come to repentance. But the Day of the LORD will come like a thief. The heavens will disappear with a roar; the elements will be destroyed by fire, and the earth and everything done in it will be laid bare. Since everything will be destroyed in this way, what kind of people ought you to be? You ought to live holy and godly lives as you look forward to the Day of GOD and speed its coming. That Day will bring about the destruction of the heavens by fire, and the elements will melt in the heat. But in keeping with His promise we are looking forward to a new heaven and a new earth, where righteousness dwells. So then, dear friends, since you are looking forward to this, make every effort to be found spotless, blameless and at peace with Him," 2 Peter 3:1-14.

The Word Of The LORD
Jerusalem—An Adulterous Wife
Ezekiel 16

"The word of the LORD came to me: [2] "Son of man, confront Jerusalem with her detestable practices [3] and say, 'This is what the Sovereign LORD says to Jerusalem: Your ancestry and birth were in the land of the

Canaanites; your father was an Amorite and your mother a Hittite. [4] On the day you were born your cord was not cut, nor were you washed with water to make you clean, nor were you rubbed with salt or wrapped in cloths. [5] No one looked on you with pity or had compassion enough to do any of these things for you. Rather, you were thrown out into the open field, for on the day you were born you were despised. [6] "Then I passed by and saw you kicking about in your blood, and as you lay there in your blood I said to you, "Live!" [7] I made you grow like a plant of the field. You grew and developed and entered puberty. Your breasts had formed and your hair had grown, yet you were stark naked. [8] "'Later I passed by, and when I looked at you and saw that you were old enough for love, I spread the corner of my garment over you and covered your naked body. I gave you my solemn oath and entered into a covenant with you, declares the Sovereign LORD, and you became mine. [9] "'I bathed you with water and washed the blood from you and put ointments on you. [10] I clothed you with an embroidered dress and put sandals of fine leather on you. I dressed you in fine linen and covered you with costly garments. [11] I adorned you with jewelry: I put bracelets on your arms and a necklace around your neck, [12] and I put a ring on your nose, earrings on your ears and a beautiful crown on your head. [13] So you were adorned with gold and silver; your clothes were of fine linen and costly fabric and embroidered cloth. Your food was honey, olive oil and the finest flour. You became very beautiful and rose to be a queen. [14] And your fame spread among the nations on account of your beauty, because the splendor I had given you made your beauty perfect, declares the Sovereign LORD. [15] But you trusted in your beauty and used your fame to become a prostitute. You lavished your favors on anyone who passed by and your beauty became his. [16] You took some of your garments to make gaudy high places, where you carried on your prostitution. You went to him, and he possessed your beauty. [17] You also took the fine jewelry I gave you, the jewelry made of my gold and silver, and you made for yourself male idols and engaged in prostitution with them. [18] And you took your embroidered clothes to put on them, and you offered my oil and incense before them. [19] Also the food I provided for you—the flour, olive oil and honey I gave you to eat—you offered as fragrant incense before them. That is what happened, declares the Sovereign LORD. [20] And you took your sons and daughters whom you bore to me and sacrificed them as food to the idols. Was your prostitution not enough? [21] You slaughtered my children and sacrificed them to the idols. [22] In all your detestable practices and your prostitution you did not remember the days of your youth, when you were naked and bare, kicking about in your blood. [23] Woe! Woe to you, declares the Sovereign LORD. In addition to all your other wickedness, [24] you built a mound for yourself and made a lofty shrine in every public square. [25] At every street corner you built your lofty shrines and degraded your beauty, spreading your legs with increasing promiscuity to anyone who passed by. [26] You engaged in prostitution with the Egyptians, your neighbors with large genitals, and aroused my anger with your increasing promiscuity. [27] So I stretched out my hand against you and reduced your territory; I gave you over to the greed of your enemies, the daughters of the Philistines, who were shocked by your lewd conduct. [28] You engaged in prostitution with the Assyrians too, because you were insatiable; and even after that, you still were not satisfied. [29] Then you increased your promiscuity to include Babylonia, a land of merchants, but even with this you were not satisfied. [30] "'I am filled with fury against you, declares the Sovereign LORD, when you do all these things, acting like a brazen prostitute! [31] When you built your mounds at every street corner and made your lofty shrines in every public square, you were unlike a prostitute, because you scorned payment. [32] You adulterous wife! You prefer strangers to your own husband! [33] All prostitutes receive gifts, but you give gifts to all your lovers, bribing them to come to you from everywhere for your illicit favors. [34] So in your prostitution you are the opposite of others; no one runs after you for your favors. You are the very opposite, for you give payment and none is given to you. [35] "'Therefore, you prostitute, hear the word of the LORD! [36] This is what the Sovereign LORD says: Because you poured out your lust and exposed your naked body in your promiscuity with your lovers, and because of all your detestable idols, and because you gave them your children's blood, [37] therefore I am going to gather all your lovers, with whom you found pleasure, those you loved as well as those you hated. I will gather them against you from all around and will strip you in front of them, and they will see you stark naked. [38] I will sentence you to the punishment of women who commit adultery and who shed blood; I will bring on you the blood vengeance of my wrath and jealous anger. [39] Then I will deliver you into the hands of your lovers, and they will tear down your mounds and destroy your lofty shrines. They will strip you of your clothes and take your fine jewelry and leave you stark naked. [40] They will bring a mob against you, who will stone you and hack you to pieces with their swords. [41] They will burn down your houses and inflict punishment on you in the sight of many women. I will put a stop to your prostitution, and you will no longer pay your lovers. [42] Then my wrath against you will subside and my jealous anger will turn away from you; I will be calm and no longer angry. [43] Because you did not remember the days of your youth but enraged me with all these things, I will surely bring down on your head what you have done, declares the Sovereign LORD. Did you not add lewdness to all your other detestable practices? [44] Everyone who quotes proverbs will quote this proverb about you: "Like mother, like daughter." [45] You are a true daughter of your mother, who despised her husband and her children; and you are a true sister of your sisters, who despised their husbands and their children. Your mother was a Hittite and your father an Amorite. [46] Your older sister was Samaria, who lived to the north of you with her daughters; and your younger sister, who lived to the south of you with her daughters, was Sodom. [47] You not only followed their ways and copied their detestable practices, but in all your ways you soon became more depraved than they. [48] As surely as I live, declares the Sovereign LORD, your sister Sodom and her daughters never did what you and your daughters have done. [49] Now this was the sin of your sister Sodom: She and her daughters were arrogant, overfed and unconcerned; they did not help the poor and needy. [50] They were haughty and did detestable things before me. Therefore, I did away with them as you have seen. [51] Samaria did not commit half the sins you did. You have done more detestable things than they, and have made your sisters seem righteous by all these things you have done. [52] Bear your disgrace, for you have furnished some justification for your sisters. Because your sins were more vile than theirs, they appear more righteous than you. So then, be ashamed and bear your disgrace, for you have made your sisters appear righteous. [53] "'However, I will restore the fortunes of Sodom and her daughters and of Samaria and her daughters, and your fortunes along with them, [54] so that you may bear your disgrace and be ashamed of all you have done in giving them comfort. [55] And your sisters, Sodom with her daughters and Samaria with her daughters, will return to what they were before; and you and your daughters will return to what you were before. [56] You would not even mention your sister Sodom in the day of your pride, [57] before your wickedness was uncovered. Even so, you are now scorned by the daughters of Edom and all her neighbors and the daughters of the Philistines—all those around you who despise you. [58] You will bear the consequences of your lewdness and your detestable practices, declares the LORD. [59] "'This is what the Sovereign LORD says: I will deal with you as you deserve, because you have despised my oath by breaking the covenant. [60] Yet I will remember the covenant I made with you in the days of your youth, and I will establish an everlasting covenant with you. [61] Then you will remember your ways and be ashamed when you receive your sisters, both those who are older than you and those who are younger. I will give them to you as daughters, but not on the basis of my covenant with you. [62] So I will establish my covenant with you, and you will know that I am the LORD. [63] Then, when I make atonement for you for all you have done, you will remember and be ashamed and never again open your mouth because of your humiliation, declares the Sovereign LORD.'"

Insights In Prophecy
Unlock The Ancient Mysteries Of Daniel & Revelation
BIBLE DISCOVERY SERIES

Lesson 27

LAMENT OVER BABYLON: THE FINALITY OF JERUSALEM'S DEMISE

Read Revelation 18

- **Learn Why The Blood Of The Prophets Seals Jerusalem's Demise**
- **The Three Woes Condemn The Great City**

The beloved city Jerusalem, over four thousand years old, is holy to all three of the world's monotheistic religions—Judaism, Christianity, and Islam. The history of each faith includes conquering the city at one time or another, and holding preeminence over the capital. Jerusalem remains a sacred destination for

pilgrimages and prayers by all three religions. The city abounds with holy symbols and fascinating buildings, including synagogues, churches and mosques; but, the spiritual center of the city is the Temple Mount. All three of the traditions have made use of the Temple Mount. This, in no small measure, explains why its story has been one of strife, war and debate. Everything that happens in and around the Temple Mount and Western Wall, each piece of ground that is disturbed, each artifact that is dug up, stirs ancient hopes and spurs renewed resentment. With the unease shared particularly between Israelis and Arabs, Jerusalem's international attraction proves it to be a city of provocation and continued clashes.

The Temple Mount is the most sacred site in Judaism and epicenter of Bible prophecy and final events. These 36 acres are where the two Temples of Jewish history once stood, with growing hope for building the third Temple. The first was built by King Solomon in 957 B.C. to house the Ark of the Covenant, which safeguarded the Ten Commandments in a special room called "The Holy of Holies". For Muslims, Haram al-Sharif (Noble Sanctuary) is the third holiest site in Islam after Mecca and Medina in Saudi Arabia. On the Temple Mount complex, you'll find two Islamic structures—the Dome of the Rock and the al-Aqsa Mosque. For Christians, the Temple Mount is significant because the second Temple located there was where Jesus often taught and prayed. Jerusalem is the focal point of His ministry, and the revered location of Messiah's death, resurrection and return.

However, the Scriptures expose Jerusalem's checkered history; when the Israelites obeyed Yahweh, the city was blessed and preserved, but other times when they rejected the prophets' counsel the city and Temple were overrun by Israel's enemies. In the previous lesson on Revelation 17, we solidified the *Great City, Babylon's* identity to be Jerusalem. Jesus warned of her destruction long ago when He told His disciples that not one stone would be left upon another (Matthew 24:1-2). In spite of Jerusalem's two historic calamities (586 B.C. and 70 A.D.), along with the many prophetic warnings about Jerusalem's end-time desolation throughout the Biblical Scriptures, few Bible students believe the warnings; only a minority link the derogatory names in the book of Revelation to Jerusalem. "Egypt" and "Sodom" are offensive titles assigned to the great city, where also our "LORD was crucified" (Revelation 11:7-9); and, where the two witnesses, Moses and Elijah, will also be martyred and left to rot in her streets. No matter what prophetic view you hold, we likely agree that at some point the old city must be destroyed in a fiery blaze before the New Jerusalem takes its place; there is no evidence for both, standing side by side, on the New Earth. Mystery Babylon will sadly meet her final doom—sooner than most imagine.

A Brief History of Jerusalem
Source: Israel Ministry of Foreign Affairs, October 2007

King David made Jerusalem the capital of his kingdom and the religious center of the Jewish people in 1003 BCE. Some forty years later, his son Solomon built the Temple (the religious and national center of the people of Israel) and transformed the city into the prosperous capital of an empire extending from the Euphrates to Egypt. Exiled by Babylonian king Nebuchadnezzar in 586 BCE, who conquered Jerusalem and destroyed the Temple, the Jews were allowed to return and rebuild the city and the Temple some 50 years later by the Persian King Cyrus.

Alexander the Great conquered Jerusalem in 332 BCE. The later desecration of the Temple and attempts to suppress Jewish religious identity under the Seleucid ruler Antiochus IV resulted in a revolt led by Judah Maccabee, who rededicated the Temple (164 BCE) and re-established Jewish independence under the Hasmonean dynasty. A century later, Pompey imposed Roman rule on Jerusalem. King Herod, installed as ruler of Judah by the Romans (37 - 4 BCE), established cultural institutions in Jerusalem, erected magnificent public buildings and refashioned the Temple into an edifice of splendor.

Jewish revolt against Rome broke out in 66 CE, as Roman rule after Herod's death became increasingly oppressive. In 70 CE, Roman legions under Titus conquered the city and destroyed the Temple. Jewish independence was briefly restored during the Bar Kochba revolt (132-135), but again the Romans prevailed. Jews were forbidden to enter the city, renamed Aelia Capitolina. After Byzantine conquest of the city (313), Jerusalem was transformed into a Christian center under Emperor Constantine, with the Church of the Holy Sepulcher the first of many grandiose structures built in the city. Muslim armies invaded the country in 634, and four years later Caliph Omar captured Jerusalem. Only during the reign of Abdul Malik, who built the Dome of the Rock (691), did Jerusalem briefly become the seat of a caliph.

The Crusaders conquered Jerusalem in 1099, massacred its Jewish and Muslim inhabitants, and established the city as the capital of the Crusader. Synagogues were destroyed, old churches were rebuilt and many mosques were turned into Christian shrines. Crusader rule over Jerusalem ended in 1187, when the city fell to Saladin. In 1247 Jerusalem fell once more to Egypt, now ruled by the Mamluks, until the conquest by the Ottoman Turks in 1517. Suleiman the Magnificent rebuilt the city walls (1537). After his death, the central authorities in Constantinople took little interest in Jerusalem and the city declined.

Jerusalem began to thrive once more in the latter half of the 19th century. Growing numbers of Jews returning to their land, waning Ottoman power and revitalized European interest in the Holy Land led to renewed development of Jerusalem. The British army led by General Allenby conquered Jerusalem in [November] 1917. From 1922 to 1948, Jerusalem was the administrative seat of the British authorities in the Land of Israel (Palestine), which had been entrusted to Great Britain by the League of Nations.

Upon termination of the British Mandate on May 14, 1948, and in accordance with the UN resolution of November 29, 1947, Israel proclaimed its independence, with Jerusalem as its capital. Opposing its establishment, the Arab countries launched an all-out assault on the new state, resulting in the 1948-49 War of Independence. The armistice lines drawn at the end of the war divided Jerusalem into two, with Jordan occupying the Old City and areas to the north and south, and Israel retaining the western and southern parts of the city.

When the Six-Day War broke out in June 1967 Israel contacted Jordan through the UN as well as the American Embassy, and made it clear that if Jordan refrained from attacking Israel, Israel would not attack Jordan. Nevertheless, the Jordanians attacked west Jerusalem and occupied the former High Commissioner's building. Following heavy fighting, the IDF recovered the compound and removed the Jordanian army from east Jerusalem, resulting in the reunification of the city. After the liberation of the city by the IDF, the walls dividing the city were torn down. Three weeks later, the Knesset enacted legislation unifying the city and extending Israeli sovereignty over the eastern part of the city.

The reunification of the city was also a fundamental moment in the history of religious tolerance, opening the city of Jerusalem to worshippers of all faiths, permitting Jews to return to the Western Wall and other holy sites, and allowing Israeli Muslims and Christians to visit those sacred places in eastern Jerusalem from which they too had been barred since 1948. One year later, in 1968, it was decided that the day marking the liberation and reunification of Jerusalem—28 Iyar according to the Jewish lunar calendar—would be a national holiday in Israel. On Jerusalem Day we celebrate the reunification of the city and the Jewish people's connection with Jerusalem throughout the ages.

Almighty God has hidden the identity of the prostitute city until closer to the time when the wayward woman will meet her doom. The most descriptive title for this mysterious city in the book of Revelation, which in itself communicates secrecy, is found in Revelation 17:5.

"MYSTERY"
BABYLON THE GREAT
THE MOTHER OF PROSTITUTES
AND OF THE ABOMINATIONS OF THE EARTH

Although a mystery, two promises are given in the Word of God for those who are searching Daniel and Revelation for insight into this and other prophetic secrets: "None of the wicked will understand, but those who are wise will understand," Daniel 12:10; and, "Blessed is the one who reads the words of this prophecy, and blessed are those who hear it and take to heart what is written in it, because the time is near," Revelation 1:3. The wise, willing to take God at His word, will perceive the identity of secret Babylon, and her last-day apostasy. And, it is with sorrow that we must speak the truth on this matter. We are committed in this lesson series to find the truths in God's Word, even painful truths.

Babylon is not the city of Rome, as many surmise, although Catholicism's deceptions will accelerate in the last days; the focus of the Hebrew Scriptures is JERUSALEM. In fact, so great is Jerusalem's failure during the final days of human history that the whole chapter of the Revelation 18 Apocalypse is devoted to describing her fiery ruin. As noted, twice when God's people rejected the Holy One of Israel in the past, the Temple was burnt to the ground and the city ravaged. The false prophets boldly declared that Yahweh loved His people and city too much to allow her destruction. "'Peace, peace,' they say, when there is no peace," Jeremiah 6:14. As the chosen people through Abraham, the Israelites could not comprehend that God would judge His city, allowing the killing of His people, and destruction of the beautiful Sanctuary through the swords and fiery blaze of foreigners. Likewise, our modern generation will not believe that Jerusalem will fall in ruins, even though there are vibrant warnings. Today, Jerusalem sits on the brink of devastation that will change the landscape of the beloved city and the course of human history. At any moment, Jerusalem will suffer an epic earthquake resulting in loss of lives and massive ruins. The Temple Mount and structures will collapse in shambles, and daily worship at the Western Wall and Temple Mount will be taken away; then, the 1,290 counting days will begin. During the last half of *The Kingdom Calendar* counting periods the city will be partially rebuilt, but as the 1,290 days come to an end Israel's leadership will allow the False Shepherd onto the Temple Mount to set up his abomination. This will usher in the final and fiery desolation of Jerusalem.

1. John's attention turns to the Messenger who will descend down from Heaven with great authority. What is said of His power and glorious brilliance (18:1)? _____

The whole planet will be lit with His splendid radiance. The Sun of Righteousness will rise from the east with healing in His wings (Malachi 4:1-2). "The LORD God is a sun and shield," Psalm 84:11. Psalm 80:3-7 expresses Israel's cry for deliverance at the shining of Messiah's face: "Awaken Your might; come and save us. Restore us, O God; make Your face shine upon us, that we may be saved. O LORD God Almighty, how long will Your anger smolder against the prayers of Your people? You have fed them with the bread of tears; You have made them drink tears by the bowlful. You have made us a source of contention to our neighbors, and our enemies mock us. Restore us, O God Almighty; make Your face shine upon us, that we may be saved."

Psalm 94:1-2 continues the theme of Yeshua's glory on the Day of the LORD: "O LORD, the God who avenges, O God who avenges, shine forth. Rise up, O Judge of the earth; pay back to the proud what they deserve." Supernatural phenomena on earth and in the sky will accompany His arrival. With His brilliant glory too bright to peer into, He will illuminate Planet Earth that sits in darkness and despondency. Along with judgment of the wicked, His return is always associated with the light of salvation for His people (Luke 1:78, John 1:4, 9, John 12:46, 2 Peter 1:19, Revelation 2:28).

2. His voice is "mighty" and He "shouted" a taunting, exultant dirge over Babylon as though she had already fallen. How does this description compare to the Angel who John saw earlier "coming down to earth" in Revelation 10:1-3? _____

This Messenger we identified through the evidence of Scripture to be Michael in Revelation 10 (Lesson 17). At the time of Great Tribulation, the Messenger of the Covenant will stand for the protection of His people (Daniel 12:1-2), and will descend in wind and storm to visit the Abominator in the Sanctuary (Malachi 3:1-2), for judgment always begins with God's household (1 Peter 4:17). He will cry with deafening thunder around the globe, and breaking the darkness His glory will fill the eastern skies (Ezekiel 43:2-4, 7), although His countenance will not be seen; then, the Great Tribulation will commence.

Jeremiah adds these chilling words: "See, I am beginning to bring disaster on the city [Jerusalem] that bears My Name, and will you indeed go unpunished? You will not go unpunished, for I am calling down a sword upon all who live on the earth, declares the LORD Almighty. Now prophesy all these words against them and say to them: "'The LORD will roar from on high; He will thunder from His holy dwelling and roar mightily against His land. He will shout like those who tread the grapes, shout against all who live on the earth. The tumult will resound to the ends of the earth, for the LORD will bring charges against the nations; He will bring judgment on all mankind and put the wicked to the sword,'" declares the LORD. This is what the LORD Almighty says: "Look! Disaster is spreading from nation to nation; a mighty storm is rising from the ends of the earth," Jeremiah 25:29-32.

3. What is the result of the Archangel's voice (1 Thessalonians 4:16-17)? _____
_____

While most commentators disassociate the Archangel's loud resurrection shout from the voice of Messiah, John 5:25 identifies the voice that gives life to dead bodies and scattered ashes: "a time is coming and has now come when the dead will hear the voice of the Son of God and those who hear will live." The righteous dead in Christ will be raised first to be taken to Heaven during the short but Great Tribulation, before they return with Yeshua at the Great Day of the LORD (Day 1,335). On earth the 144,000, who are still alive and are left behind for the short duration that remains, must run for safety.

4. Babylon is about to fall. What messages does Heaven's Messenger shout to the righteous elect "who are still alive and are left" to flee from Mystery Babylon—Jerusalem (v. 2)? _____

Babylon the great is fallen in sin, which is an amplification of the angelic warning of Revelation 14:8— "Babylon is fallen, is fallen, that great city, because she has made all nations drink of the wine of the wrath of her fornication." Israel's decision to allow Antichrist into the city and onto the Temple Mount in an intimate religious relationship to set up the abomination is spiritual fornication, and this choice brings disaster first to Jerusalem, then Israel, followed by the whole world of nations. Every sinner must drink from Jerusalem's cup of wrath.

5. The Hebrew prophets described a similar destruction in history, and again at the Day of Vengeance and Eternal Jubilee (Isaiah 13:19-22; 34:8-15). How? _____

When the Wicked One is allowed to enter Jerusalem and onto the Temple Mount, he brings with him the demonic train of evil spirits. Once the blessed Holy City of God's Divine Presence, Jerusalem will become the habitation of devils. Her destruction will be sealed, and all that will remain is ruin and prickly thorns when the wrath of God is complete. No human will live there, or anywhere else on Planet Earth, after the plagues and Armageddon. Desolation will replace the once bustling cities. Jesus warned the unrepentant generation of His day, "When an impure spirit comes out of a person, it goes through arid places seeking rest and does not find it. Then it says, 'I will return to the house I left.' When it arrives, it finds the house unoccupied, swept clean and put in order. Then it goes and takes with it seven other spirits more wicked than itself, and they go in and live there. And the final condition of that person is worse than the first. That is how it will be with this wicked generation," Matthew 12:43-46.

In the meantime, Revelation 18:3 tells us the nations will become intoxicated by Jerusalem's relationship with Rome's pagan Christianity during the counting periods. The International City of Peace will be rich with financial resources and international aid, and through her conformity to Antichrist's plan the financial markets evidently rebound to some degree under global governance and domestic strategies.

6. What three groups are specifically identified as getting caught up in the united nation's agreement to follow the religious edicts of the Lawless One? _____

The three include all nations (worldwide population at large), the kings of the earth (politicians and statesmen around the globe) and merchants (businesspeople involved in employment and industry). The bottom line is "nearly everybody" on Planet Earth, while few in comparison will speak out against the popular views of those days.

7. Reading Revelation 18:4-6, what warning will be given to the elect through the Son of God? _____

_____

The message will be given—Jerusalem must be deserted by all human inhabitants; the armies from the East are coming. Heaven exhorts all who will listen to leave the city in haste, unless they too share in her sins and fiery affliction (Jeremiah 51:45; 50:8; Isaiah 48:20; Mark 13:14-20). Those who are alive and remain must leave Babylon in haste, so that they will not be caught in her demise, when she receives double punishment (Isaiah 40:2).

8. Review the nine passages below. How do they compare to the historical warnings to Babylon of old, and Babylon (Jerusalem) of the last days? _____

_____

_____

_____

~ Jeremiah 50:15, 29: "Shout against her on every side! She surrenders, her towers fall, her walls are torn down. Since this is the vengeance of the LORD, take vengeance on her; do to her as she has done to others... Summon archers against Babylon, all those who draw the bow. Encamp all around her; let no one escape. Repay her for her deeds; do to her as she has done. For she has defied the LORD, the Holy One of Israel."

~ Jeremiah 51:6-9: "Flee from Babylon! Run for your lives! Do not be destroyed because of her sins. It is time for the LORD's vengeance; he will pay her what she deserves. Babylon was a gold cup in the LORD's hand; she made the whole earth drunk. The nations drank her wine; therefore they have now gone mad. Babylon will suddenly fall and be broken. Wail over her! Get balm for her pain; perhaps she can be healed.

We would have healed Babylon, but she cannot be healed; let us leave her and each go to his own land, for her judgment reaches to the skies, it rises as high as the clouds."

~ Psalm 137:8: "O Daughter of Babylon, doomed to destruction, happy is He who repays you for what you have done to us."

~ Daniel 9:26: "After the sixty-two `sevens,' the anointed one [Elijah] will be cut off and will have nothing. The people of the Ruler [Antichrist] who will come will destroy the city [Jerusalem] and the Sanctuary. The end will come like a flood: War will continue until the end, and desolations have been decreed."

~ Matthew 24:16: "Then let those who are in Judea flee to the mountains."

~ Luke 21:20-22: "When you see Jerusalem being surrounded by armies, you will know that its desolation is near. Then let those who are in Judea flee to the mountains, let those in the city get out, and let those in the country not enter the city. For this is the time of punishment in fulfillment of all that has been written."

~ 2 Corinthians 6:17: "Therefore come out from them and be separate, says the LORD. Touch no unclean thing, and I will receive you."

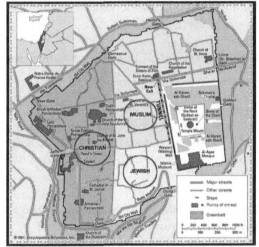

The Three Religions of Jerusalem Will Be Permanently Split Apart When The City Is Divided By The Massive Earthquake

~ Revelation 16:17-21: "The Seventh Angel poured out His bowl into the air, and out of the Temple came a loud voice from the throne, saying, "It is done!" Then there came flashes of lightning, rumblings, peals of thunder and a severe earthquake. No earthquake like it has ever occurred since man has been on earth, so tremendous was the [global earth] quake. The great city [Jerusalem] split into three parts [dividing the three great religions—Judaism, Christianity and Islam], and the cities of the nations collapsed. God remembered Babylon the Great and gave her the cup filled with the wine of the fury of His wrath. Every island fled away and the mountains could not be found. From the sky huge hailstones of about a hundred pounds each fell upon men. And they cursed God on account of the plague of hail, because the plague was so terrible."

~ Revelation 17:4; 14:8: "The woman [Jerusalem] was dressed in purple and scarlet, and was glittering with gold, precious stones and pearls" given her by her political/religious lovers. "She held a golden cup in her hand, filled with abominable things and the filth of her adulteries... A second angel followed and said, "Fallen! Fallen is Babylon the Great, which made all the nations drink the maddening wine of her adulteries."

Figuratively speaking, Jerusalem—the pinnacle city will glorify herself; she will live in the luxury of donated wealth, military protection and a rebuilding plan as the days of counting progress, while other cities around the globe will collapse under catastrophes, strife, famine and disease during the appointed times.

9. What will Jerusalem's residents think in their hearts, according to Revelation 18:7? _____

_____

She (her leaders) boasts in her heart with complete confidence of God's divine protection in spite of her turpitudes: "I sit as queen" exalted among the nations, "I am not a widow" my Husband still protects, "and I will never mourn" since I will live forever. Isaiah 47:7-9 adds, "You said, `I will continue forever—the eternal queen!' But you did not consider these things or reflect on what might happen. Now then, listen, you wanton creature, lounging in your security and saying to yourself, 'I am, and there is none besides me. I will never be a widow or suffer the loss of children.' Both of these will overtake you in a moment, on a single day: loss of children and widowhood. They will come upon you in full measure, in spite of your many sorceries and all your potent spells."

10. How does the prophet Zephaniah describe Jerusalem's sins (2:15-3:4)? _____

_____

11. What warning does Paul give Gentiles, especially those living at the end of the age, concerning the past sins of Israel (2 Corinthians 10:1-7, 11-12)? _____

_____

Paul states that although the Israelites personally experienced the miracles of God, delivering them from Egypt—including the parting sea, and manna and water in the desert—this did not seal their safety. God was not pleased with their evil habits and idol worship, so the destroying angel visited them.

This is an example for those who pretend to follow God. Paul adds that these historical events "were written down as warnings to us, on whom the fulfillment of the ages has come. So, if you think you are standing firm, be careful that you don't fall!" The temptation to disregard God's Commandments in adoration of the Papal leader and his idolatry will be overwhelming. The masses will give into the fear of survival, trading the eternal for momentary food and shelter.

12. Isaiah stated that Babylon's destruction would come "on a single day." Compare this to Revelation 18:8. What type of judgment will God pass upon her? _____

God's judgment will not be prolonged. Her plagues will come in one day, including death, mourning, famine, and a blistering and consuming fire (Isaiah 10:16-18; Ezekiel 12:25; 13:10-16).

13. What purpose is Jerusalem destroyed in the context of the Eternal Jubilee and the declaration of rest (Jeremiah 50:34)? _____

The Land of Israel will have a long-deserved rest from sin and sinners. The Redeemer will recover His land and bring down the sinful city, along with all sinners around the globe. The ransom was paid in full with His own blood two thousand years ago. Yeshua will cry with loud voice and proclaim liberty; then the land will be brought to rest. Evil men will not listen to the prophets' warnings, but now they hear Messiah's doom.

Consider the first of three woes in this chapter described in Revelation 18:9-10. Jerusalem's downfall will come not only in one day, but in one hour. The whole world will mourn in sorrow; but particularly, the political leaders will cry out for their loss. The International City of Peace will have been their great hope for global unity. The nations invested their hope in the great city's acceptance of the Vatican ruler to give the world freedom from strife, but he will not save Jerusalem; rather, his actions will destroy her. So breathtaking will be her demise, that the nations will be "terrified at her torment, and they will stand far off" in abject fear, because of the obliteration of the city and mass destruction in Israel when God withdraws His hand of protection (Jeremiah 22:8-9; Jeremiah 50:46; Daniel 9:26; Luke 21:20).

14. How does Luke describe not only the upheaval and horror that will overtake Israel at the climax of time, but the whole world (21:25-26)? What does the prophet Zephaniah predict (1:2-9)? _____
_____
_____

Politicians & Financiers Mourn The Worldwide Economic Collapse

The statesmen mourn, and the global financiers join in the sorrow of Jerusalem's demise and the final collapse of the world's economies (Revelation 18:11-17) at the second woe. They cry like babies over the great city, which had been rebuilt and dressed with the beautiful Temple edifice, adorned with priceless golden vessels and the best investment of building stones money could buy, with fine linen and blue, purple and scarlet curtains. "In one hour such great wealth has been brought to ruin!" Like the quick fall of the stock market in a single day, so will the global marketplace be brought to a halt to cry and lament this terrible event; all this on the heels of their celebration just days earlier over the death of God's last two prophets (Revelation 11:10).

15. How does James describe the foolishness of greed, money and power at this future moment in time (5:1-6)? _____

16. What is James' counsel to the last-day victors (5:7-8)? _____

The Merchants Mourn While The Martyrs Rejoice

The final woe evokes sorrow over Jerusalem's demise, because of Jew's global influence over importing and exporting goods. The ancient sea captains, representing today's modern merchants, will join the capitalists and political leaders in weeping over the loss of Jerusalem (18:17-19). However, the righteous martyrs in Heaven rejoice over *God's sovereign judgment* of the great city for the recorded killing of His prophets and saints during her long history, and at the end of the two prophet's 1,260-day ministry. These faithful now celebrate God's judgment of Jerusalem for killing of God's "apostles"—those individuals whom Jesus personally called and sent out to enlarge the early groups of believers; and finally, for the cruelty dealt to the prophets whom God sent to Israel and the city over the course of human history, including Yeshua.

The shout is heard, "Rejoice over her, O Heaven! Rejoice, *saints* and *apostles* and *prophets*! God has judged her for the way she treated you," Revelation 18:20. Jubilation over the fall of Babylon will reach Heaven itself (Jeremiah 51:48; Isaiah 44:23). The great multitude of martyrs from all nationalities, whether common or renowned, will have triumphed over the Man of Lawlessness, his mark and image. To "rejoice" in the original language means to "keep festival," and no doubt Jerusalem's destruction will occur during the High Holy Days at the fall Festival season, as orchestrated by God.

Just before her demise, the innumerable multitude of all nations will be resurrected to life, escaping the Great Tribulation by being transported to stand before God's throne (Revelation 7:9, 14; 15:1-2); and, there to reign with Him (20:4). This large group of sacrificial victims, who will sacrifice their lives during the final trial (Daniel 7:9, 8:24; 11:33; Matthew 24:9; 2 Timothy 2:11-12), petition God as Abel's blood cried out from the ground (Genesis 4:10) with the probing question, "how long, Sovereign LORD... until you judge the inhabitants of the earth and avenge our blood?" Revelation 6:10-11. They were told just a little longer until the full count of the martyred victors is complete. Once raised and taken home, the throne room will be filled with this great multitude of overcomers; then, the angels will depart with the trumpet and vial judgments.

17. Yeshua warned Jerusalem, and the generation living in His day, about mistreating His servants (Matthew 23:34-39). How does His warning of punishment for future generations accumulate for the deaths of the righteous throughout the ages, especially if they too join in the killing of God's prophets and righteous ones? _____

Examples of Israel's apostasy to idolatry and killing of the prophets have been written in God's Word, as an example for those living in the last days. If such counsel is ignored (and sadly, it will be), the final generation is all the more responsible for the final wrath of God upon the beloved city for their disobedience and murders. Those who inhabit the city (Jew and Gentile alike) will not evade the anger of a jealous God during the Great Tribulation.

The Mighty Angel's Cry Against The Traitorous Wife

Angels play a significant role throughout the book of Revelation. Revelation 18:21-23 depicts the Mighty Angel whose responsibility it is to assure Jerusalem's desolation. He picks up a large boulder the size of a millstone and in divine anger pitches it into the sea as symbolic recognition that Babylon's fate is sealed. She will sink out of sight, lost in the depths (Jeremiah 51:62-64). The Messenger declares, "With such violence the great city of Babylon will be thrown down, never to be found again." Jesus earlier warned, "and if anyone causes one of these little ones who believe in me to sin, it would be better for him to be thrown into the sea with a large millstone tied around his neck," Mark 9:42.

There is no choice; either the residents will flee from the city for their lives for the short but very destructive  Great Tribulation or stay with stubborn pride and die in Jerusalem. With heart-felt sorrow we learn that talented musicians will never play instruments in her again. No workman of any trade will drive into her to deliver goods or open their doors for business. The churning echo of automobiles and machinery will never be heard again. Homes and businesses filled with lights of hope, denoting life and activity, will be extinguished forever. Not one lamp or candle will be lit again. Bar mitzvahs, bat mitzvahs and weddings will never be performed within her gates; never again a joyous celebration of laughter and glee. All that will remain is desolation and dead silence.

We must stand firm on God's prophetic warnings all the way to the end; otherwise, we may be taken in by her spell. The prophecies indicate that our neighbors, friends and relatives will likely forsake God's Law to earn food and shelter. The voices of many will tug at us to join them in their sin of idolatry, fornication and murder. If we do not enlist with them, betrayal may rise up in our own homes, churches, synagogues and neighborhoods (Matthew 24:10), and those closest to us may regretfully seek our demise. This is the treacherous reality of the last days.

18. Due to the magnitude of Jerusalem's sins, she will have to suffer the vengeance of eternal fire, as did Sodom and Gomorrah long ago (Jude 7). How did Jeremiah predict a similar fate of desolation for Israel, because she would not listen to God's warnings in the past (7:33-34; 25:10)? _____

_____

Revelation 18:24 offers this heart-wrenching commentary: In Jerusalem "is found the blood of prophets and of the saints, and of all who have been killed on the earth." This is the reason Jerusalem, as we know it today, could not be the seat of the majestic throne of God. Too much blood has been shed in the land— the blood of Yeshua, and the death of the God's saints and prophets at the hands of evil men and demons. This is confirmed in Jeremiah 19:3-4, 7-8; Lamentations 1:1, 8; and, Matthew 23:29-38. In Matthew's account, Jesus' spoke in disgust and condemnation of Jerusalem's religious leaders of His day for their denunciation of His prophets, and His own rejection and death on the cross He knew was forthcoming. This criticism far exceeds anything written in this lesson:

"Woe to you, teachers of the law and Pharisees, you hypocrites! You build tombs for the prophets and decorate the graves of the righteous. And you say, 'If we had lived in the days of our ancestors, we would not have taken part with them in shedding the blood of the prophets.' So you testify against yourselves that you are the descendants of those who murdered the prophets. Go ahead, then, and complete what your ancestors started! "You snakes! You brood of vipers! How will you escape being condemned to hell? Therefore, I am sending you prophets and sages and teachers. Some of them you will kill and crucify; others you will flog in your synagogues and pursue from town to town. And so upon you will come all the righteous blood that has been shed on earth, from the blood of righteous Abel to the blood of Zechariah son of Berekiah, whom you murdered between the temple and the altar. Truly I tell you, all this will come on this generation. "Jerusalem, Jerusalem, you who kill the prophets and stone those sent to you, how often I have longed to gather your children together, as a hen gathers her chicks under her wings, and you were not willing. Look, your house is left to you desolate.

If the religious and political leaders of modern Jerusalem would reject Antichrist, the Man of Sin, and keep him from the Temple Mount, and if they would sigh and cry for all the abominations of the wicked, the city might be spared. However, prophecy already proclaims her downfall; few citizens, politicians or religious leaders will believe the warnings of God's Word, because their minds will be set only on following the mysterious Leader of the nations, whom they believe God has sent to save mankind.

Lamentations 4:12-14 sums up the matter eloquently: "The kings of the earth did not believe, nor did any of the world's people, that enemies and foes could enter the gates of Jerusalem. But it happened because of the sins of her [false] prophets and the iniquities of her [beguiling] priests, who shed within her the blood of the righteous. Now they grope through the streets like men who are blind. They are so defiled with blood that no one dares to touch their garments." Israel's/Jerusalem's pattern of disobedience is well documented. Down through the centuries she has rejected the Laws of God and have been involved in acts of adultery and prostitution (Jeremiah 3:20; Hosea 2:13; 3:1). Prophets have not been able to stop her through either punishment or counsel; she persists on in detestable acts, climbing into bed with the political leaders instead of staying true to her Husband.

It is said, "Lesbian, gay, bisexual, and transgender (LGBT) rights in Israel is the most advanced in the Middle East and one of the most advanced in Asia. Same-sex sexual activity was legalized in 1988, although the former law against buggery had not been enforced since a court decision of 1963. Israel became the first in Asia to recognize unregistered cohabitation between same-sex couples, making it the only country in Asia to recognize any same-sex union thus far. Gays and lesbians are also allowed to serve openly in the military. Recent polls have indicated that most Israelis support same-sex marriage, despite some social conservatism. Tel Aviv has frequently been referred to by publishers as one of the gayest friendly cities in the world, famous for its annual Pride Parade and gay beach, earning it the nickname "the gay capital of the Middle East" by *Out* magazine," Wikipedia (2016).

The unfaithful wife brings upon herself the sentence of death. Through the ages Jerusalem has murdered God's prophets; then, adding insult she rejected her Husband-Messiah two thousand years ago and delighted in His death. However, because of His patience one last time God will send His two prophets—Moses and Elijah—to inform and warn her. Still the people won't listen. Instead, most in Israel will join the world in celebration of the murder of God's last two anointed ones, giving their full attention to the Pope. By their actions, Jerusalem's doom will be sealed. Elohim will have no choice but to let her go; for, although He loved her deeply, she cannot live on while others suffer the flames of judgment that will fall upon every other city across the globe. Just as Jesus warned long ago, "O Jerusalem, Jerusalem, the one who kills the prophets and stones those who are sent to her! How often I wanted to gather your children together, as a hen gathers her chicks under her wings, but you were not willing! See! Your house is left to you desolate," Matthew 23:37-38. In the last days, the two witnesses will issue this warning once again.

The doctrine of divine retribution was recorded by the ancient Bible writers, particularly in the Psalms, and John developed this theme in the book of Revelation into an apocalyptic triumph of the righteous over their enemies and persecutors. Once Jerusalem—the Mother of Prostitutes & Abominations is stoned at the hands of her political lovers, illustrated by the three woes of Revelation 18, Messiah will be released from His marital-covenant obligation to His rebellious wife. She will die a permanent death, never to be rebuilt; then, the door will be opened for the celestial wedding between the Bridegroom and the New Jerusalem—the beautiful Golden City, which will take the place of the wayward wife. Once earth's Jerusalem is destroyed, the marriage festivities will begin in Heaven (Revelation 19:7-8; 21:2). The New Bride will be adorned when the overcomers enter her gates at the Sukkot celebration (Pt. 20) during the Great Tribulation. This joyous event will be covered in our next lesson.

---NOTES---

THE JUDGE

השופט

Insights In Prophecy
Unlock The Ancient Mysteries Of Daniel & Revelation
BIBLE DISCOVERY SERIES

Lesson 28

MARRIAGE OF THE LAMB TO THE NEW JERUSALEM

Read Revelation 19

- Discover The Marriage Participants—Bride, Groom & Guests
- Consider When The New Jerusalem Will Become The Eternal Home

During the appointed time of the end, the nations will look to Jerusalem—the epicenter of international events—with great hope for global peace and religious unity. However, near the end of the struggle for world dominion, the Man of Lawlessness will be allowed to enter onto the Jerusalem Temple Mount with the approval of Israel's religious and political leaders, and there proclaim himself Savior of mankind;

nevertheless, Messiah will suddenly come to His Temple to cleanse it of this treacherous idolatry. For this sin and for rejecting the two prophets' warnings, Jerusalem and her citizens who remain will meet their fiery doom.

On the *Day of Visitation*, the *countless multitudes* of martyred overcomers from all nationalities will be resurrected and transported to Heaven's Temple to stand before God's throne. The word is pronounced in Heaven that the prostitute city has burned in divine retribution. A loud roar of celebration echoes from the multitude of redeemed, "Hallelujah! Salvation and glory and power belong to our God, for true and just are His judgments. He has condemned the great prostitute who corrupted the earth by her adulteries. He has avenged on her the blood of His servants." And again, the group shouts, "Hallelujah! The smoke from her goes up for ever and ever," Revelation 19:1-3, signifying Jerusalem's total desolation from which she will never recover.

The Great Multitude Celebrates The Unfaithful Wife's Death

1. How is the "great multitude" identified in the book of prophecy (Revelation 7:9, 14-17; 15:2; 20:4)?

_____

_____

As last-day victors who remain loyal while enduring persecution and martyrdom, who are promised several amazing and personal rewards from Messiah, found in the first few chapters of Revelation (2:7; 2:11; 2:17; 2:26-28; 3:5; 3:12; 3:21). This innumerable steadfast group is made up of all nationalities—Jew and Gentile believers alike. They will escape as the Great Tribulation begins, because they will patiently endure at loss of life itself; and doing so, they overcome the Beast, his image and his mark (3:10). Their sacrifice for Yeshua is repaid; they will serve God in the Holy of Holies—a special honor for those who are victorious and clothed in white robes.

2. What are the main reasons for the great city Jerusalem's devastation in 586 BC and 70 AD, and again in the future appointed time of the end (Jeremiah 22:8-9, 17; Matthew 23:31-38; Revelation 18:24)? _____

_____

_____

Insights In Prophecy
Unlock The Ancient Mysteries Of Daniel & Revelation
BIBLE DISCOVERY SERIES

The people abandoned God's Covenant—the Ten Commandments and are called out for their sins: dishonest gain; shedding innocent blood, including the blood of prophets, wise men and teachers; oppression and extortion; and ultimately, their adoration of Antichrist. Jerusalem's leaders are particularly condemned for the killing of the innocent down through the ages, and the residents of the city celebrate with the rest of the world when God's last two prophets are murdered. Showing even greater distain, they leave them as rubbish in the street. For this reason, all Heaven repays with shouts of festivity when the city falls shortly thereafter, because "God has avenged on her the blood of His servants" the prophets (v. 2).

3. "The smoke from her goes up for ever and ever," (Revelation 19:3). Should we expect Babylon's smoke will literally rise for all eternity? _____

No. This statement is idiomatic—an "expression" unique to a particular language and culture, not to be taken literally. Common sense tells us that smoke rising forever is figurative, expressing the finality of the city's demise.

We would understand this to mean that Jerusalem's destruction is complete, and she will never be rebuilt again. Not one stone is left upon another. Jude 7 is similar in that the prophet said "Sodom and Gomorrah and the surrounding towns… suffered the punishment of *eternal fire*." Again, the *fire* was not eternal—the flames died out shortly after the fiery destruction hit, but the *results* were eternal; these towns have never been reconstructed. Therefore, unlike the rebuilding of Jerusalem after her destruction in both 586 BC and 70 AD, and the modern-day rebuilding of the great city during the 70 Weeks prophecy, the city will never be restored again after her ultimate destruction during the Great Tribulation. Her structures and homes will be leveled to their foundations and fire will destroy the prostitute city; no tools will be lifted, or machinery turned on to rebuild her streets, walls or buildings.

In Revelation 19:4, the twenty-four redeemed elders (Revelation 5:8-9), who sit as jury during the Courtroom Judgment (Daniel 7:9-10), fall down in worship along with the four living creatures in concert with the multitude of redeemed. They add their approval to the judgment of Babylon, the great city.

4. What New City is being prepared, that will replace this sinful city with greater splendor than ever seen before (Revelation 21:1-2)? _____

5. In Revelation 19:5-6 a voice calls up what group of people to respond in adoration to Almighty? ____ _____

The cry is for the "servants"—those who reverence Almighty—"both small and great!" to lift their voices in adoration, identified as the great multitude of Revelation 7:9-10.

In Revelation 7:7, the Word says they have escaped or "come out of the Great Tribulation" and are transport to Heaven at Yom Kippur for a special ceremony, which is soon to begin. 1 Corinthians 15:20-24 shows us that "resurrection" paves the way for God's retribution: "all die, so in Christ all will be made alive" in resurrection. "But each in his own turn: Christ, the firstfruits" two thousand years ago "then, when He comes" back, "those who belong to Him" will be raised to life. "Then *the end* will come."

280

Insights In Prophecy
Unlock The Ancient Mysteries Of Daniel & Revelation
BIBLE DISCOVERY SERIES

The Great Multitude Celebrates The Wedding Between New Bride & Bridegroom

6. Revelation 19:7-9 defines the celebration in Heaven. The redeemed shout in unified praise over rebellious Jerusalem's annihilation, then Almighty calls upon the innumerable crowd to lift their voices in festivity for the wedding of the Lamb is about to begin. Why? _____

The Bride has made herself ready for the wedding, because she is adorned in "fine linen, bright and clean... the righteous acts of the saints."

The great multitude of saints will step through the gates during Sukkot and into the New Jerusalem—the

place Messiah has prepared for them (John 14:1-3). The Bride (Revelation 21:9-10)—the beautiful New Jerusalem—for so long absent of her wedding attire, will be clothed with the beauty and glorious light of her redeemed citizens. For the great "multitudes who sleep in the dust of the earth will awake" to be taken to Heaven for the wedding event, and... "those who are wise will shine like the brightness of the heavens... like the stars for ever and ever," Daniel 12:2-3. The Bride will finally be clothed in fine linen, for the persecuted saints are themselves clothed in white robes (Revelation 3:4-5; 6:9-11; 7:9); in contrast, the prostitute city wears "purple and scarlet, and is glittering with gold, precious stones and pearls," given her by Antichrist and her political lovers, in whom Israel trusted more than Messiah and His two anointed prophets—the two rejected, despised and killed (Revelation 17:4).

On that great wedding day under the Chuppah of God's protection—the canopy covering under which a Jewish couple stand during their Jewish wedding ceremony, the union will be complete between Yeshua the Bridegroom and the New Jerusalem Bride and invited guests, who are dressed in their gifted wedding garments. The Groom, Bride and children (Matthew 5:9, 44-45) of the Most High will continue in celebration for the seven days of Sukkot—the Feast of Tabernacles, known also as the Feast of the Nations (Zechariah 14:16)—followed by the eighth day Shemini Atzeret/Simchat Torah celebrations (Leviticus 23:39-43).

7. How did Jesus promise this home coming and wedding for His followers before He left the earth (John 14:1-3)? _____

"I am going there to prepare a place— New Jerusalem "for you. And if I go and prepare a place for you" to live, "I will come back and take you" to Heaven "with Me" at the Yom Kippur trumpet blast "that you also may be where I am."

8. The three passages below teach the gemmed New Jerusalem in Heaven will replace the old stone and mortar Jerusalem. They also share the believers' anticipation of entering the City as guests for the wedding celebration between Jesus and His Bride. How is this truth revealed? _____
_____
_____

~ Hebrews 11:10, 16: "For he [Abraham] was looking forward to the city [New Jerusalem] with foundations, whose architect and builder is God... they [people of faith] were longing for a better country—a heavenly one. Therefore, God is not ashamed to be called their God, for He has prepared a city for them."

~ Hebrews 12:22: "But you have come to Mount Zion, to the heavenly Jerusalem, the city of the living God. You have come to thousands upon thousands of angels in joyful assembly."

~ Hebrews 13:14: "For here [on earth] we do not have an enduring city [which goes on forever], but we are looking for the city [New Jerusalem] that is to come."

Jesus entered the Temple courts in Jerusalem and spoke several parables of warning to the chief priests and elders of that day. The rabbis were cautioned: "The kingdom of God will be taken away from you and given to a people who will produce its fruit," Matthew 21:43. Then, He enlightened minds through the Parable of the Wedding Banquet in Matthew 22:1-14. Jesus said the king (Heavenly Father) prepared a wedding for his son (Christ), and he sent his servants (the prophets) to invite the guests (Israelites, scribes and Pharisees) who would not accept the invitation. They even killed the king's servants (the prophets) who were personally sent with notices. So the king (Almighty) sent his armies and destroyed the murderers and burned up their city (Jerusalem), then he extended the invitation to the poor, maimed and blind (of all nations), and the wedding was furnished with guests.

Because of the stubborn attitudes of those who were first invited to the marriage, a great multitude of all nations (the primary focus is on Gentiles, but also believing Jews) will be the invited guests to both witness and be a part of the wedding ceremony between Messiah and His Bride—the New Jerusalem.

Marriage Supper Of The Lamb

Revelation 19:9 announces, "Blessed are those who are invited to the wedding supper of the Lamb! These are the true words of God," and therefore, can be depended upon. A second beatitude also identifies why this set apart group is so honored. Revelation 20:6 says, "Blessed and holy are those who have part in the first resurrection. The second death has no power over them, but they will be *priests* of God and of Christ and will reign with Him for a thousand [1,000] years." The first resurrection—comprised of the great multitude of all nations—is not all the righteous of all ages, but primarily the victorious ones who become Temple servants in Heaven's sanctuary; those who triumphed over the Beast, his image and mark of the last days at the cost of life itself (20:4).

9. How did John respond to the Angel's announcement of salvation (Revelation 19:10)? _____
_____

The prophet John was a disciple and dear friend of Jesus during His lifetime on earth. However, when he first saw Yeshua in vision with all His brilliance and glory John "fell at His feet as though dead" in fear (Revelation 1:16-17). Obviously, John knew the Savior's face and would prostrate to worship the King, his one and only Savior. Here John again "fell to worship" the Angel a second time, who had just proclaimed salvation. The prophet would not have worshiped just any messenger from Heaven, only his Master and LORD. The Messenger could be none other than Michael—a title for our Messenger King, and the One who visited with John in Revelation 17:1 to show him the final revelations about Babylon's destruction and the climactic wedding in Heaven to the City Bride.

10. What did Michael say to John that would continue to hide, but then eventually reveal, His identity in final unsealing of prophecy (v. 10)? _____

Although John knew that Jesus deserved his worship, Michael would not at that time allow John to worship Him while fulfilling His duty as a humble Messenger of future trials. Although equal with the Father, for this visionary period He considered Himself in a prophet's role; so Yeshua told him "do not do it!" Rather, He wanted John to stand eye to eye as a prophet—equal in service to the Father. Therefore, He said to John that He was "a fellow servant" and "brother" with him, and with all those who would hold to the testimony of Jesus—the book of Revelation. Revelation's messages were identified as coming from the Spirit, the Divine source of prophecy and Revealer of future events in minute detail thousands of years before they would come to pass (1:2).

11. Philippians 2:5-8 helps us identify our Messiah as "fellow servant" and "brother". How? _____
_____

It is written, "Christ Jesus: Who, being in very nature God, did not consider equality with God something to be grasped, but made Himself nothing, taking the very nature of *a servant*, being made in human likeness. And being found in appearance as *a man*." In other words, God's Son humbled Himself, leaving behind the worship due Him, to come to earth in the "appearance as" a human being. Although Divine, He appeared to be a mere man—as a "brother". In this way, He identified with us and with our struggles against evil, and ultimately provided the way of escape. No other angelic messenger could identify with the prophet as his "brother". What other messenger could so move John the disciple with words of salvation that he would fall prostrate in worship before him? Only Yeshua, John's long-time beloved friend, his Savior and LORD.

As mankind can identify with the incarnate Jesus, so too can Heaven's countless angels. Christ fulfills His role in the "appearance" and duties of the Archangel, so that none of His created beings will feel exempt from His devoted love and association. This does not make Him any less God, for He was with the Father from the beginning. On the contrary, this makes Him Supremely God, the originator and proponent of love through His continuous acts of humility, as the Messenger to men and Military Commander of the angelic army.

Jesus had acted in similar meekness during an episode recorded in Matthew 19:16-17 (KJV). A man approached and addressed Him as "Good Master" and asked a question about eternal life. Instead of taking the glory to Himself, Jesus instead replied, "why callest thou Me good? there is none good but One, that is, God" the Father. Again, He displayed humility, when the seeker had attempted to show Him honor. In this way, the glory would be transferred to the Father and away from Him as the Son of Man. These acts of humility are not found in the lives of the future world leader or Satan, who both seek worship and honor for personal gain. Their pride contrasts the humble Savior; nonetheless, His gentleness will end when He returns as Judge of sin and all sinners.

As the Messenger of the Covenant, I AM visited with thunder at Mount Sinai to deliver the Law to Moses (Acts 7:30-31, 35, 38). Soon He will return again, and His voice will be heard in thunderous echo when all mystery will be completed (10:7). "But who can abide the Day of His coming?" Malachi 3:1-2.

12. The invitation to the marriage supper of the Lamb—He who will take away the sin of the world (John 1:49) in one final battle, has been associated with the heavenly banquet where the saints sit down for a magnificent meal. This celebration will surely occur. However, the context of the supper in Revelation 19 indicates the event is about what (vs. 17-18)? _____

A marvelous banquet will be held in Heaven at the Kingdom meal (Matthew 8:11; 26:29; Luke 22:18, 30) and wedding banquet; however, the Revelation passage points to a very different meal—the consumption of evil men—when all the rebellious ones will be devoured who have hated, persecuted and killed God's servants during the final days, and despised Yeshua's salvation. Zephaniah 1:7-8, 12, 17-18 also speaks of this meal: "Hold thy peace at the presence of the LORD GOD: for the Day of the LORD is at hand: for the LORD hath prepared a sacrifice, He hath bid His guests. And it shall come to pass in the Day of the LORD's sacrifice, that I will punish the princes, and the king's children... And it shall come to pass at that time, that I will search Jerusalem with candles, and punish the men that are settled on their lees: that say in their heart, The LORD will not do good, neither will he do evil... And I will bring distress upon men that they shall walk like blind men, because they have sinned against the LORD: and their blood shall be poured out as dust, and their flesh as the dung. Neither their silver nor their gold shall be able to deliver them in the Day of the LORD's wrath; but the whole land shall be devoured by the fire of His jealousy: for He shall make even a speedy riddance of all them that dwell in the land."

The Rider Of The White Horse

The remaining verses of Revelation 19 take us to the final moments of the appointed time counting days—Day 1,335.

13. Who is found on the white horse of royalty and battle (v. 11)? _____

On the magnificent stallion sits Faithful and True; He is true to His word, and honest in His dealings with mankind. He will judge and make war.

14. What does He look like, and what is He wearing (vs. 12-13)? _____
_____

He has eyes of blazing fire (1:14; 2:18)—our God is a consuming fire (Hebrews 12:29); on His head many crowns—He is King over all the earth (Psalm 44:4; 72:1; Isaiah 32:1; 43:15; Jeremiah 23:5; Zechariah 13:9; John 1:49). A name is written on Him that no man knows; a name that depicts His role as King and avenger of His people. The robe dipped in blood signifies His sacrifice and His military conquest (Isaiah 63:2-4), and He is called the "Word of God" (John 1:1-3)—the Creator who spoke all things into existence (Colossians 1:15-17; 1 John 1:1; Philippians 2:6).

15. Who is seen following the Conquering Messiah? How are they identified? _____

The armies of Heaven follow Him, also riding on white horses and they are "dressed in fine linen, white and clean." Obviously, these individuals are symbolized wearing righteous garments; they are the redeemed from among men and have been invited guests to the Sukkot wedding and feast at the Tabernacle.

16. How do the following verses prove the army is made up of the victors, who at that time will have been resurrected and taken to Heaven, while the living (sealed for protection—Revelation 7:2-4) remain on earth for the short but Great Tribulation, until the plagues are completed (1 Thessalonians 3:13; 4:14-17; Jude 14-15; Revelation 3:4; 19:8)? _____
_____

17. In addition to the horse riders, who also joins the fine-linen warriors returning though the universe toward earth, who gather together the scattered elect—the 144,000 (Matthew 13:39-41; 24:30-31)? __
_____

18. A sharp sword is symbolized as coming from the mouth of the King (Revelation 19:15). What does the sword and rod of iron signify (2 Thessalonians 2:8; Revelation 1:16; 2:27)? _____

_____

While Jesus rode into Jerusalem the first time in humility on a donkey to be killed by rebellious Israel at the hands of Romans, at His second coming He will return as conquering King on a white stallion and in fierce anger. The Father will accompany His Son as well, remaining on His glorious throne (Matthew 16:27; 26:64; Luke 9:26). The crowned King's victory over human enemies, Satan and evil angels will be swift and decisive; He will destroy all the nations of the world and the powers of the air, and with it all wickedness will be subjugated.

19. Revelation 14:19-20 portrays war's devastation to that of grapes stomped in a winepress. How is it described? _____

"They were trampled in the winepress outside the city [Jerusalem], and blood flowed out of the press, rising as high as the horses' bridles for a distance of 1,600 stadia." As feet stomp on tiny grapes to expel the juices, so will the blood of the rebellious be spilled out, for they have brought the curse of sin upon themselves. The 1,600 stadia represent about 200 miles, indicating the severity of widespread death and the numbers of dead to be vast. Revelation 19:16 provides another of the many titles assigned to Messiah through the ages. This is a name of triumph over all the great men of the earth—the kings, politicians and wealthy aristocrats: His name is KING OF KINGS AND LORD OF LORDS.

The Marriage Supper Served

20. In Revelation 19:17 an angel stands in front of the sun, signifying pronounced darkness. Zechariah 1:14-18 describes this fateful Day. How? _____

_____

21. The call rings out for the flying vultures to descend to the supper of God (Revelation 19:18-19), where they will eat the flesh of the dead (Matthew 24:26-28). What people are included in this feast?

_____

From the least to the greatest, all the unfaithful will pay for the wages of sin—death. No human flesh will survive the wrath of God to enter an earth-bound millennium, as many teach. The Hebrew Scriptures communicate that all sin and sinners will be annihilated, including all wicked politicians, commanders and marshaled forces of military might along with their machinery. "*All people*," no matter their standing in society, "*free and slave, small and great*" will be food for the vultures. Ezekiel 39:17-20 describes in the poetry of finality this feast of politicians and military personnel that have positioned themselves to fight against the returning King and His army: "Son of man, this is what the Sovereign LORD says: Call out to every kind of bird and all the wild animals: 'Assemble and come together from all around to the sacrifice I am preparing for you, the great sacrifice on the mountains of Israel. There you will eat flesh and drink blood. You will eat the flesh of mighty men and drink the blood of the princes of the earth as if they were rams and lambs, goats and bulls—all of them fattened animals from Bashan. At the sacrifice I am preparing for you, you will eat fat till you are glutted and drink blood till you are drunk. At *My table you will eat your fill* of horses and riders, mighty men and soldiers of every kind,' declares the Sovereign LORD."

Isaiah 34:1-3, 8-10 also adds more about this military conquest: "Come near, you nations, and listen; pay attention, you peoples! Let the earth hear, and all that is in it, the world, and all that comes out of it! The

LORD is angry with all nations; His wrath is on all their armies. He will totally destroy them, He will give them over to slaughter. Their slain will be thrown out, their dead bodies will stink; the mountains will be soaked with their blood. For the LORD has a Day of vengeance, a year of retribution, to uphold Zion's cause. Edom's streams will be turned into pitch, her dust into burning sulfur; her land will become blazing pitch! It will not be quenched night or day; its smoke will rise forever. From generation to generation it will lie desolate; no one will ever pass through it again."

22. Zechariah 14:2 and Isaiah 66:6 locate Armageddon near what city? _____
What does Joel 3:2, 12 reveal? _____

The Valley of Jehoshaphat, east of Jerusalem. In Revelation 19:20-21 the Beast and the False Prophet, who performed deceptive miracles to cause the masses to take the mark and worship idols and demons, will be thrown into this lake of fire.

23. Where does Peter locate this destructive fire (2 Peter 3:10)? _____

24. Why will Judah and the rest of the world burn (Amos 2:4-5)? _____
_____

25. How does Joel 2:1-5, 11 describe the terrible destruction by fire on the Day of the LORD? _____
_____

26. What is the Beast's doom, along with all others, whom the Bible identifies as the remaining "remnant" of sinners (Revelation 19:21: 2 Thessalonians 2:8; Psalm 37:20; 104:35)? _____
_____

27. What insight does Isaiah 1:28, Zephaniah 3:8 and Luke 17:29-30 add? _____
_____

28. What will the Kingdom saints see as they look back over their shoulders on their ascent to Heaven and the New Jerusalem, following the aftermath of the Armageddon battle (Jeremiah 4:23-29)? _____
_____

The earth will be nothing but a desolate planet—formless and empty. The sun, moon and stars will no longer shine, the mountains and hills will be removed from their foundations, all birds will fly away, the land will be a dry wasteland, all towns will sit in ruins of war and no one will live in them—all are dead. This will not be the full end of the world; that will occur at the end of the thousand years.

Surely God has "set a day," an appointed time, when He will judge earth's inhabitants for their rebellion (Acts 17:31; Habakkuk 2:3). Do you recognize the signs of the time (Luke 12:56)? Time is running out, and our futures are about to change. We want to be on the right side of that final battle, by being right with the King today, and having done all to stand. "Finally, be strong in the LORD and in His mighty power. Put on the full armor of God, so that you can take your stand against the devil's schemes. For our struggle is not against flesh and blood, but against the rulers, against the authorities, against the powers of this dark world and against the spiritual forces of evil in the heavenly realms. Therefore, put on the full armor of God, so that when the day of evil comes, you may be able to stand your ground, and after you have done everything, to stand. Stand firm then, with the belt of truth buckled around your waist, with the breastplate of righteousness in place, and with your feet fitted with the readiness that comes from the gospel of peace. In addition to all this, take up the shield of faith, with which you can extinguish all the flaming arrows of the evil one. Take the helmet of salvation and the sword of the Spirit, which is the word of God. And pray in the Spirit on all occasions with all kinds of prayers and requests. With this in mind, be alert and always keep on praying for all the LORD's people," Ephesians 6:10-18.

The following two very respected rabbis in the Modern Orthodox stream of Judaism, who do not adhere to the book of Revelation, testify to the timing of the wedding between the Bride—Jerusalem with her righteous saints, and the Bridegroom—Yeshua, at Sukkot, the Feast of Tabernacles during the Great Tribulation (*The Kingdom Calendar*—Pt. 20).

Sukkot From A Jewish Perspective

Think of Sukkot as a Joyous Wedding Under the Chuppah
by Rabbi Judah Dardik, Modern Orthodox

"September and October are big holiday months. In acts of great effort and dedication, millions of Jews across the world reorganize their school, work and personal schedules to carve out extra time for holiday meals, extensive (and hopefully inspiring) synagogue services and other religious get-togethers. And just as the intensity of Yom Kippur passes and our thoughts naturally turn to a return to "normal" life, along comes Sukkot."

"Funny timing on this one. Some holidays fall out on a certain spot on the calendar as a result of the time of year in which they occurred. For example, the Jewish people were freed from Egyptian slavery in the spring, and so we celebrate Passover at that time. We received the Torah just over seven weeks later, which accounts for the timing of Shavuot. Yom Kippur was the date on which we received a second chance with the gift of the second set of tablets inscribed with the Ten Commandments. Forever after we look for a reprieve, another chance, on that date."

"By contrast, Sukkot has no particular date associated with it. As a holiday that recalls the care HaShem displayed towards us during 40 years of wandering in the desert, it could have been celebrated any time. We lived for decades in thatched huts, and appreciate the Divine care that assured our protection and survival in that hostile environment. But this was a daily occurrence, suitable for commemoration on any day of the year. Why have it now, just when we are overloaded with holidays as it is?"

"In the search for clues, it makes sense to keep an eye open for anything unusual in the Torah's description of the holiday. A glance through the text reveals a repeated theme: We are commanded on three separate occasions to be joyous on Sukkot. There is no such specific command with regard to Shabbat nor with almost any other holiday, and yet we are thrice reminded to be happy on this holiday."

"Perhaps instead of thinking of Sukkot as a repeating historical event on the calendar, we should consider it a personal event that happens to come back each year. It is preceded by some days of serious thought, places us outside under a canopy, involves seven days of rejoicing, and culminates in the dancing of Simchat Torah. Sound at all familiar? Might it resemble the description of a Jewish wedding?"

"The historical cycle of holidays begins with Passover, which was an experience of getting to know HaShem and then "going out" together in early courtship. The relationship proceeded over the ensuing weeks to get quite a bit more serious, with formal commitment to one another (engagement) on Shavuot. The episode of the Golden Calf may display our early insecurity in the relationship and our first "big fight," a consequence of flirtation with infidelity. It is well past time to think seriously about this upcoming wedding, and that may be the explanation for the timing of the celebration of Sukkot."

"Perhaps our Torah places Sukkot months later, near the High Holy Days, to give it the proper context and mindset. After months of engagement, we spend the days before the "wedding" in clear-headed contemplation of both the gravity and overwhelming joy of being in a dynamic, vibrant and deeply committed relationship. We even fast on Yom Kippur, just as many brides and grooms do before their big day."

"And now for the wedding day of Sukkot. It's an outdoor chuppah, bedecked with greenery, flowers, decorations, and a view of the stars. Seven days of feasting and rejoicing (the Sheva Brachot) follow, including the dance sets of Simchat Torah."

"When we first met, we thought we "knew this was the one." Then we got engaged, all the more confident. But we never truly know why we would want to spend our lives with someone until we do so, and so the holiday of joy is the one of finally being together. Rosh Hashanah and Yom Kippur are very heavy events, but they are also a prelude to joy. Let the wedding commence!"

Judaism: Sukkot and the Wedding Feast
By Rabbi Dr. Shlomo Riskin, Modern Orthodox

"The Sacred Marriage between G-d and Israel has been, at best, put off, postponed. And so it is with us… We are in exile, our King is in exile, the Sacred Marriage between G-d and Israel has been, at best, put off, postponed. Shall we request to partake of the wedding feast? We can only pray for the wedding to take place as soon as possible."

"On Rosh HaShanah we pray that G-d be proclaimed King over the entire world, that the Sacred Marriage, which will bring unity to the world, shall come about immediately. On Yom Kippur we are transported to the Holy Temple, the nuptial canopy; the High Priest proclaims everyone purified, we hear the triumphant trumpet-shofar of the Almighty, we cry out: 'Hear Oh Israel, the LORD our G-d, The LORD is One, Blessed be the Name of His glorious Kingdom forever, the LORD (of Israel) he is G-d (of the world)."

"But alas, this is all a dream - a glorious dream - but not yet a reality. And so immediately after we awaken from the dream, with the blast of the shofar, we must build our modest sukkah, symbol of the exile of the Divine Presence, move into that sukkah with our entire family, and pray that the 'Merciful One re-establish for us the fallen tabernacle of King David' and transform our small sukkah into the Eternal Temple; at that time all nations will flock to attend the Sacred Marriage of the Divine and the redemption of all humanity."

Insights In Prophecy
Unlock The Ancient Mysteries Of Daniel & Revelation
BIBLE DISCOVERY SERIES

Lesson 29

LESSON 29

THE MILLENNIAL DELAY OF JUDGMENT

Read Revelation 20

- **Consider The Activities Of The Millennial (1,000 Year) Period**
- **Examine The Location Of The Lake Of Fire**

The Hebrew prophets often wrote about the conquering Messiah, the Day of the LORD, and the Kingdom of God as one single climactic event. However, John the Revelator introduced a new period not written of prior to the Apocalypse—a one-thousand-year period. Twice in the Scriptures the writers spoke about the concept of God's delay in reference to a "thousand years": Psalm 90:4, 13 says, "For a *thousand years* in  Your sight are like yesterday when it is past, and like a watch in the night... Relent, LORD! How long will it be? Have compassion on your servants." Then, Peter repeated God's perspective on time: "But do not forget this one thing, dear friends: With the LORD a day is like a *thousand years*, and a *thousand years* are like a day. The LORD is not slow in keeping His promise, as some understand slowness. Instead He is patient with you, not wanting anyone to perish, but everyone to come to repentance." 2 Peter 3:8-9.

John's disclosure of time—what looks to be a postponement of the Great White Throne Judgment, the restoration of the new earth, and arrival of the New Jerusalem—can clarify an otherwise baffling series of ancient Bible predictions. The apostles anticipated the conquering Mashiach in their day, and were surprised by the delay. Why? Because the Scriptures spoke repeatedly of Messiah's victory, while the evidence for the suffering and sacrificed Christ lay in obscure passages, as a veiled mystery of God.

Once Yeshua's victory was gained at the cross, and with His resurrection and ascension, He might have immediately returned in power to defeat Satan and take His rightful kingdom. However, God's plan included a two-thousand-year postponement that many more individuals might be saved, based on the reality of His great sacrifice at Calvary. Should we then be surprised that a further suspension will push back the final sentences of reward or punishment?

Much like the other visions of Revelation, chapter 20 is not entirely chronological. For example, in Revelation 21:2 John sees the New Jerusalem descending out of Heaven; then, at verse 10, he repeats the movement of the City of God to earth, but with added details. Therefore, we must reconstruction the events of chapter 20 that brings the one thousand years to an end, the descent of the New Jerusalem, the Great White Throne Judgment, the final battle and fiery demise of sinners and the old earth, the recreation of Planet Earth, and eternal peace.

1. What is symbolized in the key, great chain and Abyss (Revelation 20:1-3)? _____

_____

Satan is bound for one thousand years. The Devil is judged as unfit to reign any longer by the Heavenly tribunal (Daniel 7:9-10, 26), and he will be stripped of his status as prince and power of the air (Ephesians

6:12), but will be bound alive and alone that he might ponder his wickedness and where his decisions have brought him.

John learns that Satan is the "dragon" and "ancient serpent". The *cunning wisdom* of the serpent is an attribute that distinguishes the serpent from other creatures (Genesis 3:1). Jesus recommended to His disciples to be as wise as serpents (Matthew 10:16). A snake bites with poisonous venom through his mouth and fangs, and his heart is under the throat and very near his head. Maybe for this reason God told the Serpent in the Garden of Eden, "I will put enmity between you and the woman, and between your offspring and hers; He will *crush your head*, and you will strike His heel," Genesis 3:15. The low and lonely dust would be the hated serpent's trail, and the dark desolate Abyss will be the Serpent's cursed abode.

Revelation 12:9 calls the Devil a Serpent, both because he cloaked himself in the body of a charming serpent when he seduced the first woman, and because he will hide his intentions once again through the mouth of an enchanting world ruler during the counting periods of the appointed time (2 Corinthians 11:14-15). He has a serpentine disposition, being a subtle, crafty and dangerous enemy to mankind, and he will mix truth with error as he did in the Garden; and, thereby march multitudes of souls head-long into eternal judgment.

The Dragon signifies very "old serpents grown with age to a prodigious size" with wings, says the Cruden's Concordance, which are often found in uninhabited places, in the ruins of cities and in rubbish (Isaiah 13:22; 34:13; Jeremiah 9:11). In Revelation 12:9 Satan is not only called the Dragon for his great strength and bloody cruelty against believers, but also to signify the Serpent grown to full strength of evil. He is so enormous that he can give others authority to rule (Revelation 13:2-4), and push the entire world's governments in the direction he chooses; his tail overthrows a third of the righteous angels in battle and flings them to their demise (Revelation 12:3-4; 7-9); and yet, he cannot fully overcome Messiah, whose heel he can only bruise. Satan is seized and bound for one thousand years. His release will be only short-lived, for the Dragon's head will eventually be crushed (Isaiah 27:1; Isaiah 51:9), and his fiery demise is foretold— "a horrible end and [he] will be no more," Ezekiel 28:17-19.

2. Although sketchy in details, what did John connect to the one thousand years as the primary reason for the lengthy delay (Revelation 20:4)? _____

A group will be given authority to judge, just as the twenty-four elders described earlier (Revelation 4:4).

Paul spoke of how saints would eventually judge; that is, make decisions in behalf of both mankind and angels (1 Corinthians 6:2-3), and thereby render important verdicts. Yeshua also promised His disciples "twelve thrones" from which they would be "judging the twelve tribes of Israel," (Matthew 19:28).

3. A specific group is described as being resurrected back to life who "reigned with Christ a thousand years," (Revelation 20:4). Who are they? _____

This are the victorious overcomers of the last days; more specifically, the martyrs of the appointed time identified as having been "beheaded" for having endured against Antichrist's worship, image and mark to follow the "testimony of Jesus" (recorded in the book of Revelation—Revelation 1:1-3; Matthew 24:13; Hebrews 3:12-15).

4. The prophet Daniel writes of a resurrection at the onset of the "time of distress," the Great Tribulation (12:2-3). Who are included? _____

Daniel speaks of "many"—both saints and sinners—coming to life from the dusty earth, which also represents a limited group.

Revelation 1:7 says that "every eye will see Him, even those who pierced Him." Evidently, Messiah's most cruel adversaries will be raised to life temporarily to see His triumphant return. Revelation 7:9-14 also identifies an enormous group of all nationalities—a "great multitude"—as coming out of the Great Tribulation, taken up to stand triumphant in the heavenly Temple. These victorious martyrs are found in Heaven before the seven plagues are poured out (Revelation 12:10-11; 15:1-8).

5. The "rest of the dead" remain in death's sleep—those not included in the "first resurrection." How long? (Revelation 20:5)? _____

Outside of the last-day martyrs, no other believers are identified as being included in the first resurrection in Revelation 20. Messiah will call whom He chooses for the first resurrection. The evidence shows that all remaining saints and sinners who have been laid to rest in the course of human history will not come to life until the one thousand years are finished.

6. What is the blessing for those who are raised in the first resurrection (Revelation 20:6)? _____
_____

The second death has no power over them; their destiny has already been sealed.

This "great multitude" of victors cannot be condemned or judged unworthy of God's kingdom at the Great White Throne Judgment, for they have already proven themselves by faithful witness as "holy" and worthy

to become "priests of God and of Christ" in His holy Temple above. This group of leaders has a position of priestly honor in God's Sanctuary: "they are before the throne of God and serve Him day and night in His Temple," Revelation 7:14-15. "To him who loves us and has freed us from our sins by His blood, and has made us to be a kingdom and priests to serve His God and Father—to Him be glory and power for ever and ever!" Revelation 1:5-6. Yeshua confirms there will be diverse positions
from the least to the greatest among the redeemed in the Kingdom, "Whosoever therefore shall break one of these least commandments, and shall teach men so, he shall be called the least in the kingdom of heaven: but whosoever shall do and teach them, the same shall be called great in the kingdom of heaven," Matthew 5:19.

7. Hebrews 9:27 depicts the progression of life, death and judgment. How? _____
_____

When life ends there is death's sleep, then resurrection to judgment for either eternal punishment or eternal reward. God knows how to reserve the fallen angels and wicked men for the long-foretold day of judgment to be punished (2 Peter 2:4; Jude 6; 2 Peters 2:9). We all must appear before the judgment seat of God to give an accounting of our actions and decisions (Romans 14:10-12; 2 Corinthians 5:10).

Death Is Called Sleep In The Hebrew Scriptures

~ Daniel 12:2, "Multitudes who *sleep* in the dust of the earth will awake: some to everlasting life, others to shame and everlasting contempt."

~ John 11:11-14, "After he had said this, he went on to tell them, "Our friend Lazarus has fallen *asleep*; but I am going there to wake him up." His disciples replied, "LORD, if he sleeps, he will get better." Jesus had been *speaking of his death*, but his disciples thought he meant natural sleep. So then he told them plainly, "Lazarus is dead.""

~ 1 Corinthians 15:51, "Listen, I tell you a mystery: We will not all *sleep*, but we will all be changed."

~ 1 Thessalonians 4:13, "Brothers and sisters, we do not want you to be uninformed about those who *sleep in death*, so that you do not grieve like the rest of mankind, who have no hope."

~ Ephesians 5:14, "This is why it is said: "*Wake up, sleeper*, rise from the dead, and Christ will shine on you.""

The Millennium Debate

Although a popular view, Revelation 20 is silent about a reign of Jesus over Planet Earth during the one-thousand-year millennium. Almighty God will release His trumpet and vial plagues that will crush earth's ecological system. Global wide earthquakes will level cities, and islands will disappear. The sea and fresh water will be polluted. The whole planet will be brought to devastation and ruin, to be finished off one-thousand years later by a worldwide fire, which will need a total makeover.

A few probing questions need to be asked: 1) if the one-thousand-year Messianic reign occurs on earth, the Scriptures would speak about a global restoration at the beginning of the millennium. 2) Imagine how beautiful the planet would be by the end of one thousand years of Messiah's rule. Why would God then destroy His great handiwork by fire at the end of the millennium? 3) If Jesus promised that He would go and prepare a place for His followers—the New Jerusalem, and He would come again (at His return) and *receive us to Himself*, that where He is (in Heaven) there we would also be (John 14:2), why would He relegate the saints to a war-torn, dusty planet *without* the New Jerusalem for one thousand years?

The New Jerusalem is the hope of believers (Hebrews 11:10, 16; 13:14). So real is this hope that according to God's Word the faithful are called "aliens and strangers on earth," Hebrews 11:13, and they long for a "better country—a heavenly one. Therefore, God is not ashamed to be called their God, for He has prepared a city [New Jerusalem] for them," Hebrews 11:16. "An inheritance that can never perish, spoil or fade— kept [reserved] in Heaven for you who through faith are shielded by God's power until the coming of the salvation that is ready to be revealed in the last time," 1 Peter 1:4-5.

At the Second Coming of Christ the world will be bombarded by fire and brimstone. Jeremiah saw the vast devastation that would be left behind (4:23-29), and he wrote, "I looked at the earth, and it was formless and empty; and at the heavens, and their light was gone... I looked and there was no people; every bird in the sky had flown away... all the towns lay in ruins before the LORD, before His fierce anger."

The General Resurrection

Once the one thousand years have expired, Messiah, the New Jerusalem and her inhabitants will slip through the portal and come down from Heaven to this dark, desolate planet; then, lit with God's glory the universal resurrection will occur. At the voice of God the sea—great bodies of water—will expel all the dead found in them, and hell (Greek: "hades", meaning the "graves") will release their lifeless victims—all the dead of all ages who had not come forth in the first resurrection will rise up from their dispersed abodes by the life-giving power of Messiah's loud voice (Revelation 20:13).

8. Who are included in this general resurrection (John 5:28-29)? _____

Those who have done good and those who have done evil will rise. Jesus taught there would be a future judgment for separating the righteous and unrighteous in the parables of the tares and the net (Matthew 13:37-43; 47-50).

9. How does Paul support the idea of a general resurrection of both good and evil persons (Acts 24:15)?
_____

The Great White Throne Judgment

Revelation 20:11-12 takes us to the point of Judgment at the end of one thousand years. The dead of all ages and of all nationalities will be raised to life to stand before the Judge of the Universe to receive those things done during their lifetimes. We do not have the details as to how this is all accomplished, whether those who are righteous are raised first followed by the wicked; we do not know; nor, do we know the length of time involved for this process. We do not know how God will judge those who lived before the person of Jesus Christ was revealed, as opposed to those who came after the life, death and resurrection of the Son of God. Only God knows the heart of each man, woman and child.

10. What types of books are opened for the evidence to be presented (Daniel 7:10; 12:1; Revelation 3:5; 13:8; 17:8; 21:27; 22:19; Exodus 32:32; Psalm 69:28; Psalm 139:16; Malachi 3:16)? _____
_____

Both the Lamb's Book of Life—with the names of the redeemed, and the Books of Remembrance, focused on the thoughts, decisions and actions done in this lifetime. For the repentant, the sins of each individual have been blotted out (Acts 3:19); but, for the unrepentant, and because of their unbelief, their sins will remain in the books, which will condemn them.

11. The two groups will be separated (Matthew 25:32-41). How? _____
_____

"When the Son of Man comes in His glory, and all the holy angels with Him, then He will sit on the throne of His glory. All the nations will be gathered before Him, and He will separate them one from another, as a shepherd divides his sheep from the goats. And He will set the sheep on His right hand, but the goats on the left. Then the King will say to those on His right hand, 'Come, you blessed of My Father, inherit the kingdom prepared for you from the foundation of the world... Then He will also say to those on the left hand, 'Depart from Me, you cursed, into the everlasting fire prepared for the devil and his angels,'" Matthew 25:31-34, 41. As we have learned in previous lessons, the ashes are eternal, but not the fire.

12. What additional obligation does Christ expect of those who know Him personally, that will be considered when it comes time for the judgment (Matthew 10:32; Luke 12:8)? _____

13. What happens to the individuals whose names are not found in the Book of Life, along with death itself and all graves (Revelation 20:14-15)? _____

All sinners will be destroyed, and death will be eliminated forever, never to enter paradise, our homes or families again in God's eternal kingdom.

Graves will never be excavated again. There will be no torturing fire in the universe, as many believe, where anguishing fires burn and blister unsaved loved ones for billions and billions, upon billions of years, where Satan and demons rule. How do we know? "Surely the Day is coming; it will burn like a furnace. All the arrogant and every evildoer will be stubble, and that Day that is coming will set them on fire, says the LORD Almighty. Not a root or a branch will be left to them... then you will trample down the wicked; they will be ashes under the soles of your feet on the day when I do these things, says the LORD Almighty," Malachi 4:1-3.

The Angry Mob & Satan's Doom

The Great White Throne Judgment brings all men and women to their knees. "Every knee will bow before Me, says the LORD, every tongue will confess to God... each... will give an account of himself to God," Romans 14:11-12. "At the name of Jesus every knee should bow... and every tongue confess that Jesus Christ is LORD, to the glory of God the Father," Philippians 2:10-11. The righteous will inherit the City of God, while the wicked will be left out. This vast multitude of all ages, spread out around the globe as the sand of the sea, know they have been condemned. They see the redeemed in the city, the gates are closed, and they are outside. They scream in sorrow for all they have lost forever, and cry with weeping and gnashing of teeth.

Satan sees his opportunity to prepare for one last massive battle for supremacy, and will deceive the nations

to help (Revelation 20:7-10). He will marshal all the armies of rebellion under his banner, and through them endeavor to execute his plan. By rejecting faith in the Creator and His salvation they arbitrarily accepted the side of the rebel. They are ready to receive his suggestions and to do his bidding. His words and wonders inspire to raise a vast army who follow him to the City of the saints, the New Jerusalem. The innumerable mob, including kings, generals and valiant armies who once conquered nations, believe that they might be able to overthrow the City and save their souls.

The armies surround the Holy City, ready for the onset of war, then the command is given, and they surge forward. They march across the breath of the earth, but fire will come down from heaven and devoured them (Revelation 20:9). "Every warrior's boot used in battle and every garment rolled in blood will be destined for burning, will be fuel for the fire... The LORD is angry with all nations; His wrath is upon all their armies. He will totally destroy them, He will give them over to slaughter," Isaiah 9:5; 34:2. "On the wicked He will rain fiery coals and burning sulfur," Psalm 11:6.

The earth itself will be vast lake of fire. "But the Day of the LORD will come... The heavens will disappear with a roar; the elements will be destroyed by fire, and the earth and everything in it will be laid bare... that Day will bring about the destruction of the heavens by fire, and the elements will melt in the heat. But in keeping with His promise we are looking forward to a new heaven and a new earth, the home of righteousness," 2 Peter 3:10-13. "The present heavens and earth are reserved for fire, begin kept for the Day of Judgment and destruction of ungodly men," says 2 Peter 3:7.

It's possible that many are destroyed in a moment, while others suffer for a longer period. Everyone is punished according to their works. Satan's punishment will no doubt be more severe than those he has deceived. He, along with Antichrist and the False Prophet, in poetic terms, "will be tormented day and night for ever and ever," Revelation 20:10. No escape from the power of the flame will be possible; their doom is certain.

The prophet Ezekiel speaks directly to Satan about his demise: "Your heart became proud on account of your beauty, and you corrupted your wisdom because of your splendor. So I threw you to the earth; I made a spectacle of you before kings. By your many sins and dishonest trade you have desecrated your sanctuaries. So *I made a fire come out from you, and it consumed you, and I reduced you to ashes on the ground in the sight of all who were watching. All the nations who knew you are appalled at you; you have come to a horrible end and will be no more*," (28:17-19).

"For the LORD your God is a consuming fire," Deuteronomy 4:14; Hebrews12:29. The full penalty of the God's Law will be visited, and the demands of justice will be met. "What do you conspire against the LORD? He will make an *utter end of it.* Affliction will not rise up a second time," Nahum 1:9 (NKJV).

---- NOTES----

CONSUMING FIRE

צריכת אש

Insights In Prophecy
Unlock The Ancient Mysteries Of Daniel & Revelation
BIBLE DISCOVERY SERIES

Lesson 30

NEW JERUSALEM: GOD'S ETERNAL JUBILEE HOME

LESSON 30

Read Revelation 21 & 22

- Admire The Beautiful City & God's Completed Plan Of Redemption
- Celebrate That Planet Earth Becomes The Throne Of The Universe

The apostle Peter writes that the present skies above and earth beneath are "reserved for fire, being kept for the Day of Judgment and destruction of ungodly men." The *lake of fire*, referred to in Revelation 20, will burn until all sin and sinners are destroyed. In that inexpressible period of global fire, all of God's children will be safe within the fortified City of God. The heavens will "disappear with a roar, the elements will be destroyed by fire, and the earth and everything in it will be laid bare... that Day will bring about the destruction of the heavens by fire, and the elements will melt in the heat. But in keeping with His promise we are looking forward to a new heaven and a new earth, the home of righteousness," (2 Peter 3:7, 10-13).

Once the fire burns out, the Spirit of God will move. The earth and atmosphere will be changed into a lovely habitation of Eden's beauty. No sea will separate peoples and races. Fascinating creatures of various

designs and species will be brought into existence at the voice of God, each with a pleasant temperament.

Luscious green grass, trees and foliage will blossom fresh and will remain so throughout the generations. All the redeemed will gladly live by God's commandments, for He has written His Law in their hearts (Jeremiah 31:33; Hebrews 8:10; 10:16)—to love God first and foremost, and others as themselves. Mankind's natural tendency will then always be to do what is right, and the temptation to sin will disappear.

The prophet saw in vision a total restructure of the skies above and Planet Earth renewed, for the first heaven and earth had passed away before his eyes (Revelation 21:1-2).

1. What does John next see coming down to earth? _____

2. She is identified as "a Bride beautifully dressed for her Husband," Yeshua. When will the wedding, the union of Bride and Groom, take place in Heaven prior to this point in time (Revelation 19:1-8)? _____
_____

Just after the "prostitute"—the great city that symbolizes Messiah's wayward wife (Jeremiah 3:14, 20)—is destroyed during the Great Tribulation just after the world's end-time leader sets up his abomination on the Temple Mount.

As with men who indulge in illicit sex with prostitutes, the nations will ultimately *despise* the woman, Jerusalem, after having used her. Once they get what they want—Antichrist's access to the Temple Mount—the nations will turn on her. First, the two witnesses are killed and the "anointed one is cut off and will have no one" (f26, NIV) left to warn of the coming destruction, the nations will attack Jerusalem and leave her desolate and naked (Daniel 9:26; Revelation 17:16-18).

Soon after the prostitute is destroyed, the wedding will take place in Heaven at the Feast of Tabernacles, before Messiah returns visibly in the clouds to destroy all sinners at the Armageddon battle. The gates of the City of God—the New Jerusalem will be opened up for the first time, and Yeshua Messiah will walk in with the redeemed who have just been raised to life at the trumpet blast and the loud voice of the Archangel. In the symbolism of marriage, this intimate connection will last for the ages to come between the New Jerusalem—the Bride inhabited by star-bright citizens who adorn her dressed in white linen (Revelation 19:7-8; Daniel 12:3; Matthew 13:43) and her Groom—Messiah in His radiant glory (Matthew 17:2; Revelation 1:16). At the end of the millennium, the City will descend to earth and God and His Son will abide forever on the earth made new; and for this reason, this planet and the saints purchased by the blood of the Most Holy One will always maintain a special relationship, no matter how many other worlds are created in the vast universe throughout the ceaseless ages.

3. What is the proclamation given in Revelation 21:3-4? _____

God's dwelling is going to be with mankind. He will transfer His throne from Heaven to this location. Elohim will also wipe away all sadness and tears. There will be no more death, mourning, crying or pain, for the old order of things will pass away. Once sin and sinners are destroyed from existence along with all traces of sin, the former will not be remembered again. By God's grace He will wipe the pain and loss from our hearts, and replace it with joy.

In Revelation 21:5-8 God proclaims He is making all things new! You can count on it, God declares, so "write this down" as an everlasting record. The "Alpha and the Omega"—from the first to the last alphabet of all speech and communication, the "Beginning and the End"—the One who has always existed and will always exist, is in complete control.

4. God proclaims—"It is done," then peace and rest fills the soul. What four times in the Scriptures (see below) does God's *finished work* bring rest? _____

~ Genesis 2:1-3: *After His creative work, so He added an extra day—the seventh day Sabbath—that mankind might join in the weekly rest.*

~ John 19:30-31: *After His redemptive work, so He rested in the grave during the Sabbath hours in honor of His creative labor.*

~ Revelation 16:17: *After His investigative judgment work and blotting out of sin from the courts of Heaven, so He will add on the seventh millennial (1,000 year) Sabbath day before final judgment.*

~ Revelation 21:6: *After His judgment and re-creation, so that mankind might rest in an Eternal Jubilee of peace and joy.*

5. What three promises are given to the saints in Revelation 19:6-7? _____

The three promises are: 1) access to the springs of living water at no cost (eternal life); 2) inheritance (although undeserved) of all that God will create for our enjoyment; and, 3) the official adoption as sons and daughters of God (to live in intimate companionship in God's home).

Believers are first chosen, predestined and then adopted as the very sons and daughters of God (Ephesians 1:4-5). For this reason, they will receive the privileges of protection, provision of daily needs, guidance, and audience with God the Father and the Son, and the heavenly inheritance—a place to call home, which no one can take away.

In contrast, Revelation 21:8 identifies eight types of people who will be destroyed in the lake of fire—the second death. They represent some of the sins that God hates, and behavior which cannot be tolerated. They are 1) cowardly individuals who deny Christ before others; 2) those who waver in their faith; 3) the vile person who practices known sins; 4) individuals who destroy without just cause; 5) the sexually immoral; 6) those who practice astrology and magic arts; 7) those who worship stone images and man-made creations 8) and, the deliberately deceptive.

The Seventh Angel Introduces The Bride Wife

Revelation 21:9-10 reveals how One of the seven angels—Michael, the Seventh Angel, for later in the vision He declares, "Behold I am coming soon," 22:7—invites John to "Come, I will show you the Bride, the Wife of the Lamb." He picks up John and carries him away to a great and high mountain. There he sees "the Holy City, Jerusalem, coming down out of Heaven from God."

Under similar circumstances, One of the seven angels earlier showed John another woman in Revelation 17:1. He said, "Come, I will show you the punishment of the great prostitute; the woman you saw is the great city that rules over the kings of the earth," (18). He picks up John and carries him away to the parched and desolate "wilderness". There he sees the "woman sitting on the scarlet beast that was covered with blasphemous names and had seven heads and ten horns"—MYSTERY BABYLON THE GREAT THE MOTHER OF PROSTITUTES AND OF THE ABOMINATIONS OF THE EARTH. Although we have often prayed for the peace of Jerusalem, because she is loved for her connection to Messiah and God's plan of redemption, the modern-day city has fallen from grace. How sad a commentary about a city teeming with religious and political leaders who should know the Scriptures, who should stand firm against Antichrist, and proclaim God's Commandments against idolatry and sin, but they will not.

Both women are decked in gold, precious stones and pearls (Revelation 17:4; Revelation 21:11)—one from the wealth of the nations who prostitute with her, the other from the wealth of Messiah—her Groom. Both are measured by the prophet John (Revelation 11:1; Revelation 21:15)—one for temporary man-made construction and judgment, the other for eternal God-designed splendor. The old city's residents long ago rejoiced at the death of the King of the Jews and again at the end when His two witnesses are killed (Revelation 11:8-10), but the New City will delight in her King and the salvation of His children! The old city will invite Antichrist, demons and abominations into the heart of the city (2 Thessalonians 2:4; Revelation 18:2), while the New City will take in only those with pure hearts and lives (Revelation 21:27). The earth-bound woman is "clothed with the sun [and] with the moon (Revelation 12:1), the heavenly woman "has no need of the sun or the moon to shine on it, for the glory of God gives it light, and the Lamb is its lamp," Revelation 21:23.

Insights In Prophecy
Unlock The Ancient Mysteries Of Daniel & Revelation
BIBLE DISCOVERY SERIES

The Beautiful Bride-Wife Described

Revelation 21:11-20 is a detailed description of the New Jerusalem, starting with her brilliance. She will shine with God's glory, brighter than the sun. Messiah's wife will be like a magnificent shining jewel on top

of a great mountain. She will be enormous in size and will be seen from great distances. The City will be closely connected to her roots, for her foundations will have on them the names of the twelve apostles of Christ, and the twelve gates the twelve tribes of the nation of Israel.

By all accounts, her walls will be about 200 feet in thickness; and yet, her magnificent gates, not made of steel or wood but of single pearls, will always be open for one and all to enter. The walls will be built not of base materials, but from colorful precious stones of every kind—jasper, sapphire, chalcedony, emerald, sardonyx, carnelian, chrysolite, beryl, topaz, chrysoprase, jacinth and amethyst. The street will be laid with "pure gold" like transparent glass.

6. What is the New Jerusalem no longer in need of, according to Revelation 21:21-24? _____

No Temple—for God the Father and the Lamb are to be openly worshipped, with no separation from the citizens of Heaven. Both sun and moon will be gone, for the glory of God the Father gives it light and the Lamb is its lamp. The skies above and the structure of the universe will be altered and enhanced by our Creator, once the final order is completed.

By all accounts, the City is laid out in a perfect cubicle square (1,400 miles four-square)—as long as it is wide—like the Holy of Holies compartment of the Temple. The City itself will replace the walled Sanctuary, for she will have no Temple with veil, doors or barriers to separate worshipers from Almighty God.

Revelation 21:25-27 teaches the gates will never be shut at the end of the day, for the great day of the LORD will never close. The sun will no longer drop in the western skies where shadows of sin once found dark corners to thrive in. The glory and honor of all races and nationalities will traverse inside of Jerusalem. Nothing impure, such as deceivers and shameful characters, will ever step through her gates; only those whose names are written in the Lamb's Book of Life—the recorded and documented children of the New City.

7. What important river flows from the throne of God and the Lamb (Revelation 22:1-5)? _____
_____

The River of the Water of Life will flow from the source of life itself. The saints will never thirst again; the fountain of youth will remain as our eternal drink.

8. What life-giving tree adorns each side of the river? _____

The Tree of Life will yield twelve crops of fruit.

The saints will never hunger for want of food again. The life-giving water and fruit will always remind the children of God of their eternal dependence of God's grace; meaning, eternal life will never be self-determining, independent of the water and food available in the City and from God's throne. Dependence on God will always remain, as a Father lovingly provides and cares for his sons and daughters.

9. The curse of separation between God and man, which includes the inability to serve God in open face to face communication, will be gone. When did the curse of verse 3 first begin, and what did the entire affliction consist of (Genesis 3:14-24)? _____
_____

~ The serpent's curse to run on its belly and eat dust—Lucifer would be lowered from his position of heavenly power, and eventually destroyed.
~ The woman's curse of increased pains in child birth, and her subordinate role of submission to males.
~ The man's curse of sweat-filled labor to produce food in sometimes selfish soil, thorns and thistles.
~ Mankind's curse of death, of returning to dust from where we were first taken. Of mankind's banishment from the thriving Garden of Eden, and from the Tree of Life with it's life-giving properties.

Verse 6 states that overcomers will rule forever. So true are these words spoken by the Angel that He affirmed, "these words are trustworthy and true," for it was the LORD, the God of the prophets, who has sent His Angel to show His servants the things which will soon take place.

10. What promise does the Angel proclaim in Revelation 22:7? _____
_____

"Behold, I am coming soon! Blessed is he who keeps the words of the prophecy in this book."

11. How does this compare to the Mighty Angel—the Seventh Angel in Revelation 10:1-7? _____
_____

The Seventh Angel is said to "come down" from Heaven to earth. He has been identified as none other than Yeshua, our Messiah, because His splendid characteristics could only apply to the Son of God. He also swears His promise is trustworthy that "there will be no more delay" in the final unfolding of God's mysterious plan.

12. What is John's response once he hears the Messenger's promised return (22:8)? _____
_____

The prophet falls at His feet in worship for the second time, as recorded in the book of Revelation. John was a personal companion and a part of the inner circle with Jesus while He was on the earth. Only in honor and worship of His Savior would he prostrate himself—this was no ordinary angelic messenger.

13. Why did Michael stop John from further worship at that time (22:9)? _____

After having declared, "I am coming soon!" Yeshua identified with John as a "fellow servant with you and with your brothers the prophets and of all who keep the words of this book." Jesus would not accept worship above those who will also suffer for keeping the words of the book of Revelation. He said "Worship God!" The honor would be His Father's, not His own at that moment in John's vision.

14. John had once before fallen down at the Messenger's feet (Revelation 19:9-10). What had the Angel stated just before John's reaction of worship? _____
_____ **Does Michael once again turn the attention to the Father in 22:9?** _____

Blessed are those who are invited to the wedding supper of the Lamb! These are the true words of God." John responds in humble honor of the Messenger, for he wants desperately to be found worthy to be invited to the supper at Messiah's return. Michael, as is found later in the book, adds that He is a "fellow servant" with John who holds to the testimony of Jesus—the book of Revelation.

When the prophet first saw Messiah with all His brilliance and shining glory in his first vision, John "fell at His feet as though dead" in trepidation and fear (Revelation 1:16-17). Obviously, John knew the Savior's face and would prostrate to worship Christ the King and Him only. Here John again "fell to worship" the One who had just proclaimed salvation. The prophet would not have bowed in worship to anyone other than his Master and LORD. Therefore, the Messenger could be none other than Yeshua, one of the seven messengers, who had come to John in Revelation 17:1 to give him some of the final revelations about Babylon's destruction, and the promised wedding in Heaven.

Although deserved, Michael would not allow John to worship Him while fulfilling His duty as a prophet messenger. Rather, He wanted John to stand eye to eye and to identify with Him as an equal in service for God. Therefore, He said He was "a fellow servant" and "brother" with John, and with all those who would hold to the testimony of Jesus. This message is identified as coming from the Spirit, the divine source of prophecy—the revealer of future events, given in minute detail, thousands of years before events occur (1:2).

15. Philippians 2:5-8, Deuteronomy 18:15-18 and Acts 3:20-22 help us identify this Angel Messenger, whom John worships as the "fellow servant" and "brother" the prophet. How? _____

_____

It is written, "Christ Jesus: Who, being in very nature God, did not consider equality with God something to be grasped, but *made Himself nothing*, taking the very nature of a *servant, being made in human likeness*. And being found *in appearance as a man*." In other words, God's only Son humbled Himself, leaving behind the worship due Him in Heaven, to come to earth in the "appearance as" a human being. Although Divine, He appeared to be a mere man—as a "brother". In this way, He identified with us and with our struggles against evil, and ultimately provided the way of escape. What other angelic messenger could identify with the prophet as a "brother"? What other angel could so move John with words of salvation that he would fall prostrate in worship before him? Only Yeshua.

As mankind can now identify with Jesus, so too can Heaven's countless millions of angelic citizens. Christ fulfills His role in the appearance and duties of Michael, so that none of His created beings will feel exempt from His devoted association. This does not make Him any less divine, for He was with the Father from the beginning of time. On the contrary, this makes Him Supremely God, the originator and proponent of love through His continuous acts of humility.

Jesus had acted in similar meekness during an episode recorded in Matthew 19:16-17 (KJV). A man approached and addressed Him as "Good Master" and asked a question about eternal life. Instead of taking the glory to Himself, Messiah instead replied, "why callest thou Me good? there is none good but One, that is, God [the Father]." Again, this was showing humility, when the individual had attempted to shown Him honor. In this way the glory would be transferred to His Father. This very act of humility would never be found in the Evil One, who always seeks the glory for himself.

The Messenger of the Covenant visited Moses on Mount Sinai to deliver the Law of God (Acts 7:30-31, 35, 38). Now, He will come again and His voice will be heard in thunderous echo when all mystery will be completed (10:7). "But who can abide the Day of His coming?" Malachi 3:1-2.

16. What did the Angel tell John not to do with the scroll of information he would be writing (Revelation 22:10)? _____

"Do not seal up the words of the prophecy of this book, because the time is near." God does not do anything significant that involves mankind, unless He first reveals it to His servants the prophets (Amos 3:7).

17. How does John's unsealed book contrast the message Michael earlier delivered to the prophet Daniel about his book of prophecy in Daniel 12:4, 9? _____

Daniel's book would not be understood until the end of time is upon us, while John's book must remain an opened explanation of Daniel's obscure predictions. Revelation would open to the readers their understanding of Daniel's mysterious writings. Both books merge together; Revelation is the book of Daniel's visions, unsealed.

18. The declaration of Revelation 22:11-12 occurs when? _____

These words are spoken at the close of the Courtroom Judgment Daniel 7:9-10, just before Jesus returns. How do we know? He says, "Behold I am coming soon ["quickly," KJV]!" The time will arrive when probation closes, and destinies will be sealed forever. Hence, the words are spoken from on high, "let him who does wrong continue to do wrong; let him who is vile continue to be vile; let him who does right continue to do right; and let him who is holy continue to be holy." Only two groups of people will remain—the unrighteous and righteous. These are words associated with the approaching Day of Atonement when all those written in the book are delivered, and the unrepentant are forever cut off from the camp of the saints (Leviticus 23:27-29; Daniel 12:1). John writes (22:14), "Blessed are those who wash their robes ["do His commandments," KJV], that they may have the right to the Tree of Life and may go through the gate into the City" of God.

19. 1 John 2:3-4 reinforces this idea. How? _____

Those who obey God show they have a genuine faith, while the disobedient reveal they lack faith and love for Jesus. The saints are washing their robes in the blood of the Lamb, who gave Himself for them. They follow in His footsteps of service and obedience to the Father's will.

20. What specific types of sinners will find themselves outside of the City (22:15)? _____

~ *dogs—prostitutes involved in immoral activities both sexually and religiously*
~ *magic arts—involvement in the occult*
~ *sexually immoral—homosexuals, adulterers and fornicators*
~ *murderers—those who destroy without just cause*
~ *idolaters—worshipers of images*
~ *liars—those who love and practice falsehood*

Jesus personally identifies Himself as the Messenger whom John has been communicating with. He states that He has sent His angel, likely Gabriel (Daniel 8:16; Luke 1:19), as a medium for the various visions John received.

Messiah confirms, "I am the Root and the Offspring of David (Revelation 5:5), the bright and Morning Star." The morning star appears near dawn, in the hours of darkness as the night is ending. Jesus is the light of the world—the glimmer of hope in the shadows of night. His loosening of the sealed book of prophecy has made the testimony of Jesus possible for all who will take note and listen to its warnings. It is the great light shining at this midnight hour of earth's history.

The generous invitation is given, "The Spirit and the Bride [New Jerusalem] say, Come! And let him who hears say Come! Whoever is thirsty, let him come, and whoever wishes, let him take the free gift of the water of life" found in the City, flowing from the throne of God. The invitation to the City of God is open to all; however, many are called but few are chosen (Matthew 20:16).

21. The warning is given not to tamper with the book of prophecy (22:18-19). Why? _____
_____

The book must remain unchanged, as penned by John. So vital is every word of the book that, just as the Law of God, no scribe dare add or take away even the "smallest letter, not the least stroke of a pen," (Matthew 5:18).

Supplementary to the warning is the threat of plagues described in the book of Revelation, even the taking away the transgressor's share in the Tree of Life and the Holy City; or, as the King James Version more threatening reads: "God shall take away his part out of the Book of Life."

22. How does Yeshua conclude the prophetic book (Revelation 22:20-21)? _____

With a promise. He reiterates once again that He is coming soon, or quickly. This has two meanings. First, to God a thousand years is as one day (2 Peter 3:8), and so, from Heaven's perspective His coming was only a day or two away. Second, when Christ leaves the gates of Heaven, His return will be as quick as stepping through an opened door at the parting of the sky. His arrival will be swift.

John expresses that blessed hope of every overcomer who has anxiously awaited the King, since the fall of mankind... "Come, LORD Jesus"; then, he finishes his apocalyptic scroll with a prayer, "The grace of the LORD Jesus be with God's people. Amen."

The Book of Daniel
King James Version (KJV)

Chapter 1

In the third year of the reign of Jehoiakim king of Judah came Nebuchadnezzar king of Babylon unto Jerusalem, and besieged it.

2 And the Lord gave Jehoiakim king of Judah into his hand, with part of the vessels of the house of God: which he carried into the land of Shinar to the house of his god; and he brought the vessels into the treasure house of his god.

3 And the king spake unto Ashpenaz the master of his eunuchs, that he should bring certain of the children of Israel, and of the king's seed, and of the princes;

4 Children in whom was no blemish, but well favoured, and skilful in all wisdom, and cunning in knowledge, and understanding science, and such as had ability in them to stand in the king's palace, and whom they might teach the learning and the tongue of the Chaldeans.

5 And the king appointed them a daily provision of the king's meat, and of the wine which he drank: so nourishing them three years, that at the end thereof they might stand before the king.

6 Now among these were of the children of Judah, Daniel, Hananiah, Mishael, and Azariah:

7 Unto whom the prince of the eunuchs gave names: for he gave unto Daniel the name of Belteshazzar; and to Hananiah, of Shadrach; and to Mishael, of Meshach; and to Azariah, of Abednego.

8 But Daniel purposed in his heart that he would not defile himself with the portion of the king's meat, nor with the wine which he drank: therefore he requested of the prince of the eunuchs that he might not defile himself.

9 Now God had brought Daniel into favour and tender love with the prince of the eunuchs.

10 And the prince of the eunuchs said unto Daniel, I fear my lord the king, who hath appointed your meat and your drink: for why should he see your faces worse liking than the children which are of your sort? then shall ye make me endanger my head to the king.

11 Then said Daniel to Melzar, whom the prince of the eunuchs had set over Daniel, Hananiah, Mishael, and Azariah,

12 Prove thy servants, I beseech thee, ten days; and let them give us pulse to eat, and water to drink.

13 Then let our countenances be looked upon before thee, and the countenance of the children that eat of the portion of the king's meat: and as thou seest, deal with thy servants.

14 So he consented to them in this matter, and proved them ten days.

15 And at the end of ten days their countenances appeared fairer and fatter in flesh than all the children which did eat the portion of the king's meat.

16 Thus Melzar took away the portion of their meat, and the wine that they should drink; and gave them pulse.

17 As for these four children, God gave them knowledge and skill in all learning and wisdom: and Daniel had understanding in all visions and dreams.

18 Now at the end of the days that the king had said he should bring them in, then the prince of the eunuchs brought them in before Nebuchadnezzar.

19 And the king communed with them; and among them all was found none like Daniel, Hananiah, Mishael, and Azariah: therefore stood they before the king.

20 And in all matters of wisdom and understanding, that the king enquired of them, he found them ten times better than all the magicians and astrologers that were in all his realm.

21 And Daniel continued even unto the first year of king Cyrus.

Chapter 2

And in the second year of the reign of Nebuchadnezzar Nebuchadnezzar dreamed dreams, wherewith his spirit was troubled, and his sleep brake from him.

² Then the king commanded to call the magicians, and the astrologers, and the sorcerers, and the Chaldeans, for to shew the king his dreams. So they came and stood before the king.

³ And the king said unto them, I have dreamed a dream, and my spirit was troubled to know the dream.

⁴ Then spake the Chaldeans to the king in Syriack, O king, live for ever: tell thy servants the dream, and we will shew the interpretation.

⁵ The king answered and said to the Chaldeans, The thing is gone from me: if ye will not make known unto me the dream, with the interpretation thereof, ye shall be cut in pieces, and your houses shall be made a dunghill.

⁶ But if ye shew the dream, and the interpretation thereof, ye shall receive of me gifts and rewards and great honour: therefore shew me the dream, and the interpretation thereof.

⁷ They answered again and said, Let the king tell his servants the dream, and we will shew the interpretation of it.

⁸ The king answered and said, I know of certainty that ye would gain the time, because ye see the thing is gone from me.

⁹ But if ye will not make known unto me the dream, there is but one decree for you: for ye have prepared lying and corrupt words to speak before me, till the time be changed: therefore tell me the dream, and I shall know that ye can shew me the interpretation thereof.

¹⁰ The Chaldeans answered before the king, and said, There is not a man upon the earth that can shew the king's matter: therefore there is no king, lord, nor ruler, that asked such things at any magician, or astrologer, or Chaldean.

¹¹ And it is a rare thing that the king requireth, and there is none other that can shew it before the king, except the gods, whose dwelling is not with flesh.

¹² For this cause the king was angry and very furious, and commanded to destroy all the wise men of Babylon.

¹³ And the decree went forth that the wise men should be slain; and they sought Daniel and his fellows to be slain.

¹⁴ Then Daniel answered with counsel and wisdom to Arioch the captain of the king's guard, which was gone forth to slay the wise men of Babylon:

¹⁵ He answered and said to Arioch the king's captain, Why is the decree so hasty from the king? Then Arioch made the thing known to Daniel.

¹⁶ Then Daniel went in, and desired of the king that he would give him time, and that he would shew the king the interpretation.

¹⁷ Then Daniel went to his house, and made the thing known to Hananiah, Mishael, and Azariah, his companions:

¹⁸ That they would desire mercies of the God of heaven concerning this secret; that Daniel and his fellows should not perish with the rest of the wise men of Babylon.

¹⁹ Then was the secret revealed unto Daniel in a night vision. Then Daniel blessed the God of heaven.

²⁰ Daniel answered and said, Blessed be the name of God for ever and ever: for wisdom and might are his:

²¹ And he changeth the times and the seasons: he removeth kings, and setteth up kings: he giveth wisdom unto the wise, and knowledge to them that know understanding:

²² He revealeth the deep and secret things: he knoweth what is in the darkness, and the light dwelleth with him.

²³ I thank thee, and praise thee, O thou God of my fathers, who hast given me wisdom and might, and hast made known unto me now what we desired of thee: for thou hast now made known unto us the king's matter.

[24] Therefore Daniel went in unto Arioch, whom the king had ordained to destroy the wise men of Babylon: he went and said thus unto him; Destroy not the wise men of Babylon: bring me in before the king, and I will shew unto the king the interpretation.

[25] Then Arioch brought in Daniel before the king in haste, and said thus unto him, I have found a man of the captives of Judah, that will make known unto the king the interpretation.

[26] The king answered and said to Daniel, whose name was Belteshazzar, Art thou able to make known unto me the dream which I have seen, and the interpretation thereof?

[27] Daniel answered in the presence of the king, and said, The secret which the king hath demanded cannot the wise men, the astrologers, the magicians, the soothsayers, shew unto the king;

[28] But there is a God in heaven that revealeth secrets, and maketh known to the king Nebuchadnezzar what shall be in the latter days. Thy dream, and the visions of thy head upon thy bed, are these;

[29] As for thee, O king, thy thoughts came into thy mind upon thy bed, what should come to pass hereafter: and he that revealeth secrets maketh known to thee what shall come to pass.

[30] But as for me, this secret is not revealed to me for any wisdom that I have more than any living, but for their sakes that shall make known the interpretation to the king, and that thou mightest know the thoughts of thy heart.

[31] Thou, O king, sawest, and behold a great image. This great image, whose brightness was excellent, stood before thee; and the form thereof was terrible.

[32] This image's head was of fine gold, his breast and his arms of silver, his belly and his thighs of brass,

[33] His legs of iron, his feet part of iron and part of clay.

[34] Thou sawest till that a stone was cut out without hands, which smote the image upon his feet that were of iron and clay, and brake them to pieces.

[35] Then was the iron, the clay, the brass, the silver, and the gold, broken to pieces together, and became like the chaff of the summer threshingfloors; and the wind carried them away, that no place was found for them: and the stone that smote the image became a great mountain, and filled the whole earth.

[36] This is the dream; and we will tell the interpretation thereof before the king.

[37] Thou, O king, art a king of kings: for the God of heaven hath given thee a kingdom, power, and strength, and glory.

[38] And wheresoever the children of men dwell, the beasts of the field and the fowls of the heaven hath he given into thine hand, and hath made thee ruler over them all. Thou art this head of gold.

[39] And after thee shall arise another kingdom inferior to thee, and another third kingdom of brass, which shall bear rule over all the earth.

[40] And the fourth kingdom shall be strong as iron: forasmuch as iron breaketh in pieces and subdueth all things: and as iron that breaketh all these, shall it break in pieces and bruise.

[41] And whereas thou sawest the feet and toes, part of potters' clay, and part of iron, the kingdom shall be divided; but there shall be in it of the strength of the iron, forasmuch as thou sawest the iron mixed with miry clay.

[42] And as the toes of the feet were part of iron, and part of clay, so the kingdom shall be partly strong, and partly broken.

[43] And whereas thou sawest iron mixed with miry clay, they shall mingle themselves with the seed of men: but they shall not cleave one to another, even as iron is not mixed with clay.

[44] And in the days of these kings shall the God of heaven set up a kingdom, which shall never be destroyed: and the kingdom shall not be left to other people, but it shall break in pieces and consume all these kingdoms, and it shall stand for ever.

[45] Forasmuch as thou sawest that the stone was cut out of the mountain without hands, and that it brake in pieces the iron, the brass, the clay, the silver, and the gold; the great God hath made known to the king what shall come to pass hereafter: and the dream is certain, and the interpretation thereof sure.

[46] Then the king Nebuchadnezzar fell upon his face, and worshipped Daniel, and commanded that they should offer an oblation and sweet odours unto him.

[47] The king answered unto Daniel, and said, Of a truth it is, that your God is a God of gods, and a Lord of kings, and a revealer of secrets, seeing thou couldest reveal this secret.

[48] Then the king made Daniel a great man, and gave him many great gifts, and made him ruler over the whole province of Babylon, and chief of the governors over all the wise men of Babylon.

[49] Then Daniel requested of the king, and he set Shadrach, Meshach, and Abednego, over the affairs of the province of Babylon: but Daniel sat in the gate of the king.

Chapter 3

Nebuchadnezzar the king made an image of gold, whose height was threescore cubits, and the breadth thereof six cubits: he set it up in the plain of Dura, in the province of Babylon.

[2] Then Nebuchadnezzar the king sent to gather together the princes, the governors, and the captains, the judges, the treasurers, the counsellors, the sheriffs, and all the rulers of the provinces, to come to the dedication of the image which Nebuchadnezzar the king had set up.

[3] Then the princes, the governors, and captains, the judges, the treasurers, the counsellors, the sheriffs, and all the rulers of the provinces, were gathered together unto the dedication of the image that Nebuchadnezzar the king had set up; and they stood before the image that Nebuchadnezzar had set up.

[4] Then an herald cried aloud, To you it is commanded, O people, nations, and languages,

[5] That at what time ye hear the sound of the cornet, flute, harp, sackbut, psaltery, dulcimer, and all kinds of musick, ye fall down and worship the golden image that Nebuchadnezzar the king hath set up:

[6] And whoso falleth not down and worshippeth shall the same hour be cast into the midst of a burning fiery furnace.

[7] Therefore at that time, when all the people heard the sound of the cornet, flute, harp, sackbut, psaltery, and all kinds of musick, all the people, the nations, and the languages, fell down and worshipped the golden image that Nebuchadnezzar the king had set up.

[8] Wherefore at that time certain Chaldeans came near, and accused the Jews.

[9] They spake and said to the king Nebuchadnezzar, O king, live for ever.

[10] Thou, O king, hast made a decree, that every man that shall hear the sound of the cornet, flute, harp, sackbut, psaltery, and dulcimer, and all kinds of musick, shall fall down and worship the golden image:

[11] And whoso falleth not down and worshippeth, that he should be cast into the midst of a burning fiery furnace.

[12] There are certain Jews whom thou hast set over the affairs of the province of Babylon, Shadrach, Meshach, and Abednego; these men, O king, have not regarded thee: they serve not thy gods, nor worship the golden image which thou hast set up.

[13] Then Nebuchadnezzar in his rage and fury commanded to bring Shadrach, Meshach, and Abednego. Then they brought these men before the king.

[14] Nebuchadnezzar spake and said unto them, Is it true, O Shadrach, Meshach, and Abednego, do not ye serve my gods, nor worship the golden image which I have set up?

[15] Now if ye be ready that at what time ye hear the sound of the cornet, flute, harp, sackbut, psaltery, and dulcimer, and all kinds of musick, ye fall down and worship the image which I have made; well: but if ye worship not, ye shall be cast the same hour into the midst of a burning fiery furnace; and who is that God that shall deliver you out of my hands?

[16] Shadrach, Meshach, and Abednego, answered and said to the king, O Nebuchadnezzar, we are not careful to answer thee in this matter.

[17] If it be so, our God whom we serve is able to deliver us from the burning fiery furnace, and he will deliver us out of thine hand, O king.

[18] But if not, be it known unto thee, O king, that we will not serve thy gods, nor worship the golden image which thou hast set up.

¹⁹ Then was Nebuchadnezzar full of fury, and the form of his visage was changed against Shadrach, Meshach, and Abednego: therefore he spake, and commanded that they should heat the furnace one seven times more than it was wont to be heated.

²⁰ And he commanded the most mighty men that were in his army to bind Shadrach, Meshach, and Abednego, and to cast them into the burning fiery furnace.

²¹ Then these men were bound in their coats, their hosen, and their hats, and their other garments, and were cast into the midst of the burning fiery furnace.

²² Therefore because the king's commandment was urgent, and the furnace exceeding hot, the flames of the fire slew those men that took up Shadrach, Meshach, and Abednego.

²³ And these three men, Shadrach, Meshach, and Abednego, fell down bound into the midst of the burning fiery furnace.

²⁴ Then Nebuchadnezzar the king was astonished, and rose up in haste, and spake, and said unto his counsellors, Did not we cast three men bound into the midst of the fire? They answered and said unto the king, True, O king.

²⁵ He answered and said, Lo, I see four men loose, walking in the midst of the fire, and they have no hurt; and the form of the fourth is like the Son of God.

²⁶ Then Nebuchadnezzar came near to the mouth of the burning fiery furnace, and spake, and said, Shadrach, Meshach, and Abednego, ye servants of the most high God, come forth, and come hither. Then Shadrach, Meshach, and Abednego, came forth of the midst of the fire.

²⁷ And the princes, governors, and captains, and the king's counsellors, being gathered together, saw these men, upon whose bodies the fire had no power, nor was an hair of their head singed, neither were their coats changed, nor the smell of fire had passed on them.

²⁸ Then Nebuchadnezzar spake, and said, Blessed be the God of Shadrach, Meshach, and Abednego, who hath sent his angel, and delivered his servants that trusted in him, and have changed the king's word, and yielded their bodies, that they might not serve nor worship any god, except their own God.

²⁹ Therefore I make a decree, That every people, nation, and language, which speak any thing amiss against the God of Shadrach, Meshach, and Abednego, shall be cut in pieces, and their houses shall be made a dunghill: because there is no other God that can deliver after this sort.

³⁰ Then the king promoted Shadrach, Meshach, and Abednego, in the province of Babylon.

Chapter 4

Nebuchadnezzar the king, unto all people, nations, and languages, that dwell in all the earth; Peace be multiplied unto you.

² I thought it good to shew the signs and wonders that the high God hath wrought toward me.

³ How great are his signs! and how mighty are his wonders! his kingdom is an everlasting kingdom, and his dominion is from generation to generation.

⁴ I Nebuchadnezzar was at rest in mine house, and flourishing in my palace:

⁵ I saw a dream which made me afraid, and the thoughts upon my bed and the visions of my head troubled me.

⁶ Therefore made I a decree to bring in all the wise men of Babylon before me, that they might make known unto me the interpretation of the dream.

⁷ Then came in the magicians, the astrologers, the Chaldeans, and the soothsayers: and I told the dream before them; but they did not make known unto me the interpretation thereof.

⁸ But at the last Daniel came in before me, whose name was Belteshazzar, according to the name of my God, and in whom is the spirit of the holy gods: and before him I told the dream, saying,

⁹ O Belteshazzar, master of the magicians, because I know that the spirit of the holy gods is in thee, and no secret troubleth thee, tell me the visions of my dream that I have seen, and the interpretation thereof.

¹⁰ Thus were the visions of mine head in my bed; I saw, and behold a tree in the midst of the earth, and the height thereof was great.

[11] The tree grew, and was strong, and the height thereof reached unto heaven, and the sight thereof to the end of all the earth:

[12] The leaves thereof were fair, and the fruit thereof much, and in it was meat for all: the beasts of the field had shadow under it, and the fowls of the heaven dwelt in the boughs thereof, and all flesh was fed of it.

[13] I saw in the visions of my head upon my bed, and, behold, a watcher and an holy one came down from heaven;

[14] He cried aloud, and said thus, Hew down the tree, and cut off his branches, shake off his leaves, and scatter his fruit: let the beasts get away from under it, and the fowls from his branches:

[15] Nevertheless leave the stump of his roots in the earth, even with a band of iron and brass, in the tender grass of the field; and let it be wet with the dew of heaven, and let his portion be with the beasts in the grass of the earth:

[16] Let his heart be changed from man's, and let a beast's heart be given unto him; and let seven times pass over him.

[17] This matter is by the decree of the watchers, and the demand by the word of the holy ones: to the intent that the living may know that the most High ruleth in the kingdom of men, and giveth it to whomsoever he will, and setteth up over it the basest of men.

[18] This dream I king Nebuchadnezzar have seen. Now thou, O Belteshazzar, declare the interpretation thereof, forasmuch as all the wise men of my kingdom are not able to make known unto me the interpretation: but thou art able; for the spirit of the holy gods is in thee.

[19] Then Daniel, whose name was Belteshazzar, was astonied for one hour, and his thoughts troubled him. The king spake, and said, Belteshazzar, let not the dream, or the interpretation thereof, trouble thee. Belteshazzar answered and said, My lord, the dream be to them that hate thee, and the interpretation thereof to thine enemies.

[20] The tree that thou sawest, which grew, and was strong, whose height reached unto the heaven, and the sight thereof to all the earth;

[21] Whose leaves were fair, and the fruit thereof much, and in it was meat for all; under which the beasts of the field dwelt, and upon whose branches the fowls of the heaven had their habitation:

[22] It is thou, O king, that art grown and become strong: for thy greatness is grown, and reacheth unto heaven, and thy dominion to the end of the earth.

[23] And whereas the king saw a watcher and an holy one coming down from heaven, and saying, Hew the tree down, and destroy it; yet leave the stump of the roots thereof in the earth, even with a band of iron and brass, in the tender grass of the field; and let it be wet with the dew of heaven, and let his portion be with the beasts of the field, till seven times pass over him;

[24] This is the interpretation, O king, and this is the decree of the most High, which is come upon my lord the king:

[25] That they shall drive thee from men, and thy dwelling shall be with the beasts of the field, and they shall make thee to eat grass as oxen, and they shall wet thee with the dew of heaven, and seven times shall pass over thee, till thou know that the most High ruleth in the kingdom of men, and giveth it to whomsoever he will.

[26] And whereas they commanded to leave the stump of the tree roots; thy kingdom shall be sure unto thee, after that thou shalt have known that the heavens do rule.

[27] Wherefore, O king, let my counsel be acceptable unto thee, and break off thy sins by righteousness, and thine iniquities by shewing mercy to the poor; if it may be a lengthening of thy tranquillity.

[28] All this came upon the king Nebuchadnezzar.

[29] At the end of twelve months he walked in the palace of the kingdom of Babylon.

[30] The king spake, and said, Is not this great Babylon, that I have built for the house of the kingdom by the might of my power, and for the honour of my majesty?

[31] While the word was in the king's mouth, there fell a voice from heaven, saying, O king Nebuchadnezzar, to thee it is spoken; The kingdom is departed from thee.

³² And they shall drive thee from men, and thy dwelling shall be with the beasts of the field: they shall make thee to eat grass as oxen, and seven times shall pass over thee, until thou know that the most High ruleth in the kingdom of men, and giveth it to whomsoever he will.

³³ The same hour was the thing fulfilled upon Nebuchadnezzar: and he was driven from men, and did eat grass as oxen, and his body was wet with the dew of heaven, till his hairs were grown like eagles' feathers, and his nails like birds' claws.

³⁴ And at the end of the days I Nebuchadnezzar lifted up mine eyes unto heaven, and mine understanding returned unto me, and I blessed the most High, and I praised and honoured him that liveth for ever, whose dominion is an everlasting dominion, and his kingdom is from generation to generation:

³⁵ And all the inhabitants of the earth are reputed as nothing: and he doeth according to his will in the army of heaven, and among the inhabitants of the earth: and none can stay his hand, or say unto him, What doest thou?

³⁶ At the same time my reason returned unto me; and for the glory of my kingdom, mine honour and brightness returned unto me; and my counsellors and my lords sought unto me; and I was established in my kingdom, and excellent majesty was added unto me.

³⁷ Now I Nebuchadnezzar praise and extol and honour the King of heaven, all whose works are truth, and his ways judgment: and those that walk in pride he is able to abase.

Chapter 5

Belshazzar the king made a great feast to a thousand of his lords, and drank wine before the thousand.

² Belshazzar, whiles he tasted the wine, commanded to bring the golden and silver vessels which his father Nebuchadnezzar had taken out of the temple which was in Jerusalem; that the king, and his princes, his wives, and his concubines, might drink therein.

³ Then they brought the golden vessels that were taken out of the temple of the house of God which was at Jerusalem; and the king, and his princes, his wives, and his concubines, drank in them.

⁴ They drank wine, and praised the gods of gold, and of silver, of brass, of iron, of wood, and of stone.

⁵ In the same hour came forth fingers of a man's hand, and wrote over against the candlestick upon the plaister of the wall of the king's palace: and the king saw the part of the hand that wrote.

⁶ Then the king's countenance was changed, and his thoughts troubled him, so that the joints of his loins were loosed, and his knees smote one against another.

⁷ The king cried aloud to bring in the astrologers, the Chaldeans, and the soothsayers. And the king spake, and said to the wise men of Babylon, Whosoever shall read this writing, and shew me the interpretation thereof, shall be clothed with scarlet, and have a chain of gold about his neck, and shall be the third ruler in the kingdom.

⁸ Then came in all the king's wise men: but they could not read the writing, nor make known to the king the interpretation thereof.

⁹ Then was king Belshazzar greatly troubled, and his countenance was changed in him, and his lords were astonied.

¹⁰ Now the queen by reason of the words of the king and his lords came into the banquet house: and the queen spake and said, O king, live for ever: let not thy thoughts trouble thee, nor let thy countenance be changed:

¹¹ There is a man in thy kingdom, in whom is the spirit of the holy gods; and in the days of thy father light and understanding and wisdom, like the wisdom of the gods, was found in him; whom the king Nebuchadnezzar thy father, the king, I say, thy father, made master of the magicians, astrologers, Chaldeans, and soothsayers;

¹² Forasmuch as an excellent spirit, and knowledge, and understanding, interpreting of dreams, and shewing of hard sentences, and dissolving of doubts, were found in the same Daniel, whom the king named Belteshazzar: now let Daniel be called, and he will shew the interpretation.

Insights In Prophecy
Unlock The Ancient Mysteries Of Daniel & Revelation
BIBLE DISCOVERY SERIES

¹³ Then was Daniel brought in before the king. And the king spake and said unto Daniel, Art thou that Daniel, which art of the children of the captivity of Judah, whom the king my father brought out of Jewry?
¹⁴ I have even heard of thee, that the spirit of the gods is in thee, and that light and understanding and excellent wisdom is found in thee.
¹⁵ And now the wise men, the astrologers, have been brought in before me, that they should read this writing, and make known unto me the interpretation thereof: but they could not shew the interpretation of the thing:
¹⁶ And I have heard of thee, that thou canst make interpretations, and dissolve doubts: now if thou canst read the writing, and make known to me the interpretation thereof, thou shalt be clothed with scarlet, and have a chain of gold about thy neck, and shalt be the third ruler in the kingdom.
¹⁷ Then Daniel answered and said before the king, Let thy gifts be to thyself, and give thy rewards to another; yet I will read the writing unto the king, and make known to him the interpretation.
¹⁸ O thou king, the most high God gave Nebuchadnezzar thy father a kingdom, and majesty, and glory, and honour:
¹⁹ And for the majesty that he gave him, all people, nations, and languages, trembled and feared before him: whom he would he slew; and whom he would he kept alive; and whom he would he set up; and whom he would he put down.
²⁰ But when his heart was lifted up, and his mind hardened in pride, he was deposed from his kingly throne, and they took his glory from him:
²¹ And he was driven from the sons of men; and his heart was made like the beasts, and his dwelling was with the wild asses: they fed him with grass like oxen, and his body was wet with the dew of heaven; till he knew that the most high God ruled in the kingdom of men, and that he appointeth over it whomsoever he will.
²² And thou his son, O Belshazzar, hast not humbled thine heart, though thou knewest all this;
²³ But hast lifted up thyself against the Lord of heaven; and they have brought the vessels of his house before thee, and thou, and thy lords, thy wives, and thy concubines, have drunk wine in them; and thou hast praised the gods of silver, and gold, of brass, iron, wood, and stone, which see not, nor hear, nor know: and the God in whose hand thy breath is, and whose are all thy ways, hast thou not glorified:
²⁴ Then was the part of the hand sent from him; and this writing was written.
²⁵ And this is the writing that was written, MENE, MENE, TEKEL, UPHARSIN.
²⁶ This is the interpretation of the thing: MENE; God hath numbered thy kingdom, and finished it.
²⁷ TEKEL; Thou art weighed in the balances, and art found wanting.
²⁸ PERES; Thy kingdom is divided, and given to the Medes and Persians.
²⁹ Then commanded Belshazzar, and they clothed Daniel with scarlet, and put a chain of gold about his neck, and made a proclamation concerning him, that he should be the third ruler in the kingdom.
³⁰ In that night was Belshazzar the king of the Chaldeans slain.
³¹ And Darius the Median took the kingdom, being about threescore and two years old.

Chapter 6
It pleased Darius to set over the kingdom an hundred and twenty princes, which should be over the whole kingdom;
² And over these three presidents; of whom Daniel was first: that the princes might give accounts unto them, and the king should have no damage.
³ Then this Daniel was preferred above the presidents and princes, because an excellent spirit was in him; and the king thought to set him over the whole realm.
⁴ Then the presidents and princes sought to find occasion against Daniel concerning the kingdom; but they could find none occasion nor fault; forasmuch as he was faithful, neither was there any error or fault found in him.

⁵ Then said these men, We shall not find any occasion against this Daniel, except we find it against him concerning the law of his God.

⁶ Then these presidents and princes assembled together to the king, and said thus unto him, King Darius, live for ever.

⁷ All the presidents of the kingdom, the governors, and the princes, the counsellors, and the captains, have consulted together to establish a royal statute, and to make a firm decree, that whosoever shall ask a petition of any God or man for thirty days, save of thee, O king, he shall be cast into the den of lions.

⁸ Now, O king, establish the decree, and sign the writing, that it be not changed, according to the law of the Medes and Persians, which altereth not.

⁹ Wherefore king Darius signed the writing and the decree.

¹⁰ Now when Daniel knew that the writing was signed, he went into his house; and his windows being open in his chamber toward Jerusalem, he kneeled upon his knees three times a day, and prayed, and gave thanks before his God, as he did aforetime.

¹¹ Then these men assembled, and found Daniel praying and making supplication before his God.

¹² Then they came near, and spake before the king concerning the king's decree; Hast thou not signed a decree, that every man that shall ask a petition of any God or man within thirty days, save of thee, O king, shall be cast into the den of lions? The king answered and said, The thing is true, according to the law of the Medes and Persians, which altereth not.

¹³ Then answered they and said before the king, That Daniel, which is of the children of the captivity of Judah, regardeth not thee, O king, nor the decree that thou hast signed, but maketh his petition three times a day.

¹⁴ Then the king, when he heard these words, was sore displeased with himself, and set his heart on Daniel to deliver him: and he laboured till the going down of the sun to deliver him.

¹⁵ Then these men assembled unto the king, and said unto the king, Know, O king, that the law of the Medes and Persians is, That no decree nor statute which the king establisheth may be changed.

¹⁶ Then the king commanded, and they brought Daniel, and cast him into the den of lions. Now the king spake and said unto Daniel, Thy God whom thou servest continually, he will deliver thee.

¹⁷ And a stone was brought, and laid upon the mouth of the den; and the king sealed it with his own signet, and with the signet of his lords; that the purpose might not be changed concerning Daniel.

¹⁸ Then the king went to his palace, and passed the night fasting: neither were instruments of musick brought before him: and his sleep went from him.

¹⁹ Then the king arose very early in the morning, and went in haste unto the den of lions.

²⁰ And when he came to the den, he cried with a lamentable voice unto Daniel: and the king spake and said to Daniel, O Daniel, servant of the living God, is thy God, whom thou servest continually, able to deliver thee from the lions?

²¹ Then said Daniel unto the king, O king, live for ever.

²² My God hath sent his angel, and hath shut the lions' mouths, that they have not hurt me: forasmuch as before him innocency was found in me; and also before thee, O king, have I done no hurt.

²³ Then was the king exceedingly glad for him, and commanded that they should take Daniel up out of the den. So Daniel was taken up out of the den, and no manner of hurt was found upon him, because he believed in his God.

²⁴ And the king commanded, and they brought those men which had accused Daniel, and they cast them into the den of lions, them, their children, and their wives; and the lions had the mastery of them, and brake all their bones in pieces or ever they came at the bottom of the den.

²⁵ Then king Darius wrote unto all people, nations, and languages, that dwell in all the earth; Peace be multiplied unto you.

²⁶ I make a decree, That in every dominion of my kingdom men tremble and fear before the God of Daniel: for he is the living God, and stedfast for ever, and his kingdom that which shall not be destroyed, and his dominion shall be even unto the end.

²⁷ He delivereth and rescueth, and he worketh signs and wonders in heaven and in earth, who hath delivered Daniel from the power of the lions.

²⁸ So this Daniel prospered in the reign of Darius, and in the reign of Cyrus the Persian.

Chapter 7

In the first year of Belshazzar king of Babylon Daniel had a dream and visions of his head upon his bed: then he wrote the dream, and told the sum of the matters.

² Daniel spake and said, I saw in my vision by night, and, behold, the four winds of the heaven strove upon the great sea.

³ And four great beasts came up from the sea, diverse one from another.

⁴ The first was like a lion, and had eagle's wings: I beheld till the wings thereof were plucked, and it was lifted up from the earth, and made stand upon the feet as a man, and a man's heart was given to it.

⁵ And behold another beast, a second, like to a bear, and it raised up itself on one side, and it had three ribs in the mouth of it between the teeth of it: and they said thus unto it, Arise, devour much flesh.

⁶ After this I beheld, and lo another, like a leopard, which had upon the back of it four wings of a fowl; the beast had also four heads; and dominion was given to it.

⁷ After this I saw in the night visions, and behold a fourth beast, dreadful and terrible, and strong exceedingly; and it had great iron teeth: it devoured and brake in pieces, and stamped the residue with the feet of it: and it was diverse from all the beasts that were before it; and it had ten horns.

⁸ I considered the horns, and, behold, there came up among them another little horn, before whom there were three of the first horns plucked up by the roots: and, behold, in this horn were eyes like the eyes of man, and a mouth speaking great things.

⁹ I beheld till the thrones were cast down, and the Ancient of days did sit, whose garment was white as snow, and the hair of his head like the pure wool: his throne was like the fiery flame, and his wheels as burning fire.

¹⁰ A fiery stream issued and came forth from before him: thousand thousands ministered unto him, and ten thousand times ten thousand stood before him: the judgment was set, and the books were opened.

¹¹ I beheld then because of the voice of the great words which the horn spake: I beheld even till the beast was slain, and his body destroyed, and given to the burning flame.

¹² As concerning the rest of the beasts, they had their dominion taken away: yet their lives were prolonged for a season and time.

¹³ I saw in the night visions, and, behold, one like the Son of man came with the clouds of heaven, and came to the Ancient of days, and they brought him near before him.

¹⁴ And there was given him dominion, and glory, and a kingdom, that all people, nations, and languages, should serve him: his dominion is an everlasting dominion, which shall not pass away, and his kingdom that which shall not be destroyed.

¹⁵ I Daniel was grieved in my spirit in the midst of my body, and the visions of my head troubled me.

¹⁶ I came near unto one of them that stood by, and asked him the truth of all this. So he told me, and made me know the interpretation of the things.

¹⁷ These great beasts, which are four, are four kings, which shall arise out of the earth.

¹⁸ But the saints of the most High shall take the kingdom, and possess the kingdom for ever, even for ever and ever.

¹⁹ Then I would know the truth of the fourth beast, which was diverse from all the others, exceeding dreadful, whose teeth were of iron, and his nails of brass; which devoured, brake in pieces, and stamped the residue with his feet;

²⁰ And of the ten horns that were in his head, and of the other which came up, and before whom three fell; even of that horn that had eyes, and a mouth that spake very great things, whose look was more stout than his fellows.

²¹ I beheld, and the same horn made war with the saints, and prevailed against them;

²² Until the Ancient of days came, and judgment was given to the saints of the most High; and the time came that the saints possessed the kingdom.

²³ Thus he said, The fourth beast shall be the fourth kingdom upon earth, which shall be diverse from all kingdoms, and shall devour the whole earth, and shall tread it down, and break it in pieces.

²⁴ And the ten horns out of this kingdom are ten kings that shall arise: and another shall rise after them; and he shall be diverse from the first, and he shall subdue three kings.

²⁵ And he shall speak great words against the most High, and shall wear out the saints of the most High, and think to change times and laws: and they shall be given into his hand until a time and times and the dividing of time.

²⁶ But the judgment shall sit, and they shall take away his dominion, to consume and to destroy it unto the end.

²⁷ And the kingdom and dominion, and the greatness of the kingdom under the whole heaven, shall be given to the people of the saints of the most High, whose kingdom is an everlasting kingdom, and all dominions shall serve and obey him.

²⁸ Hitherto is the end of the matter. As for me Daniel, my cogitations much troubled me, and my countenance changed in me: but I kept the matter in my heart.

Chapter 8

In the third year of the reign of king Belshazzar a vision appeared unto me, even unto me Daniel, after that which appeared unto me at the first.

² And I saw in a vision; and it came to pass, when I saw, that I was at Shushan in the palace, which is in the province of Elam; and I saw in a vision, and I was by the river of Ulai.

³ Then I lifted up mine eyes, and saw, and, behold, there stood before the river a ram which had two horns: and the two horns were high; but one was higher than the other, and the higher came up last.

⁴ I saw the ram pushing westward, and northward, and southward; so that no beasts might stand before him, neither was there any that could deliver out of his hand; but he did according to his will, and became great.

⁵ And as I was considering, behold, an he goat came from the west on the face of the whole earth, and touched not the ground: and the goat had a notable horn between his eyes.

⁶ And he came to the ram that had two horns, which I had seen standing before the river, and ran unto him in the fury of his power.

⁷ And I saw him come close unto the ram, and he was moved with choler against him, and smote the ram, and brake his two horns: and there was no power in the ram to stand before him, but he cast him down to the ground, and stamped upon him: and there was none that could deliver the ram out of his hand.

⁸ Therefore the he goat waxed very great: and when he was strong, the great horn was broken; and for it came up four notable ones toward the four winds of heaven.

⁹ And out of one of them came forth a little horn, which waxed exceeding great, toward the south, and toward the east, and toward the pleasant land.

¹⁰ And it waxed great, even to the host of heaven; and it cast down some of the host and of the stars to the ground, and stamped upon them.

¹¹ Yea, he magnified himself even to the prince of the host, and by him the daily sacrifice was taken away, and the place of the sanctuary was cast down.

¹² And an host was given him against the daily sacrifice by reason of transgression, and it cast down the truth to the ground; and it practised, and prospered.

¹³ Then I heard one saint speaking, and another saint said unto that certain saint which spake, How long shall be the vision concerning the daily sacrifice, and the transgression of desolation, to give both the sanctuary and the host to be trodden under foot?

¹⁴ And he said unto me, Unto two thousand and three hundred days; then shall the sanctuary be cleansed.

¹⁵ And it came to pass, when I, even I Daniel, had seen the vision, and sought for the meaning, then, behold, there stood before me as the appearance of a man.

¹⁶ And I heard a man's voice between the banks of Ulai, which called, and said, Gabriel, make this man to understand the vision.

¹⁷ So he came near where I stood: and when he came, I was afraid, and fell upon my face: but he said unto me, Understand, O son of man: for at the time of the end shall be the vision.

¹⁸ Now as he was speaking with me, I was in a deep sleep on my face toward the ground: but he touched me, and set me upright.

¹⁹ And he said, Behold, I will make thee know what shall be in the last end of the indignation: for at the time appointed the end shall be.

²⁰ The ram which thou sawest having two horns are the kings of Media and Persia.

²¹ And the rough goat is the king of Grecia: and the great horn that is between his eyes is the first king.

²² Now that being broken, whereas four stood up for it, four kingdoms shall stand up out of the nation, but not in his power.

²³ And in the latter time of their kingdom, when the transgressors are come to the full, a king of fierce countenance, and understanding dark sentences, shall stand up.

²⁴ And his power shall be mighty, but not by his own power: and he shall destroy wonderfully, and shall prosper, and practise, and shall destroy the mighty and the holy people.

²⁵ And through his policy also he shall cause craft to prosper in his hand; and he shall magnify himself in his heart, and by peace shall destroy many: he shall also stand up against the Prince of princes; but he shall be broken without hand.

²⁶ And the vision of the evening and the morning which was told is true: wherefore shut thou up the vision; for it shall be for many days.

²⁷ And I Daniel fainted, and was sick certain days; afterward I rose up, and did the king's business; and I was astonished at the vision, but none understood it.

Chapter 9

In the first year of Darius the son of Ahasuerus, of the seed of the Medes, which was made king over the realm of the Chaldeans;

² In the first year of his reign I Daniel understood by books the number of the years, whereof the word of the LORD came to Jeremiah the prophet, that he would accomplish seventy years in the desolations of Jerusalem.

³ And I set my face unto the Lord God, to seek by prayer and supplications, with fasting, and sackcloth, and ashes:

⁴ And I prayed unto the LORD my God, and made my confession, and said, O Lord, the great and dreadful God, keeping the covenant and mercy to them that love him, and to them that keep his commandments;

⁵ We have sinned, and have committed iniquity, and have done wickedly, and have rebelled, even by departing from thy precepts and from thy judgments:

⁶ Neither have we hearkened unto thy servants the prophets, which spake in thy name to our kings, our princes, and our fathers, and to all the people of the land.

⁷ O LORD, righteousness belongeth unto thee, but unto us confusion of faces, as at this day; to the men of Judah, and to the inhabitants of Jerusalem, and unto all Israel, that are near, and that are far off, through all the countries whither thou hast driven them, because of their trespass that they have trespassed against thee.

⁸ O Lord, to us belongeth confusion of face, to our kings, to our princes, and to our fathers, because we have sinned against thee.

⁹ To the Lord our God belong mercies and forgivenesses, though we have rebelled against him;

¹⁰ Neither have we obeyed the voice of the LORD our God, to walk in his laws, which he set before us by his servants the prophets.

¹¹ Yea, all Israel have transgressed thy law, even by departing, that they might not obey thy voice; therefore the curse is poured upon us, and the oath that is written in the law of Moses the servant of God, because we have sinned against him.

¹² And he hath confirmed his words, which he spake against us, and against our judges that judged us, by bringing upon us a great evil: for under the whole heaven hath not been done as hath been done upon Jerusalem.

¹³ As it is written in the law of Moses, all this evil is come upon us: yet made we not our prayer before the LORD our God, that we might turn from our iniquities, and understand thy truth.

¹⁴ Therefore hath the LORD watched upon the evil, and brought it upon us: for the LORD our God is righteous in all his works which he doeth: for we obeyed not his voice.

¹⁵ And now, O Lord our God, that hast brought thy people forth out of the land of Egypt with a mighty hand, and hast gotten thee renown, as at this day; we have sinned, we have done wickedly.

¹⁶ O LORD, according to all thy righteousness, I beseech thee, let thine anger and thy fury be turned away from thy city Jerusalem, thy holy mountain: because for our sins, and for the iniquities of our fathers, Jerusalem and thy people are become a reproach to all that are about us.

¹⁷ Now therefore, O our God, hear the prayer of thy servant, and his supplications, and cause thy face to shine upon thy sanctuary that is desolate, for the Lord's sake.

¹⁸ O my God, incline thine ear, and hear; open thine eyes, and behold our desolations, and the city which is called by thy name: for we do not present our supplications before thee for our righteousnesses, but for thy great mercies.

¹⁹ O Lord, hear; O Lord, forgive; O Lord, hearken and do; defer not, for thine own sake, O my God: for thy city and thy people are called by thy name.

²⁰ And whiles I was speaking, and praying, and confessing my sin and the sin of my people Israel, and presenting my supplication before the LORD my God for the holy mountain of my God;

²¹ Yea, whiles I was speaking in prayer, even the man Gabriel, whom I had seen in the vision at the beginning, being caused to fly swiftly, touched me about the time of the evening oblation.

²² And he informed me, and talked with me, and said, O Daniel, I am now come forth to give thee skill and understanding.

²³ At the beginning of thy supplications the commandment came forth, and I am come to shew thee; for thou art greatly beloved: therefore understand the matter, and consider the vision.

²⁴ Seventy weeks are determined upon thy people and upon thy holy city, to finish the transgression, and to make an end of sins, and to make reconciliation for iniquity, and to bring in everlasting righteousness, and to seal up the vision and prophecy, and to anoint the most Holy.

²⁵ Know therefore and understand, that from the going forth of the commandment to restore and to build Jerusalem unto the Messiah the Prince shall be seven weeks, and threescore and two weeks: the street shall be built again, and the wall, even in troublous times.

²⁶ And after threescore and two weeks shall Messiah be cut off, but not for himself: and the people of the prince that shall come shall destroy the city and the sanctuary; and the end thereof shall be with a flood, and unto the end of the war desolations are determined.

²⁷ And he shall confirm the covenant with many for one week: and in the midst of the week he shall cause the sacrifice and the oblation to cease, and for the overspreading of abominations he shall make it desolate, even until the consummation, and that determined shall be poured upon the desolate.

Chapter 10

In the third year of Cyrus king of Persia a thing was revealed unto Daniel, whose name was called Belteshazzar; and the thing was true, but the time appointed was long: and he understood the thing, and had understanding of the vision.

² In those days I Daniel was mourning three full weeks.

³ I ate no pleasant bread, neither came flesh nor wine in my mouth, neither did I anoint myself at all, till three whole weeks were fulfilled.

⁴ And in the four and twentieth day of the first month, as I was by the side of the great river, which is Hiddekel;

⁵ Then I lifted up mine eyes, and looked, and behold a certain man clothed in linen, whose loins were girded with fine gold of Uphaz:

⁶ His body also was like the beryl, and his face as the appearance of lightning, and his eyes as lamps of fire, and his arms and his feet like in colour to polished brass, and the voice of his words like the voice of a multitude.

⁷ And I Daniel alone saw the vision: for the men that were with me saw not the vision; but a great quaking fell upon them, so that they fled to hide themselves.

⁸ Therefore I was left alone, and saw this great vision, and there remained no strength in me: for my comeliness was turned in me into corruption, and I retained no strength.

⁹ Yet heard I the voice of his words: and when I heard the voice of his words, then was I in a deep sleep on my face, and my face toward the ground.

¹⁰ And, behold, an hand touched me, which set me upon my knees and upon the palms of my hands.

¹¹ And he said unto me, O Daniel, a man greatly beloved, understand the words that I speak unto thee, and stand upright: for unto thee am I now sent. And when he had spoken this word unto me, I stood trembling.

¹² Then said he unto me, Fear not, Daniel: for from the first day that thou didst set thine heart to understand, and to chasten thyself before thy God, thy words were heard, and I am come for thy words.

¹³ But the prince of the kingdom of Persia withstood me one and twenty days: but, lo, Michael, one of the chief princes, came to help me; and I remained there with the kings of Persia.

¹⁴ Now I am come to make thee understand what shall befall thy people in the latter days: for yet the vision is for many days.

¹⁵ And when he had spoken such words unto me, I set my face toward the ground, and I became dumb.

¹⁶ And, behold, one like the similitude of the sons of men touched my lips: then I opened my mouth, and spake, and said unto him that stood before me, O my lord, by the vision my sorrows are turned upon me, and I have retained no strength.

¹⁷ For how can the servant of this my lord talk with this my lord? for as for me, straightway there remained no strength in me, neither is there breath left in me.

¹⁸ Then there came again and touched me one like the appearance of a man, and he strengthened me,

¹⁹ And said, O man greatly beloved, fear not: peace be unto thee, be strong, yea, be strong. And when he had spoken unto me, I was strengthened, and said, Let my lord speak; for thou hast strengthened me.

²⁰ Then said he, Knowest thou wherefore I come unto thee? and now will I return to fight with the prince of Persia: and when I am gone forth, lo, the prince of Grecia shall come.

²¹ But I will shew thee that which is noted in the scripture of truth: and there is none that holdeth with me in these things, but Michael your prince.

Chapter 11

Also I in the first year of Darius the Mede, even I, stood to confirm and to strengthen him.

² And now will I shew thee the truth. Behold, there shall stand up yet three kings in Persia; and the fourth shall be far richer than they all: and by his strength through his riches he shall stir up all against the realm of Grecia.

³ And a mighty king shall stand up, that shall rule with great dominion, and do according to his will.

⁴ And when he shall stand up, his kingdom shall be broken, and shall be divided toward the four winds of heaven; and not to his posterity, nor according to his dominion which he ruled: for his kingdom shall be plucked up, even for others beside those.

[5] And the king of the south shall be strong, and one of his princes; and he shall be strong above him, and have dominion; his dominion shall be a great dominion.

[6] And in the end of years they shall join themselves together; for the king's daughter of the south shall come to the king of the north to make an agreement: but she shall not retain the power of the arm; neither shall he stand, nor his arm: but she shall be given up, and they that brought her, and he that begat her, and he that strengthened her in these times.

[7] But out of a branch of her roots shall one stand up in his estate, which shall come with an army, and shall enter into the fortress of the king of the north, and shall deal against them, and shall prevail:

[8] And shall also carry captives into Egypt their gods, with their princes, and with their precious vessels of silver and of gold; and he shall continue more years than the king of the north.

[9] So the king of the south shall come into his kingdom, and shall return into his own land.

[10] But his sons shall be stirred up, and shall assemble a multitude of great forces: and one shall certainly come, and overflow, and pass through: then shall he return, and be stirred up, even to his fortress.

[11] And the king of the south shall be moved with choler, and shall come forth and fight with him, even with the king of the north: and he shall set forth a great multitude; but the multitude shall be given into his hand.

[12] And when he hath taken away the multitude, his heart shall be lifted up; and he shall cast down many ten thousands: but he shall not be strengthened by it.

[13] For the king of the north shall return, and shall set forth a multitude greater than the former, and shall certainly come after certain years with a great army and with much riches.

[14] And in those times there shall many stand up against the king of the south: also the robbers of thy people shall exalt themselves to establish the vision; but they shall fall.

[15] So the king of the north shall come, and cast up a mount, and take the most fenced cities: and the arms of the south shall not withstand, neither his chosen people, neither shall there be any strength to withstand.

[16] But he that cometh against him shall do according to his own will, and none shall stand before him: and he shall stand in the glorious land, which by his hand shall be consumed.

[17] He shall also set his face to enter with the strength of his whole kingdom, and upright ones with him; thus shall he do: and he shall give him the daughter of women, corrupting her: but she shall not stand on his side, neither be for him.

[18] After this shall he turn his face unto the isles, and shall take many: but a prince for his own behalf shall cause the reproach offered by him to cease; without his own reproach he shall cause it to turn upon him.

[19] Then he shall turn his face toward the fort of his own land: but he shall stumble and fall, and not be found.

[20] Then shall stand up in his estate a raiser of taxes in the glory of the kingdom: but within few days he shall be destroyed, neither in anger, nor in battle.

[21] And in his estate shall stand up a vile person, to whom they shall not give the honour of the kingdom: but he shall come in peaceably, and obtain the kingdom by flatteries.

[22] And with the arms of a flood shall they be overflown from before him, and shall be broken; yea, also the prince of the covenant.

[23] And after the league made with him he shall work deceitfully: for he shall come up, and shall become strong with a small people.

[24] He shall enter peaceably even upon the fattest places of the province; and he shall do that which his fathers have not done, nor his fathers' fathers; he shall scatter among them the prey, and spoil, and riches: yea, and he shall forecast his devices against the strong holds, even for a time.

[25] And he shall stir up his power and his courage against the king of the south with a great army; and the king of the south shall be stirred up to battle with a very great and mighty army; but he shall not stand: for they shall forecast devices against him.

[26] Yea, they that feed of the portion of his meat shall destroy him, and his army shall overflow: and many shall fall down slain.

[27] And both of these kings' hearts shall be to do mischief, and they shall speak lies at one table; but it shall not prosper: for yet the end shall be at the time appointed.

[28] Then shall he return into his land with great riches; and his heart shall be against the holy covenant; and he shall do exploits, and return to his own land.

[29] At the time appointed he shall return, and come toward the south; but it shall not be as the former, or as the latter.

[30] For the ships of Chittim shall come against him: therefore he shall be grieved, and return, and have indignation against the holy covenant: so shall he do; he shall even return, and have intelligence with them that forsake the holy covenant.

[31] And arms shall stand on his part, and they shall pollute the sanctuary of strength, and shall take away the daily sacrifice, and they shall place the abomination that maketh desolate.

[32] And such as do wickedly against the covenant shall he corrupt by flatteries: but the people that do know their God shall be strong, and do exploits.

[33] And they that understand among the people shall instruct many: yet they shall fall by the sword, and by flame, by captivity, and by spoil, many days.

[34] Now when they shall fall, they shall be holpen with a little help: but many shall cleave to them with flatteries.

[35] And some of them of understanding shall fall, to try them, and to purge, and to make them white, even to the time of the end: because it is yet for a time appointed.

[36] And the king shall do according to his will; and he shall exalt himself, and magnify himself above every god, and shall speak marvellous things against the God of gods, and shall prosper till the indignation be accomplished: for that that is determined shall be done.

[37] Neither shall he regard the God of his fathers, nor the desire of women, nor regard any god: for he shall magnify himself above all.

[38] But in his estate shall he honour the God of forces: and a god whom his fathers knew not shall he honour with gold, and silver, and with precious stones, and pleasant things.

[39] Thus shall he do in the most strong holds with a strange god, whom he shall acknowledge and increase with glory: and he shall cause them to rule over many, and shall divide the land for gain.

[40] And at the time of the end shall the king of the south push at him: and the king of the north shall come against him like a whirlwind, with chariots, and with horsemen, and with many ships; and he shall enter into the countries, and shall overflow and pass over.

[41] He shall enter also into the glorious land, and many countries shall be overthrown: but these shall escape out of his hand, even Edom, and Moab, and the chief of the children of Ammon.

[42] He shall stretch forth his hand also upon the countries: and the land of Egypt shall not escape.

[43] But he shall have power over the treasures of gold and of silver, and over all the precious things of Egypt: and the Libyans and the Ethiopians shall be at his steps.

[44] But tidings out of the east and out of the north shall trouble him: therefore he shall go forth with great fury to destroy, and utterly to make away many.

[45] And he shall plant the tabernacles of his palace between the seas in the glorious holy mountain; yet he shall come to his end, and none shall help him.

Chapter 12

And at that time shall Michael stand up, the great prince which standeth for the children of thy people: and there shall be a time of trouble, such as never was since there was a nation even to that same time: and at that time thy people shall be delivered, every one that shall be found written in the book.

[2] And many of them that sleep in the dust of the earth shall awake, some to everlasting life, and some to shame and everlasting contempt.

[3] And they that be wise shall shine as the brightness of the firmament; and they that turn many to righteousness as the stars for ever and ever.

⁴ But thou, O Daniel, shut up the words, and seal the book, even to the time of the end: many shall run to and fro, and knowledge shall be increased.

⁵ Then I Daniel looked, and, behold, there stood other two, the one on this side of the bank of the river, and the other on that side of the bank of the river.

⁶ And one said to the man clothed in linen, which was upon the waters of the river, How long shall it be to the end of these wonders?

⁷ And I heard the man clothed in linen, which was upon the waters of the river, when he held up his right hand and his left hand unto heaven, and sware by him that liveth for ever that it shall be for a time, times, and an half; and when he shall have accomplished to scatter the power of the holy people, all these things shall be finished.

⁸ And I heard, but I understood not: then said I, O my Lord, what shall be the end of these things?

⁹ And he said, Go thy way, Daniel: for the words are closed up and sealed till the time of the end.

¹⁰ Many shall be purified, and made white, and tried; but the wicked shall do wickedly: and none of the wicked shall understand; but the wise shall understand.

¹¹ And from the time that the daily sacrifice shall be taken away, and the abomination that maketh desolate set up, there shall be a thousand two hundred and ninety days.

¹² Blessed is he that waiteth, and cometh to the thousand three hundred and five and thirty days.

¹³ But go thou thy way till the end be: for thou shalt rest, and stand in thy lot at the end of the days.

Insights In Prophecy

Unlock The Ancient Mysteries Of Daniel & Revelation

BIBLE DISCOVERY SERIES

Insights In Prophecy
Unlock The Ancient Mysteries Of Daniel & Revelation
BIBLE DISCOVERY SERIES

Matthew 24
King James Version (KJV)

Chapter 24

And Jesus went out, and departed from the temple: and his disciples came to him for to shew him the buildings of the temple.

[2] And Jesus said unto them, See ye not all these things? verily I say unto you, There shall not be left here one stone upon another, that shall not be thrown down.

[3] And as he sat upon the mount of Olives, the disciples came unto him privately, saying, Tell us, when shall these things be? and what shall be the sign of thy coming, and of the end of the world?

[4] And Jesus answered and said unto them, Take heed that no man deceive you.

[5] For many shall come in my name, saying, I am Christ; and shall deceive many.

[6] And ye shall hear of wars and rumours of wars: see that ye be not troubled: for all these things must come to pass, but the end is not yet.

[7] For nation shall rise against nation, and kingdom against kingdom: and there shall be famines, and pestilences, and earthquakes, in divers places.

[8] All these are the beginning of sorrows.

[9] Then shall they deliver you up to be afflicted, and shall kill you: and ye shall be hated of all nations for my name's sake.

[10] And then shall many be offended, and shall betray one another, and shall hate one another.

[11] And many false prophets shall rise, and shall deceive many.

[12] And because iniquity shall abound, the love of many shall wax cold.

[13] But he that shall endure unto the end, the same shall be saved.

[14] And this gospel of the kingdom shall be preached in all the world for a witness unto all nations; and then shall the end come.

[15] When ye therefore shall see the abomination of desolation, spoken of by Daniel the prophet, stand in the holy place, (whoso readeth, let him understand:)

[16] Then let them which be in Judaea flee into the mountains:

[17] Let him which is on the housetop not come down to take any thing out of his house:

[18] Neither let him which is in the field return back to take his clothes.

[19] And woe unto them that are with child, and to them that give suck in those days!

[20] But pray ye that your flight be not in the winter, neither on the sabbath day:

[21] For then shall be great tribulation, such as was not since the beginning of the world to this time, no, nor ever shall be.

[22] And except those days should be shortened, there should no flesh be saved: but for the elect's sake those days shall be shortened.

[23] Then if any man shall say unto you, Lo, here is Christ, or there; believe it not.

[24] For there shall arise false Christs, and false prophets, and shall shew great signs and wonders; insomuch that, if it were possible, they shall deceive the very elect.

[25] Behold, I have told you before.

[26] Wherefore if they shall say unto you, Behold, he is in the desert; go not forth: behold, he is in the secret chambers; believe it not.

[27] For as the lightning cometh out of the east, and shineth even unto the west; so shall also the coming of the Son of man be.

[28] For wheresoever the carcase is, there will the eagles be gathered together.

[29] Immediately after the tribulation of those days shall the sun be darkened, and the moon shall not give her light, and the stars shall fall from heaven, and the powers of the heavens shall be shaken:

[30] And then shall appear the sign of the Son of man in heaven: and then shall all the tribes of the earth mourn, and they shall see the Son of man coming in the clouds of heaven with power and great glory.

[31] And he shall send his angels with a great sound of a trumpet, and they shall gather together his elect from the four winds, from one end of heaven to the other.

[32] Now learn a parable of the fig tree; When his branch is yet tender, and putteth forth leaves, ye know that summer is nigh:

[33] So likewise ye, when ye shall see all these things, know that it is near, even at the doors.

[34] Verily I say unto you, This generation shall not pass, till all these things be fulfilled.

[35] Heaven and earth shall pass away, but my words shall not pass away.

[36] But of that day and hour knoweth no man, no, not the angels of heaven, but my Father only.

[37] But as the days of Noah were, so shall also the coming of the Son of man be.

[38] For as in the days that were before the flood they were eating and drinking, marrying and giving in marriage, until the day that Noe entered into the ark,

[39] And knew not until the flood came, and took them all away; so shall also the coming of the Son of man be.

[40] Then shall two be in the field; the one shall be taken, and the other left.

[41] Two women shall be grinding at the mill; the one shall be taken, and the other left.

[42] Watch therefore: for ye know not what hour your Lord doth come.

[43] But know this, that if the goodman of the house had known in what watch the thief would come, he would have watched, and would not have suffered his house to be broken up.

[44] Therefore be ye also ready: for in such an hour as ye think not the Son of man cometh.

[45] Who then is a faithful and wise servant, whom his lord hath made ruler over his household, to give them meat in due season?

[46] Blessed is that servant, whom his lord when he cometh shall find so doing.

[47] Verily I say unto you, That he shall make him ruler over all his goods.

[48] But and if that evil servant shall say in his heart, My lord delayeth his coming;

[49] And shall begin to smite his fellowservants, and to eat and drink with the drunken;

[50] The lord of that servant shall come in a day when he looketh not for him, and in an hour that he is not aware of,

[51] And shall cut him asunder, and appoint him his portion with the hypocrites: there shall be weeping and gnashing of teeth.

Insights In Prophecy
Unlock The Ancient Mysteries Of Daniel & Revelation
BIBLE DISCOVERY SERIES

The Book of Revelation
King James Version (KJV)

Chapter 1

The Revelation of Jesus Christ, which God gave unto him, to shew unto his servants things which must shortly come to pass; and he sent and signified it by his angel unto his servant John:

[2] Who bare record of the word of God, and of the testimony of Jesus Christ, and of all things that he saw.

[3] Blessed is he that readeth, and they that hear the words of this prophecy, and keep those things which are written therein: for the time is at hand.

[4] John to the seven churches which are in Asia: Grace be unto you, and peace, from him which is, and which was, and which is to come; and from the seven Spirits which are before his throne;

[5] And from Jesus Christ, who is the faithful witness, and the first begotten of the dead, and the prince of the kings of the earth. Unto him that loved us, and washed us from our sins in his own blood,

[6] And hath made us kings and priests unto God and his Father; to him be glory and dominion for ever and ever. Amen.

[7] Behold, he cometh with clouds; and every eye shall see him, and they also which pierced him: and all kindreds of the earth shall wail because of him. Even so, Amen.

[8] I am Alpha and Omega, the beginning and the ending, saith the Lord, which is, and which was, and which is to come, the Almighty.

[9] I John, who also am your brother, and companion in tribulation, and in the kingdom and patience of Jesus Christ, was in the isle that is called Patmos, for the word of God, and for the testimony of Jesus Christ.

[10] I was in the Spirit on the Lord's day, and heard behind me a great voice, as of a trumpet,

[11] Saying, I am Alpha and Omega, the first and the last: and, What thou seest, write in a book, and send it unto the seven churches which are in Asia; unto Ephesus, and unto Smyrna, and unto Pergamos, and unto Thyatira, and unto Sardis, and unto Philadelphia, and unto Laodicea.

[12] And I turned to see the voice that spake with me. And being turned, I saw seven golden candlesticks;

[13] And in the midst of the seven candlesticks one like unto the Son of man, clothed with a garment down to the foot, and girt about the paps with a golden girdle.

[14] His head and his hairs were white like wool, as white as snow; and his eyes were as a flame of fire;

[15] And his feet like unto fine brass, as if they burned in a furnace; and his voice as the sound of many waters.

[16] And he had in his right hand seven stars: and out of his mouth went a sharp twoedged sword: and his countenance was as the sun shineth in his strength.

[17] And when I saw him, I fell at his feet as dead. And he laid his right hand upon me, saying unto me, Fear not; I am the first and the last:

[18] I am he that liveth, and was dead; and, behold, I am alive for evermore, Amen; and have the keys of hell and of death.

[19] Write the things which thou hast seen, and the things which are, and the things which shall be hereafter;

[20] The mystery of the seven stars which thou sawest in my right hand, and the seven golden candlesticks. The seven stars are the angels of the seven churches: and the seven candlesticks which thou sawest are the seven churches.

Chapter 2

Unto the angel of the church of Ephesus write; These things saith he that holdeth the seven stars in his right hand, who walketh in the midst of the seven golden candlesticks;

2 I know thy works, and thy labour, and thy patience, and how thou canst not bear them which are evil: and thou hast tried them which say they are apostles, and are not, and hast found them liars:

3 And hast borne, and hast patience, and for my name's sake hast laboured, and hast not fainted.

4 Nevertheless I have somewhat against thee, because thou hast left thy first love.

5 Remember therefore from whence thou art fallen, and repent, and do the first works; or else I will come unto thee quickly, and will remove thy candlestick out of his place, except thou repent.

6 But this thou hast, that thou hatest the deeds of the Nicolaitanes, which I also hate.

7 He that hath an ear, let him hear what the Spirit saith unto the churches; To him that overcometh will I give to eat of the tree of life, which is in the midst of the paradise of God.

8 And unto the angel of the church in Smyrna write; These things saith the first and the last, which was dead, and is alive;

9 I know thy works, and tribulation, and poverty, (but thou art rich) and I know the blasphemy of them which say they are Jews, and are not, but are the synagogue of Satan.

10 Fear none of those things which thou shalt suffer: behold, the devil shall cast some of you into prison, that ye may be tried; and ye shall have tribulation ten days: be thou faithful unto death, and I will give thee a crown of life.

11 He that hath an ear, let him hear what the Spirit saith unto the churches; He that overcometh shall not be hurt of the second death.

12 And to the angel of the church in Pergamos write; These things saith he which hath the sharp sword with two edges;

13 I know thy works, and where thou dwellest, even where Satan's seat is: and thou holdest fast my name, and hast not denied my faith, even in those days wherein Antipas was my faithful martyr, who was slain among you, where Satan dwelleth.

14 But I have a few things against thee, because thou hast there them that hold the doctrine of Balaam, who taught Balac to cast a stumblingblock before the children of Israel, to eat things sacrificed unto idols, and to commit fornication.

15 So hast thou also them that hold the doctrine of the Nicolaitanes, which thing I hate.

16 Repent; or else I will come unto thee quickly, and will fight against them with the sword of my mouth.

17 He that hath an ear, let him hear what the Spirit saith unto the churches; To him that overcometh will I give to eat of the hidden manna, and will give him a white stone, and in the stone a new name written, which no man knoweth saving he that receiveth it.

18 And unto the angel of the church in Thyatira write; These things saith the Son of God, who hath his eyes like unto a flame of fire, and his feet are like fine brass;

19 I know thy works, and charity, and service, and faith, and thy patience, and thy works; and the last to be more than the first.

20 Notwithstanding I have a few things against thee, because thou sufferest that woman Jezebel, which calleth herself a prophetess, to teach and to seduce my servants to commit fornication, and to eat things sacrificed unto idols.

21 And I gave her space to repent of her fornication; and she repented not.

22 Behold, I will cast her into a bed, and them that commit adultery with her into great tribulation, except they repent of their deeds.

23 And I will kill her children with death; and all the churches shall know that I am he which searcheth the reins and hearts: and I will give unto every one of you according to your works.

24 But unto you I say, and unto the rest in Thyatira, as many as have not this doctrine, and which have not known the depths of Satan, as they speak; I will put upon you none other burden.

25 But that which ye have already hold fast till I come.

26 And he that overcometh, and keepeth my works unto the end, to him will I give power over the nations:

27 And he shall rule them with a rod of iron; as the vessels of a potter shall they be broken to shivers: even as I received of my Father.

28 And I will give him the morning star.

²⁹ He that hath an ear, let him hear what the Spirit saith unto the churches.

Chapter 3

And unto the angel of the church in Sardis write; These things saith he that hath the seven Spirits of God, and the seven stars; I know thy works, that thou hast a name that thou livest, and art dead.

² Be watchful, and strengthen the things which remain, that are ready to die: for I have not found thy works perfect before God.

³ Remember therefore how thou hast received and heard, and hold fast, and repent. If therefore thou shalt not watch, I will come on thee as a thief, and thou shalt not know what hour I will come upon thee.

⁴ Thou hast a few names even in Sardis which have not defiled their garments; and they shall walk with me in white: for they are worthy.

⁵ He that overcometh, the same shall be clothed in white raiment; and I will not blot out his name out of the book of life, but I will confess his name before my Father, and before his angels.

⁶ He that hath an ear, let him hear what the Spirit saith unto the churches.

⁷ And to the angel of the church in Philadelphia write; These things saith he that is holy, he that is true, he that hath the key of David, he that openeth, and no man shutteth; and shutteth, and no man openeth;

⁸ I know thy works: behold, I have set before thee an open door, and no man can shut it: for thou hast a little strength, and hast kept my word, and hast not denied my name.

⁹ Behold, I will make them of the synagogue of Satan, which say they are Jews, and are not, but do lie; behold, I will make them to come and worship before thy feet, and to know that I have loved thee.

¹⁰ Because thou hast kept the word of my patience, I also will keep thee from the hour of temptation, which shall come upon all the world, to try them that dwell upon the earth.

¹¹ Behold, I come quickly: hold that fast which thou hast, that no man take thy crown.

¹² Him that overcometh will I make a pillar in the temple of my God, and he shall go no more out: and I will write upon him the name of my God, and the name of the city of my God, which is new Jerusalem, which cometh down out of heaven from my God: and I will write upon him my new name.

¹³ He that hath an ear, let him hear what the Spirit saith unto the churches.

¹⁴ And unto the angel of the church of the Laodiceans write; These things saith the Amen, the faithful and true witness, the beginning of the creation of God;

¹⁵ I know thy works, that thou art neither cold nor hot: I would thou wert cold or hot.

¹⁶ So then because thou art lukewarm, and neither cold nor hot, I will spue thee out of my mouth.

¹⁷ Because thou sayest, I am rich, and increased with goods, and have need of nothing; and knowest not that thou art wretched, and miserable, and poor, and blind, and naked:

¹⁸ I counsel thee to buy of me gold tried in the fire, that thou mayest be rich; and white raiment, that thou mayest be clothed, and that the shame of thy nakedness do not appear; and anoint thine eyes with eyesalve, that thou mayest see.

¹⁹ As many as I love, I rebuke and chasten: be zealous therefore, and repent.

²⁰ Behold, I stand at the door, and knock: if any man hear my voice, and open the door, I will come in to him, and will sup with him, and he with me.

²¹ To him that overcometh will I grant to sit with me in my throne, even as I also overcame, and am set down with my Father in his throne.

²² He that hath an ear, let him hear what the Spirit saith unto the churches.

Chapter 4

After this I looked, and, behold, a door was opened in heaven: and the first voice which I heard was as it were of a trumpet talking with me; which said, Come up hither, and I will shew thee things which must be hereafter.

² And immediately I was in the spirit: and, behold, a throne was set in heaven, and one sat on the throne.

³ And he that sat was to look upon like a jasper and a sardine stone: and there was a rainbow round about the throne, in sight like unto an emerald.

⁴ And round about the throne were four and twenty seats: and upon the seats I saw four and twenty elders sitting, clothed in white raiment; and they had on their heads crowns of gold.

⁵ And out of the throne proceeded lightnings and thunderings and voices: and there were seven lamps of fire burning before the throne, which are the seven Spirits of God.

⁶ And before the throne there was a sea of glass like unto crystal: and in the midst of the throne, and round about the throne, were four beasts full of eyes before and behind.

⁷ And the first beast was like a lion, and the second beast like a calf, and the third beast had a face as a man, and the fourth beast was like a flying eagle.

⁸ And the four beasts had each of them six wings about him; and they were full of eyes within: and they rest not day and night, saying, Holy, holy, holy, LORD God Almighty, which was, and is, and is to come.

⁹ And when those beasts give glory and honour and thanks to him that sat on the throne, who liveth for ever and ever,

¹⁰ The four and twenty elders fall down before him that sat on the throne, and worship him that liveth for ever and ever, and cast their crowns before the throne, saying,

¹¹ Thou art worthy, O Lord, to receive glory and honour and power: for thou hast created all things, and for thy pleasure they are and were created.

Chapter 5

And I saw in the right hand of him that sat on the throne a book written within and on the backside, sealed with seven seals.

² And I saw a strong angel proclaiming with a loud voice, Who is worthy to open the book, and to loose the seals thereof?

³ And no man in heaven, nor in earth, neither under the earth, was able to open the book, neither to look thereon.

⁴ And I wept much, because no man was found worthy to open and to read the book, neither to look thereon.

⁵ And one of the elders saith unto me, Weep not: behold, the Lion of the tribe of Judah, the Root of David, hath prevailed to open the book, and to loose the seven seals thereof.

⁶ And I beheld, and, lo, in the midst of the throne and of the four beasts, and in the midst of the elders, stood a Lamb as it had been slain, having seven horns and seven eyes, which are the seven Spirits of God sent forth into all the earth.

⁷ And he came and took the book out of the right hand of him that sat upon the throne.

⁸ And when he had taken the book, the four beasts and four and twenty elders fell down before the Lamb, having every one of them harps, and golden vials full of odours, which are the prayers of saints.

⁹ And they sung a new song, saying, Thou art worthy to take the book, and to open the seals thereof: for thou wast slain, and hast redeemed us to God by thy blood out of every kindred, and tongue, and people, and nation;

¹⁰ And hast made us unto our God kings and priests: and we shall reign on the earth.

¹¹ And I beheld, and I heard the voice of many angels round about the throne and the beasts and the elders: and the number of them was ten thousand times ten thousand, and thousands of thousands;

¹² Saying with a loud voice, Worthy is the Lamb that was slain to receive power, and riches, and wisdom, and strength, and honour, and glory, and blessing.

¹³ And every creature which is in heaven, and on the earth, and under the earth, and such as are in the sea, and all that are in them, heard I saying, Blessing, and honour, and glory, and power, be unto him that sitteth upon the throne, and unto the Lamb for ever and ever.

¹⁴ And the four beasts said, Amen. And the four and twenty elders fell down and worshipped him that liveth for ever and ever.

Chapter 6

And I saw when the Lamb opened one of the seals, and I heard, as it were the noise of thunder, one of the four beasts saying, Come and see.

2 And I saw, and behold a white horse: and he that sat on him had a bow; and a crown was given unto him: and he went forth conquering, and to conquer.

3 And when he had opened the second seal, I heard the second beast say, Come and see.

4 And there went out another horse that was red: and power was given to him that sat thereon to take peace from the earth, and that they should kill one another: and there was given unto him a great sword.

5 And when he had opened the third seal, I heard the third beast say, Come and see. And I beheld, and lo a black horse; and he that sat on him had a pair of balances in his hand.

6 And I heard a voice in the midst of the four beasts say, A measure of wheat for a penny, and three measures of barley for a penny; and see thou hurt not the oil and the wine.

7 And when he had opened the fourth seal, I heard the voice of the fourth beast say, Come and see.

8 And I looked, and behold a pale horse: and his name that sat on him was Death, and Hell followed with him. And power was given unto them over the fourth part of the earth, to kill with sword, and with hunger, and with death, and with the beasts of the earth.

9 And when he had opened the fifth seal, I saw under the altar the souls of them that were slain for the word of God, and for the testimony which they held:

10 And they cried with a loud voice, saying, How long, O Lord, holy and true, dost thou not judge and avenge our blood on them that dwell on the earth?

11 And white robes were given unto every one of them; and it was said unto them, that they should rest yet for a little season, until their fellowservants also and their brethren, that should be killed as they were, should be fulfilled.

12 And I beheld when he had opened the sixth seal, and, lo, there was a great earthquake; and the sun became black as sackcloth of hair, and the moon became as blood;

13 And the stars of heaven fell unto the earth, even as a fig tree casteth her untimely figs, when she is shaken of a mighty wind.

14 And the heaven departed as a scroll when it is rolled together; and every mountain and island were moved out of their places.

15 And the kings of the earth, and the great men, and the rich men, and the chief captains, and the mighty men, and every bondman, and every free man, hid themselves in the dens and in the rocks of the mountains;

16 And said to the mountains and rocks, Fall on us, and hide us from the face of him that sitteth on the throne, and from the wrath of the Lamb:

17 For the great day of his wrath is come; and who shall be able to stand?

Chapter 7

And after these things I saw four angels standing on the four corners of the earth, holding the four winds of the earth, that the wind should not blow on the earth, nor on the sea, nor on any tree.

2 And I saw another angel ascending from the east, having the seal of the living God: and he cried with a loud voice to the four angels, to whom it was given to hurt the earth and the sea,

3 Saying, Hurt not the earth, neither the sea, nor the trees, till we have sealed the servants of our God in their foreheads.

4 And I heard the number of them which were sealed: and there were sealed an hundred and forty and four thousand of all the tribes of the children of Israel.

5 Of the tribe of Juda were sealed twelve thousand. Of the tribe of Reuben were sealed twelve thousand. Of the tribe of Gad were sealed twelve thousand.

6 Of the tribe of Aser were sealed twelve thousand. Of the tribe of Nephthalim were sealed twelve thousand. Of the tribe of Manasses were sealed twelve thousand.

⁷ Of the tribe of Simeon were sealed twelve thousand. Of the tribe of Levi were sealed twelve thousand. Of the tribe of Issachar were sealed twelve thousand.

⁸ Of the tribe of Zabulon were sealed twelve thousand. Of the tribe of Joseph were sealed twelve thousand. Of the tribe of Benjamin were sealed twelve thousand.

⁹ After this I beheld, and, lo, a great multitude, which no man could number, of all nations, and kindreds, and people, and tongues, stood before the throne, and before the Lamb, clothed with white robes, and palms in their hands;

¹⁰ And cried with a loud voice, saying, Salvation to our God which sitteth upon the throne, and unto the Lamb.

¹¹ And all the angels stood round about the throne, and about the elders and the four beasts, and fell before the throne on their faces, and worshipped God,

¹² Saying, Amen: Blessing, and glory, and wisdom, and thanksgiving, and honour, and power, and might, be unto our God for ever and ever. Amen.

¹³ And one of the elders answered, saying unto me, What are these which are arrayed in white robes? and whence came they?

¹⁴ And I said unto him, Sir, thou knowest. And he said to me, These are they which came out of great tribulation, and have washed their robes, and made them white in the blood of the Lamb.

¹⁵ Therefore are they before the throne of God, and serve him day and night in his temple: and he that sitteth on the throne shall dwell among them.

¹⁶ They shall hunger no more, neither thirst any more; neither shall the sun light on them, nor any heat.

¹⁷ For the Lamb which is in the midst of the throne shall feed them, and shall lead them unto living fountains of waters: and God shall wipe away all tears from their eyes.

Chapter 8

And when he had opened the seventh seal, there was silence in heaven about the space of half an hour.

² And I saw the seven angels which stood before God; and to them were given seven trumpets.

³ And another angel came and stood at the altar, having a golden censer; and there was given unto him much incense, that he should offer it with the prayers of all saints upon the golden altar which was before the throne.

⁴ And the smoke of the incense, which came with the prayers of the saints, ascended up before God out of the angel's hand.

⁵ And the angel took the censer, and filled it with fire of the altar, and cast it into the earth: and there were voices, and thunderings, and lightnings, and an earthquake.

⁶ And the seven angels which had the seven trumpets prepared themselves to sound.

⁷ The first angel sounded, and there followed hail and fire mingled with blood, and they were cast upon the earth: and the third part of trees was burnt up, and all green grass was burnt up.

⁸ And the second angel sounded, and as it were a great mountain burning with fire was cast into the sea: and the third part of the sea became blood;

⁹ And the third part of the creatures which were in the sea, and had life, died; and the third part of the ships were destroyed.

¹⁰ And the third angel sounded, and there fell a great star from heaven, burning as it were a lamp, and it fell upon the third part of the rivers, and upon the fountains of waters;

¹¹ And the name of the star is called Wormwood: and the third part of the waters became wormwood; and many men died of the waters, because they were made bitter.

¹² And the fourth angel sounded, and the third part of the sun was smitten, and the third part of the moon, and the third part of the stars; so as the third part of them was darkened, and the day shone not for a third part of it, and the night likewise.

¹³ And I beheld, and heard an angel flying through the midst of heaven, saying with a loud voice, Woe, woe, woe, to the inhabiters of the earth by reason of the other voices of the trumpet of the three angels, which are yet to sound!

Chapter 9

And the fifth angel sounded, and I saw a star fall from heaven unto the earth: and to him was given the key of the bottomless pit.

² And he opened the bottomless pit; and there arose a smoke out of the pit, as the smoke of a great furnace; and the sun and the air were darkened by reason of the smoke of the pit.

³ And there came out of the smoke locusts upon the earth: and unto them was given power, as the scorpions of the earth have power.

⁴ And it was commanded them that they should not hurt the grass of the earth, neither any green thing, neither any tree; but only those men which have not the seal of God in their foreheads.

⁵ And to them it was given that they should not kill them, but that they should be tormented five months: and their torment was as the torment of a scorpion, when he striketh a man.

⁶ And in those days shall men seek death, and shall not find it; and shall desire to die, and death shall flee from them.

⁷ And the shapes of the locusts were like unto horses prepared unto battle; and on their heads were as it were crowns like gold, and their faces were as the faces of men.

⁸ And they had hair as the hair of women, and their teeth were as the teeth of lions.

⁹ And they had breastplates, as it were breastplates of iron; and the sound of their wings was as the sound of chariots of many horses running to battle.

¹⁰ And they had tails like unto scorpions, and there were stings in their tails: and their power was to hurt men five months.

¹¹ And they had a king over them, which is the angel of the bottomless pit, whose name in the Hebrew tongue is Abaddon, but in the Greek tongue hath his name Apollyon.

¹² One woe is past; and, behold, there come two woes more hereafter.

¹³ And the sixth angel sounded, and I heard a voice from the four horns of the golden altar which is before God,

¹⁴ Saying to the sixth angel which had the trumpet, Loose the four angels which are bound in the great river Euphrates.

¹⁵ And the four angels were loosed, which were prepared for an hour, and a day, and a month, and a year, for to slay the third part of men.

¹⁶ And the number of the army of the horsemen were two hundred thousand thousand: and I heard the number of them.

¹⁷ And thus I saw the horses in the vision, and them that sat on them, having breastplates of fire, and of jacinth, and brimstone: and the heads of the horses were as the heads of lions; and out of their mouths issued fire and smoke and brimstone.

¹⁸ By these three was the third part of men killed, by the fire, and by the smoke, and by the brimstone, which issued out of their mouths.

¹⁹ For their power is in their mouth, and in their tails: for their tails were like unto serpents, and had heads, and with them they do hurt.

²⁰ And the rest of the men which were not killed by these plagues yet repented not of the works of their hands, that they should not worship devils, and idols of gold, and silver, and brass, and stone, and of wood: which neither can see, nor hear, nor walk:

²¹ Neither repented they of their murders, nor of their sorceries, nor of their fornication, nor of their thefts.

Chapter 10

And I saw another mighty angel come down from heaven, clothed with a cloud: and a rainbow was upon his head, and his face was as it were the sun, and his feet as pillars of fire:

² And he had in his hand a little book open: and he set his right foot upon the sea, and his left foot on the earth,

³ And cried with a loud voice, as when a lion roareth: and when he had cried, seven thunders uttered their voices.

⁴ And when the seven thunders had uttered their voices, I was about to write: and I heard a voice from heaven saying unto me, Seal up those things which the seven thunders uttered, and write them not.

⁵ And the angel which I saw stand upon the sea and upon the earth lifted up his hand to heaven,

⁶ And sware by him that liveth for ever and ever, who created heaven, and the things that therein are, and the earth, and the things that therein are, and the sea, and the things which are therein, that there should be time no longer:

⁷ But in the days of the voice of the seventh angel, when he shall begin to sound, the mystery of God should be finished, as he hath declared to his servants the prophets.

⁸ And the voice which I heard from heaven spake unto me again, and said, Go and take the little book which is open in the hand of the angel which standeth upon the sea and upon the earth.

⁹ And I went unto the angel, and said unto him, Give me the little book. And he said unto me, Take it, and eat it up; and it shall make thy belly bitter, but it shall be in thy mouth sweet as honey.

¹⁰ And I took the little book out of the angel's hand, and ate it up; and it was in my mouth sweet as honey: and as soon as I had eaten it, my belly was bitter.

¹¹ And he said unto me, Thou must prophesy again before many peoples, and nations, and tongues, and kings.

Chapter 11

And there was given me a reed like unto a rod: and the angel stood, saying, Rise, and measure the temple of God, and the altar, and them that worship therein.

² But the court which is without the temple leave out, and measure it not; for it is given unto the Gentiles: and the holy city shall they tread under foot forty and two months.

³ And I will give power unto my two witnesses, and they shall prophesy a thousand two hundred and threescore days, clothed in sackcloth.

⁴ These are the two olive trees, and the two candlesticks standing before the God of the earth.

⁵ And if any man will hurt them, fire proceedeth out of their mouth, and devoureth their enemies: and if any man will hurt them, he must in this manner be killed.

⁶ These have power to shut heaven, that it rain not in the days of their prophecy: and have power over waters to turn them to blood, and to smite the earth with all plagues, as often as they will.

⁷ And when they shall have finished their testimony, the beast that ascendeth out of the bottomless pit shall make war against them, and shall overcome them, and kill them.

⁸ And their dead bodies shall lie in the street of the great city, which spiritually is called Sodom and Egypt, where also our Lord was crucified.

⁹ And they of the people and kindreds and tongues and nations shall see their dead bodies three days and an half, and shall not suffer their dead bodies to be put in graves.

¹⁰ And they that dwell upon the earth shall rejoice over them, and make merry, and shall send gifts one to another; because these two prophets tormented them that dwelt on the earth.

¹¹ And after three days and an half the spirit of life from God entered into them, and they stood upon their feet; and great fear fell upon them which saw them.

¹² And they heard a great voice from heaven saying unto them, Come up hither. And they ascended up to heaven in a cloud; and their enemies beheld them.

[13] And the same hour was there a great earthquake, and the tenth part of the city fell, and in the earthquake were slain of men seven thousand: and the remnant were affrighted, and gave glory to the God of heaven.

[14] The second woe is past; and, behold, the third woe cometh quickly.

[15] And the seventh angel sounded; and there were great voices in heaven, saying, The kingdoms of this world are become the kingdoms of our Lord, and of his Christ; and he shall reign for ever and ever.

[16] And the four and twenty elders, which sat before God on their seats, fell upon their faces, and worshipped God,

[17] Saying, We give thee thanks, O LORD God Almighty, which art, and wast, and art to come; because thou hast taken to thee thy great power, and hast reigned.

[18] And the nations were angry, and thy wrath is come, and the time of the dead, that they should be judged, and that thou shouldest give reward unto thy servants the prophets, and to the saints, and them that fear thy name, small and great; and shouldest destroy them which destroy the earth.

[19] And the temple of God was opened in heaven, and there was seen in his temple the ark of his testament: and there were lightnings, and voices, and thunderings, and an earthquake, and great hail.

Chapter 12

And there appeared a great wonder in heaven; a woman clothed with the sun, and the moon under her feet, and upon her head a crown of twelve stars:

[2] And she being with child cried, travailing in birth, and pained to be delivered.

[3] And there appeared another wonder in heaven; and behold a great red dragon, having seven heads and ten horns, and seven crowns upon his heads.

[4] And his tail drew the third part of the stars of heaven, and did cast them to the earth: and the dragon stood before the woman which was ready to be delivered, for to devour her child as soon as it was born.

[5] And she brought forth a man child, who was to rule all nations with a rod of iron: and her child was caught up unto God, and to his throne.

[6] And the woman fled into the wilderness, where she hath a place prepared of God, that they should feed her there a thousand two hundred and threescore days.

[7] And there was war in heaven: Michael and his angels fought against the dragon; and the dragon fought and his angels,

[8] And prevailed not; neither was their place found any more in heaven.

[9] And the great dragon was cast out, that old serpent, called the Devil, and Satan, which deceiveth the whole world: he was cast out into the earth, and his angels were cast out with him.

[10] And I heard a loud voice saying in heaven, Now is come salvation, and strength, and the kingdom of our God, and the power of his Christ: for the accuser of our brethren is cast down, which accused them before our God day and night.

[11] And they overcame him by the blood of the Lamb, and by the word of their testimony; and they loved not their lives unto the death.

[12] Therefore rejoice, ye heavens, and ye that dwell in them. Woe to the inhabiters of the earth and of the sea! for the devil is come down unto you, having great wrath, because he knoweth that he hath but a short time.

[13] And when the dragon saw that he was cast unto the earth, he persecuted the woman which brought forth the man child.

[14] And to the woman were given two wings of a great eagle, that she might fly into the wilderness, into her place, where she is nourished for a time, and times, and half a time, from the face of the serpent.

[15] And the serpent cast out of his mouth water as a flood after the woman, that he might cause her to be carried away of the flood.

[16] And the earth helped the woman, and the earth opened her mouth, and swallowed up the flood which the dragon cast out of his mouth.

¹⁷ And the dragon was wroth with the woman, and went to make war with the remnant of her seed, which keep the commandments of God, and have the testimony of Jesus Christ.

Chapter 13

And I stood upon the sand of the sea, and saw a beast rise up out of the sea, having seven heads and ten horns, and upon his horns ten crowns, and upon his heads the name of blasphemy.
² And the beast which I saw was like unto a leopard, and his feet were as the feet of a bear, and his mouth as the mouth of a lion: and the dragon gave him his power, and his seat, and great authority.
³ And I saw one of his heads as it were wounded to death; and his deadly wound was healed: and all the world wondered after the beast.
⁴ And they worshipped the dragon which gave power unto the beast: and they worshipped the beast, saying, Who is like unto the beast? who is able to make war with him?
⁵ And there was given unto him a mouth speaking great things and blasphemies; and power was given unto him to continue forty and two months.
⁶ And he opened his mouth in blasphemy against God, to blaspheme his name, and his tabernacle, and them that dwell in heaven.
⁷ And it was given unto him to make war with the saints, and to overcome them: and power was given him over all kindreds, and tongues, and nations.
⁸ And all that dwell upon the earth shall worship him, whose names are not written in the book of life of the Lamb slain from the foundation of the world.
⁹ If any man have an ear, let him hear.
¹⁰ He that leadeth into captivity shall go into captivity: he that killeth with the sword must be killed with the sword. Here is the patience and the faith of the saints.
¹¹ And I beheld another beast coming up out of the earth; and he had two horns like a lamb, and he spake as a dragon.
¹² And he exerciseth all the power of the first beast before him, and causeth the earth and them which dwell therein to worship the first beast, whose deadly wound was healed.
¹³ And he doeth great wonders, so that he maketh fire come down from heaven on the earth in the sight of men,
¹⁴ And deceiveth them that dwell on the earth by the means of those miracles which he had power to do in the sight of the beast; saying to them that dwell on the earth, that they should make an image to the beast, which had the wound by a sword, and did live.
¹⁵ And he had power to give life unto the image of the beast, that the image of the beast should both speak, and cause that as many as would not worship the image of the beast should be killed.
¹⁶ And he causeth all, both small and great, rich and poor, free and bond, to receive a mark in their right hand, or in their foreheads:
¹⁷ And that no man might buy or sell, save he that had the mark, or the name of the beast, or the number of his name.
¹⁸ Here is wisdom. Let him that hath understanding count the number of the beast: for it is the number of a man; and his number is Six hundred threescore and six.

Chapter 14

And I looked, and, lo, a Lamb stood on the mount Sion, and with him an hundred forty and four thousand, having his Father's name written in their foreheads.
² And I heard a voice from heaven, as the voice of many waters, and as the voice of a great thunder: and I heard the voice of harpers harping with their harps:
³ And they sung as it were a new song before the throne, and before the four beasts, and the elders: and no man could learn that song but the hundred and forty and four thousand, which were redeemed from the earth.

⁴ These are they which were not defiled with women; for they are virgins. These are they which follow the Lamb whithersoever he goeth. These were redeemed from among men, being the firstfruits unto God and to the Lamb.

⁵ And in their mouth was found no guile: for they are without fault before the throne of God.

⁶ And I saw another angel fly in the midst of heaven, having the everlasting gospel to preach unto them that dwell on the earth, and to every nation, and kindred, and tongue, and people,

⁷ Saying with a loud voice, Fear God, and give glory to him; for the hour of his judgment is come: and worship him that made heaven, and earth, and the sea, and the fountains of waters.

⁸ And there followed another angel, saying, Babylon is fallen, is fallen, that great city, because she made all nations drink of the wine of the wrath of her fornication.

⁹ And the third angel followed them, saying with a loud voice, If any man worship the beast and his image, and receive his mark in his forehead, or in his hand,

¹⁰ The same shall drink of the wine of the wrath of God, which is poured out without mixture into the cup of his indignation; and he shall be tormented with fire and brimstone in the presence of the holy angels, and in the presence of the Lamb:

¹¹ And the smoke of their torment ascendeth up for ever and ever: and they have no rest day nor night, who worship the beast and his image, and whosoever receiveth the mark of his name.

¹² Here is the patience of the saints: here are they that keep the commandments of God, and the faith of Jesus.

¹³ And I heard a voice from heaven saying unto me, Write, Blessed are the dead which die in the Lord from henceforth: Yea, saith the Spirit, that they may rest from their labours; and their works do follow them.

¹⁴ And I looked, and behold a white cloud, and upon the cloud one sat like unto the Son of man, having on his head a golden crown, and in his hand a sharp sickle.

¹⁵ And another angel came out of the temple, crying with a loud voice to him that sat on the cloud, Thrust in thy sickle, and reap: for the time is come for thee to reap; for the harvest of the earth is ripe.

¹⁶ And he that sat on the cloud thrust in his sickle on the earth; and the earth was reaped.

¹⁷ And another angel came out of the temple which is in heaven, he also having a sharp sickle.

¹⁸ And another angel came out from the altar, which had power over fire; and cried with a loud cry to him that had the sharp sickle, saying, Thrust in thy sharp sickle, and gather the clusters of the vine of the earth; for her grapes are fully ripe.

¹⁹ And the angel thrust in his sickle into the earth, and gathered the vine of the earth, and cast it into the great winepress of the wrath of God.

²⁰ And the winepress was trodden without the city, and blood came out of the winepress, even unto the horse bridles, by the space of a thousand and six hundred furlongs.

Chapter 15

And I saw another sign in heaven, great and marvellous, seven angels having the seven last plagues; for in them is filled up the wrath of God.

² And I saw as it were a sea of glass mingled with fire: and them that had gotten the victory over the beast, and over his image, and over his mark, and over the number of his name, stand on the sea of glass, having the harps of God.

³ And they sing the song of Moses the servant of God, and the song of the Lamb, saying, Great and marvellous are thy works, Lord God Almighty; just and true are thy ways, thou King of saints.

⁴ Who shall not fear thee, O Lord, and glorify thy name? for thou only art holy: for all nations shall come and worship before thee; for thy judgments are made manifest.

⁵ And after that I looked, and, behold, the temple of the tabernacle of the testimony in heaven was opened:

⁶ And the seven angels came out of the temple, having the seven plagues, clothed in pure and white linen, and having their breasts girded with golden girdles.

⁷ And one of the four beasts gave unto the seven angels seven golden vials full of the wrath of God, who liveth for ever and ever.

⁸ And the temple was filled with smoke from the glory of God, and from his power; and no man was able to enter into the temple, till the seven plagues of the seven angels were fulfilled.

Chapter 16

And I heard a great voice out of the temple saying to the seven angels, Go your ways, and pour out the vials of the wrath of God upon the earth.

² And the first went, and poured out his vial upon the earth; and there fell a noisome and grievous sore upon the men which had the mark of the beast, and upon them which worshipped his image.

³ And the second angel poured out his vial upon the sea; and it became as the blood of a dead man: and every living soul died in the sea.

⁴ And the third angel poured out his vial upon the rivers and fountains of waters; and they became blood.

⁵ And I heard the angel of the waters say, Thou art righteous, O Lord, which art, and wast, and shalt be, because thou hast judged thus.

⁶ For they have shed the blood of saints and prophets, and thou hast given them blood to drink; for they are worthy.

⁷ And I heard another out of the altar say, Even so, Lord God Almighty, true and righteous are thy judgments.

⁸ And the fourth angel poured out his vial upon the sun; and power was given unto him to scorch men with fire.

⁹ And men were scorched with great heat, and blasphemed the name of God, which hath power over these plagues: and they repented not to give him glory.

¹⁰ And the fifth angel poured out his vial upon the seat of the beast; and his kingdom was full of darkness; and they gnawed their tongues for pain,

¹¹ And blasphemed the God of heaven because of their pains and their sores, and repented not of their deeds.

¹² And the sixth angel poured out his vial upon the great river Euphrates; and the water thereof was dried up, that the way of the kings of the east might be prepared.

¹³ And I saw three unclean spirits like frogs come out of the mouth of the dragon, and out of the mouth of the beast, and out of the mouth of the false prophet.

¹⁴ For they are the spirits of devils, working miracles, which go forth unto the kings of the earth and of the whole world, to gather them to the battle of that great day of God Almighty.

¹⁵ Behold, I come as a thief. Blessed is he that watcheth, and keepeth his garments, lest he walk naked, and they see his shame.

¹⁶ And he gathered them together into a place called in the Hebrew tongue Armageddon.

¹⁷ And the seventh angel poured out his vial into the air; and there came a great voice out of the temple of heaven, from the throne, saying, It is done.

¹⁸ And there were voices, and thunders, and lightnings; and there was a great earthquake, such as was not since men were upon the earth, so mighty an earthquake, and so great.

¹⁹ And the great city was divided into three parts, and the cities of the nations fell: and great Babylon came in remembrance before God, to give unto her the cup of the wine of the fierceness of his wrath.

²⁰ And every island fled away, and the mountains were not found.

²¹ And there fell upon men a great hail out of heaven, every stone about the weight of a talent: and men blasphemed God because of the plague of the hail; for the plague thereof was exceeding great.

Chapter 17

And there came one of the seven angels which had the seven vials, and talked with me, saying unto me, Come hither; I will shew unto thee the judgment of the great whore that sitteth upon many waters:

² With whom the kings of the earth have committed fornication, and the inhabitants of the earth have been made drunk with the wine of her fornication.

³ So he carried me away in the spirit into the wilderness: and I saw a woman sit upon a scarlet coloured beast, full of names of blasphemy, having seven heads and ten horns.

⁴ And the woman was arrayed in purple and scarlet colour, and decked with gold and precious stones and pearls, having a golden cup in her hand full of abominations and filthiness of her fornication:

⁵ And upon her forehead was a name written, MYSTERY, BABYLON THE GREAT, THE MOTHER OF HARLOTS AND ABOMINATIONS OF THE EARTH.

⁶ And I saw the woman drunken with the blood of the saints, and with the blood of the martyrs of Jesus: and when I saw her, I wondered with great admiration.

⁷ And the angel said unto me, Wherefore didst thou marvel? I will tell thee the mystery of the woman, and of the beast that carrieth her, which hath the seven heads and ten horns.

⁸ The beast that thou sawest was, and is not; and shall ascend out of the bottomless pit, and go into perdition: and they that dwell on the earth shall wonder, whose names were not written in the book of life from the foundation of the world, when they behold the beast that was, and is not, and yet is.

⁹ And here is the mind which hath wisdom. The seven heads are seven mountains, on which the woman sitteth.

¹⁰ And there are seven kings: five are fallen, and one is, and the other is not yet come; and when he cometh, he must continue a short space.

¹¹ And the beast that was, and is not, even he is the eighth, and is of the seven, and goeth into perdition.

¹² And the ten horns which thou sawest are ten kings, which have received no kingdom as yet; but receive power as kings one hour with the beast.

¹³ These have one mind, and shall give their power and strength unto the beast.

¹⁴ These shall make war with the Lamb, and the Lamb shall overcome them: for he is Lord of lords, and King of kings: and they that are with him are called, and chosen, and faithful.

¹⁵ And he saith unto me, The waters which thou sawest, where the whore sitteth, are peoples, and multitudes, and nations, and tongues.

¹⁶ And the ten horns which thou sawest upon the beast, these shall hate the whore, and shall make her desolate and naked, and shall eat her flesh, and burn her with fire.

¹⁷ For God hath put in their hearts to fulfil his will, and to agree, and give their kingdom unto the beast, until the words of God shall be fulfilled.

¹⁸ And the woman which thou sawest is that great city, which reigneth over the kings of the earth.

Chapter 18

And after these things I saw another angel come down from heaven, having great power; and the earth was lightened with his glory.

² And he cried mightily with a strong voice, saying, Babylon the great is fallen, is fallen, and is become the habitation of devils, and the hold of every foul spirit, and a cage of every unclean and hateful bird.

³ For all nations have drunk of the wine of the wrath of her fornication, and the kings of the earth have committed fornication with her, and the merchants of the earth are waxed rich through the abundance of her delicacies.

⁴ And I heard another voice from heaven, saying, Come out of her, my people, that ye be not partakers of her sins, and that ye receive not of her plagues.

⁵ For her sins have reached unto heaven, and God hath remembered her iniquities.

⁶ Reward her even as she rewarded you, and double unto her double according to her works: in the cup which she hath filled fill to her double.

⁷ How much she hath glorified herself, and lived deliciously, so much torment and sorrow give her: for she saith in her heart, I sit a queen, and am no widow, and shall see no sorrow.

[8] Therefore shall her plagues come in one day, death, and mourning, and famine; and she shall be utterly burned with fire: for strong is the Lord God who judgeth her.

[9] And the kings of the earth, who have committed fornication and lived deliciously with her, shall bewail her, and lament for her, when they shall see the smoke of her burning,

[10] Standing afar off for the fear of her torment, saying, Alas, alas that great city Babylon, that mighty city! for in one hour is thy judgment come.

[11] And the merchants of the earth shall weep and mourn over her; for no man buyeth their merchandise any more:

[12] The merchandise of gold, and silver, and precious stones, and of pearls, and fine linen, and purple, and silk, and scarlet, and all thyine wood, and all manner vessels of ivory, and all manner vessels of most precious wood, and of brass, and iron, and marble,

[13] And cinnamon, and odours, and ointments, and frankincense, and wine, and oil, and fine flour, and wheat, and beasts, and sheep, and horses, and chariots, and slaves, and souls of men.

[14] And the fruits that thy soul lusted after are departed from thee, and all things which were dainty and goodly are departed from thee, and thou shalt find them no more at all.

[15] The merchants of these things, which were made rich by her, shall stand afar off for the fear of her torment, weeping and wailing,

[16] And saying, Alas, alas that great city, that was clothed in fine linen, and purple, and scarlet, and decked with gold, and precious stones, and pearls!

[17] For in one hour so great riches is come to nought. And every shipmaster, and all the company in ships, and sailors, and as many as trade by sea, stood afar off,

[18] And cried when they saw the smoke of her burning, saying, What city is like unto this great city!

[19] And they cast dust on their heads, and cried, weeping and wailing, saying, Alas, alas that great city, wherein were made rich all that had ships in the sea by reason of her costliness! for in one hour is she made desolate.

[20] Rejoice over her, thou heaven, and ye holy apostles and prophets; for God hath avenged you on her.

[21] And a mighty angel took up a stone like a great millstone, and cast it into the sea, saying, Thus with violence shall that great city Babylon be thrown down, and shall be found no more at all.

[22] And the voice of harpers, and musicians, and of pipers, and trumpeters, shall be heard no more at all in thee; and no craftsman, of whatsoever craft he be, shall be found any more in thee; and the sound of a millstone shall be heard no more at all in thee;

[23] And the light of a candle shall shine no more at all in thee; and the voice of the bridegroom and of the bride shall be heard no more at all in thee: for thy merchants were the great men of the earth; for by thy sorceries were all nations deceived.

[24] And in her was found the blood of prophets, and of saints, and of all that were slain upon the earth.

Chapter 19

And after these things I heard a great voice of much people in heaven, saying, Alleluia; Salvation, and glory, and honour, and power, unto the Lord our God:

[2] For true and righteous are his judgments: for he hath judged the great whore, which did corrupt the earth with her fornication, and hath avenged the blood of his servants at her hand.

[3] And again they said, Alleluia And her smoke rose up for ever and ever.

[4] And the four and twenty elders and the four beasts fell down and worshipped God that sat on the throne, saying, Amen; Alleluia.

[5] And a voice came out of the throne, saying, Praise our God, all ye his servants, and ye that fear him, both small and great.

[6] And I heard as it were the voice of a great multitude, and as the voice of many waters, and as the voice of mighty thunderings, saying, Alleluia: for the Lord God omnipotent reigneth.

7 Let us be glad and rejoice, and give honour to him: for the marriage of the Lamb is come, and his wife hath made herself ready.

8 And to her was granted that she should be arrayed in fine linen, clean and white: for the fine linen is the righteousness of saints.

9 And he saith unto me, Write, Blessed are they which are called unto the marriage supper of the Lamb. And he saith unto me, These are the true sayings of God.

10 And I fell at his feet to worship him. And he said unto me, See thou do it not: I am thy fellowservant, and of thy brethren that have the testimony of Jesus: worship God: for the testimony of Jesus is the spirit of prophecy.

11 And I saw heaven opened, and behold a white horse; and he that sat upon him was called Faithful and True, and in righteousness he doth judge and make war.

12 His eyes were as a flame of fire, and on his head were many crowns; and he had a name written, that no man knew, but he himself.

13 And he was clothed with a vesture dipped in blood: and his name is called The Word of God.

14 And the armies which were in heaven followed him upon white horses, clothed in fine linen, white and clean.

15 And out of his mouth goeth a sharp sword, that with it he should smite the nations: and he shall rule them with a rod of iron: and he treadeth the winepress of the fierceness and wrath of Almighty God.

16 And he hath on his vesture and on his thigh a name written, KING OF KINGS, AND LORD OF LORDS.

17 And I saw an angel standing in the sun; and he cried with a loud voice, saying to all the fowls that fly in the midst of heaven, Come and gather yourselves together unto the supper of the great God;

18 That ye may eat the flesh of kings, and the flesh of captains, and the flesh of mighty men, and the flesh of horses, and of them that sit on them, and the flesh of all men, both free and bond, both small and great.

19 And I saw the beast, and the kings of the earth, and their armies, gathered together to make war against him that sat on the horse, and against his army.

20 And the beast was taken, and with him the false prophet that wrought miracles before him, with which he deceived them that had received the mark of the beast, and them that worshipped his image. These both were cast alive into a lake of fire burning with brimstone.

21 And the remnant were slain with the sword of him that sat upon the horse, which sword proceeded out of his mouth: and all the fowls were filled with their flesh.

Chapter 20

And I saw an angel come down from heaven, having the key of the bottomless pit and a great chain in his hand.

2 And he laid hold on the dragon, that old serpent, which is the Devil, and Satan, and bound him a thousand years,

3 And cast him into the bottomless pit, and shut him up, and set a seal upon him, that he should deceive the nations no more, till the thousand years should be fulfilled: and after that he must be loosed a little season.

4 And I saw thrones, and they sat upon them, and judgment was given unto them: and I saw the souls of them that were beheaded for the witness of Jesus, and for the word of God, and which had not worshipped the beast, neither his image, neither had received his mark upon their foreheads, or in their hands; and they lived and reigned with Christ a thousand years.

5 But the rest of the dead lived not again until the thousand years were finished. This is the first resurrection.

6 Blessed and holy is he that hath part in the first resurrection: on such the second death hath no power, but they shall be priests of God and of Christ, and shall reign with him a thousand years.

7 And when the thousand years are expired, Satan shall be loosed out of his prison,

⁸ And shall go out to deceive the nations which are in the four quarters of the earth, Gog, and Magog, to gather them together to battle: the number of whom is as the sand of the sea.

⁹ And they went up on the breadth of the earth, and compassed the camp of the saints about, and the beloved city: and fire came down from God out of heaven, and devoured them.

¹⁰ And the devil that deceived them was cast into the lake of fire and brimstone, where the beast and the false prophet are, and shall be tormented day and night for ever and ever.

¹¹ And I saw a great white throne, and him that sat on it, from whose face the earth and the heaven fled away; and there was found no place for them.

¹² And I saw the dead, small and great, stand before God; and the books were opened: and another book was opened, which is the book of life: and the dead were judged out of those things which were written in the books, according to their works.

¹³ And the sea gave up the dead which were in it; and death and hell delivered up the dead which were in them: and they were judged every man according to their works.

¹⁴ And death and hell were cast into the lake of fire. This is the second death.

¹⁵ And whosoever was not found written in the book of life was cast into the lake of fire.

Chapter 21

And I saw a new heaven and a new earth: for the first heaven and the first earth were passed away; and there was no more sea.

² And I John saw the holy city, new Jerusalem, coming down from God out of heaven, prepared as a bride adorned for her husband.

³ And I heard a great voice out of heaven saying, Behold, the tabernacle of God is with men, and he will dwell with them, and they shall be his people, and God himself shall be with them, and be their God.

⁴ And God shall wipe away all tears from their eyes; and there shall be no more death, neither sorrow, nor crying, neither shall there be any more pain: for the former things are passed away.

⁵ And he that sat upon the throne said, Behold, I make all things new. And he said unto me, Write: for these words are true and faithful.

⁶ And he said unto me, It is done. I am Alpha and Omega, the beginning and the end. I will give unto him that is athirst of the fountain of the water of life freely.

⁷ He that overcometh shall inherit all things; and I will be his God, and he shall be my son.

⁸ But the fearful, and unbelieving, and the abominable, and murderers, and whoremongers, and sorcerers, and idolaters, and all liars, shall have their part in the lake which burneth with fire and brimstone: which is the second death.

⁹ And there came unto me one of the seven angels which had the seven vials full of the seven last plagues, and talked with me, saying, Come hither, I will shew thee the bride, the Lamb's wife.

¹⁰ And he carried me away in the spirit to a great and high mountain, and shewed me that great city, the holy Jerusalem, descending out of heaven from God,

¹¹ Having the glory of God: and her light was like unto a stone most precious, even like a jasper stone, clear as crystal;

¹² And had a wall great and high, and had twelve gates, and at the gates twelve angels, and names written thereon, which are the names of the twelve tribes of the children of Israel:

¹³ On the east three gates; on the north three gates; on the south three gates; and on the west three gates.

¹⁴ And the wall of the city had twelve foundations, and in them the names of the twelve apostles of the Lamb.

¹⁵ And he that talked with me had a golden reed to measure the city, and the gates thereof, and the wall thereof.

¹⁶ And the city lieth foursquare, and the length is as large as the breadth: and he measured the city with the reed, twelve thousand furlongs. The length and the breadth and the height of it are equal.

¹⁷ And he measured the wall thereof, an hundred and forty and four cubits, according to the measure of a man, that is, of the angel.

¹⁸ And the building of the wall of it was of jasper: and the city was pure gold, like unto clear glass.

¹⁹ And the foundations of the wall of the city were garnished with all manner of precious stones. The first foundation was jasper; the second, sapphire; the third, a chalcedony; the fourth, an emerald;

²⁰ The fifth, sardonyx; the sixth, sardius; the seventh, chrysolyte; the eighth, beryl; the ninth, a topaz; the tenth, a chrysoprasus; the eleventh, a jacinth; the twelfth, an amethyst.

²¹ And the twelve gates were twelve pearls: every several gate was of one pearl: and the street of the city was pure gold, as it were transparent glass.

²² And I saw no temple therein: for the Lord God Almighty and the Lamb are the temple of it.

²³ And the city had no need of the sun, neither of the moon, to shine in it: for the glory of God did lighten it, and the Lamb is the light thereof.

²⁴ And the nations of them which are saved shall walk in the light of it: and the kings of the earth do bring their glory and honour into it.

²⁵ And the gates of it shall not be shut at all by day: for there shall be no night there.

²⁶ And they shall bring the glory and honour of the nations into it.

²⁷ And there shall in no wise enter into it any thing that defileth, neither whatsoever worketh abomination, or maketh a lie: but they which are written in the Lamb's book of life.

Chapter 22

And he shewed me a pure river of water of life, clear as crystal, proceeding out of the throne of God and of the Lamb.

² In the midst of the street of it, and on either side of the river, was there the tree of life, which bare twelve manner of fruits, and yielded her fruit every month: and the leaves of the tree were for the healing of the nations.

³ And there shall be no more curse: but the throne of God and of the Lamb shall be in it; and his servants shall serve him:

⁴ And they shall see his face; and his name shall be in their foreheads.

⁵ And there shall be no night there; and they need no candle, neither light of the sun; for the Lord God giveth them light: and they shall reign for ever and ever.

⁶ And he said unto me, These sayings are faithful and true: and the Lord God of the holy prophets sent his angel to shew unto his servants the things which must shortly be done.

⁷ Behold, I come quickly: blessed is he that keepeth the sayings of the prophecy of this book.

⁸ And I John saw these things, and heard them. And when I had heard and seen, I fell down to worship before the feet of the angel which shewed me these things.

⁹ Then saith he unto me, See thou do it not: for I am thy fellowservant, and of thy brethren the prophets, and of them which keep the sayings of this book: worship God.

¹⁰ And he saith unto me, Seal not the sayings of the prophecy of this book: for the time is at hand.

¹¹ He that is unjust, let him be unjust still: and he which is filthy, let him be filthy still: and he that is righteous, let him be righteous still: and he that is holy, let him be holy still.

¹² And, behold, I come quickly; and my reward is with me, to give every man according as his work shall be.

¹³ I am Alpha and Omega, the beginning and the end, the first and the last.

¹⁴ Blessed are they that do his commandments, that they may have right to the tree of life, and may enter in through the gates into the city.

¹⁵ For without are dogs, and sorcerers, and whoremongers, and murderers, and idolaters, and whosoever loveth and maketh a lie.

¹⁶ I Jesus have sent mine angel to testify unto you these things in the churches. I am the root and the offspring of David, and the bright and morning star.

[17] And the Spirit and the bride say, Come. And let him that heareth say, Come. And let him that is athirst come. And whosoever will, let him take the water of life freely.

[18] For I testify unto every man that heareth the words of the prophecy of this book, If any man shall add unto these things, God shall add unto him the plagues that are written in this book:

[19] And if any man shall take away from the words of the book of this prophecy, God shall take away his part out of the book of life, and out of the holy city, and from the things which are written in this book.

[20] He which testifieth these things saith, Surely I come quickly. Amen. Even so, come, Lord Jesus.

[21] The grace of our Lord Jesus Christ be with you all. Amen.

Made in the USA
Middletown, DE
22 September 2019